ARTIFICIAL INTELLIGENCE

39.95

ARTIFICIAL INTELLIGENCE

An Applications-oriented Approach

Daniel Schutzer

VAN NOSTRAND REINHOLD COMPANY
_____NEW YORK

Copyright © 1987 by Van Nostrand Reinhold Company Inc.

Library of Congress Catalog Card Number 86-13291

ISBN 0-442-28034-3

All rights reserved. No part of this work covered by the copyright hereon may be reproduced or used in any form or by any means—graphic, electronic, or mechanical, including photocopying, recording, taping, or information storage and retrieval systems—without written permission of the publisher.

Printed in the United States of America

Designed by Beth Tondreau

Van Nostrand Reinhold Company Inc.
115 Fifth Avenue
New York, New York 10003

Van Nostrand Reinhold Company Limited
Molly Millars Lane
Wokingham, Berkshire RG11 2PY, England

Van Nostrand Reinhold
480 La Trobe Street
Melbourne, Victoria 3000, Australia

Macmillan of Canada
Division of Canada Publishing Corporation
164 Commander Boulevard
Agincourt, Ontario M1S 3C7, Canada

16 15 14 13 12 11 10 9 8 7 6 5 4 3 2

Library of Congress Cataloging-in-Publication Data

Schutzer, Daniel, 1940–
  Artificial intelligence.

  Bibliography: p.
  Includes index.
  1. Artificial intelligence. I. Title.
Q335.S4116 1986   006.3   86-13291
ISBN 0-442-28034-3

Contents

PREFACE	vii
ACKNOWLEDGMENTS	ix
1. INTRODUCTION	1
Definition of Artificial Intelligence	1
Key Attributes	2
Historical Background	7
2. THEORIES AND CONCEPTS	13
Knowledge Representation	14
Predicate Calculus	18
Production Rules	23
Frames and Scripts	27
Semantic Networks	31
Dealing with Uncertainty	36
Inference and Deduction	42
Formal Reasoning	44
Forward Chaining and Backward Chaining	52
Frame-based Representations in Complex Reasoning	57
Reasoning with Uncertainty	59
Problem Solving	67
Search Strategies	72
Planning	81
Learning	86
3. TOOLS AND TECHNIQUES	94
LISP	95
Logic Programming and PROLOG	110
Other Languages and Higher-Order Software Tools	122
LISP Machines and Other Special Hardware	123
4. CURRENT APPLICATIONS	130
Expert Systems	131
Machine Perception	142
Natural Language Processing	146

Speech Understanding	164
Vision and Image Understanding	174
Robotics	188
5. SYSTEMS IMPLICATIONS	195
6. FUTURE PROSPECTS	205
Appendix A. Summary of A.I. Research	223
Appendix B. Commercially Offered Expert Systems	232
Appendix C. Commercially Offered Natural Language Systems	247
Appendix D. Speech Synthesis Systems	251
Appendix E. Robot Programming Systems	259
GLOSSARY	263
BIBLIOGRAPHY	266
INDEX	290

Preface

Although artificial intelligence has been studied academically since the late 1950s, the subject has recently generated wider interest because commercial applications now seem to be practical. One major factor in the successful transition of artificial intelligence from academia to industry is the dramatic advances in computer hardware that have occurred in the last two decades. Computer prices and sizes have plummeted, whereas memory capacity and processing speeds have increased to the point that personal microcomputers today possess all the power of the mainframes used by artificial intelligence researchers in the late 1950s and early 1960s. Because artificial intelligence applications tend to be computer-intensive, requiring a great deal of computer resources, the technological advances in the computer industry as a whole have increased the likelihood of successful commercialization.

Another important factor in the likely success of the commercialization of artificial intelligence is the increased maturity of the field itself. Although artificial intelligence is still far from being well understood, certain key unifying concepts and principles have emerged, and several important tools and techniques have been developed in support of these concepts. Much of this book is devoted to an exposition of these unifying concepts and principles and of the supporting tools and techniques that have been developed to facilitate their practical application.

Increased understanding and improved tools have produced many important successful prototypes, and these successes have captured the interest and investment dollars of both industry and government. Numerous projects have been initiated in diverse fields; many of these projects are reviewed herein. Several new companies specialize in artificial intelligence. In addition, artificial intelligence groups have been set up in many established companies, including many Fortune 500 firms. These activities have already led to several commercial successes and offerings, primarily in the area of expert systems and natural language processing. Concrete examples of these successes are studied in this book.

Since 1983, a private industry consortium has set up the Microelectronics and Computer Technology Corporation (MCC) to develop new advanced computer technologies that apply artificial intelligence (A.I.) technologies. On the government side, the Defense Science Board has ranked artificial intelligence and robotics in the top ten military technologies for the 1980s. Anticipated applications include surveillance; weapons delivery, command, and control; maintenance; and training. The Department of Defense research agency DARPA has initiated an artificial intelligence–based supercomputer project, the Strategic Computing Program, which is intended to provide the necessary computer power for many military applications of artificial intelligence.

Interest in A.I. is worldwide. In June 1982, Japan launched a ten-year program to produce a fifth-generation computer system—a knowledge-information processing system (KIPS) based on A.I. concepts and principles. In early 1983, Japan began a project to develop a next-generation robot capable of advanced, autonomous decision making. Researchers in the robot project draw upon, among other things, results from the fifth-generation computer project. Great Britain has started a national A.I. project called the Alvey Project, and the European Common Market has initiated the ESPRIT program; interest and investment dollars are also evident in such countries as the Soviet Union, France, Germany, Austria, Italy, and Canada.

Artificial Intelligence examines these activities and discusses future trends and prospects that might result from them (as well as from complementary advances in computer hardware and software). A revolution in the way we process information is now taking place. This book offers fresh insights into how these directions and trends may affect the reader's field and into how new concepts, principles, tools, and techniques may best be exploited and applied to the reader's own work.

Acknowledgments

I wish to thank my students for their insights and penetrating questions, which helped to shape this book. I would also like to thank my editor, Linda Venator, for her invaluable suggestions and critiques of the book. Finally, I would like to dedicate the book to my loving wife, Myra, without whose patience and support it could not have been written, and to our children, Eric, Richard, and Pamela.

1 ▪ Introduction

DEFINITION OF ARTIFICIAL INTELLIGENCE

Artificial intelligence (A.I.) is a field of study concerned with designing and programming machines to accomplish tasks that people accomplish using their intelligence. A.I. also attempts to understand how human beings think, by studying the behavior of machine designs and programs that model current hypotheses and conjectures about some aspect of the human cognitive process. Thus stated, this field of endeavor is almost as old as the human species.

Our understanding of what constitutes intelligence is vague, and definitions of human intelligence are imprecise. The most widely accepted standard measure is the IQ (intelligence quotient) test, but the validity of this test as a true gauge of a person's intrinsic intelligence (potential or achieved) is still hotly contested in many quarters. Consequently, it should not be too surprising to learn that the definition of machine (or artificial) intelligence is equally vague.

Many attempts have been made to define and demonstrate more precisely what is meant by artificial intelligence. Turing (1963) proposed the following test of machine intelligence: if a person engaged in a typewritten discourse with a machine hidden behind a curtain could not determine whether the conversation was with another person or with a machine, the machine could be said to exhibit intelligence. Early A.I. programs addressed this challenge with mixed success. Another attempt to demonstrate machine intelligence involved programming a computer to solve portions of an IQ test. The attempt to define what behavioral characteristics a machine must possess to be considered intelligent, however, is best considered as an evolutionary process; advances in machine intelligence often result in more exact redefinitions of intelligent behavior.

But *Artificial Intelligence* is less concerned with the philosophical question of what constitutes intelligence than with the narrower question of which theories, concepts, tools, techniques, and models produced from research in this field can be applied to building better computer-based systems (including "smart" robots). To this end, the book concentrates on attributes and features of A.I. that distinguish it from the more conventional algorithmic computer problem-solving methods.

A.I. is a mind-set, a way of looking at and solving problems from a particular point of view. The concepts, methods, and techniques discussed in this book have been developed as a consequence of approaching problems from the relatively heuristic point of view that distinguishes the field of artificial intelligence from other computer science and systems engineering disciplines. The strengths and weaknesses associated with this approach, as well as the methodologies and techniques it has produced, are critically examined so as to enable the reader to recognize attributes and characteristics of a problem that identify it as most suitable for solution through heuristic programming or A.I. processing techniques.

Certain software tools and special hardware are available today to assist in applying these concepts, methods, and techniques; obtaining them and getting more information about them are discussed in later chapters. The current status and maturity of these tools and techniques are assessed, and past and existing examples of where this technology has been applied are reviewed. Finally, some forecasts of likely futures for this technology are explored.

■ KEY ATTRIBUTES

More than anything else, artificial intelligence represents a particular problem-solving mind-set that differs from more traditional algorithmic-oriented approaches. Much of the difference is traceable to the nature of the problems A.I. researchers tackle. A.I. research has concentrated on solving problems that are demonstrably solvable by human beings but for which no currently well-formulated, computationally feasible methodology exists. This class of problems includes:

- How we learn
- How we play games
- How we communicate with one another
- How we perceive (see, hear, speak, listen, write)
- How we create

Thus, A.I. has been concerned with human mental activities that are among the least well understood.

The approaches taken to solve these problems can best be characterized as informal, symbolic, and conceptual rather than as quantitative. Solutions are generally nonoptimal and are reached principally through approximate rules of thumb (for example, if A and B, then C), and through logical or plausible inferences based on these rules (for example, if A implies B and B implies C, then A implies C), rather than through calculation or step-by-step procedures.

Because A.I. has developed largely in the research community and because the methodologies needed to solve problems of interest to this group are poorly understood, A.I. has been largely a trial-and-error science. Consequently, the techniques developed have been designed with change and evolution in mind. The methods employed tend to be nonprocedural, flexible, and adaptive in nature; additional knowledge (facts and rules) can be added, deleted, or modified easily without system design modification. Furthermore, A.I. system architecture usually facilitates evaluating, examining, and analyzing proposed changes before their permanent addition.

The knowledge is often expressed in an object-oriented representation (where data, procedures, and rules are combined into conceptual units and communicate with each other through messages), rather than a system of separate data, separate procedure-oriented knowledge representations. One reason the problems under investigation are not amenable to well-understood quantitative methodologies is because the data are dirty. Available information is often noisy, full of uncertainty and errors, incomplete, and often inconsistent.

Many researchers attracted to A.I. are cognitive psychologists by training or inclination who are interested in understanding how human beings think. They observe and study people in various problem-solving situations and attempt to formulate theories and hypotheses at the macro level (not at the level of neural connections) to explain observed behavior. They develop computer models that test these hypotheses by attempting to duplicate the observed behaviors. These models and theories have strongly influenced the A.I. field, inspiring many A.I. concepts and techniques.

Of course, many other A.I. researchers are not concerned with whether or not their approach faithfully models the way human beings solve problems; they are concerned only that their programs work. These researchers are justified in seeking more novel, machine-unique solutions by the fact that (at least for the current crop of computer hardware) the computer and the human brain differ in several basic ways. The human brain has about 40 billion neurons (a neuron can be thought of as representing approximately 1 byte of information), whereas today's computers typically have main memories ranging from about 2 million bytes (2 Mbytes) for personal microcomputers to several hundred million bytes for large mainframes. Since we believe that decision making, learning, and other "intelligence-oriented" functions use only a comparatively small percentage of the brain's total capacity—typically 10 to 30 percent—the equivalent of only about 10 billion bytes (10 Gbytes) of neural memory probably are available to a human being for intelligence-oriented functions. This, however, represents a far greater capacity than that of today's computers. Moreover, each neuron has from 1,000 to 10,000 inputs and outputs, with over 100 trillion interconnections. By contrast, today's computer components are relatively sparsely interconnected, with no more than 4 inputs per logic gate. On the other hand, neural impulses typically travel at a speed of about 10 miles per hour, whereas electrons in an electronic circuit can travel at the speed of light. Finally, the brain's neurons generally fire on a majority threshold basis, whereas computer components work on a binary logic basis.

The final assessment of computer problem solving and the human paradigm has not yet been made. A case supporting the notion that computers should not necessarily emulate human problem-solving techniques is the current crop of chess-playing machines. These are specially designed machines that can rapidly anticipate many more moves than most people can, but they possess little strategic planning capability. They certainly do not play chess the way people do, yet they perform reasonably well against human opponents. They do, however, have recognizable shortcomings, and researchers are attempting to supplement current chess-playing machine designs with human-style approaches, including strategic planning, the setting of intermediate goals, and associated tactics.

In summary, although A.I. has much in common with other computer science disciplines, it differs from more conventional computer science areas in the following respects:

1. Viewpoint (plausible and logical reasoning, instead of quantitative calculation)
2. Subject matter (mental activity—very knowledge-intensive)
3. Tolerance for errors and imprecise data
4. Symbolic manipulation (instead of numeric orientation)
5. Evolutionary design principles (nonprocedural, anticipating addition and change)
6. Knowledge-based design

7. Inference and deduction capabilities (has a line of reasoning and can explain itself)
8. Heuristic or approximate problem-solving approach

Of course, any of these individual attributes can be found in more conventional computer science disciplines; for example, compilers do symbolic processing. Taken together, however, these attributes characterize a unique, human-style approach to problem solving that differs substantially from the mainstream computational approach.

A GENERIC A.I. SYSTEM

Typical A.I. system architecture is pictured in figure 1-1. It includes a knowledge base (in which the problem-domain knowledge is explicitly represented as a collection of facts, rules, and relationships about the

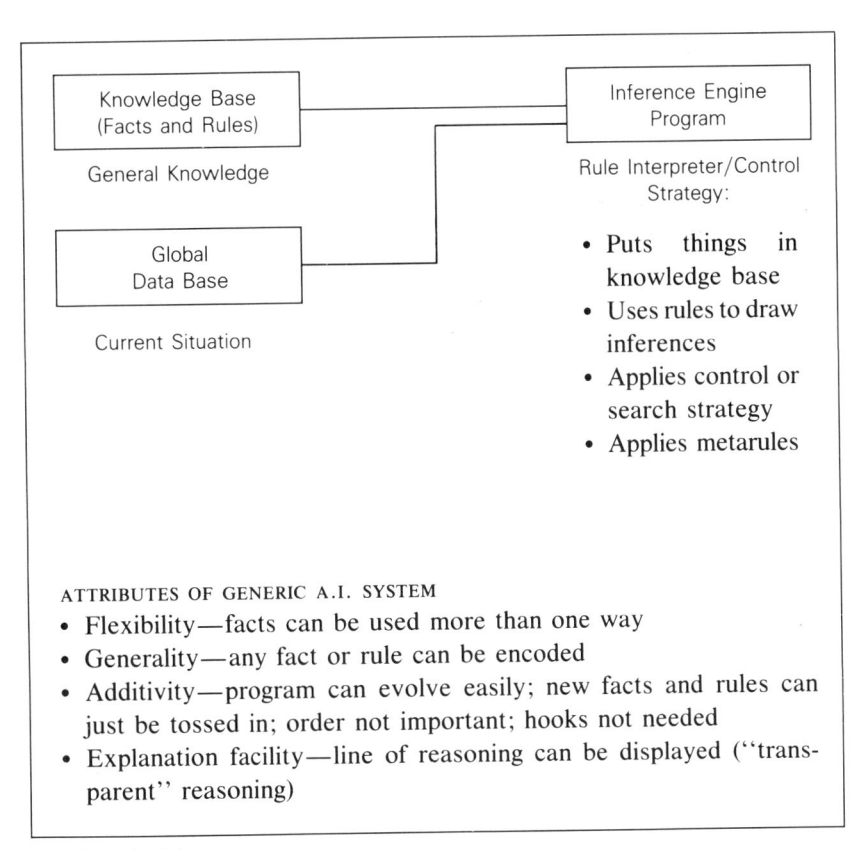

```
┌─────────────────────────┐         ┌─────────────────────────┐
│   Knowledge Base        │─────────│   Inference Engine      │
│   (Facts and Rules)     │         │   Program               │
└─────────────────────────┘         └─────────────────────────┘
     General Knowledge                Rule Interpreter/Control
                                      Strategy:

┌─────────────────────────┐           • Puts things in
│       Global            │─────────    knowledge base
│      Data Base          │           • Uses rules to draw
└─────────────────────────┘             inferences
     Current Situation                • Applies control or
                                        search strategy
                                      • Applies metarules
```

ATTRIBUTES OF GENERIC A.I. SYSTEM
- Flexibility—facts can be used more than one way
- Generality—any fact or rule can be encoded
- Additivity—program can evolve easily; new facts and rules can just be tossed in; order not important; hooks not needed
- Explanation facility—line of reasoning can be displayed ("transparent" reasoning)

1-1. Generic A.I. system.

problem-domain objects and concepts), a global data base (which contains assertions about the current case/problem under consideration, expressing the current state of knowledge about the particular problem being solved), and an inference engine program (which represents the control or procedural knowledge that updates the global data base, feeds information to the global data base, determines how to use the rules in the knowledge base to draw conclusions, and establishes the sequence in which different rules in the knowledge base are brought to bear in solving the problem).

In A.I. systems, program control is generally not a predefined, step-by-step procedure in which order is important. It is more of a trial-and-error procedure in which searches are made of a space of candidate solutions, and heuristics are used to prune the combinational growth that occurs in most complex real-world problem searches. The inference engine applies the control or search strategy; it determines when to apply which rules against what part of the data base to produce an output or to reach a goal or conclusion. This strategy is often expressed by heuristic rules of thumb that are pattern-invoked, triggered by the specifics of the problem state, called metarules. This approach is characterized by:

- *Flexibility:* facts can be used in more than one way.
- *Generality:* any fact or rule can be encoded.
- *Additivity:* the program can evolve easily, with new facts and rules added randomly. The order is not critical, and hooks are not needed. The program tolerates incomplete answers, occasional errors, misses, and less than optimum results.
- *Transparent reasoning:* often these programs are run interactively and provide, upon request, an explanation in human language of the line of reasoning used—how a particular conclusion was reached or why additional information was requested.

Because the knowledge base is usually an explicit (declarative) representation of the domain knowledge, it is maintained in a form that makes it accessible for more than one kind of use. For example, the knowledge base might contain a description of the various pieces in the game of chess, their legal moves, a few strategic concepts such as the importance of controlling the center of the board, and a list of successful opening moves. The global data base contains the evolving state of the particular chess game being played. The knowledge base can be used by the inference engine to determine the next move to make. It can also be used to answer questions about the game being played and the current situation.

The size and quality of the knowledge base is important in determining system performance. Generally, the greater the knowledge, the higher the quality of the system's problem-solving ability and the better the performance of the system. Of course, the larger the number of rules to consider, the more computer processing time and memory are required. This processing overhead can sometimes be reduced through a clever control or search strategy, much as a human expert can be efficient in determining which of the many facts and rules to apply to a particular problem situation.

The inference engine is generally a separate subsystem that interprets the contents of the knowledge base for one or more purposes and applies problem-domain-specific procedural knowledge to focus and limit what would otherwise be a large search.

Artificial intelligence encompasses many different ideas and disciplines. Another way to characterize A.I. is by the fields of study it encompasses. The January 1982 Computing reviews classification system by Samet and Ralston defines A.I. as including:

- Expert systems
- Game playing
- Automatic programming
- Deduction and theorem proving
- Knowledge representation
- Learning
- Natural language processing
- Problem solving
- Robotics
- Vision and scene understanding

■ HISTORICAL BACKGROUND

Artificial intelligence research has gone on almost since the introduction of the digital computer. It is based on the idea that all intelligent activity can be formalized and described by some sort of computable function—that is, that all human intelligence can, in principle, be mimicked by a digital computer. In a sense, A.I. carries the banner first raised by the ancient Greeks, who believed in the fundamental rationality of human beings.

Work in A.I. began in earnest in the 1950s, with great expectations that important successes would be achieved quickly. Industry anticipated early commercialization. Most of the seminal work during this period was done at Rand-Carnegie (by researchers that included Alan Newell, Herb Simon, and J.C. Shaw) and at MIT (by researchers that included Marvin Minsky and John McCarthy). The initial problems undertaken included games and theorem proving. The timeline below identifies the succession of developments.

1950—Claude Shannon designed a chess-playing program that introduced the "game tree" concept.

1955—Alan Newell, J.C. Shaw, and Herb Simon showed that chess playing was analogous to the problem of proving theorems in symbolic logic.

1956—A Dartmouth workshop, organized by John McCarthy, coined the term *artificial intelligence*.

1957—Newell and his associates developed their Logic Theorist program, which proved theorems in symbolic logic using heuristic rather than exhaustive techniques. They invented IPL (Information Processing Language), the first list-processing language, to assist them in this work.

1958—Newell and his associates developed a chess program in IPL. They also developed the famous General Problem Solver (GPS), which served as an executive for managing the general searches used to solve problems in elementary logic, chess, high-school algebra word problems, and question-answering systems.

1958—John McCarthy developed programs capable of question-answering and developed the computer language LISP. LISP is currently the language of choice for most A.I. researchers.

1959—McCarthy worked on systems capable of deductive reasoning and information retrieval.

Research at this time centered on developing and understanding general problem-solving strategies, known as "weak methods." The problems proved much more difficult, and the general problem-solving approaches too weak to allow their solution on the existing computer hardware within reasonable time constraints.

By the early 1960s, few practical applications of A.I. had emerged, industry's interest had dissipated, and general disillusionment with A.I. research prevailed. Research continued in a few academic centers, namely Carnegie-Mellon, Stanford, MIT, and SRI (Stanford Research Institute). During this period, research began to move in a different direction. It addressed problems of much narrower scope and augmented the general problem-solving methodology (the weak methods) with very specific knowledge. The developments of the 1960s are listed below.

Early 1960s—T.G. Evans wrote a program that could successfully answer IQ test problems, reasoning by analogy.

Early 1960s—D.G. Bobrow wrote STUDENT, a program capable of solving high-school algebra word problems.

Early 1960s—Work began on DENDRAL by Joshua Lederberg, Bruce Buchanan, and Edward Feigenbaum at Stanford. DENDRAL inferred the structure of molecules, using mass spectrography data and a large-domain knowledge base. It was the first successful expert system and is still widely used today.

1961–65—A.L. Samuel of IBM worked on a checkers-playing program.

1961—Jim Slagle at MIT developed SAINT, a program that could perform symbolic integration. It eventually led to MACSYMA some ten years later, developed by W.A. Martin, J. Moses, and Carl Engelman. MACSYMA solves all algebraic and calculus problems at the symbolic level. A commercial success, it is currently offered as a feature on a variety of different manufacturers' computers.

1962—G.W. Ernst made the first A.I. computer-controlled robot. It had a mechanical arm with shoulder, elbow, and grabber.

1963—Alan Newell, J.C. Shaw, and Herb Simon worked on chess-playing programs.

1964—B. Raphael worked on question-answering systems using trivial data bases.

Mid-1960s—Marvin Minsky and S. Papert began their computer vision work. From this work came many ideas, including the "society of the mind" theory of Minsky, Papert, and Patrick Winston: programs should not be centralized but should be designed with parts, as heterarchies.

1967—R. Greenblatt and his associates continued research in chess playing, which led eventually to commercial chess-playing machines.

By the 1970s, the new research directions began to bear fruit. The research community grew to include researchers at institutions such as Yale, BBN, Rutgers, Rand, and the University of Illinois. This period is typified by the work of Terry Winograd in the SHRDLU program, which simulated the colored block world and was based on PLANNER, the programming language developed by C.E. Hewitt. Its narrow domain and relatively large data base resulted in a system that was surprisingly natural in its communication with people. The approach that emerged from its success was to build more narrowly focused systems that used relatively simple problem-solving methodologies but were very knowledge-intensive. These systems had large domain-specific knowledge bases and extensive procedural problem-domain-specific knowledge.

By the end of the 1970s, the fields of expert systems and natural language processing had begun to emerge. Research produced an increasing number of successes. Pioneering work was done in areas of machine perception, notably computer vision and speech understanding. By the end of the 1970s, A.I. research had already affected many fields, including programming techniques, psychology, mathematics, chemistry, genetic engineering, geology, oil exploration, medicine, and business. Many of these applications are summarized in figure 1-2 and in Appendix A. They include such systems as:

- ROBOT—a natural-language front end that led to the commercial product INTELLECT; developed by AIC (Artificial Intelligence Corporation)
- R1—a computer configuration expert; built by DEC and Carnegie-Mellon
- DENDRAL—a system that performs organic compound analysis; built by Stanford
- PUFF—pulmonary disease test interpretation; built by Stanford
- HAIL—circuit board layout and assembly; built by Hazeltine
- CAT—locomotive maintenance; built by General Electric
- DIPMETER ADVISOR—oil-drilling analysis; built by Schlumberger
- ACE—telephone cable fault diagnosis; built by Bell Telephone and Columbia University

In the 1980s previous successes, coupled with dramatic advances in hardware performance and reductions in hardware cost and size, have made large-scale commercialization of A.I. likely. With the maturing of A.I., computers will evolve from number crunchers and text crunchers to graphics crunchers and knowledge crunchers. The emphasis is shifting from machines that compute to machines that communicate.

Special A.I. hardware and software development tools have begun to emerge, and commercial applications are multiplying. A.I. products are increasingly being offered on the more traditional mainstream computer product lines. The latest surge in product offerings has been toward providing lower-cost production delivery hardware and software vehicles that can be integrated and interfaced with the existing base of conventional commercial computer hardware (such as IBM mainframes and personal computers) and software (traditional data base systems, programming languages, and operating systems). At the same time, research has begun to address fundamental issues of learning, memory structure, knowledge representation, and knowledge acquisition.

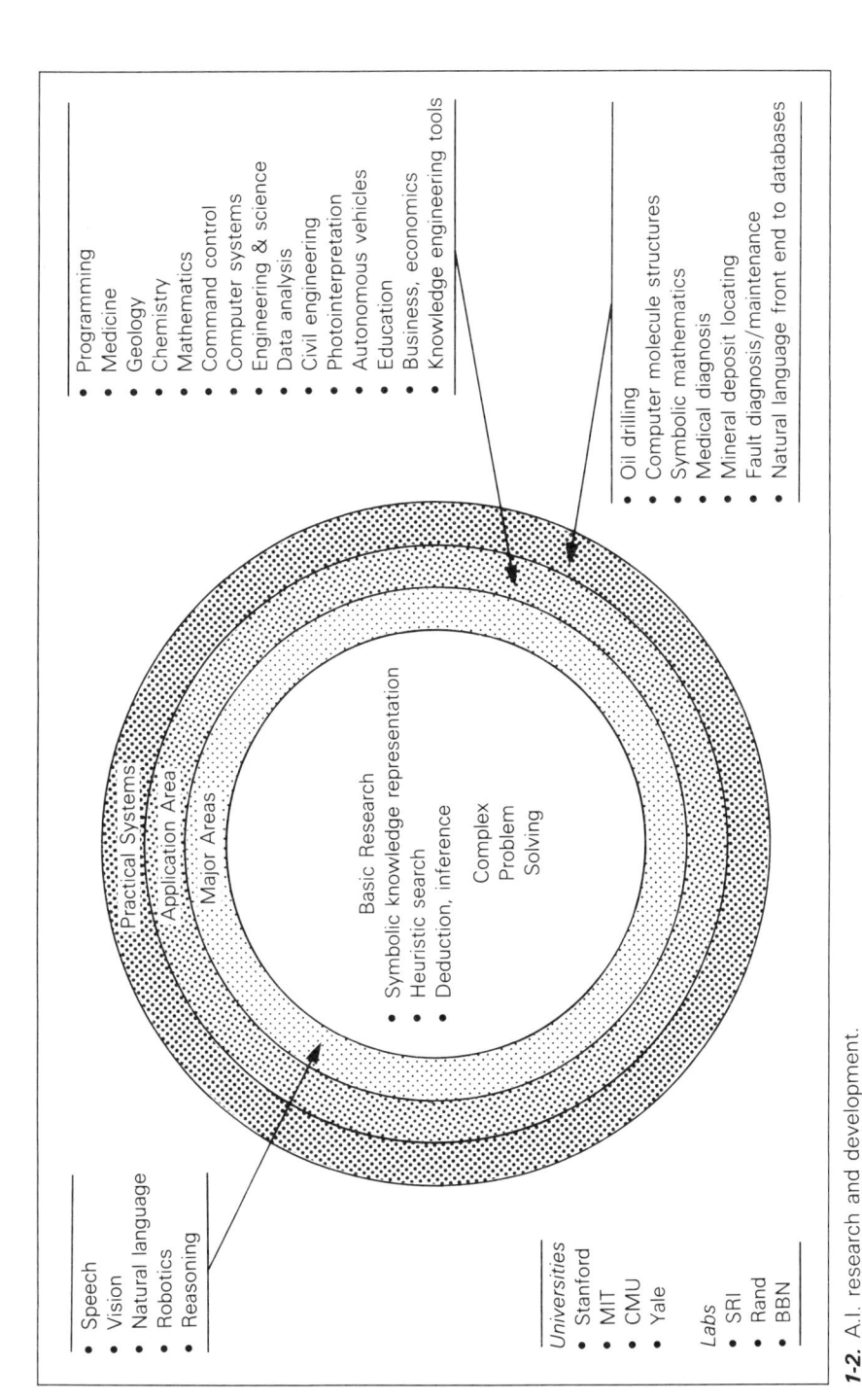

- Speech
- Vision
- Natural language
- Robotics
- Reasoning

Universities
- Stanford
- MIT
- CMU
- Yale

Labs
- SRI
- Rand
- BBN

Practical Systems
Application Area
Major Areas

Basic Research
- Symbolic knowledge representation
- Heuristic search
- Deduction, inference

Complex Problem Solving

- Programming
- Medicine
- Geology
- Chemistry
- Mathematics
- Command control
- Computer systems
- Engineering & science
- Data analysis
- Civil engineering
- Photointerpretation
- Autonomous vehicles
- Education
- Business, economics
- Knowledge engineering tools

- Oil drilling
- Computer molecule structures
- Symbolic mathematics
- Medical diagnosis
- Mineral deposit locating
- Fault diagnosis/maintenance
- Natural language front end to databases

1-2. A.I. research and development.

The A.I. market today has grown from a $250-million business in 1982 to a $750-million business in 1985 and is projected to be more than a $4-billion industry by 1990, comprising 20 to 25 percent of the computer industry. Currently, 50 percent of the business involves specialized A.I. hardware (LISP machines, symbolic processors); 10 percent, expert systems (this area is expected to increase its share in future); 24 percent, vision processing; 5 percent, voice recognition; 8 percent, natural language applications; and 3 percent, A.I. programming languages.

Interest has resurfaced in industry, as well. Among the Fortune 500 companies that have A.I. research groups are DEC, IBM, Texas Instruments, Xerox, Sperry-Rand, Schlumberger, Hewlett Packard, General Motors, Westinghouse, Hughes, Boeing, General Electric, AT&T, Martin Marietta, Lockheed, and E-Systems. New companies have formed, too, many of them spinoffs from university research, providing specialized teaching, consulting, and application-building, and offering software products—primarily expert system building tools and natural language interface systems. These companies include Teknowledge, Smart Systems, Computer Thought, Artificial Intelligence Corp., Cognitive Systems, Automatix, Octek, AI & DS, JAYCOR, PAR, Syntelligence, APEX, Intellicorp, Inference Corp., Symbolics, and LMI.

2 ▪ Theories and Concepts

To program a computer to solve nonquantitative problems dealing with such intangibles as ideas, concepts, and their relationships, a formalism capable of representing and manipulating these relatively abstract entities must be devised. This requires structuring and processing tools that go beyond the data, text, and numerical manipulation- and computation-oriented systems and languages that prevail today. We call these more powerful structures *knowledge bases,* and the manipulative operations on these knowledge bases, *inference engine programs.*

An artificial intelligence system is capable not merely of storing and manipulating data, but also of acquiring, representing, and manipulating knowledge. This manipulation includes the ability to deduce or infer new knowledge—new relationships about facts and concepts—from existing knowledge and to use representation and manipulation skills to solve complex problems that are often nonquantitative in nature. The key issues confronting the designer of an A.I. system are knowledge acquisition, knowledge representation, and knowledge manipulation (which occur primarily through inference and deduction) and the often search-oriented control strategy or inference engine (which determines the items of knowledge to be accessed, the deductions to be made, and the order of steps to be used). These ideas are illustrated in figure 2-1.

This chapter discusses some popular knowledge-representation schemes and inference mechanisms that have proved successful, at least for the limited class of A.I. applications currently in use. Selecting a representation that is capable of good description and can be easily applied to complex problem solving is of major importance to the success of the A.I. program. An important lesson learned over the course of many attempts to build successful A.I. programs is that often relatively few, relatively simple control decisions are all that are required to produce complex behavior as long as a rich, complex knowledge base is available

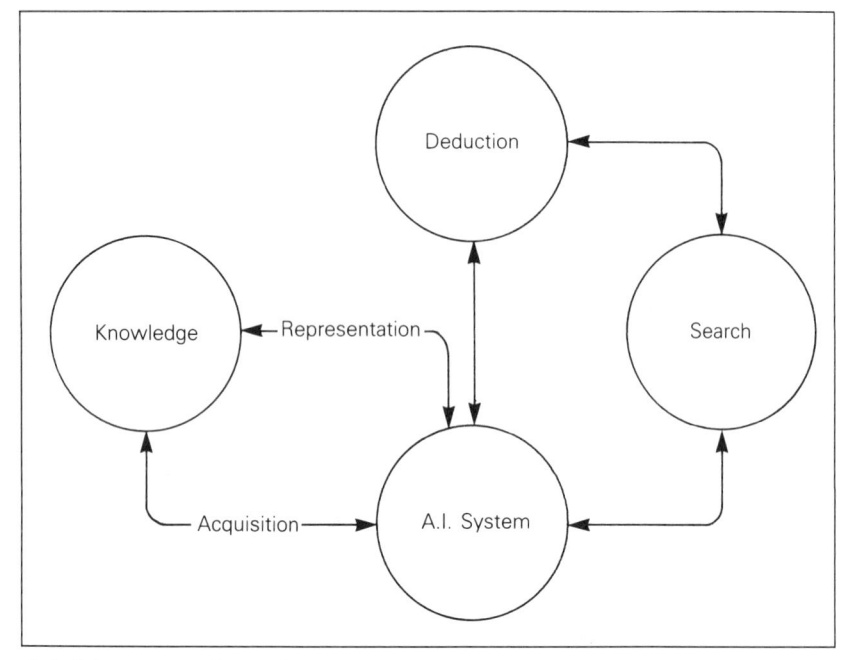

2-1. A.I. conceptual overview.

to drive the program. In short, a high degree of control sophistication is often not required for intelligent behavior, but a rich, well-structured representation of a large set of a priori data and hypotheses is.

■ KNOWLEDGE REPRESENTATION

The choice of a scheme for the representation of knowledge is critical to successful problem solving. It can affect the number of states in the problem domain and thus can either increase or decrease the complexity of the problem.

Consider the 8-puzzle game illustrated in figure 2-2. The 8-puzzle is a three-by-three-unit square in which eight numbered one-unit-square tiles are placed. The ninth square remains empty. A tile adjacent to the empty square can be slid into the empty space. The game consists of moving the tiles from a starting position to a specified goal position, such as increasing numerical order. Each problem state could be described in terms of the position of all eight tiles, and a move could be specified

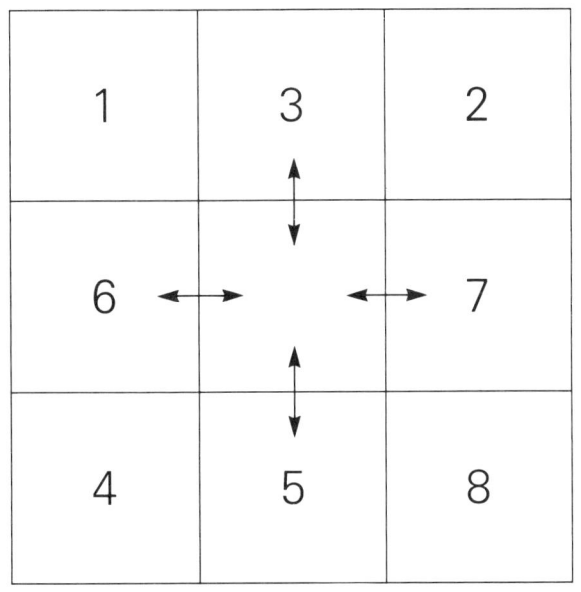

2-2. Eight-puzzle game.

by naming the tile that gets slid into the empty square; alternatively, a move could be specified in terms of whether the empty square is relocated up, down, to the right, or to the left. In the first representation scheme, a large number of moves must be considered for each starting state, even though many of these moves are not physically possible and others are physically redundant. In the second representation scheme, only the appropriate four nonredundant moves for the current problem state are considered.

Some problems, by their nature, have a fairly natural representation; for example, the game of tic-tac-toe seems most naturally represented by a three-by-three-unit square of Xs and Os, as illustrated in figure 2-3. Usually, however, no clear, natural means of representing the knowledge associated with a given problem emerges. In fact, for many problems, experts must use more than one scheme to represent the knowledge in the problem domain, much as an architect usually uses many types of sketches, blueprints, and other descriptive devices to represent an evolving design.

The bases for making the proper choice of representation for a particular problem are still poorly understood. No methodology exists for sys-

X	O	
O	O	X
X	X	O

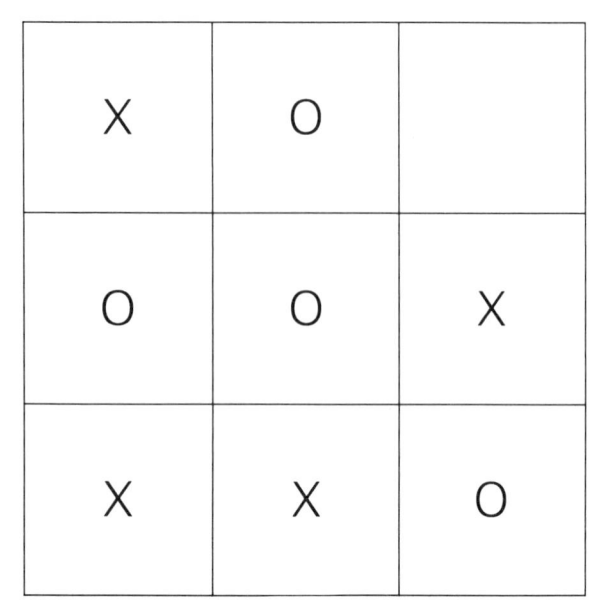

2-3. Tic-tac-toe.

tematically starting at an initial representation of the knowledge associated with a given problem and successively refining and improving that representation. Rather, successful selection of the proper knowledge representation seems to be based on experience gained through attempts to solve similar problems and on experience in using the various knowledge representation schemes under consideration.

We will discuss four knowledge representation approaches that currently form the basis for most successful A.I. applications: predicate calculus; production rules; frames and scripts; and semantic networks. These approaches are extensions of various data structures in current use in more conventional data processing systems—namely, lists, tables, hierarchies, sets, rings, networks, and matrices (see figure 2-4). To these data structure schemes are added the formalisms necessary for representing and denoting entities, events, and objects, as well as relationships among them that are associated with the semantics of the problem domain. This is where predicate calculus, production rules, frames and scripts, and semantic networks enter the picture.

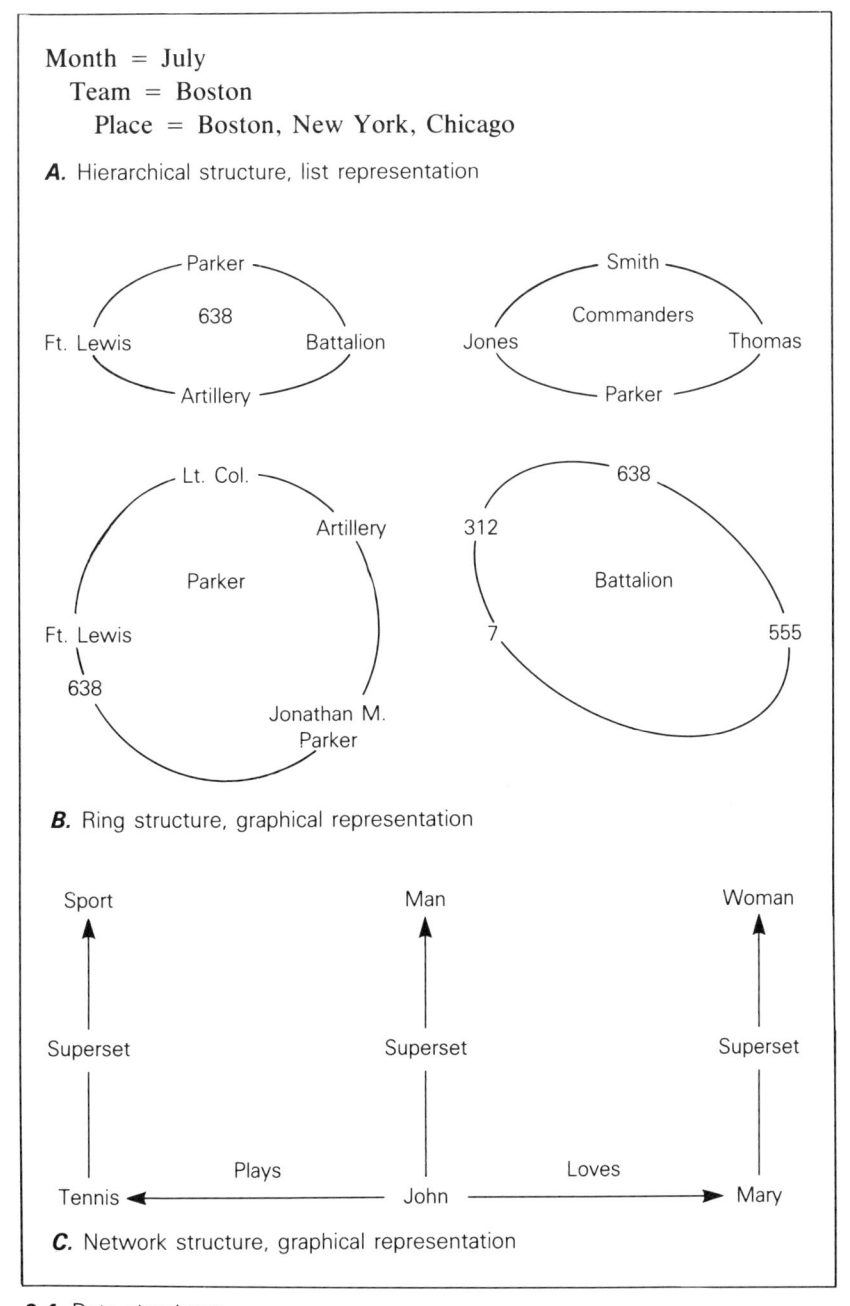

Knowledge Representation ■ **17**

Month = July
  Team = Boston
    Place = Boston, New York, Chicago

A. Hierarchical structure, list representation

            ⎯ Parker ⎯
              638
Ft. Lewis   Battalion
          ⎯ Artillery ⎯

            ⎯ Smith ⎯
           Commanders
Jones   Thomas
          ⎯ Parker ⎯

      ⎯ Lt. Col. ⎯
            Artillery
      Parker
Ft. Lewis
 638
        Jonathan M.
          Parker

         638
312
      Battalion
7   555

B. Ring structure, graphical representation

Sport   Man   Woman
↑   ↑   ↑
Superset   Superset   Superset
│   │   │
         Plays   Loves
Tennis ◀⎯⎯⎯⎯ John ⎯⎯⎯⎯▶ Mary

C. Network structure, graphical representation

2-4. Data structures.

■ PREDICATE CALCULUS

The idea of using a formal language capable of representing and mathematically manipulating logical thought is appealing and has historical precedent. It is appealing because it suggests a powerful way of deriving new knowledge from old, through mathematical deduction. Historically, the development and the use of formal logic systems to investigate the nature of reasoning and knowledge have played an important role in Western thought. The development of a formal mathematics of logic dates to the last half of the nineteenth century, with the work of Boole, Frege, and Russell; it was extended in the twentieth century by such philosophers as Quine, Carnap, and Tarski.

Formal mathematical logical systems were some of the first representation schemes to be used in artificial intelligence and are currently being applied to artificial intelligence problems by researchers such as McCarthy. First-order logic and predicate calculus are currently the most commonly used mathematical logic systems. They form the bases for the PROLOG language. Using this formalism, we can conclude that a new statement is true by proving that it follows from statements already known to be true. The technique can then be extended, as we shall see, to deriving answers to questions and finding solutions to problems.

Both these logic systems are concerned with both the form (or syntax) of statements and the determination of truth through the syntactic manipulation of these well-formed formulas of logic. In this formal treatment of logic, the representation and the processing of the formulas to reach deductions constitute two separate steps. In fact, the representational syntax of predicate calculus can be adapted for use with a different or modified processing scheme.

The most fundamental concept in logic is that of truth. A properly formed statement (or proposition) has only one of two possible values: true or false. Propositional logic adds to this concept of truth various connectives, or logical operators. Chief among them are:

- The logical *and*, often denoted by the symbol $\wedge$ or & and called the conjunction of two logical propositions
- The logical *or*, often denoted by the symbol $\vee$ and called the disjunction of two logical propositions
- The negation, or *not* connective, often denoted by the symbol $\sim$
- The *implies* connective, often denoted by the symbol $\rightarrow$ or $>$
- The *equivalent* connective, often denoted by the symbol $=$ or $\leftrightarrow$

These connectives are defined by the truth table[1] shown below.

p	q	$p \wedge q$	$p \vee q$	$p \rightarrow q$	$\sim p$	$p \leftrightarrow q$
t	t	t	t	t	f	t
t	f	f	t	f	f	f
f	t	f	t	t	t	f
f	f	f	f	t	t	t

In this table t stands for true, f stands for false, and p and q represent two propositions.

We will represent these propositions and connectives in a LISP-like structure in which the connective (or logical operator) appears first, followed by the applicable proposition(s), and the whole expression is enclosed by parentheses. For example:

> **(and p q)** represents the logical *and* of statements p and q. It is true only if both p and q are true.
>
> **(or p q)** represents the logical *or* of statements p and q. It is true if either p or q is true.
>
> **(not p)** represents the logical *not* of statement p. It is true if p is false.
>
> **(implies p q)** represents that statement p implies statement q. It states that q is true if p is true. Here we only really care about what happens to q when p is true; the assignment of a value to this expression when p is false is somewhat arbitrary. By convention, its truth value is defined as true if q is true or if p is false. In this way, (implies p q) can be replaced by the equivalent expression (or (not p) q).
>
> **(equ p q)** represents that statements p and q are equivalent. It is true if statements p and q are either both true or both false.

From syntactic combinations of variables and connectives, we can build arbitrarily complex sentences of logic and treat these just as we would expressions of mathematics. Various transformations of these representations are valid. They are summarized below:

(not (not p)) = p
(not (and p q)) = (or (not p) (not q))

---

1. From *The Handbook of Artificial Intelligence,* edited by A. Barr and E. Feigenbaum (Los Altos, CA: William Kaufmann, Inc., 1981). Reprinted with permission.

(not (or p q)) = (and (not p) (not q))
(implies p q) = (or (not p) q)
(and p (or q r)) = (or (and p q) (and p r))
(or p (and q r)) = (and (or p q) (or p r))
$p \leftrightarrow q$ = (or (and p q) (and (not p) (not q)))
$p \leftrightarrow q$ = (and implies p q) (implies q p))

A propositional sentence is said to be a *tautology* if it is true for all possible values of the sentence constants. It is said to be a *fallacy* or *contradiction* if the sentence is false regardless of the assignment of values.

In propositional calculus, we encounter the first rules of inference. An inference rule allows the deduction of new sentences from previously given sentences. The best known inference rule, *modus ponens*, states that, if we know that two sentences of the form p and $p \rightarrow q$ are true, we can infer that sentence q is also true. Thus *modus ponens* allows us to replace sentences p and $p \rightarrow q$ with the single statement q, eliminating the connective $\rightarrow$. Consequently, *modus ponens* is called the $\rightarrow$ elimination rule.

Predicate calculus is an extension of propositional logic that makes the latter applicable to artificial intelligence by allowing us to specify objects, to postulate relationships between objects, and to generalize these relationships over classes of objects. Statements about objects, whether by themselves or in relation to other objects, are called *predicates*. A predicate is applied to a specific number of arguments and has a value of either true or false. Consider the following examples.

The predicate *color* is written as:

$$\text{(color object value)}$$

or alternatively as:

$$\text{color (object, value)}$$

It constitutes a two-argument predicate that is true if the object has the assigned value for its color. More specifically,

$$\text{(color block maroon)}$$

is a predicate that is true if the object, a block, has the color value maroon.

Predicates can be logically connected. For instance, the predicate

(or (color block maroon) (color block purple))

is true if the block has either the color value maroon or the color value purple.

Another example of a logical connection of predicates is:

(implies (material block iron) (heavy block))

which states that the object block is heavy if the object block is made of the material, iron.

We also may wish to express these predicates as being true for all members, or some members, of a given set. This is achieved through the use of variables and the two quantifiers: *for all* or $\forall$, and *there exists* or $\exists$.

Consider the following predicate:

(for all (X) (implies (in X box) (color X red)))

This predicate states that, for all X, X is the color red if X is in the box. Here we have distinguished variables from constants by writing the variables in capital letters and the constants in lowercase letters. Some systems, such as the rule-based system OPS-5, distinguish variables from constants by writing a *?* as a prefix for all variables. Using this system, we would rewrite the last expression as:

(for all (?x) (implies (in ?x box) (color ?x red)))

An example of the other type of quantifier is:

(exists (X) (and (in X box) (color X red)))

which states that at least one value for the variable X exists for which it is true that X is in the box and its color is red.

First-order logic extends predicate calculus by introducing the notion of *operators* or *functions*. Functions, like predicates or truth functions, have a fixed number of arguments. Unlike predicates, however, they not only have the values true and false, they also can *return* objects related to their arguments for which the function is true. Each of the arguments of a function can be a variable, a constant, or another function.

In fact, a function can include itself—a circumstance called *recursion*. For example, the function defined as:

(father (father (john)))

would be John's paternal grandfather.

First-order logic permits quantification over objects but not over predicates or functions. For example, the statement "All predicates have only one argument" cannot be expressed in first-order logic; expressing it would require use of a higher-order logic.

So far, we have considered the parts of speech and the grammar of the language of logic. To be able to express a problem to be solved in this language, we need to agree upon and define the problem vocabulary: the names of the various objects, their values, and their relationships. Second, we need to provide the inference rules for processing and manipulating these predicates and functions, to allow the deduction of new knowledge.

The inference mechanism normally associated with predicate calculus is the process of resolution, formal reasoning, which is discussed later in this chapter. Other inferencing schemes can be applied, however, without altering the basic predicate calculus syntax and grammar. Examples of systems whose internal syntactical representation formalism is based primarily on first-order predicate calculus, using an inferencing mechanism other than pure resolution, are the OPS and EMYCIN production rule systems and the KLONE semantic network system.

Some of the attractive features of a logic-based knowledge representation scheme are:

1. It is often a natural way to express knowledge about a problem.
2. It is precise. It uses standard methods of expression.
3. It has the flexibility to represent a particular fact in a single way without having to consider its possible use.
4. It is modular. Logical assertions can be entered independently of each other and can grow incrementally. Moreover, they can be processed and examined independently of each other. This feature makes logic-based representation schemes particularly attractive for consideration in fifth-generation parallel-processing schemes.

Its disadvantages are:

1. It severely hampers user specification and control over the procedural portion of the problem solving. Because the scheme separates rep-

resentation and processing, the user cannot easily direct the logic-based system on how to use the stored facts and how to proceed with the problem solution—yet often this is the most critical aspect of building a practical system capable of solving problems under realistic time constraints.
2. It is unable to express uncertain and approximate relationships.

■ PRODUCTION RULES

The term *production rule system* refers to several different knowledge representation schemes based on the general underlying idea of *condition-action pairs*, which are also called *if-then pairs, situation-action pairs, production rules*, or just plain *productions*. Production rules were first proposed by E.L. Post (1943); they have undergone much theoretical and applications-oriented change in ensuing years.

Production rules were inspired by attempts to model the human cognitive process. The matching of a production rule was associated with the firing of a neuron. Production rule systems have been shown to be capable of modeling any computable procedure.

On the surface a production rule resembles a predicate calculus implication statement. A production rule is cast in the form "If this condition holds, then this action is appropriate."

A production system consists of the following parts:

1. The rule base, which is composed of a set of production rules.
2. One or more data bases, which contain whatever information is appropriate for the particular task. Some parts of the data base are permanent, whereas others only pertain to the current problem.
3. A short-term memory buffer, which represents the context or current focus of attention of the production rules.
4. The interpreter, which determines the task to do next or the production rule to fire next. Its operation is generally closely related to the resolution process.

Production systems operate in cycles that have three phases: matching, conflict resolution, and action. First the interpreter checks to see which productions match, are appropriate, and could fire. If more than one is found, a single production is selected from among them or the conflict is resolved. Finally, the action(s) indicated by the matching rule are initiated.

Unlike the actions of a purely logic-based system, such as first-order predicate calculus, these actions go beyond simple deduction of new knowledge. Moreover, they can allow arbitrary programs to be run, rather than just making a change in the context. In some systems, possible actions include the activation or deactivation of sets of other productions; even the matching process can have side effects, enabling the rule under examination to alter the context or change the control structure without ever being fired.

The actual syntax of the production rule varies greatly from system to system. Often two forms are employed in the system: an internal representation that is actually used by the system, and a more user-friendly form that allows the user to input and read rules in a more natural language-based format. Typically, a production rule has the following syntax:

(rule ⟨name⟩
　(if ⟨trigger fact 1⟩
　　⟨trigger fact 2⟩
　　　⋮
　　⟨trigger fact *n*⟩)
　(then ⟨conclusion fact1, or action 1⟩
　　　⟨conclusion fact2, or action 2⟩
　　　　⋮
　　　⟨conclusion fact *n*, or action *n*⟩)))

Each such rule could be loosely thought of as a *chunk* of knowledge — a term coined by H.A. Simon (1974).

Specific examples of production rules and facts include:

facts–

((animal is cheetah)
(animal is carnivore)
(animal has hair))   [2.1]

rules–

(rule identity 5
　(if (animal eats meat))
　(then (animal is carnivore)))   [2.2]

An example of an external rule format from the expert system MYCIN (upon which the expert system shell M-1 and S-1 is based) is:

Rule 86:
If:

1. The infection that requires therapy is meningitis, and
2. The patient does have evidence of serious skin or soft tissue infection, and
3. Organisms were not seen on the stain of the culture, and
4. The type of the infection is bacterial;

Then: There is evidence that the organism (other than those seen on cultures or smears) that might be causing the infection is staphylococcus-coag-pos (0.78) streptococcus-group-a (0.5). [2.3]

This last rule produces multiple conclusions whose likelihood of being correct is measured in terms of probabilitylike numbers that (in this instance) are not true probabilities but measures called certainty factors. Production rules differ from purely logic-based predicates and functions in their ability to handle uncertainty and incomplete knowledge.

An example from an expert system called SACON (a version of which has been built using the expert system shell M-1) is:

Rule 058[2]
If:

1. The material composing the substructure is one of: the metals, and
2. The tolerable analysis error (in percent) is between 5 and 30, and
3. The nondimensional stress of the substructure is greater than 0.9, and
4. The number of cycles in the loading to be applied is between 1,000 and 10,000;

Then: It is definite (1.0) that fatigue is one of the stress behavior phenomena in the substructure. [2.4]

---

2. From *Knowledge Engineering: The Applied Side of A.I.*, by E. Feigenbaum, ONR Series in Artificial Intelligence. Reprinted with permission.

An example of a rule used in an expert system built to diagnose a chemical spill (using the expert system shell OPS-5[3]) is:

```
(p coordinate-a        :if goal exists

   (goal
      ~name coordinate  :to coordinate
      ~status active    :which is active
    - (task-order)      :no preferred order
 →
   (make goal           :then make subgoal
      ~name order-tasks :determine order
      ~status active    :make status active
   (modify 1            :modify coord.goal
      ~status pending)))):change its status to pending    [2.5]
```

Here the syntax is more like that of a programming language; for this reason, explanatory comments are provided following the colons. At the same time, OPS-5 is one of the most efficient production rule systems. In OPS-5, attribute names are denoted by a preceding symbol ~ and are followed by their value. In the example above, this rule results in the determination of a new subgoal and in the modification of the control strategy (through a change in another rule's status).

From this short introduction, we can already identify many of the advantages and disadvantages of the production rule representation scheme. Many of these coincide with those we observed for the predicate calculus logic-based representation scheme. The advantages associated with production rule systems include:

1. *Modularity*—production rules can be added, changed, or deleted independently of one another, and they are order-independent. Therefore, production rule systems are potentially adaptable to fifth-generation parallel-processing architectures.
2. *Uniformity*—production rules impose a uniform structure on the knowledge in the rule base, making the information easier for third parties to understand.
3. *Naturalness*—production rules provide a syntax well-suited to the expression of certain kinds of knowledge. Such statements are frequently used by experts in explaining their jobs.

---

3. From *Building Expert Systems,* by F. Hayes-Roth, D.A. Waterman, and D.B. Lenat (Reading, MA: Addison-Wesley, 1983), pp. 302–6. Reprinted with permission.

Among the disadvantages of these systems are:

1. *Inefficiency*—the execution of a production rule imposes a large overhead on system resources, hampering their responsiveness to predetermined sequences of situations, and restricts their ability to take larger steps in reasoning when the situation demands it.
2. *Opacity*—it is often hard to follow the flow of control. The meaning of algorithms is less apparent than the meaning of corresponding expressions in a more traditional programming language.

■ FRAMES AND SCRIPTS

Purely logic-based and production rule–based representation schemes have the shortcoming of using processing resources inefficiently. These systems require scanning a list of facts and rules to locate a matching pattern. When an appropriate match is found, the list is updated with this new knowledge, and the cycle is then reinitiated until the goal is reached or the problem solved. The time associated with this pattern-directed inferencing process varies exponentially with the length of the list of facts and rules for logic-based and production rule–based systems. As the quantity of facts and rules grows, the need increases to consider organizing and structuring the knowledge in more efficient forms than the simple list—forms that can better direct attention and can facilitate recall and inference.

Frames and scripts represent an alternative method of structuring and organizing knowledge. As with production rule systems, there is no standard frame or script; instead, all possess some basic unifying principles of knowledge organization and representation. Frames and scripts organize knowledge into prototypal objects and stereotypical events appropriate to specific situations. The organization of this knowledge facilitates expectation-driven processing. Psychological evidence suggests that people use large collections of knowledge from previous experiences to interpret new situations in their everyday cognitive activity (Bartlett 1932).

R.C. Schank and R.P. Abelson (1977) designed scripts (framelike structures) to assist them in developing systems capable of understanding stories and news reports. For example, when we read a story about a person going to a restaurant, we anticipate that we will hear about such things as menus and waiters. And when we read that the customer ordered a meal and later left the restaurant, we conclude that the person ate a meal and paid a bill, even if we are not explicitly told so. Frames were originally proposed by Minsky (1975) as a basis for understanding visual perception, natural language dialogues, and other complex behaviors.

Frames do not preclude the use of logic sentences or production rules; rather, they integrate these representation schemes with data and more traditional program procedures in an organization of interrelated frames. The key representational mechanisms used in frames to make this kind of reasoning possible are *slots* and *links*. The slot is the place where knowledge fits within the larger context of the frame. It represents the attributes and properties associated with a given frame, and in turn has values associated with it. Slot values can be filled in, missing, or incomplete. For example, a frame for describing chairs might have slots for the number of legs and the style of back. Because the slot mechanism allows information to be missing or incomplete, it permits reasoning and deduction based on seeking confirmation of expectations; filling in the slots thus involves interpreting new data in terms of supplying the missing or incomplete values in various slots.

A link is a special kind of slot that indicates a unidirectional relationship between frames. For example, because the frame for describing chairs is a specialization of the frame dealing with the more generic concept of furniture, the chair frame might have a slot whose value is a pointer or unidirectional link to the furniture frame. If we seek some information about a chair that is not present in the chair frame, we can check the furniture frame. Since a chair is a special kind of furniture, we can expect (unless some exceptional situation exists) that the chair will inherit the properties and attributes present in the furniture frame. These ideas are illustrated in the following simple frame:

```
(henry (ako (value (man)))
   (height (value (75)))
   (weight (value (178)))
   (hobbies (value (jogging) (skiing)))
```

In this example, we see a frame called *henry* that has slots for the attributes height, weight, and hobbies. Each of these slots can have more than one value. Henry is a subset or specialization of the classification *man*, so we also have a specialized slot that links Henry to a frame representing the general category concept, man. In this example, the slot is labeled *ako* (for *a kind of*). This link tells us that Henry inherits as default values all the attributes and properties associated with the frame called *man*. Such inheritance-type links have also been called such names as *isa* and *specialization-of*. If we wish to know how many arms and legs Henry has, we first look for the information in the frame called *henry*. If we cannot find the information we seek in this frame, the *ako* link tells us that we could try the frame called *man*, which might contain information about the number of arms and legs men generally have. Henry inherits these properties by default, whether or not he corresponds to the typical man in this respect. If Henry is atypical, we can acknowledge the special case by putting the value *one arm* (for example) in the frame called *henry*. Other kinds of links can be established to depict other kinds of relationships between links. For example Henry might own a car. We could create a special *owner* link slot in the frame called *henry* to record the fact of this owner relationship and to point to the frame that depicts the type of car that Henry owns.

Demons are another important mechanism used in frames. Demons are collections of production rules, logical sentences, or more traditional programming procedures embedded in the frame that can be activated dynamically when the frame is accessed or updated. Demons can be triggered by *if-needed, if-added,* or *if-removed* situations.

The following example, which is representative of the type of scheme Schank and Abelson (1977) used to help understand stories about restaurant scenes, illustrates slots, links, and demons. As part of this scheme, Schank and Abelson introduced a specialized type of frame called a *script,* which was used to represent stereotypical events and was applied in story and text understanding.

Generic Restaurant Frame[4]

Specialization-of: Business establishment
Types:
   range: (cafeteria, seat-yourself, wait-to-be-seated)
   default: wait-to-be-seated
   if-needed: If plastic-counter Then fast-food
            If stack-trays Then cafeteria
            If wait-to-be-seated sign or reservations-made Then wait-to-be-seated
            Otherwise seat-yourself

---

4. From *The Handbook of Artificial Intelligence,* edited by A. Barr and E. Feigenbaum (Los Altos, CA: William Kaufmann, 1981). Reprinted with permission.

Location:
  range: address
  if-needed: (look at menu)
Name:
  if-needed: (look at menu)
Foodstyle:
  range: (burgers,chinese,american,seafood)
  default: american
  if-added: (update alternatives of restaurant)
Time-of-Operation:
  range: time-of-day
  default: open-evenings except Mondays
Payment-form:
  range: (cash,creditcard,check,skip-payment script)
Event-sequence:
  default: eat-at-restaurant script
Alternatives:
  range: all restaurants with same foodstyle
  if-needed: (find all restaurants with same foodstyle)

The eat-at-restaurant script might be structured as follows:

Eat-at-Restaurant Script[5]

Props: (restaurant,money,food,menu,tables,chairs)
Roles: (hungry-persons, waiters, chefs)
Point-of-view: hungry-persons
Time-of-occurrence: (times-of-operation of restaurant)
Place-of-occurrence: (location of restaurant)
Event-sequence:
  first: enter-restaurant script
  then: If (wait-to-be-seated sign or reservations) Then get-maître-d's-attention script
  then: please-be-seated script
  then: order-food script
  then: eat-food script Unless (long-wait) Then exit-restaurant-angry script
  then: pay-bill script
  finally: leave-restaurant script

5. From *The Handbook of Artificial Intelligence,* edited by A. Barr and E. Feigenbaum (Los Altos, CA: William Kaufmann, 1981).

Attached to each frame are several kinds of information, including how to use the frame, what can be expected to happen next, and what to do if expectations are not realized. The upper levels of the frame are usually fixed and represent things that are always true. The lower levels have many slots filled with data from specific instances, replacing generalized default data.

Frame representation leads naturally to a hierarchical structure in which information within frames is stored in slot substructures and in which frames are linked together to form frame groups. In fact, slots may themselves be frames or may be shared between frames. Clearly, designing a frame-based knowledge representation scheme is not a simple undertaking.

Frames and scripts can make more efficient use of processing resources to achieve goals and solve problems, by organizing knowledge into interrelated frames (each of which represents stereotyped objects and events) and by utilizing the mechanisms of slots, links, and demons. The performance of the scheme, however, is very sensitive to the organization and structure of the frames. Consequently, a great deal of care and time must be put into the design of a frame-based system if its performance is to be significantly better than that of purely logic-based or production rule–based systems.

■ SEMANTIC NETWORKS

Semantic networks are another popular scheme for representing knowledge in a more structured fashion than could be obtained by merely presenting a list of production rules or predicate sentences. Like frames and scripts, semantic networks require the grouping of chunks of knowledge into objects, concepts, or situations. Such objects, concepts, and situations are represented by *nodes* (drawn as dots, circles, or boxes in illustrations), which are related to one another by means of unidirectional arcs (drawn as arrows). In certain respects, semantic networks resemble frame-based systems: nodes are similar to frames, and arcs are similar to linking slots embedded in the frames. By the nature of their graphically-oriented notation, however, semantic networks place greater emphasis on the interrelationship of concepts, objects, and situations and less emphasis on the detailed knowledge structure associated with a given concept, object, or situation than frame-based representations do.

32 ■ *THEORIES AND CONCEPTS*

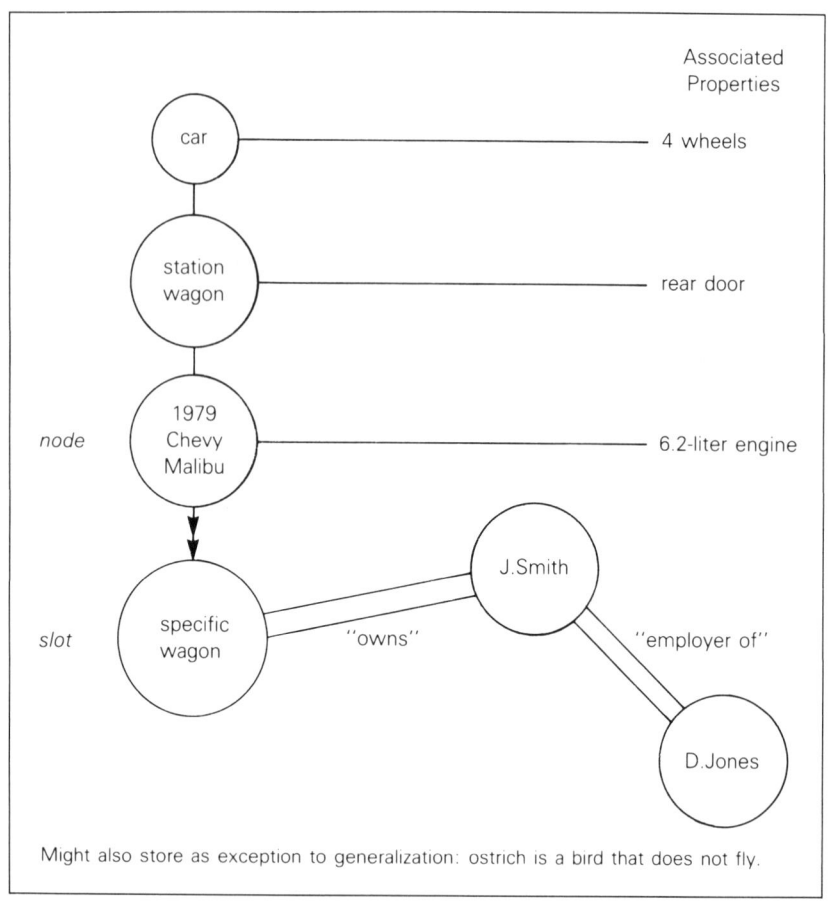

```
                                          Associated
                                          Properties

              ( car )────────────────────── 4 wheels

              ( station
                wagon )──────────────────── rear door

              ( 1979
       node    Chevy    )─────────────────── 6.2-liter engine
                Malibu )
                  ↓↓
                            ( J.Smith )
       slot  ( specific )═══"owns"═══(        )═══"employer of"
              ( wagon )                (        )
                                                  ( D.Jones )

  Might also store as exception to generalization: ostrich is a bird that does not fly.
```

2-5. Associative (or semantic) network.

The various semantic network systems currently in use vary greatly. Many have little in common except for the superficial similarity of the graphical node/arc notation. Even greater variation appears in semantic network representations than in production rule systems or frame-based systems. Early research used semantic network systems to develop psychological models of human memory (Quillian 1968) and natural language understanding (Raphael 1968). Since then, work on semantic networks has continued in these areas, as well as in expert systems work (such as PROSPECTOR).

Semantic network research is surveyed by N.V. Findler (1979). Some typical semantic networks are pictured in figures 2-5, 2-6, and 2-7. Figure 2-5 shows a semantic network where the station wagon node,

Semantic Networks ■ 33

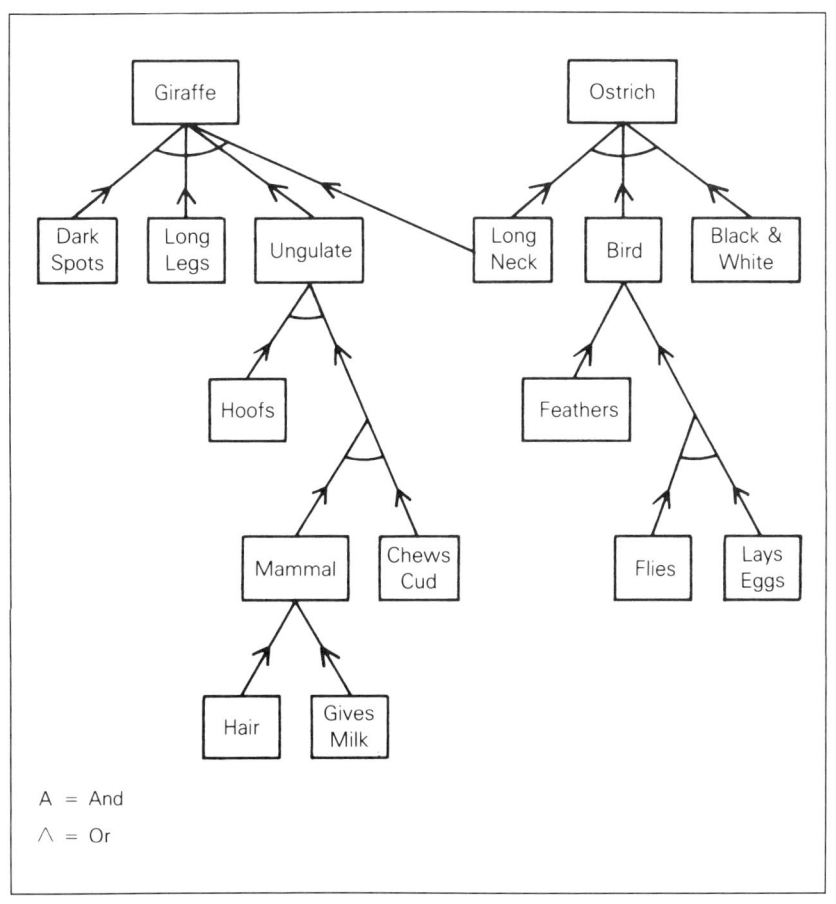

2-6. Associative network.

besides having its own unique attributes (such as possessing a rear door), inherits by default all the properties of the car node (for example, having four wheels). Likewise, the 1979 Chevy Malibu inherits by default all the properties of the station wagon node and (by inference) all those of the car node. In addition, the 1979 Chevy Malibu node has some unique properties, such as a 6.2-liter engine. An instance of the 1979 Chevy Malibu is represented in the specific wagon slot with its unique values, such as its license plates. Besides the inheritance links, two types of links are pictured in the semantic network of figure 2-5: an ownership link relating the specific wagon to its owner, J. Smith; and an employer link, relating J. Smith as the employer of D. Jones.

Figure 2-6 illustrates part of a semantic network representing the

34 ■ *THEORIES AND CONCEPTS*

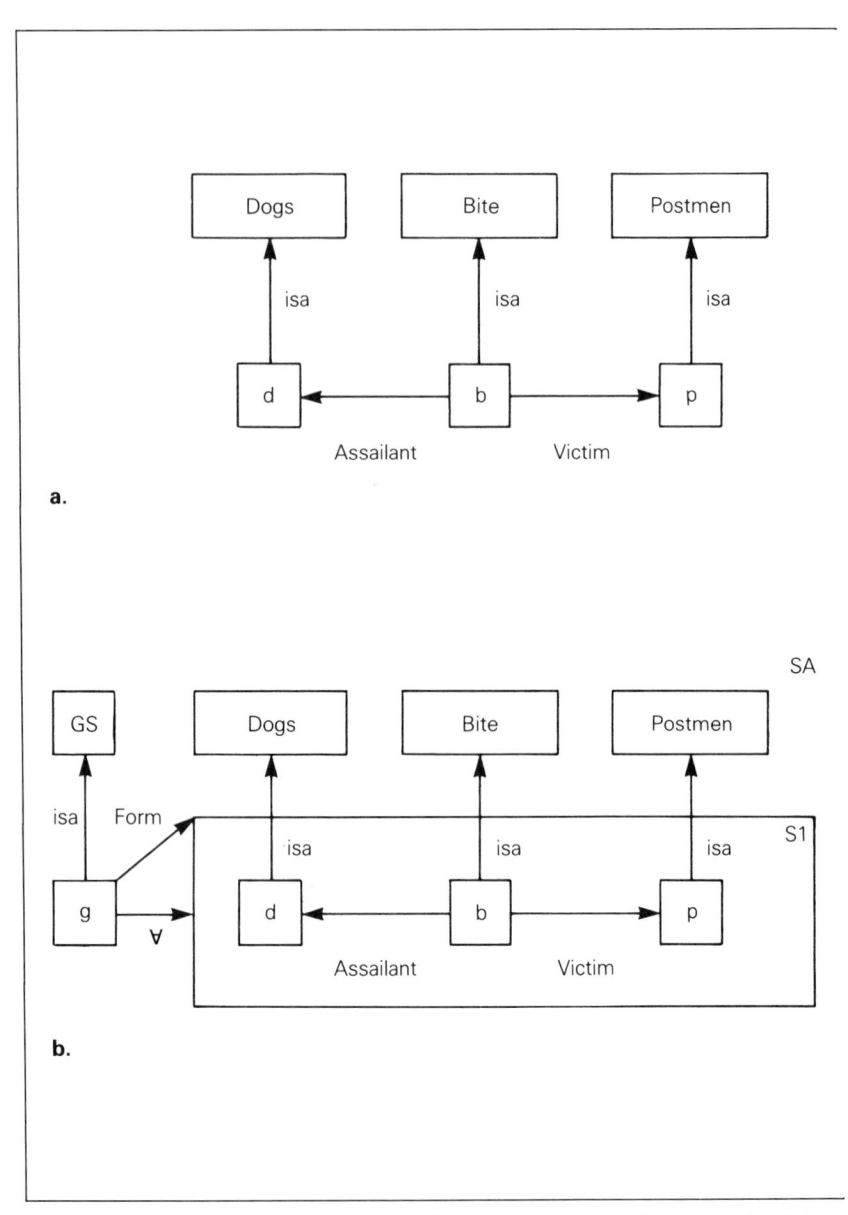

2-7. Partitioned semantic nets. (From *Artificial Intelligence,* by Elaine Rich. Published by McGraw-Hill, New York, 1983. Reprinted with permission.)

logical relationships among different animals and their parts. When the arcs are connected by a curved line, it denotes the logical *and;* otherwise the logical *or* is interpreted. For example, this figure shows that an ostrich is a bird that is black and white and has a long neck. Furthermore,

Semantic Networks ■ **35**

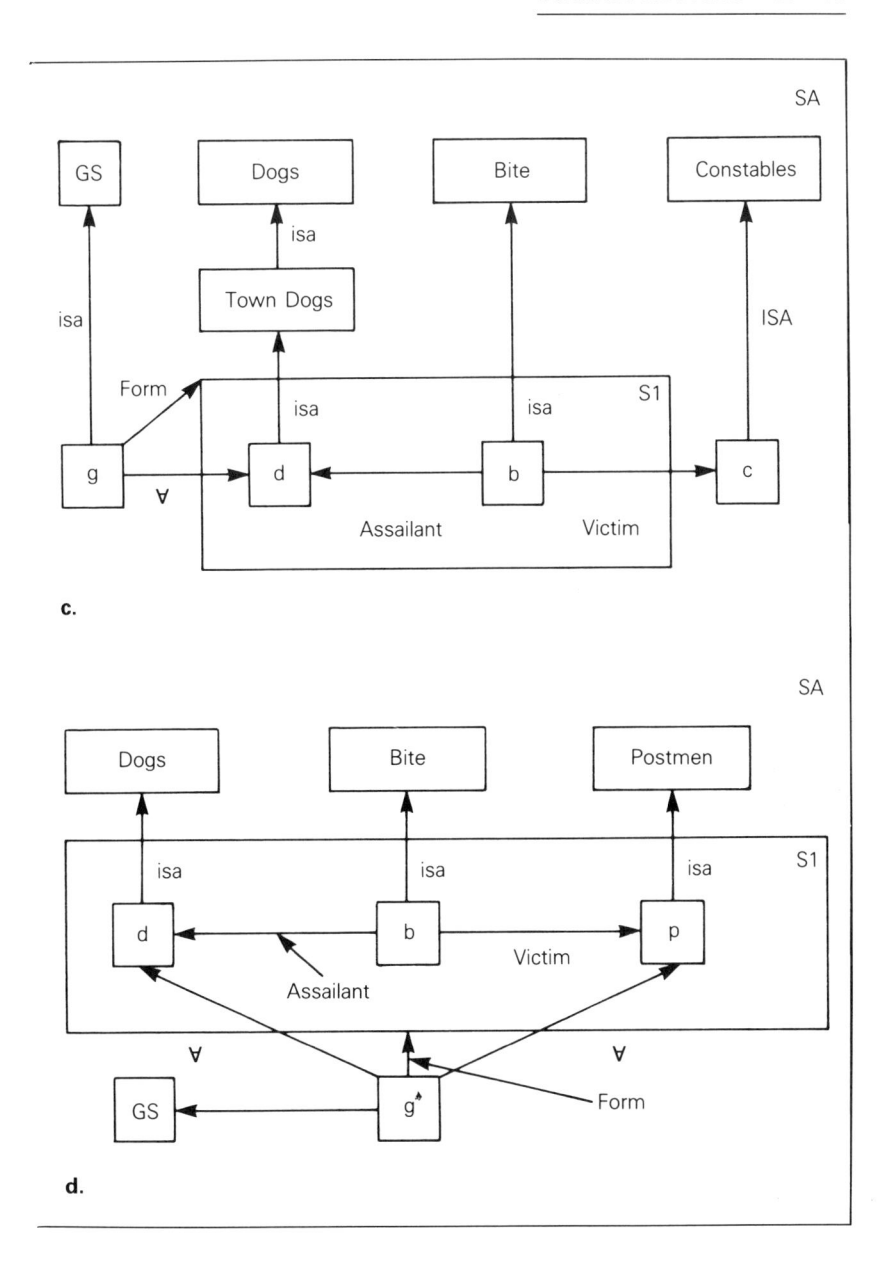

c.

[Figure c: Semantic network with nodes GS, Dogs, Bite, Constables, Town Dogs, and instances g, d, b, c within partition S1, showing isa, Form, Assailant, and Victim relations; outer partition SA]

d.

[Figure d: Semantic network with nodes Dogs, Bite, Postmen, and instances d, b, p within partition S1, and GS, g♦ outside, showing isa, Form, Assailant, Victim, and ∀ relations; outer partition SA]

a bird can be identified by either the fact that it has feathers or the fact that it flies and lays eggs.

Figure 2-7 shows how a semantic network can be partitioned to handle logical relations that include quantification, by allowing for variables

(Hendrix 1977a). Figure 2-7*a*, lacking partitioning, represents the fact that "a particular dog has bit a particular postman." The partitioning in figure 2-7*b*, on the other hand, represents the fact that "every dog has bitten a postman." Figure 2-7*c* represents the fact that "every dog in town has bitten the constable." Finally, figure 2-7*d* represents the fact that "every dog has bitten every postman."

Although it is useful to think about and work with semantic networks in terms of their graphical representation, they are usually represented in current computers using an attribute-value-memory structure (although new computer architectures resulting from fifth-generation, parallel-processing, network-based research efforts could change this (Fahlman 1980)). For example, in LISP, each node could represent an atom, the node's arcs (or links) could represent its properties, and the nodes at the other ends of the links could be values. This could be developed with the use of property lists, as shown below for the inheritance hierarchy[6] of *chair* and *my-chair*.

ATOM	PROPERTY LIST
CHAIR	((ISA FURNITURE))
MY-CHAIR	((ISA CHAIR) (COLOR TAN) (COVER COTTON) (OWNER ME))
ME	((ISA PERSON))
TAN	((ISA BROWN))
SEAT	((ISPART CHAIR))

As is the case with frames, semantic network nodes can also contain demons.

■ DEALING WITH UNCERTAINTY

As was briefly mentioned in the discussion of production rules, much of man's knowledge and many problem-solving tasks involve uncertainty. This uncertainty must be represented and successfully resolved in most

---

6. From *Artificial Intelligence*, by Elaine Rich (New York, McGraw-Hill, 1983). Reprinted with permission.

everyday problems. For example, planning tasks are characterized by uncertainty about the interactions of the plan steps. Strategic planning is further complicated by uncertainty about the opponent's intentions and actions. Perception is characterized by large quantities of noisy, ambiguous data. The input data to these tasks are often inaccurate, incomplete, from disparate sources, asynchronous, inconsistent, of varying granularity, and difficult or costly to extract. The knowledge based upon this data and used to solve a problem is thus often incomplete; it represents a kind of bounded ignorance and is occasionally incorrect.

Deciding how best to represent this uncertainty and how to manipulate knowledge in light of these uncertainties is a major issue. Various approaches have been developed and used. The certainty factors discussed later in the MYCIN production rule example is one such approach. Currently, no single approach is clearly superior in all cases to all others. Accordingly, several important ideas and approaches are discussed below, although the design choice for any individual A.I. project ultimately is the responsibility of the designer. Most of the current approaches stem from one of the following ideas:

1. *Mathematical probability*. Major contributors: Pascal, Bayes, Kolmogorov, Beryl, Savage, Difinetti.
2. *Inductive probability*. Major contributors: Bacon, Mills, Cohen.
3. *Belief functions*. Major contributors: Dempster, Shafer.
4. *Fuzzy sets*. Major contributor: Zadeh.

Mathematical probability theory was developed to help explain random physical phenomena, from games of chance to the random fluctuations of atoms and electrons. Random physical phenomena generally can be characterized by some object(s) capable of taking on one of a number of distinguishable and mutually exclusive states. Furthermore, over a large number of independent trials, the frequency of occurrence of the observed states tends to approach a stable value for each observed state. Thus if an unbiased coin is tossed a sufficiently large number of times, approximately half the tosses will come up heads and half will come up tails. After a sufficiently large number of trials, these frequencies of occurrence can be associated with probability measures that have certain mathematical properties. One is that the sum of all probabilities of all possible states must equal 1. Another is that, if an object can have n possible states and if the likelihood of these states is purely random (or equilikely), then the probability of occurrence of each of the states is $1/n$.

38 ■ THEORIES AND CONCEPTS

An important formula of probability theory is called Bayes' rule. It is useful in helping decide the true identity of a physical process that can only be observed indirectly through randomly disturbed measurements of the physical process. Consider the example of an electromagnetic communications signal that is transmitted to a remote receiver station. Suppose that the transmitted signal is a continuous wave signal of either amplitude +1 or amplitude −1. Because of random disturbances as the electromagnetic signal travels through the atmosphere, the actual signal received can be of any voltage. The observed amplitude is more likely to take on some values than others, depending on the amplitude actually transmitted.

This situation is illustrated by the two curves in figure 2-8. The curve labeled $P(x/+1)$ represents the probability that the observed amplitude

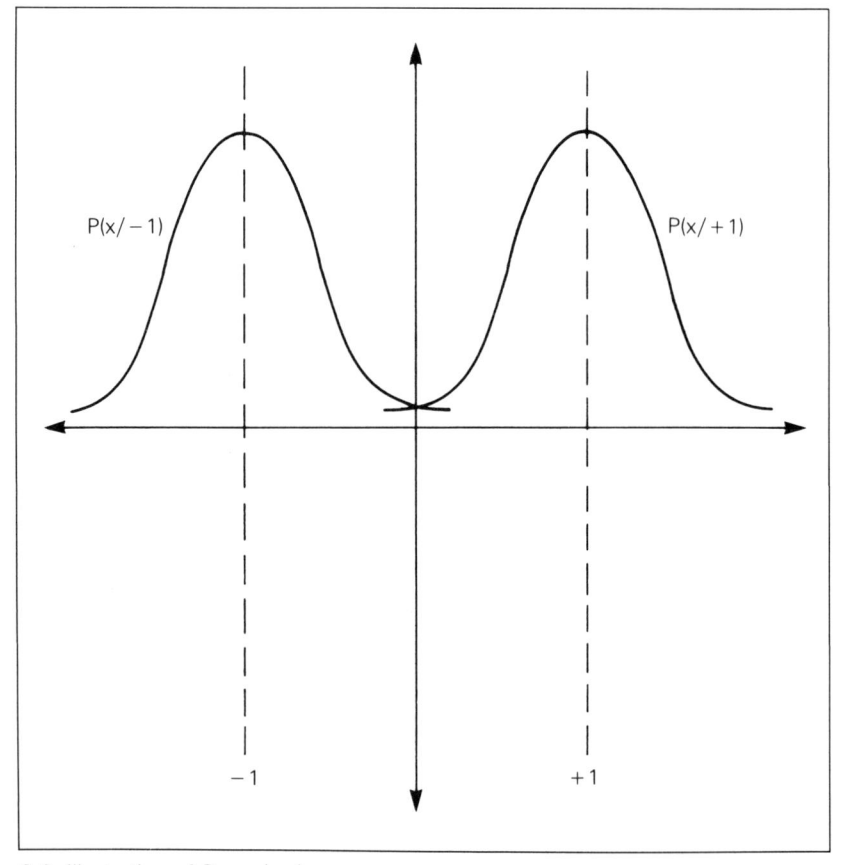

2-8. Illustration of Bayes' rule.

takes on the value x if the signal transmitted was amplitude $+1$. Similarly, the curve labeled $P(x/-1)$ represents the probability that the observed amplitude takes on the value x if the signal transmitted was amplitude -1. Both of these probabilities (known as *conditional probabilities* because they are conditional upon the actual signal amplitude transmitted) can be determined through repeated trial and measurement.

The communications problem, however, usually involves our observing a particular received signal from which we must make an informed, best decision as to the actual signal amplitude transmitted. We can measure $P(x/+1)$ and $P(x/-1)$, but we need to determine $P(H/x)$—the probability that, given the received signal x, a particular hypothesis concerning the received signal is correct. This case invites two hypotheses: H0, that the transmitted signal was amplitude -1; and H1, that the transmitted signal was amplitude $+1$. We can determine $P(H0/x)$ and $P(H1/x)$ from Bayes' rule:

$$P(H0/x) = P(x/H0)P(H0)/P(x) \qquad [2.6]$$

$$P(H1/x) = P(x/H1)P(H1)/P(x) \qquad [2.7]$$

$$P(x) = P(x/H0)P(H0) + P(x/H1)P(H1) \qquad [2.8]$$

where:

> $P(H0)$ is the a priori probability that H0 is true, amplitude is -1
> $P(H1)$ is the a priori probability that H1 is true, amplitude is $+1$
> $P(x)$ is the probability that x was received, which is equal to the sum of the probability that H0 is true and x is received plus the probability that H1 is true and x is received

Using Bayes' rule, we can solve this communications problem and all similar decision problems. By determining the conditional probabilities $P(x/H0)$ and $P(x/H1)$ and the a priori probabilities $P(H1)$ and $P(H0)$, we can establish a decision rule that will always give us a maximum probability decision. We observe the value x, and using our determined conditional and a priori probabilities, we compute the likelihood ratio:

$$P(x/H1)P(H1)/P(x/H0)P(H0)$$

If the likelihood ratio is greater than 1, hypothesis H1 is confirmed; if the likelihood ratio is less than 1, hypothesis H0 is indicated.

Bayes' rule and probability measures first began to be applied to the field of human decision making in the sciences and in games of chance.

The ideas were extended to include areas of human judgment that go far beyond assessments of the behavior of physical objects. To achieve these wider goals, the notion of a probability measure was extended to include such things as the state of ignorance—treated, for purposes of probability, as a completely random, equilikely state.

The field of decision analysis, which was developed on the basis of this school of thought, has yielded many useful ideas and approaches for making more informed decisions on subjects ranging from investments to political strategy. Among the expert systems that makes use of these principles is PROSPECTOR (Duda, Hart, and Nilsson 1976), which helps classify and discover areas where mineral deposits are most likely to exist, based on the properties of the terrain and its substructures. The extension of decision making under uncertainty beyond the realm of purely physical objects, however, does have certain shortcomings. Shafer (1976) identified many of the shortcomings and paradoxes that arise in artificial extensions of probability theory into the realms of human belief involving ignorance and judgment. The paradox below presents an illustration of one of the points they make.

Suppose that we are totally ignorant of the likelihood of there being life on Mars. We therefore assign a probability of 1/2 to the hypothesis that there is life on Mars and a probability of 1/2 to the hypothesis that there is not life on Mars. Now suppose that we are told that some minimum amount of oxygen must be present in a planet's atmosphere in order for life to be supported, but we do not know what that minimum amount is. At this juncture, we have only three possible states: one where there is sufficient oxygen but no life on Mars; one where there is sufficient oxygen and life on Mars; and one where there is insufficient oxygen and no life on Mars. Because it is impossible to have insufficient oxygen and life on Mars, the addition of the oxygen factor has effectively redivided the universe of equilikely states from two to three. Thus, without advancing from our state of ignorance, we have seen the probability that there is life on Mars shift from 1/2 to 1/3.

To overcome just such paradoxes, Dempster and Shafer developed a theory of evidential reasoning that generalizes the notion of probability theory from a single measure to a mass vector capable of measuring both the degree of support for a particular hypothesis and the degree of belief for a particular hypothesis. The former relates to the evidence against the hypothesis, the latter to the evidence for the hypothesis; the two are usually not equal. Approaches based on these notions are quite suitable to many A.I. applications, and several successful expert systems have been built on these ideas. MYCIN's confidence factor approach is an ad hoc approach that bears a close resemblance to many elements of evidential reasoning (Shortliffe and Buchanan 1984).

Another way of extending and generalizing the notions of probability theory to account for the type of inexact reasoning and categorization techniques that human beings employ to deal with abstract concepts and ideas has emerged from the work on fuzzy sets first undertaken by L.A. Zadeh (1975). As Zadeh observed, people rarely deal with clear concepts having sharp boundaries; rather, their speech and thought are based on much vaguer, fuzzier notions.

When we speak of a person as being tall, we do not maintain sharp implicit boundaries between tall, average, and short heights. Rather, each term presents a continuum of possibilities. *Tall,* for example, can be thought of as having a graded membership in all sets related to people's heights such that the degree of a height's membership, or association, in the notion of *tall* grows stronger as it approaches the upper end of the continuum. Much of human knowledge is similarly fuzzy in nature. Consider the following rule: "If a student is both very tall and athletic, then he (or she) is on the basketball team." Not only are properties such as "very tall" fuzzy, but the rule itself is fuzzy because it is fundamentally inexact. In fact, for accuracy's sake, the expert who defined this rule probably should have added "usually" in front of the rule—where *usually* would constitute yet another fuzzy term.

One last school of thought argues that none of the above measures is sufficient, and insists that logic (appropriately extended) should be the sole means for handling uncertainty. For example, if a rule is proposed that is usually true, we should first ask ourselves under what conditions the rule is inapplicable; often, we can then add these conditions to the rule. We can also extend logic to handle default reasoning by marking certain rules and the knowledge derived from these rules as tentative (for example, that John is a man and therefore has two arms). If, during the inference process, we uncover some contradictory information (for example, that John is a war veteran and lost one arm in the war), we can undo and roll back all the knowledge derived from the tentative rule. In some cases—even if we could devise a more complex rule capable of accounting for all exceptional cases—we might prefer the default reasoning approach, since it would work more efficiently most of the time.

Cohen and Grinberg (1983) have proposed a theory of endorsements, which are reasons to believe and disbelieve propositions, and Doyle (1983) has developed a theory of reasoned assumptions to allow reasoning about uncertainty without the artificiality of probabilistic representation. In these approaches, the reasoning about uncertainty is integrated into the entire knowledge base structure and inference process. For example, suppose that Mavis plans to buy a car and has narrowed her choice to either a Volkswagen Rabbit or a Chevy Malibu. She decides to pick the car that is most reliable. To make this determination, she asks her friends for their endorsements, based on their experiences (negative and positive) of cars they owned and cars they rented. Clearly, Mavis will not weight these endorsements equally; a friend who owned a Chevy for five years and never had a maintenance problem with it can offer a much more valuable endorsement than a friend who rented a Chevy for a couple of days and had no problems.

Advocates of logic-based extensions such as endorsement theories argue that probability-based schemes are not natural to people and miss many of the subtler aspects of human reasoning under uncertainty. They remind us that human beings (even statistically skilled ones) produce "probabilities" conditioned on evidence that vary sharply from probabilities produced by Bayesian conditioning rules (Tversky and Kahneman 1982). For example, people tend to be insensitive to factors that influence mathematical probabilities and sensitive to resemblances between data and a proposed classification. When asked to classify individuals as librarians or truck drivers on the basis of personality sketches, most people classified "neat, methodical, and shy" individuals as librarians, even if the prior probability of these individuals being librarians was low (there being fewer librarians than truck drivers in the world).

■ INFERENCE AND DEDUCTION

One property that sets an A.I. system apart from more conventional programs is the A.I. program's presumed ability to reason, at least to a limited extent. Being able to reason means that, once given general knowledge of a problem domain, the system can figure out what it needs to know from what it already knows. For example, if the program already knows that "all boys have a mother" and that "John is a boy," it should be able to figure out that John has a mother—without being explicitly told this fact. To know that John is a boy or that all boys have mothers merely requires retrieval of previously stored facts. To know that John has a mother requires the ability to reason from the available facts. For most complex problems, the A.I. system must be able to deduce and verify a multitude of facts beyond those it has been explicitly told, in just this manner.

There are many different forms of reasoning: formal reasoning; procedural reasoning; reasoning by analogy, generalization, and abstraction; default reasoning; abduction; and metalevel reasoning. Formal reasoning (of which mathematical logic is a prominent example) involves the syntactic manipulation of data structures to deduce new ones, in accordance with prespecified rules of inference. Formal reasoning is the type of reasoning that is most natural and most commonly used in logic-based and production rule–based representation systems. It involves deduction rules such as *modus ponens:* if P implies Q, and P is true, then Q must be true.

Procedural reasoning (for example, a program that can take the sum of two numbers) involves specialized routines or procedures for answering questions and solving problems. Procedural reasoning is most commonly used today in frame-based and semantic network–based systems; it is used to a lesser extent in conventional programs for which skeletal program shells are created that can solve a class of specific problems.

Reasoning by analogy involves the extrapolation (or the induction) of new facts from existing knowledge. For example, if Elizabeth got A grades in math and chemistry, we can infer that she probably also got a good grade in physics, since physics shares certain similarities with chemistry and math. This seems to be a very natural mode of thought for people, but so far it has been difficult to establish in an A.I. program. If this capability could be successfully implemented in a program, it would enable that program to adapt and learn by itself (Winston 1984; Michalski, Carbonell, and Mitchell 1986).

Generalization and abstraction are also natural reasoning processes for human beings that have been difficult to implement in a program, although some limited success has been achieved in constrained environments (Michalski, Carbonell, and Mitchell 1986). This area of research is thought to be at the core of most human learning. It involves induction rules, such as: if Q is true for every known instance, and if there is a large enough number of such instances, then Q is always true. If we know that robins have wings, that sparrows have wings, and that pigeons have wings, eventually we will conclude that all birds have wings. This is an example of generalization: the creation of a more abstract, generalized rule from a collection of knowledge consisting of many specialized examples, or case histories.

Conversely, we may successively refine our knowledge by making it more specific and detailed as we learn from more examples. We may initially postulate that an arch is defined as three blocks, one resting on the other two. When we are confronted with an example in which two blocks lean against each other and the third lies on top, however, we refine our definition to include the added constraint that the two supporting blocks must not be touching.

Default reasoning involves rules such as: if Q cannot be proven false, then Q is assumed to be true. Abduction involves such rules as: if P implies Q, and Q is true, then P is assumed to be true.

Metalevel reasoning involves using knowledge—particularly knowledge about the extent of your knowledge and about the importance of certain facts—in order to solve a problem. Recent research indicates that metalevel reasoning plays a key role in human cognition (Flavell 1979). Some limited success has been achieved in applying these ideas to current expert systems (Stefik 1981; Hayes-Roth, Waterman, and Lenat 1983).

One property of many of today's successful A.I. programs is their clear separation of the knowledge base from the inference processing strategy. Some support for this architecture has been found in cognitive studies of how people solve problems (Card, Moran, and Newell 1983). An advantage of such separation is that as the operators of the system gain in sophistication, they can improve the system in two relatively noninterfering ways: by adding more explicit, declarative knowledge; and by reusing the same knowledge base with progressively more sophisticated inference engines.

The division between explicitly declared knowledge and inference strategy was the motivation behind discussing, first, different approaches to knowledge representation and, second, approaches to inference and deduction. Currently, it is better to think about these two issues somewhat independently, recognizing that a knowledge representation scheme is not restricted to a single type of inference strategy (and vice versa). This approach may have to be revised, however, when more is learned about analogical reasoning, generalization, and abstraction, as well as about how human beings learn.

■ FORMAL REASONING

Most current A.I. programs are based upon the foundations of formal reasoning. In fact, the extent to which this simple paradigm has proved successful in implementing successful A.I. programs has been nothing short of amazing. Much of the human reasoning process can be successfully simulated by a program that simply stores and syntactically manipulates large collections of logical/conceptual propositions.

The foundation of this approach lies in ideas developed in the study of mathematical theorem-proving. A theorem can be represented conceptually as a statement in which we assert that a certain premise implies a given conclusion. In that sense, when we deal with logical propositions, proving a theorem equates to deriving some new fact, relationship, or implication from a given set of known logical facts, relationships, and implications.

We learned in grade school that two fundamentally different approaches can be taken in proving a theorem: we can prove that a theorem (if p, then q) is true by showing that, for all the possible combinations of states in the premise, the conclusion holds true; or we can prove that a theorem is true by showing that the contrapositive (if not q, then not p) is true, that p and not-q cannot be true and leads to a contradiction. The first approach is not particularly well suited for implementation by a formal generalized computer program. In the second approach, if two propositional clauses contradict one another, their logical conjunction ("anding") is always false, and the two clauses resolve to what is called an empty resolvent. If the negation of the theorem we wish to prove—together with the facts, relations, and implications we already know to be simultaneously true—resolves until we are left to the empty set, then the negative of the theorem and the currently known facts, relations, and implications cannot both be simultaneously true. Since the premise and its negative can never be simultaneously true, the theorem must be true. Thus, by assuming the negative of the theorem to be true, and by showing that this assumption leads to a contradiction, we can prove that the theorem must be true.

This technique, known as resolution theorem-proving, was first proposed by J.A. Robinson (1965). It forms the basis of the built-in inferencing mechanism used in PROLOG. The way this technique works mechanically is illustrated below. First, all of the logical clauses known to be true are combined and transformed into a standard conjunctive normal form such as Horn Clause notation:

(AND (OR U)
      (OR Q (NOT P))
      (OR (NOT S) (NOT R)))

Then, the clause to be proved is negated and added to the rest, resulting in an expression like the following:

```
(AND (OR (NOT U) P S (NOT Q))
     (OR U)
     (OR Q (NOT P))
     (OR (NOT S) (NOT R)))
```

Next, we search for two clauses in which the same atom (fact) appears—naked in one clause and negated in the other. This situation constitutes a contradiction; the two clauses involved are said to resolve, and the resulting expression (formed by combining everything in both clauses except for the naked atom and its negation) is called the resolvent. We then repeat the process until none of the remaining clauses resolves (if this happens, we report failure to prove the theorem; the theorem is not necessarily incorrect, but we were unable to prove it) or until all of the clauses resolve to the empty set (in this case, we report success in proving the theorem).

In the example above, the first clause (the negative) resolves with the second clause to produce the resolvent, (OR P S (NOT Q)), which in turn resolves with the third clause to produce the resolvent, (OR S), which in turn resolves with the last clause to produce the final resolvent, (OR (NOT R)). In this case, we were unable to produce the empty set, and so we were unable to prove that the theorem (AND U (NOT P) (NOT S) Q)) is true.

The Horn Clause notation used has the following characteristics: all the clauses are logically "anded" together, and each individual clause takes the form of a logical "oring," or disjunction of atoms (facts) or literals. As shown in the example above, these atoms could be represented as the negation of a fact, instead of as a naked fact.

Horn Clauses may also include variables (although none appeared in the example above), and indeed most problems of interest contain variables. Variables are always assumed to be universal when they appear in Horn Clauses; that is, each clause is assumed to be true for all possible values of the variable. When variables are involved, the resolution process includes finding a consistent string of substitutions for variables, called *variable bindings* or *instantiations,* for which all the clauses resolve.

This substitution process, illustrated in figure 2-9, is extremely important. Figure 2-9 involves proving a theorem that is so trivial that mere substitution immediately reveals the truth of the theorem without our needing to go through the formality of transforming it into Horn Clause notation and applying the resolution process. Figure 2-9 presents

{L(M,S)   (h1)

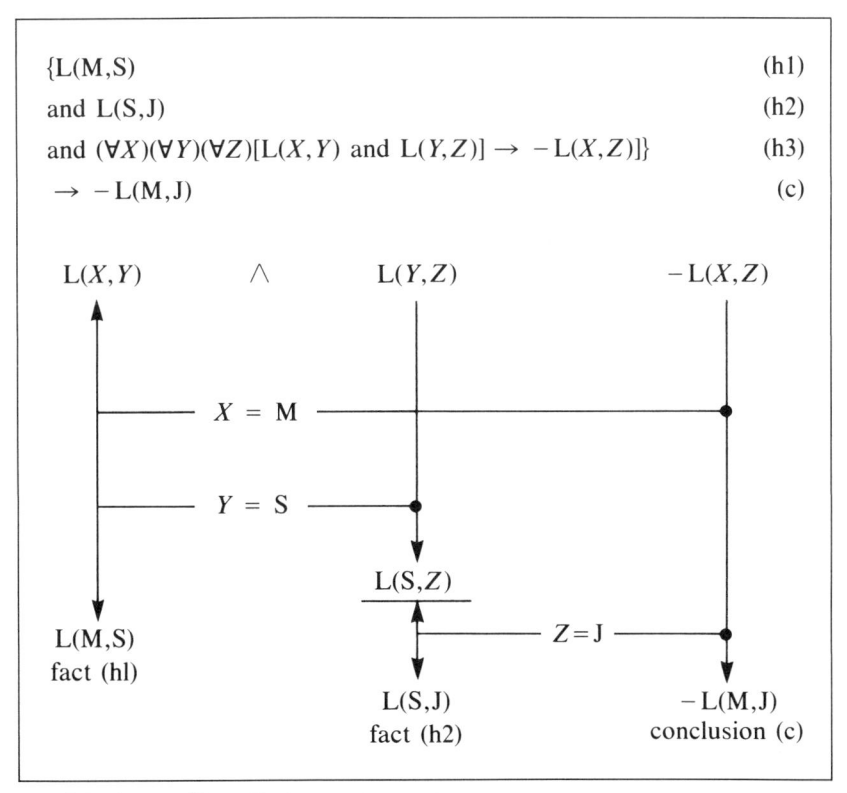

and L(S,J)   (h2)

and $(\forall X)(\forall Y)(\forall Z)[L(X,Y) \text{ and } L(Y,Z)] \to -L(X,Z)]$} (h3)

$\to -L(M,J)$ (c)

```
L(X,Y)              ∧           L(Y,Z)                    -L(X,Z)

          X = M

          Y = S
                                 L(S,Z)

L(M,S)                                          Z = J
fact (h1)
                                 L(S,J)                   -L(M,J)
                                 fact (h2)                conclusion (c)
```

2-9. Substitution. (From *Understanding Artificial Intelligence*, by Paul Gloess. Published by Alfred Publishing Company, Sherman Oaks, CA, 1981. Reprinted with permission.)

two facts and one implication, from which we would like to be able to prove a third fact. Although these facts and implication could stand for anything and the result would still apply, the logic is easier to understand if we ascribe a more concrete meaning to the relationships. For illustrative purposes, then, suppose that the predicate $L(X, Y)$ stands for the relationship "X loves Y," where X and Y are universal variables, and where M, S, and J stand for people's names—specifically, M = Mary, S = Sam, and J = Jane. In this case, the conjunction of the first two facts represents that "Mary loves Sam" and "Sam loves Jane." The implication states that "For all people, if X loves Y and Y loves Z, then X does not love Z" (the classic love triangle).

From the conjunction of the first two facts with the implication, we would like to prove the fact that "Mary does not love Jane." This is a consequence that should be obvious to us by inspection; if we wish, however, we can prove it by substitution of the variables in the implication. Since the implication is true for all X, Y, and Z, it must also be true for any specific values of X, Y, and Z. We can equate the first predicate term in the implication with the first fact by substituting the value Mary for X and the value Sam for Y. Henceforth, this substitution must apply in a consistent manner, wherever X and Y appear in the same logical expression, such as in the second predicate term of the implication—which is then L(S,Z)—and in the third predicate term of the implication—which is then ~L(M,Z). This process of *binding* the variable X to Mary and binding the variable Y to Sam is illustrated in figure 2-9. Next, we set the second predicate term equal to the second fact by binding the variable Z to Jane. In this case, the last term of the implication is –L(M,J), which matches and thus proves the desired conclusion.

Of course, we were lucky that the string of substitutions we tried resulted in immediate success. If we had instead tried to match the second fact, L(S,J), with the first term in the implication, we would have bound X to Sam and Y to Jane. This initial binding would have failed to produce the desired results, and we would have had to backtrack, undo the first set of temporary bindings, and try a different consistent set. Eventually, we would stumble upon the correct sequence of substitutions and be able to prove the hypothesized conclusion that "Mary does not love Jane." If we continued this trial-and-error procedure, sequentially trying different legitimate variable substitutions until we had exhausted all possible substitution sequences without any successful matching to the hypothesized conclusion we wished to prove, we would have failed to prove the theorem.

Figure 2-10 shows how the formal resolution process (including substitution) would apply to the same example. First, we would negate the hypothesized conclusion and transform all the clauses into Horn Clause notation. This requires transforming the implication

$$L(X,Y) \wedge L(Y,Z) \rightarrow {\sim}L(X,Z)$$

to its equivalent form:

$$\sim L(X,Y) \vee \sim L(Y,Z) \vee \sim L(X,Z)$$

Next, we would try to prove that the conjunction of all of these clauses, including the negate of the hypothesized conclusion, leads to a contradiction; that is, we would try (by trial and error) to find at least

Formal Reasoning ■ 49

Resolution

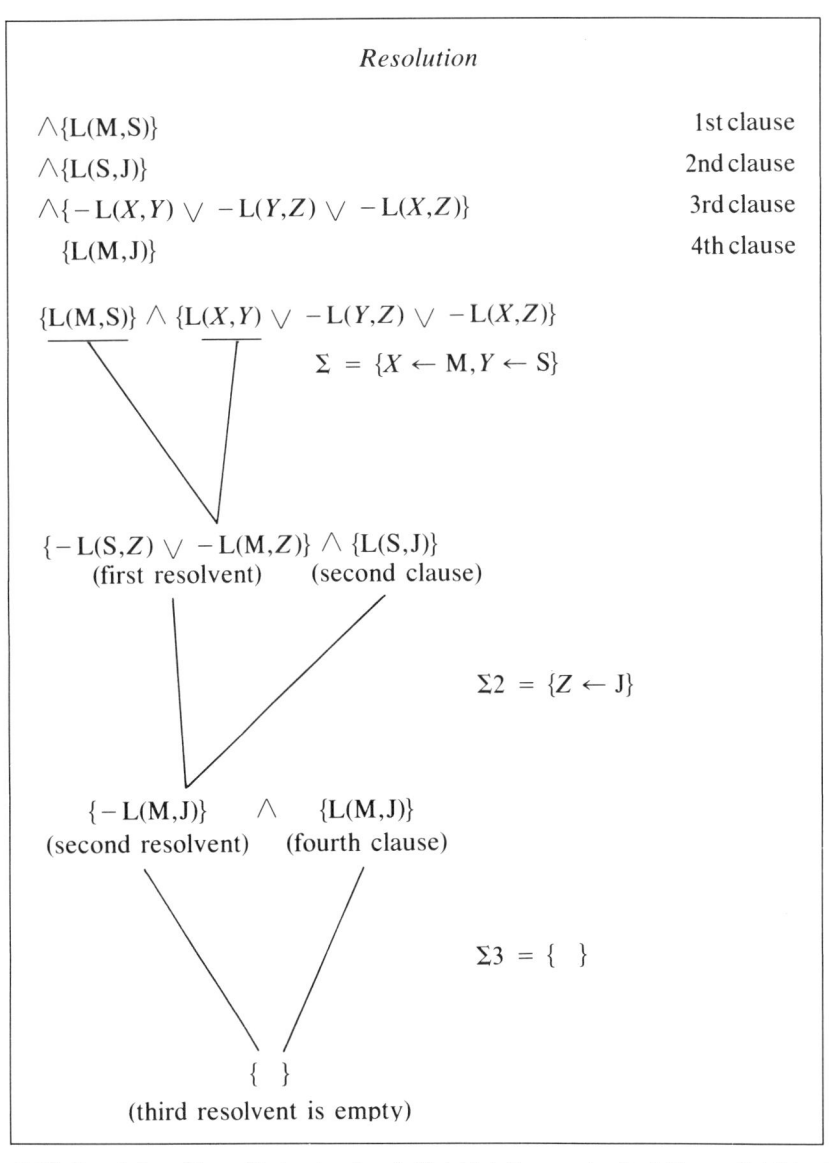

$\bigwedge \{L(M,S)\}$ 1st clause
$\bigwedge \{L(S,J)\}$ 2nd clause
$\bigwedge \{-L(X,Y) \vee -L(Y,Z) \vee -L(X,Z)\}$ 3rd clause
$\{L(M,J)\}$ 4th clause

$\{L(M,S)\} \wedge \{L(X,Y) \vee -L(Y,Z) \vee -L(X,Z)\}$

$\Sigma = \{X \leftarrow M, Y \leftarrow S\}$

$\{-L(S,Z) \vee -L(M,Z)\} \wedge \{L(S,J)\}$
(first resolvent)   (second clause)

$\Sigma 2 = \{Z \leftarrow J\}$

$\{-L(M,J)\} \wedge \{L(M,J)\}$
(second resolvent) (fourth clause)

$\Sigma 3 = \{ \}$

$\{ \}$
(third resolvent is empty)

2-10. Resolution. (From *Understanding Artificial Intelligence,* by Paul Gloess. Published by Alfred Publishing Company, Sherman Oaks, CA, 1981. Reprinted with permission.)

one legal, consistent string of variable bindings for which all of the clauses resolved to the empty (null) set. To ensure that we do not neglect any possibility, we need to adopt some methodology or strategy for systematically trying all possible variable bindings. The strategy used in figure 2-10 is to try substitutions based on the order in which the clauses appear. We will try the top clauses first, choosing variables in the clause as they appear in left-to-right order. This is called a syntactic strategy because it tries items in the order in which they appear in expressions, rather than according to any meaning associated with them.

Using this procedure, we first try to find a clause to resolve the first clause L(M,S). We accomplish this, using the leftmost clause in the implication, $\sim L(X, Y)$, by making the variable bindings Mary for X and Sam for Y. These bindings are now assumed to apply everywhere X and Y appear, yielding the resolvent:

$$\sim L(S,Z) \lor \sim L(M,Z).$$

Next, we attempt to find a clause to resolve the second clause in the list, L(S,J), with. Here we succeed, using the first term in the previous resolvent, $\sim L(S,Z)$, by making the additional binding Jane for Z. Now all the remaining clauses resolve, and we are left with the empty (null) set, proving that our hypothesized conclusion is true. Assuming it to be false leads to a contradiction. Again we were successful with the first string of variable bindings we tried, but clearly we would not have been successful with our first attempt if the clauses had been arranged in a different order, and several trials would have been required before a successful result was obtained.

The trial-and-error approach to finding clauses that resolve with appropriate variable bindings can be likened to a search up a tree of possibilities. The trunk of the tree represents the starting list of clauses. Each branch directly attached to the trunk represents a possible pair of clauses that can be resolved, along with the variable bindings that make the resolution possible. The subordinate branch attached to a main branch represents an additional resolution of a pair of clauses and an additional set of bindings. The hierarchical structuring continues until we reach the leaves of the tree, each leaf constituting either a successful search (a null state reached) or a failure. Each leaf has associated with it a unique string of variable bindings. In the trial-and-error strategy outlined above, we have chosen a search strategy that proceeds along one complete path of the tree to its end (its leaf). This is known as a depth-first strategy.

We direct or order trial-and-error searches in accordance with a refinement strategy. Refinement corresponds to working backward from the conclusion to be proved. In our example, we chose a syntactic strategy of refinement, based on the order of appearance of the clauses and of the atoms in the clause; specifically, we selected each clause in order from top to bottom, and we selected the atoms within a clause in order from left to right. PROLOG uses an inference mechanism based on the resolution principle. The refinement strategy used by PROLOG is to negate the hypothesis that is to be proved (the goal statement), place it on the top of the list, and then apply a top-to-bottom, left-to-right syntactic search strategy.

Other refinement strategies include semantic strategies and ancestry-based strategies. Semantic strategies select clauses known to be true in certain models or contexts. Here we make use of the underlying meanings of the clauses. For example, if we wished to prove that "Mary does not love Jane," we would first examine clauses that have something to do with people in love with each other, the idea being that these have some relevance to the subject matter of the hypothesis.

Ancestry-based strategies select clauses on the basis of historical precedence and past historical performance. For example, if we wish to diagnose a person's illness, we may first wish to examine clauses that relate to the common cold, since historical experience indicates that the common cold accounts for 90 percent of the cases we normally see.

Hyperresolution strategies are strategies that involve the resolution of several clauses at once. Some of these strategies are being scrutinized as the Japanese pursue their fifth-generation program and a parallel PROLOG inference engine.

In the example discussed above, we used resolution theorem-proving to show that—given the facts and implication that "Mary loves Sam," "Sam loves Jane," and "if person X loves person Y and person Y loves person Z, then person X does not love person Z"—the hypothesis "Mary does not love Jane" is true. To be useful in question-answering applications, however, the system must be able to handle a slightly different class of problems. A practical example of such question-answering applications is to ask whether there is someone that Mary does not love, and if so who the person(s) is (are) that Mary does not love. We ask this question by hypothesizing $\sim L(M,X)$, or in words, "Who is X? Who is it that Mary does not love?" The same resolution procedure outlined above can be adapted to answer this type of question. PROLOG, in fact, does just this sort of thing.

Clearly, if we attempted to prove that given the premises, there is someone X whom Mary does not love, the answer would be supplied as part of the variable bindings when we attempted to find a contradiction. One way of explicitly determining the identity of X is outlined below. First, we use the resolution process to prove that there is someone whom Mary does not love. Then we go back and replace the negated theorem with a clause that asserts, "Either the theorem is false or it is true." This statement is a tautology: it is always true, it adds no information to the existing clauses (the premises), and it does not restrict or contradict them in any way. If we now attempt to reconstruct the same proof as before, we will only be able to deduce true consequences of the premises. At the point where we previously deduced a contradiction, we must now deduce the specific consequence of the premises that was contradicted by the negation of the theorem. This consequence thus provides a precise answer to the question posed. In our example, the answer produced is ~L(M,J), or "Mary does not love Jane."

FORWARD CHAINING AND BACKWARD CHAINING

The inference control strategy employed by production rule systems is based on the formal reasoning approaches outlined in the previous section. The structure of the if-then production rule closely resembles the structure of the logical implication. The backward-chaining and forward-chaining strategies most commonly found in production rule–based expert systems are, in fact, special cases of the resolution principle just discussed.

Forward chaining involves making inferences by matching the condition sides of the if-then rules to the facts at hand. This is characteristic of deductive reasoning. The matching of a fact to the condition half of a production rule is operationally equivalent to resolving two logical clauses. Since forward chaining works from facts to conclusions, the forward-chaining inference mode has also been called the antecedent mode, event-driven mode, or data-derived mode.

The forward-chaining inference procedure is to start with a collection of facts and rules and to try, in an iterative manner, to find the available rule(s) whose condition side matches a fact (perhaps with a variable substitution or binding required). From this match, new facts are derived. We continue adding new facts and searching for matching rules until no further rules apply, or until the problem is solved and the goal state is reached. When more than one rule matches a fact, a possible conflict situation is created that must be resolved. We must decide which rule to apply first, with its associated variable bindings and its resultant new facts; then we must determine whether to try to match the new fact just derived or one of the older matches that we temporarily postponed considering.

OPS-5 is a forward-chaining production rule system that was developed at Carnegie-Mellon University and has since been used to develop many expert systems. Several commercial versions of OPS-5 are available on several different computers. OPS-5 always resolves conflicts that arise when more than one rule is applicable by picking the rule that has the most specific conditions and is triggered by the most recent facts.

Most OPS-5 programs also make heavy use of goals to direct the processing. Goals are not part of the OPS-5 language, but they serve as convenient organizing principles and can be put into the data base when appropriate for the current problem-solving strategy. A rule can then be associated with a given goal (or goals). The collection of rules applicable to the goal for a given task constitute the method for that task. OPS-5 does not scan a list of applicable rules looking for a match; rather, the rules are compiled and restructured into a hierarchy of simpler condition tests that, when completed, reveal all the matching rules (Forgy 1979).

Although the number of rules in a typical expert system design can grow into the thousands, the condition half of this set of rules is usually restricted to a much smaller number (typically, 100 or less) of conditional tests on a set of objects and object attributes. Accordingly, for most problems of interest, a much shorter time is needed to examine the hierarchy of object and object attribute matches globally than to examine each rule's condition half independently. Because of its techniques for compiling rules and because of its organizational principles, OPS-5 systems generally produce more efficient designs than many other production rule systems.

Forward-chaining systems do have some significant disadvantages. For one thing, they lack focus. Since it is data-driven, a forward-chaining production rule system tends to discover all the logical consequences of the set of facts and knowledge under investigation, whether they were requested or not. Furthermore, if the problem characteristics are such that the facts or evidence can trigger many and diverse applicable rules, the search tree is multilimbed at the outset, and the conflict resolution problem can get unwieldy. We may find the system wasting numerous computer cycles deriving facts that have no bearing on the problem under investigation.

Backward-chaining systems tend to provide the goal-oriented focus missing in forward-chaining systems. They work from the hypotheses to the facts or evidence, and for this reason backward-chaining inference mode has alternately been called consequent mode, goal-driven, and hypothesis-driven. Backward chaining starts with an unsubstantiated hypothesis and tries to prove it by finding rules that demonstrate the hypothesis and then trying to verify the facts that enable the rule to work. Thus, it replaces the hypothesis to be proved with subgoals that, if proved, will prove the hypothesis. The first step consists of searching down the conclusion side of a list of rules and identifying the ones that, with the appropriate variables, substitutions, or bindings, would match the unsubstantiated hypothesis. The next step is to try to verify the facts on the condition side that would make each rule applicable. The condition side usually consists of a compound set of conditions—one or more subgoals. If these subgoals do not match known facts, they are used to rescan the list of rules, this time to search for facts or rules whose conclusions match the subgoals. Iteration through the facts and rules continues in this manner until a complete line of reasoning has been identified that links or chains the unsubstantiated hypothesis back through subgoals until they finally connect to some known facts or evidence.

As is the case with forward chaining, this process of matching rules with variable substitutions is operationally equivalent to resolving two logical clauses. Backward chaining has the advantage of not performing unnecessary inferences. Backward chaining operates ad hoc when an expressed need, query, or goal has been raised. An example of the process is given below.

Suppose we wish to substantiate the hypothesis, "block *B* supports block *A*," or:

(SUPPORTS *B A*).

We would scan a set of facts and rules, searching for a match (with appropriate variable bindings) between the consequent side of a rule and the goal. One possible match is with the following rule:

(IF (ON ?*X* ?*Y*) then (SUPPORTS ?*Y* ?*X*)).

This rule states that if block ?*X* is on top of block ?*Y*, then block ?*Y* supports block ?*X*. (The prefix ? denotes a variable; this notation for variables is used in OPS-5.) This rule can substantiate the desired goal if we substitute *B* for ?*Y* and *A* for ?*X*, and if we can show that the condition (ON *A B*) is true. Thus in place of proving the goal (SUPPORTS *B A*), we have substituted attempting to prove the subgoal (ON *A B*).

A more complex example involves the goal:

(HATES JOHN FRED).

Here the matching rule is:

(IF (AND (LOVES ?*X* ?*Y*) (LOVES ?*Y* ?*Z*) (NOT (= ?*X* ?*Z*)))
then (HATES ?*X* ?*Z*)).

This rule can be used to prove the goal, if we can prove the following three subgoals:

Subgoal 1: (LOVES JOHN ?*Y*)
Subgoal 2: (LOVES ?*Y* FRED)
Subgoal 3: (NOT (= JOHN FRED))

All the ?*Y* must be the same, and therefore the bindings must be the same.

EMYCIN is an example of a production rule system that is based on the backward-chaining principle. EMYCIN was developed at Stanford University (it is a descendant of the medical diagnosis expert system, MYCIN). Several commercial versions of EMYCIN are currently on the market, including S-1 and M-1 from Teknowledge, and PERSONAL CONSULTANT from Texas Instruments.

Backward chaining, like forward chaining, is not trouble-free. The subgoals can grow in number and complexity, making substantiation of the ultimate goal very difficult and time-consuming. Furthermore, when we attempt to find a rule whose consequent matches a goal or subgoal, we may find that more than one possibility exists, putting us again in a conflict situation. Which rule and its resulting subgoals should we try first? Which is more likely to lead to a useful result, and which to a blind alley? The bushier the tree with the goal state as its starting point, the worse the problem. Practical backward-chaining systems employ all sorts of organizational concepts to help overcome these difficulties.

The differing strengths and weaknesses of forward and backward chaining have raised interest in efforts to integrate them into some sort of bidirectional search (goal-directed and data-driven) combining the best of both worlds. In combining both chaining modes, ambiguous or invalid input data may generate too many possible paths for pure forward-chain reasoning and too many hypotheses for pure backward chaining. Backward chaining, however, can be used to control the exponential growth of possibilities and to avoid the needless collection of facts and conclusions when the forward-chaining search tree begins to fan out excessively. The focus of backward chaining can be confined to plausible predictions with the aid of forward chaining.

An early A.I. inferencing system called PLANNER actually labeled rules as F (forward-chaining) rules and B (backward-chaining) rules. These rules were labeled on the basis of their semantic content and syntactic structure (for example, rules with very specific conditions might be labeled F rules because they are likely to apply to only a few unique situations and so are not likely to conflict with many other data-driven rules). Users of PLANNER then attempted to conduct an efficient bidirectional search applying these rules. But a bidirectional search strategy presents even greater perils, as illustrated in figure 2-11. Foremost is the danger that the path originating at the goal point and the path originating at the received evidence may pass each other and never connect, as shown. Proper control of a bidirectional search to ensure eventual connection of the two paths is very difficult. In fact, only a handful of systems have been successfully implemented using a bidirectional search stategy and these have been sufficiently structured and complex to warrant the trouble. Many of these problems involved machine perception, such as speech, image, and signal understanding. The Hearsay II speech understanding project is one such sophisticated system. The integration of a frame-based representation with production rules and logical clauses can assist in implementing these more complex reasoning strategies.

Once we depart from the fairly simple and mechanical resolution-based procedures such as those implemented in PROLOG, in pure forward-chaining systems (OPS-5), or in pure backward-chaining systems (EMYCIN, or one of its commercial versions such as S-1), a more fundamental approach to problem-solving methodology must be undertaken.

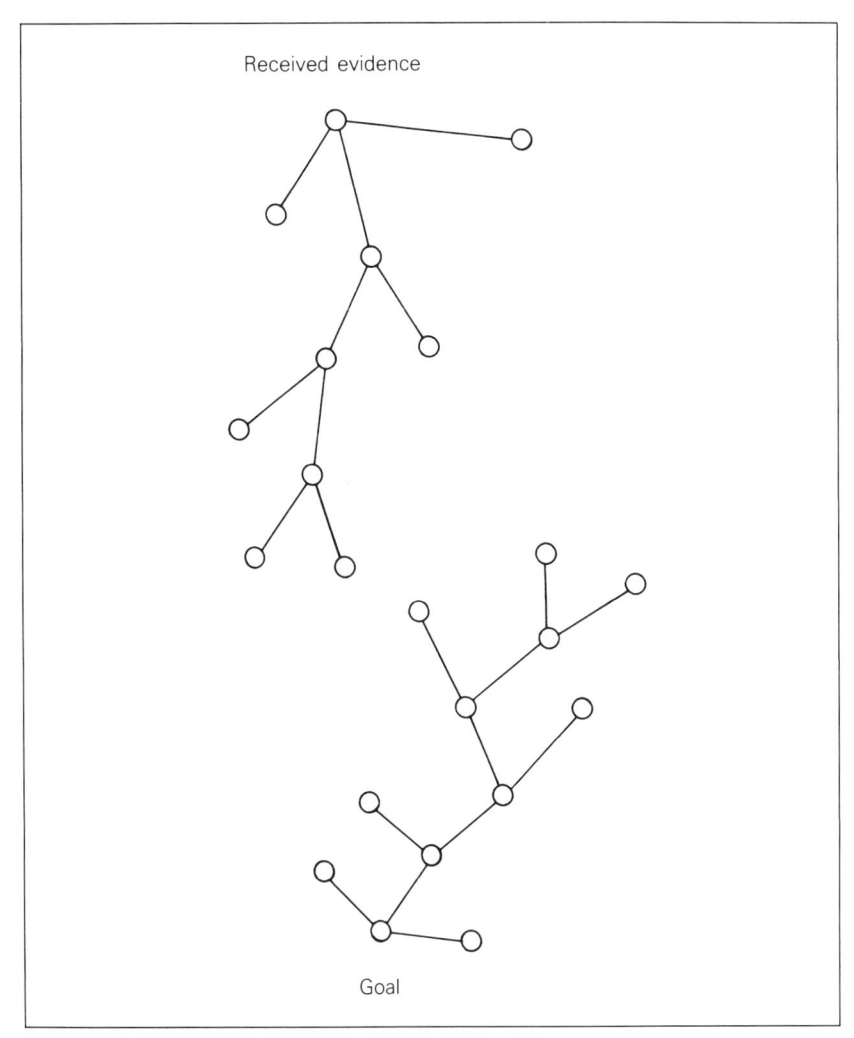

2-11. Hazards of a bidirectional search.

■ FRAME-BASED REPRESENTATIONS IN COMPLEX REASONING

A major shortcoming of production rules is their inadequacy in defining terms, describing objects, and identifying relationships. Frames provide a rich structural language for describing the objects referred to in rules and also provide an implicit underlying deductive capability through inheritance and membership links. These frame taxonomies can also be used to partition, index, and organize a system's production rules. A great deal of success has been achieved through this integration of frame and production rules to form hybrid representation facilities— for example, LOOPS (Stefik et al. 1983), KEE (Fikes and Kehler 1985), and CENTAUR (Aikins 1983). Having a hybrid capability makes it easier to construct rules, to understand rules, and to control when and for what purpose the system will use particular collections of rules.

Frame languages provide no specific facilities for declaratively describing behavior, but they allow control of behavior through mechanisms called *methods* and *active values*. Methods are procedures (often LISP procedures) attached to frames that respond to messages sent to the frames. Methods are stored as values in slots that have been identified as message responders. Active values are procedures or collections of rules attached to slots that are invoked when the slots' values are accessed and stored. Thus they behave as demons, monitoring changes and uses of values. They can also be used to compute values dynamically when needed.

Each independent rule set can be driven either in a backward-chaining mode or in a forward-chaining mode, depending on the nature of the rule set and/or the particular circumstances for which it was called/awakened. For example, a large diagnosis system could be structured into a collection of frame-based objects and rule sets such that a top-level rule set would be triggered whenever an anomalous situation triggered an alarm. This top-level monitor would typically be forward chained to identify all possible consequences of the anomalous situation in order to determine the class of problem involved. It then can call a more specialized expert rule set (depending upon the class of problem) that can further analyze and diagnose the specific problem. Often, the expert rule set could also be invoked in a backward-chaining mode to test specific hypotheses about the problem.

Frame systems provide constraint-checking procedures for determining whether a slot's value class and cardinality specifications exclude a given item from being a value of the slot. An item is excluded if the slot already has its maximum number of allowable values or if the item is not a member of the slot's value class. These procedures can be called directly by the user or by the system whenever the slot's values, value class specifications, or cardinality specifications are changed. Calls by the system result in an error's being generated if a constraint is violated.

Frames supply a powerful language for describing the objects being reasoned about by rules. They automatically perform useful sets of inferences based on these descriptions and can be used to represent the rules themselves. When used to represent a rule, the frame can contain an external view of the rule that accords with the view the user wishes to have of it, together with a parse method for converting the rule into an internal form for system use. The internal form may consist of lists of expressions that are values of condition, conclusion, and action slots, as well as descriptions such as rationalizations for the rule, records of usage, and goals for which the rule is useful. Frames can significantly help with rule management, by providing a means of modularizing, organizing, indexing, and scheduling, and invoking rules according to their intended use.

On the other hand, production rules can be used to augment the effectiveness of frame-based representations. Most frames describe prototype objects. Prototypes contain necessary but incomplete descriptions that can be used by a classifier to conclude that an item is not a member of a class but normally cannot be used to conclude that an item is a member. Production rules provide a natural way of supplementing class descriptions with sufficient descriptions for determining membership in a class.

■ REASONING WITH UNCERTAINTY

As should be clear from our earlier discussion regarding the representation of uncertainty, we still have a lot to learn about programming a computer to reason with uncertainty. Many research issues remain to be resolved, but programs have been implemented that have successfully dealt with uncertainty in their narrow problem domains. Several successful approaches are reviewed below.

MYCIN is an expert system that addresses the problem of diagnosing and treating blood diseases caused by bacterial infections. MYCIN was one of the first expert systems to use probabilistic-style reasoning. Proceeding under the assumption that medical reasoning is intuitive and not expressible in precise probabilistic terms, E.H. Shortliffe developed a rule-based inferencing scheme that includes an informal probabilistic reasoning process described below. The process involves two basic concepts: the measure of belief (MB), and the measure of disbelief (MD). In this scheme, $MB(H,E)$ is a measure of the belief in the consequent H, based on all available current evidence E; and $MD(H,E)$

is a measure of the disbelief in H, given all available current evidence E.

Mathematically, the measure of belief is the ratio of the increase of belief in the consequent or hypothesis H (due to the knowledge that E is also true) to the maximum possible increase in belief in H. The measure of disbelief is similarly defined as the ratio of the increase of disbelief in H (given knowledge of E) to the maximum possible increase in disbelief in H. For any simple antecedent or proposition E, either MD or MB must be zero; therefore, knowledge of a situation E must either increase the belief in a hypothesis and add nothing to disbelief or increase the disbelief in a hypothesis and add nothing to belief. A proposition E that does not influence H in any way has zero values for both its measure of belief and its measure of disbelief. The equations for these relationships are:

$$\text{MB}(H,E) = \begin{cases} 1 & \text{if } P(H)=1 \\ 0 & \text{if } P(H/E) \leq P(H) \\ P(H/E) - P(H) & \text{otherwise;} \end{cases}$$

$$\text{MD}(H,E) = \begin{cases} 1 & \text{if } P(H)=1 \\ 0 & \text{if } P(H/E) \geq P(H) \\ P(H) - P(H/E) & \text{otherwise;} \end{cases}$$

where:

$P(H)$ is the current probability that the consequent H is true
$P(H/E)$ is the probability that H is true, given that E is known to be true

These measures of belief and disbelief are updated individually and then combined to provide a certainty factor that is the difference of the two:

$$\text{CF}(H,E) = \text{MB}(H,E) - \text{MD}(H,E).$$

Measures of belief and disbelief are calculated for each proposition in the antecedent of a consequent to be updated. These measures are then combined under the rules of fuzzy logic (Zadeh 1965) to find the total measures of belief and disbelief on the antecedent of a rule. The certainty factor of the antecedent is then determined by combining these measures. Under the rules of fuzzy logic, the probability of a logical conjunction (*and*) of several pieces of evidence equals the minimum of the individual probability values corresponding to the evidence; the probability of a logical disjunction (*or*) corresponds to the maximum of the individual probabilities of the pieces. These certainty factors, which are calculated for the antecedent of a rule, are used to update the measures of belief and disbelief in the consequent according to the following formulas:

$$MB(H, E\&E1) = MB(H, E) + MB'(H, E1) * CF(E1, E) * (1 - MB(H, E)),$$

if MB'$(H, E) > 0$, or:

$$MD(H, E\&E1) = MD(H, E) + MD'(H, E1) * CF(E1, E) * (1 - MD(H, E)),$$

if MD'$(H, E1) > 0$. In these equations $E1$ is the new antecedent, E is the current situation, H is the consequent, and MB'$(H, E1)$ and MD'$(H, E1)$ are the maximum measures of belief and disbelief in the consequent, given that the antecedent is absolutely believed.

If all rules are assumed to increase the belief in their consequents and if endpoint conditions are ignored, then updating may be expressed as:

$$CF(H, E\&E1) = CF(H, E) + CF'(H, E1) * CF(E1, E) * (1 - CF(H, E)).$$

PROSPECTOR is a computer consultant system designed to aid geologists in evaluating the favorability of an exploration site or region for occurrences of particular types of ore deposits (Duda, Hart, and Nilsson 1976). PROSPECTOR uses three different kinds of relations— logical, plausible, and contextual—to specify how a change in probability of one assertion affects the probability of other assertions.

With logical relations, the truth (or falsity) of a hypothesis is completely determined by the truth (or falsity) of the assertions that define it. These relations include the primitive logical operations: conjunction (*and*), disjunction (*or*), and negation (*not*). As with MYCIN's measures of belief and disbelief, fuzzy set theory is employed to compute the probability of a hypothesis from the probability of its component assertions (Zadeh 1965). The logical *and* is the minimum of the probability values of the corresponding elements of evidence, and the logical *or* is the maximum of the probability values of the components.

With plausible relations, each assertion contributes votes or markers for or against the truth of the hypothesis. Each rule has associated with it a rule strength that measures the degree to which a change in the probability of the evidence changes the probability of the hypothesis. This change can be positive or negative, since each assertion can provide evidence that is either favorable or unfavorable to a hypothesis. The plausible reasoning scheme is based on Bayesian probability decision theory; the changes in probability are computed using Bayes' rule. From Bayes' rule we know that:

$$P(H/Ej) = P(Ej/H)*P(H)/P(Ej).$$

The probability of the consequent, given its antecedent Ej, is equal to the probability that the antecedent will be at its current probability (given the consequent), multiplied by the prior probability of the consequent, and divided by the prior probability of the antecedent. PROSPECTOR uses the odds-likelihood form of Bayes' rule:

$$O(H/E) = LS*O(H),$$

where the odds O is related to the probability P by the following relationships:

$$O = P/(1 - P),$$
$$P = O/(1 + O),$$

and where LS is a standard quantity in statistics known as the likelihood ratio, defined as:

$$LS = P(E/H)/P(E/\sim H),$$

where $\sim H$ means "not H."

A complementary set of equations describes the case in which E is known to be absent—that is, the case in which $\sim E$ is true:

$$O(H/\sim E) = LN*O(H),$$

where:

$$LN = P(\sim E/H)/P(\sim E/\sim H),$$

and where LN is called the necessity measure. As LN approaches zero, E becomes a logical necessity for H.

Hence, we define a plausible inference rule as:

IF E
THEN (to degree LS,LN) H,

where we must articulate E and H; supply numerical values for LS, LN, and $O(H)$; and interpret the importance of a piece of evidence as an indicator by its likelihood and necessity measures. For example, LS = 5,700 and LN = 0.0001 describe an antecedent that is a highly sufficient and highly necessary factor.

Contextual relations, the third class of relations, are used to express a condition that must be established before an assertion can be brought into the reasoning process. For example, contextual relations are used in PROSPECTOR when one assertion is geologically significant only if another assertion has already been established.

Different relations can be combined in PROSPECTOR to express more complex relationships. Consider, for example, the section of figure 2-12 dealing with establishing "suggestive morphology of igneous rocks." This section can be described in the following language: "There are four positive indicators for establishing a suggestive morphology of igneous rocks, namely intrusive breccias, stocks, dikes, and volcanic plugs." Each of these factors contributes independently to establishing a suggestive morphology of igneous rocks, although to differing degrees. The absence of any one of these four factors is unimportant (that is, LN = 1 for those rules), but if all four factors are absent (node SMIRA is false), then the probability of a suggestive morphology of igneous rocks is effectively zero (LN = 0.0002 for SMIRA).

PROSPECTOR uses a -5-to-5 certainty scale for the user to express the degree of certainty felt about the evidence requested by the system and for the program to express the degree of confidence it has computed regarding a conclusion back to the user. PROSPECTOR maps internal probability values to external certainty scores in a piecewise linear fashion, where the posterior certainty is a function of the difference between the posterior probability and the prior probability. For example, if the prior probability of a hypothesis is 0.005, and the posterior probability is 0.34276, the posterior certainty can be identified as:

$$5*(0.34276 - 0.005)/(1 - 0.005) = 1.697.$$

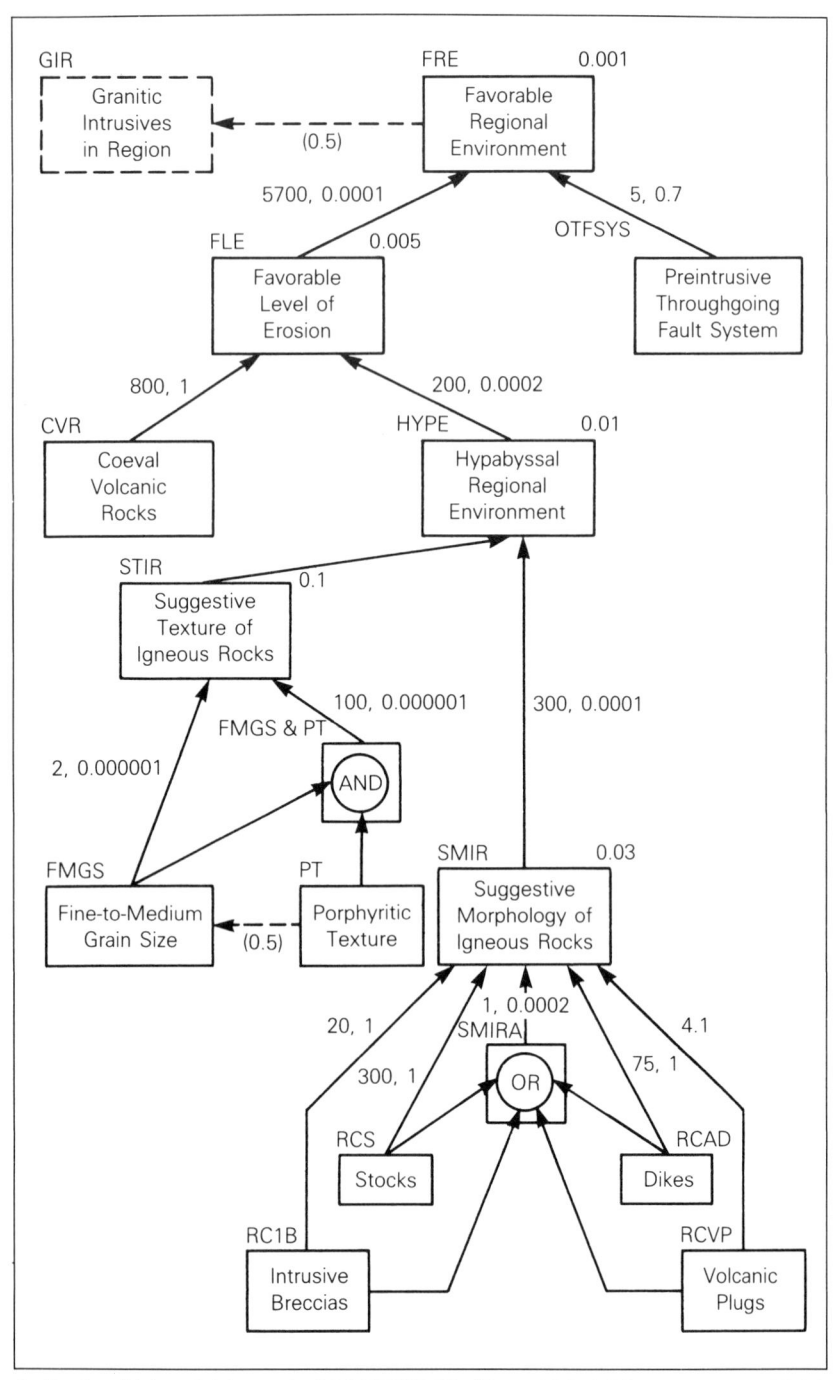

2-12. Combining Evidence in PROSPECTOR. (From "Model Design in the PROSPECTOR Consultant System for Mineral Exploration," by Richard Duda, John Gaschnig, and Peter Hart. In *Expert Systems in the Microelectronic Age*, edited by D. Michie. Published by Edinburgh University Press, Edinburgh, 1979. Reprinted with permission.)

Evidential reasoning, based on a relatively new body of mathematics known as the Shafer-Dempster theory, extends the more common Bayesian probability analysis to provide a formal semantics for the representation and manipulation of degrees of belief (Shafer 1976). It allows reasoning from evidence that can be inaccurate, incomplete, and incorrect. In the Shafer-Dempster theory, the fundamental measure of belief is represented as an interval bounding the probability of a proposition, an approach that allows the representation of ignorance as well as of uncertainty. It enables the user to express partial belief in evidence without expressing a preference for any portion of the evidence; in contrast, a Bayesian approach often requires unjustified assumptions such as representing ignorance as a uniform distribution across all possible states. Bayesian theory does not allow a distinction between ignorance and disbelief. In the Shafer-Dempster theory, bodies of evidence are represented by mass distributions of units of belief across the space of propositions. The mass distribution assigns a value of belief in the range (0,1) to each subset of the space of propositions, such that:

$$\sum_{\text{all } Fi} M(Fi) = 1$$

where $M(Fi)$ is the mass attributed to proposition Fi. This representation allows the user to specify belief at exactly the level of detail desired while remaining noncommittal toward propositions about which the user is ignorant.

The support, $\text{Spt}(Q)$, for an arbitrary proposition Q is the total belief attributed by the mass distribution to propositions that imply Q; that is:

$$\text{Spt}(Q) = \sum_{Fi \subseteq Q} M(Fi)$$

The plausibility, $\text{Pls}(Q)$, of the arbitrary proposition Q is the total belief attributed by the mass distribution to propositions that do not imply $\sim Q$; it represents the degree to which the evidence fails to refute the hypothesis:

$$\begin{aligned}\text{Pls}(Q) &= \sum_{Fi \cap Q \neq \emptyset} M(Fi) \\ &= 1 - \sum_{Fi \subseteq \sim Q} M(Fi) \\ &= 1 - \text{Spt}(\sim Q)\end{aligned}$$

For each proposition Q, a mass function defines the credibility interval $(\text{Spt}(Q), \text{Pls}(Q))$ that bounds the probability of Q. The difference $\text{Pls}(Q) - \text{Spt}(Q)$ represents the degree of ignorance. It can be shown that:

$$\text{Pls}(Q) = 1 - \text{Spt}(\sim Q),$$

and:

$$\text{Spt}(Q) \leq \text{Prob}(Q) \leq \text{Pls}(Q).$$

The probability of Q is known exactly if $\text{Spt}(Q) = \text{Pls}(Q)$. In this case, the more general Shafer-Dempster measure matches the probability measure.

The Shafer-Dempster measures can be combined to pool multiple bodies of evidence. Starting with arbitrarily complex mass distributions M1 and M2 (as long as they are not completely contradictory), the measures produce a third mass distribution Ms that represents the consensus of the two disparate prior opinions. Dempster's rule moves belief toward propositions that are supported by both bodies of evidence and away from all others. Mathematically, Ms, the consensus mass distribution, is represented as:

$$\text{Ms}(Q) = (1/1-k) \sum_{Fi \cap Fj = Q} M1(Fi)*M2(Fj),$$

where the factor k is defined as:

$$k = \sum_{Fi \cap Fj \neq \emptyset} M1(Fi)*M2(Fj).$$

Factor k can be thought of as a measure of the degree of disagreement between the two bodies of evidence represented by masses M1 and M2. If $k = 1$, the bodies of evidence represented by M1 and M2 are contradictory, and their combination is not defined.

An important property of Dempster's rule is that it is both commutative and associative. This allows bodies of evidence to be combined in any order and in any groupings (the same property holds true for MYCIN's confidence factors and for the PROSPECTOR system).

Among the disadvantages of using these statistically based inference schemes is that they usually require a lot of data, including an estimation of the probability or confidence measures. Moreover, the proper way to interpret the numbers used in these techniques is often unclear; the numbers are subjective and probably inaccurate, in the sense that an expert may assess different numbers in the same situation. Further, interpretations of the numbers may or may not be preserved by the functions that combine them; in fact, studies conducted by the MYCIN group suggest that the numbers can be modified by as much as 20 percent without significantly changing the certainty ranking of hypotheses.

Another concern is that these schemes probably differ fundamentally from the scheme human beings use, since human beings (even statistically skilled ones) produce subjective probabilities conditioned on evidence that vary sharply from probabilities produced by Bayesian conditioning rules (Tversky and Kahneman 1982). People tend to classify and to assign probabilities on the basis of similarity to stereotype members, and not on the model of games of chance. This is called the representativeness heuristic. Thus, except when truly random physical phenomena are under examination, numbers should usually serve a representation of last resort in A.I. When we understand the real content of the numbers, we abandon them for more symbolic representations.

■ PROBLEM SOLVING

Earlier sections have described how general problem solving involves a search of candidate solutions and partial solutions. For example, the problem definition could be considered as the initial state, and the knowledge base of applicable production rules could be considered as operators that transform the initial problem state into intermediate states (either subgoals that can be used to prove a hypothesis through backward chaining or new consequences that are derived by matching conditions with existing facts and rules through forward chaining). The problem-solving strategy consists of finding a sequence of state transitions that leads to a desired solution. This state space search approach to problem solving is illustrated in figure 2-13.

General-purpose search methods that do not make use of special knowledge pertinent to the specific problem domain are called *weak methods*. These uninformed search methods prove inefficient for many problems of practical interest as the number of candidate solutions requiring examination would be too large.

In the game of chess, for example, 35 possible moves can be made from a given position. An exploration of all the possibilities of 4 subsequent moves in a chess game, starting from the same initial position, would require examining over 1.4 million moves. To perform an exhaustive search of all possible moves in a typical chess game would require

68 ■ THEORIES AND CONCEPTS

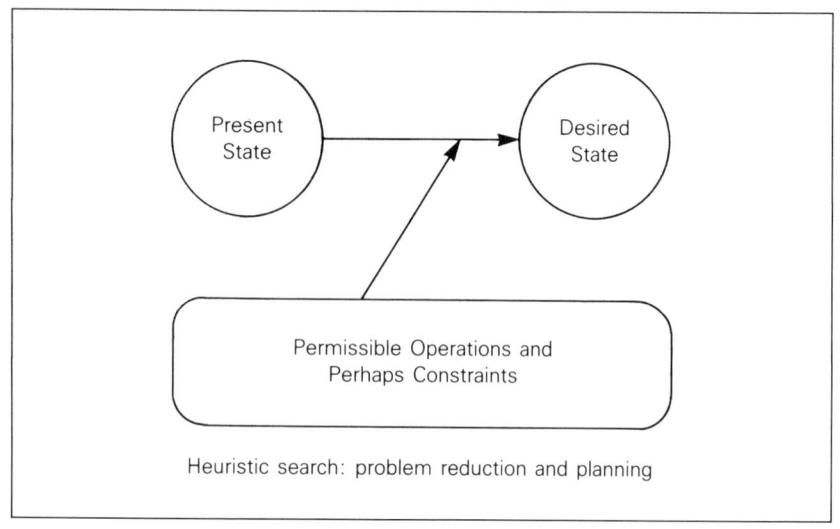

2-13. Problem solving.

examining over 10^{120} moves. If moves could be examined at the rate of 3 billion per second it would still take 10^{21} centuries to explore the whole tree of possibilities. Belle, the specially constructed chess machine developed at Bell Telephone Laboratories, can only examine moves at the rate of 160,000 per second.

This search can be reduced in two ways: through decomposition, and through heuristic search. Decomposition requires breaking up the original problem into a set of several smaller, simpler problems, each requiring far less search time than the original problem. This is known as "divide and conquer." Heuristic search involves using special task-dependent knowledge to constrain the search by eliminating searches along unlikely paths. Expertise in an area involves having the ability to use shortcuts and labor-saving techniques that less experienced persons would not know about. Experts are able to reduce the equivalent of a large search space for a general problem-solving program to a much smaller search space that can usually (but does not always) lead to a problem solution without reducing the quality of the solution. These knowledge-intensive task-dependent search limiters/reducers are known as heuristics.

The strategy for solving a problem is influenced by its characteristics. A problem that is decomposable can be broken into smaller, more manageable subproblems. If the separate problem parts are only partially decomposable, such that the subproblems can interfere with each other, we can still attempt to solve the problem by breaking it into its subparts and solving each subproblem in turn. This requires care and the making of minimum, least commitments capable of affecting future subproblems in the course of solving a particular subproblem. For example, a person who wishes to paint one wall white, one wall pink, and a third wall red, but only has two cans of paint—a red one and a white one—would be well advised to postpone mixing the two cans of paint together and painting the pink wall until after having painted one of the walls white and the other red.

It might also be necessary to make some plausible guesses in order to move forward with the solution of a given subproblem. For example, in solving an electronic circuit analysis problem in which one stage requires solving for the electric current flowing through a transistor, it may be necessary to guess at the state of the transistor (which parametric load line to use). Some guesses and commitments may have to be undone in later stages of the problem-solving process.

For any given problem or subproblem, the nature of the search control strategy and of the housekeeping required is strongly influenced by characteristics of the problem. For some classes of problems, the solution steps may be ignored. An example of this would be the case of proving some mathematical formula—logical, algebraic, or otherwise. To prove a theorem in logic, all facts and consequents must be related to each other through an interlocking logical network. We can derive all implied consequents from any starting point, given a consistent and complete set of facts and logical implications. As long as all the manipulations are legal, we never have to back up and undo any steps; we can always pick up where we left off. With algebraic equations, as long as we perform the same operations on both sides of the equal sign, we never need to backtrack, since we know that we have preserved the equality of the equation and that all operations are reversible.

Some problems may require backtracking in order to explore alternative paths. Consider the 8-puzzle game illustrated in figure 2-2. We can make a sequence of moves that leaves us in a situation from which we can only achieve our desired goal by retracting some of the more recent moves and returning to an earlier situation. Such a problem—one in which we cannot ignore past steps, but for which past steps are recoverable—dictates a search strategy that allows us to store sufficient pertinent information about earlier states to enable us to backtrack and return to an earlier, more promising state when we detect that we have reached a stalemate.

Some problems, such as playing the game of chess or controlling complex manufacturing processes, present more difficulties. In this class of problems, once we move to a new state we can no longer return to an earlier state. Once we make a chess move, we cannot retract it, even if we suddenly realize that the move opens the way for a checkmate or for the capture of an important piece of ours. If we mix our only can of red paint with our only can of white paint so that we can paint a wall pink, we have lost the opportunity to paint the remaining walls white or red.

For such a problem, we must expend considerable time in advance simulating an approximate model or abstract representation of the actual problem to avoid making any bad moves that cannot be undone. This planning process often requires a search. We model and anticipate the likely consequents of our possible actions, and then choose the action that appears to provide the desired results. If the current and future problem states are characterized by uncertainty, the strategy of the search process must take this uncertainty into account. The planning process gets much more complicated when uncertainty is involved because we can no longer simulate all possibilities.

Determining when we have solved our problem and when to stop searching is a final function of the problem characteristics. If the desired solution state is relative, recognizing when we have reached the solution state (without exploring all possible solutions) becomes much more difficult. For example, if we wish to locate the shortest route connecting ten different cities, we will find it difficult to be sure that we have located the shortest route unless we have checked all possible routes or have found a route whose total distance is equal to the minimum airline distance between the ten cities (for example, if all ten cities lie on a straight line and our route is equal to the airline distance between the two farthest cities). On the other hand, if we wish to prove that Mary is John's mother, we know that we have solved our problem when we succeed in finding a chain of rules that connects some known facts and relationships and their consequents to the conclusion that John has a mother named Mary.

It is therefore important to study searches and search strategies if we are to improve our problem-solving control. Search strategies describe the process by which a network or *and/or* tree structure is examined. For most problems, this tree is only implicitly defined; that is, the tree or network is generally not known and not completely specified at the start of the problem. Rather, only the top or starting position is known, along with rules to generate successor positions from the current position and a search termination criterion. This is illustrated in figure 2-14.

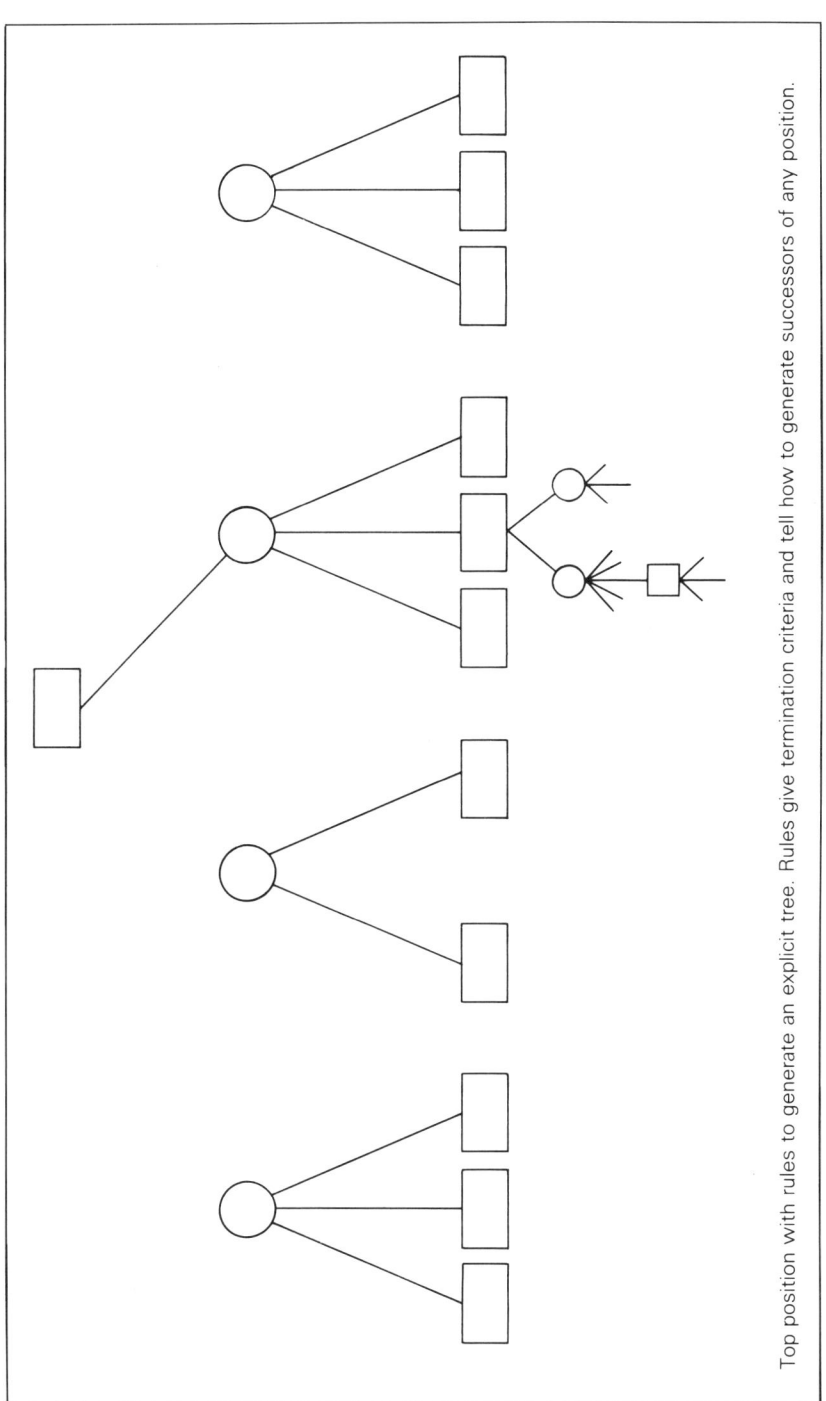

Top position with rules to generate an explicit tree. Rules give termination criteria and tell how to generate successors of any position.

2-14. Implicit trees.

■ SEARCH STRATEGIES

Some of the more basic search strategies are: breadth-first, depth-first, hill-climbing, best-first, and branch-and-bound.

A breadth-first search looks for the goal state among all nodes at a given level before going on to the next level. In a pure breadth-first search, the search proceeds along the tree, layer by layer, and no alternative is ignored. This is illustrated in figure 2-15. It is a careful and conservative approach that is particularly effective if the tree is narrow and long. It is sure to find a solution if one exists. It has not been used too often in current A.I. systems, however, because of three major problems:

1. It requires a lot of memory.
2. It requires a lot of work.
3. Irrelevant or redundant operators greatly increase the number of nodes that must be explored.

A depth-first search follows one path as far as it can go. In a pure depth-first search, selection of a route at each branch point is arbitrary; no likelihood of success is assumed in choosing a path, and alternatives are ignored as long as progress is made. If an impasse is reached such that a path can go no further and a successful solution has not yet been found, the process backs up to the nearest node and then proceeds along the path of a previously unexplored alternative. The depth-first strategy, illustrated in figure 2-16, is aggressive but dangerous: a depth-

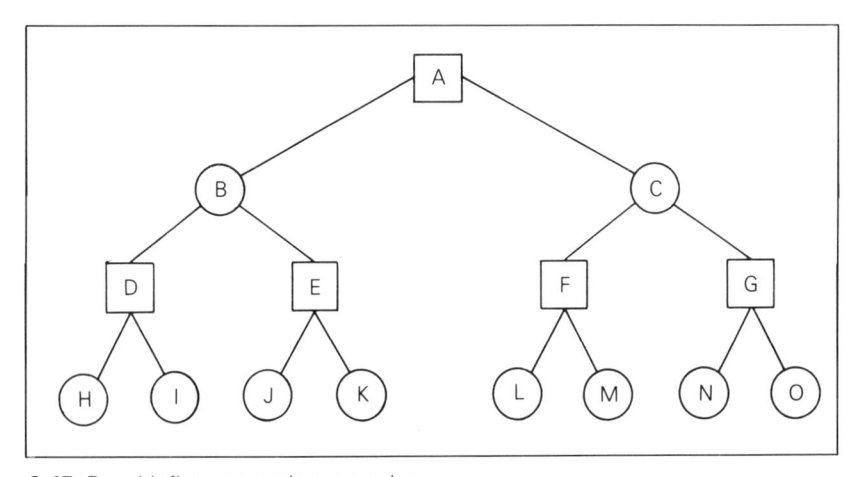

2-15. Breadth-first generation procedure.

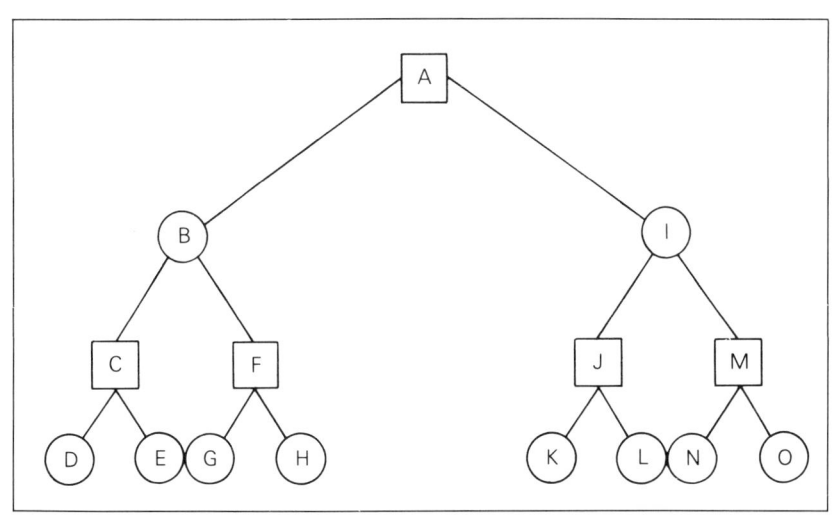

2-16. Depth-first generation procedure.

first search may reach a solution that bypasses much shorter valid paths, wasting time and yielding a less-than-optimum result. A depth-first search works best on broad and shallow problem-state trees.

Generate-and-test is a depth-first search procedure that involves generating whole potential solutions, one at a time. First a potential solution (a particular point in problem space or a path from a start space) is generated; then its validity as an actual solution is tested by having the endpoint matched to a set of acceptable goal states. If a matching solution is found, we quit; if not, we repeat the process, generating another possible solution, testing, and so on.

Hill-climbing is a depth-first search combined with a method for ordering the alternatives by measuring the probability of success at each decision point. The hill-climbing strategy is to take a step in all possible directions, move to the best point found, and then repeat the process until a spot is reached that cannot be improved upon by single-step moves. Such a strategy encounters problems with local maxima (the foothill problem), with gradients where the loci are not along the exploratory directions chosen (the ridge problem), with areas lacking any local gradient (the plateau problem), and with multidimensional problem spaces.

A best-first search is similar to hill-climbing, except that—instead of continuing in the best direction from the last decision point examined—progress continues in the best direction from the best node examined so far, no matter where it is. Best-first thus combines the advantages of depth-first and breadth-first search strategies in a single method.

The A∗ algorithm (Hart et al. 1968, 1972) is a particularly well-known implementation of the best-first search strategy. This algorithm operates by searching a directed graph in which each node represents a point in problem space. Each node contains a description of the problem state it represents, an indication of how promising it is, a parent link that points back to the best node from which it came, and a list of nodes that were generated from it. The parent link allows us to recover the solution path once the goal is found, and the list of successors allows propagation of the improvement down to its successors if a better path is found to an already existing node.

The A∗ algorithm maintains two lists of nodes: the open list, which contains nodes that have been generated and have had the heuristic function applied to them, but have not yet been examined (their successors have not been generated); and the closed list, which includes nodes that have already been examined. The algorithm uses a heuristic function to estimate the merits of each node we generate. We call it $f*$ to indicate that this function is an approximation of the true evaluation of the node. For many applications, $f*$ is defined as the sum of two components that we will call g and $h*$. The function g is a true measure of the cost of getting from the initial node to the current node. The function $h*$ is an estimate of the additional cost of getting from the current node to a goal state. This is where knowledge of the problem domain is exploited.

The operation of this algorithm proceeds in steps. At each step, the algorithm picks the most promising of the nodes that have been generated but (so far) not expanded. It then generates the successors of the chosen node, applies the heuristic function to them, and adds them to the list of open nodes (after checking to see if any of them have already been generated). The algorithm continues in this manner until the goal state is reached or until we run out of time.

As an example of the A∗ algorithm, consider a variant of the traveling salesman problem, in which the salesman wishes to visit a set of cities by selecting from the set of all roads the shortest possible route that connects all the cities and returns the salesman home. If we tried to solve this problem by exploring all possible paths, we would have $(N - 1)!$ (factorial) paths to explore, where N is the number of cities to be visited. This represents a number that grows unreasonably large as the number of cities increases to ten or more.

The nearest neighbor algorithm is a heuristic that can be implemented using the A∗ algorithm. This heuristic is not guaranteed to find the best answer, but it will almost always find a good answer in a realistic time— time proportional to N^2. In this case, a node represents a city with an estimate $h*$ of its distance to the other cities on the list (such as an approximation of the number of airline miles), and the generator expands nodes by searching different roads for one that connects the city where the salesman is currently located with the closest city on the list of as-yet unvisited cities. The merit of each path is evaluated by the function $f* = g + h*$, where g represents the actual distance already traveled from the starting city, and $h*$ represents an estimate of the distance (the airline distance) to the next closest city. We repeat this step until all the cities on the list are visited and the salesman returns home.

A disadvantage of the A* algorithm is that, if we overestimate $h*$, we cannot be sure of finding the optimum path solution unless we expand the entire graph. Under certain conditions, the A* algorithm generates the fewest nodes of any algorithm in the process of finding a solution to a problem (Gelperin 1977; Martelli 1977).

Another algorithm that implements the best-first search strategy is the agenda-driven system. This system is particularly useful when no single, simple heuristic function exists for measuring the distance between a given node and a goal. An agenda is a list of tasks that a system could perform. Each task bears a list of reasons explaining why the task is being proposed (often called justifications) and a rating representing the weight of evidence suggesting that the task would be useful. An agenda-driven system operates by choosing the most promising task from the agenda and then executing the task.

Executing the task commonly generates additional tasks. If the task is already on the agenda, it should be checked to see if it already has the current justification; if it does not, the justification should be added. If the task was not on the agenda, it should be added. The new task's rating is then computed from all its justifications.

A branch-and-bound search is used when an optimum solution is desired. As the network is explored, the path that is shortest or most likely to succeed is extended one level, creating new incomplete paths. These new paths are then evaluated along with the old ones, and again the one that is shortest or most likely to succeed is extended. This technique could be applied to problems such as the traveling salesman problem described above. It will find an optimum solution in exponential time, time equal to a number raised to the N power. This time is faster than $(N - 1)!$ but significantly slower than N^2 (the time required for the A* algorithm); the branch-and-bound algorithm, however, guarantees finding a best solution.

Means-ends analysis is a technique that allows a mixture of both forward and backward reasoning, enabling users to solve the major parts of the problem first. The General Problem Solver (Newell and

Simon 1963; Ernst and Newell 1969) was the first A.I. program to use means-ends analysis.

Means-ends analysis requires a set of operators whose ability to move the current state toward the goal state can be measured. First the user detects the differences between the current state and the goal state; then the user finds the operator that causes the greatest reduction of this difference. This operator most often will be unable to operate on the current state and will not produce the goal state. Therefore, we will have to satisfy some preconditions, by applying other operators, before being able to apply the selected operator. Once at our new state, we will repeat the process, looking now for the next-highest-priority operator to apply.

As an example of this technique, suppose that we wish to travel from a school classroom in New York to our aunt's house in Los Angeles. The distance between these two cities is approximately 3,000 miles. The operator that is most effective in reducing this difference is "fly." But this operator requires being at an airport; so because we chose the operator "fly," we have a new subgoal to satisfy, namely getting to the airport. The difference between the school and the airport is approximately 50 miles. Now the best operator to apply is "drive." This operator, however, requires us to be in our car, which is downstairs in the garage. This means that we now need to satisfy the subgoal of getting to the garage. To satisfy this subgoal, we select the operator "walk," whose precondition we already satisfy.

In general, a search strategy requires:

1. A procedure for generating successor states.
2. A procedure for evaluating which successor state to pick and when to terminate the search.
3. A procedure for backing up when an impasse is reached.

SEARCH STRATEGY EXAMPLE

Consider the depth-first minimax procedure in figure 2-17. This approach might be used in playing a special type of chess we will call *truncated chess*. In this game, the two opponents, Chris and Sandy, start out with the same number of pieces, each in a prespecified position. Chris and Sandy are each allowed two moves; Chris moves first. At the end of the game, all of Chris's remaining pieces will be added up (each different type of piece has a different weight), and if the sum exceeds a given threshold, Chris wins; if not, Sandy wins.

```
                    A ☐

        B (30)                    I (29)

   C [40]    F [30]         J [29]      [80]

 D(40) E(10) G(30) H(20)  K(21) L(29)  (5)  (80)
```

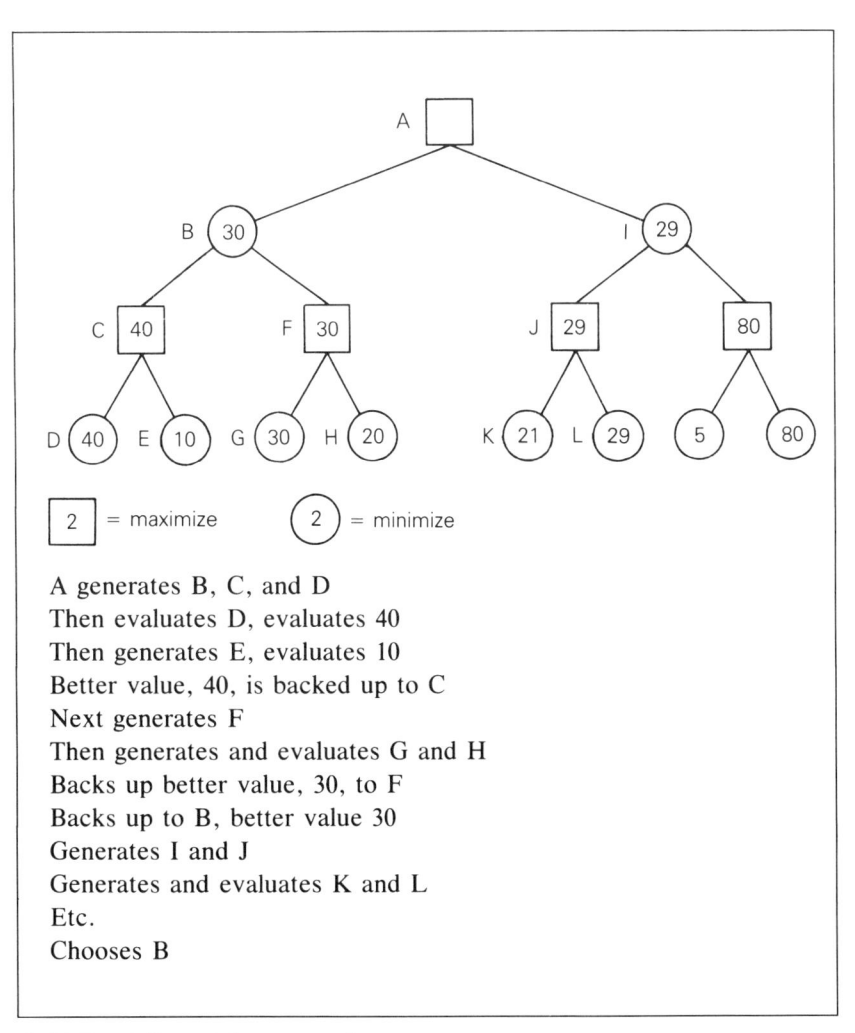

[2] = maximize   (2) = minimize

A generates B, C, and D
Then evaluates D, evaluates 40
Then generates E, evaluates 10
Better value, 40, is backed up to C
Next generates F
Then generates and evaluates G and H
Backs up better value, 30, to F
Backs up to B, better value 30
Generates I and J
Generates and evaluates K and L
Etc.
Chooses B

2-17. Depth-first minimax procedure.

Because moves are irreversible and an unpredictable opponent is involved, Chris will select moves based on a planning process that simulates Sandy's behavior—assuming that Sandy never makes mistakes and always acts to maximize points on offense and to minimize points on defense. The search tree for this game is shallow and narrow, so Chris will use an exhaustive depth-first strategy in which all the paths are fully evaluated. The tree in figure 2-17 is shown in standard minimax game theory notation, where the square denotes *maximize* and the circle denotes *minimize*. The termination nodes are evaluated exactly by taking the weighted sum of Chris's remaining pieces; these numbers are illustrated inside the circles labeled D, E, G, H, K, L, N, and O.

The first path to be considered is A-B-C-D. Evaluating A involves first evaluating B and I; evaluating B involves first evaluating C and F; and evaluating C involves first evaluating D and E. D is 40, and E is 10; therefore, since C is Chris's move and since Chris wishes to maximize points, the proper move for Chris to make is from C to D (worth 40 points). Likewise, since G and H are worth 30 and 20 points, respectively, F is worth only 30 points. Since B is a minimize node, representing Sandy's move, Sandy will choose alternative F (worth 30 points) over alternative C. The remaining paths I-J-K, I-J-L, I-M-N, and I-M-O can be evaluated according to the same logic, as shown in figure 2-17. Since A is a maximize node, Chris should pick B as the next successor state because it is worth 30 points, 1 point more than alternative I.

It was not necessary to consider and evaluate all these nodes and paths. Many could have been eliminated by means of a backward pruning procedure called the alpha-beta procedure. This modified depth-first procedure produces equivalent results by generating a smaller fraction of the tree than the depth-first minimax procedure does. For this reason, it is used when more than two or three tree levels must be inspected. The alpha-beta procedure involves establishing an alpha cutoff (maximum position) and a beta cutoff (minimum position).

To see how this works, consider our previous illustration. Having evaluated B as equal to 30, Chris sets the alpha cutoff to 30 (meaning that Chris need not settle for a node worth less than 30); then Chris begins to evaluate node I. First, from the values for K and L, J is evaluated as 29. Since I is a minimize node, I cannot be worth more that 29 because Sandy can always select node J. Thus, neither path I-M-N nor path I-M-O has to be evaluated, since node I falls below the alpha cutoff; Chris should select B as the successor to A. Similarly, in evaluating node B, Chris can establish a beta cutoff. If node F had been evaluated as 30 first, the beta cutoff for B would have been 30; this represents the best defensive move Chris can make. Since B is a minimizing node and since Sandy can always select node F as a successor, Sandy will never pick a successor whose value exceeds the beta cutoff of 30. Knowing that the value of D (one of C's successors) is 40, Chris can immediately disqualify C and its successors from further consideration.

Up until now, we have assumed that our illustrative example represents a special truncated chess game in which Chris's opponent, Sandy, behaves in an error-free (and in that sense, predictable) way. But suppose Sandy makes a few mistakes, such as selecting alternative M over alternative J as the successor to state I. If this happens, Chris may not have picked the optimum solution by using the depth-first minimax search strategy or the modified depth-first minimax search strategy. In fact, node I may turn out to be worth 80 points rather than 29—50 points more than B. Thus the evaluation function is not exact but heuristic; it approximates the actual value of each node. If the likelihood of Sandy's making a mistake becomes nonnegligible, the actual value of node I may become sufficiently large to make alternative I the preferred successor to select. By choosing I, Chris risks losing 1 point in exchange for the chance of winning an additional 50. Perhaps some random selection strategy would be preferable.

Using the weighted sum of pieces left after two plays (two moves and two countermoves) as the evaluation function in an actual game of chess would clearly be a heuristic and not an exact evaluation function. Furthermore, the evaluation would not require that a path be explored to termination, leaving the function vulnerable to counterstrategies in a real chess game; upon recognizing the predictable playing pattern that the heuristic follows, Sandy could plan five or six moves ahead and set Chris up. In a real game of chess, a more sophisticated strategy, where different paths are explored to varying depths and where substrategies are instituted, would be more effective. Nevertheless, it should be clear that searches in complex problems can be kept manageable by heuristics used to:

- Limit the number of successors generated and hypotheses considered
- Evaluate and select which nodes and paths to try, and in what order to try them
- Decide which paths and nodes to prune and remove from further consideration

This idea is summarized in figure 2-18.

DENDRAL

The expert system DENDRAL (Lindsay et al. 1980)—developed by Feigenbaum, Lederberg, and their associates—provides an excellent example of the power of heuristics to reduce search. DENDRAL infers the structure of organic compounds, using mass spectrogram and nuclear

80 ■ THEORIES AND CONCEPTS

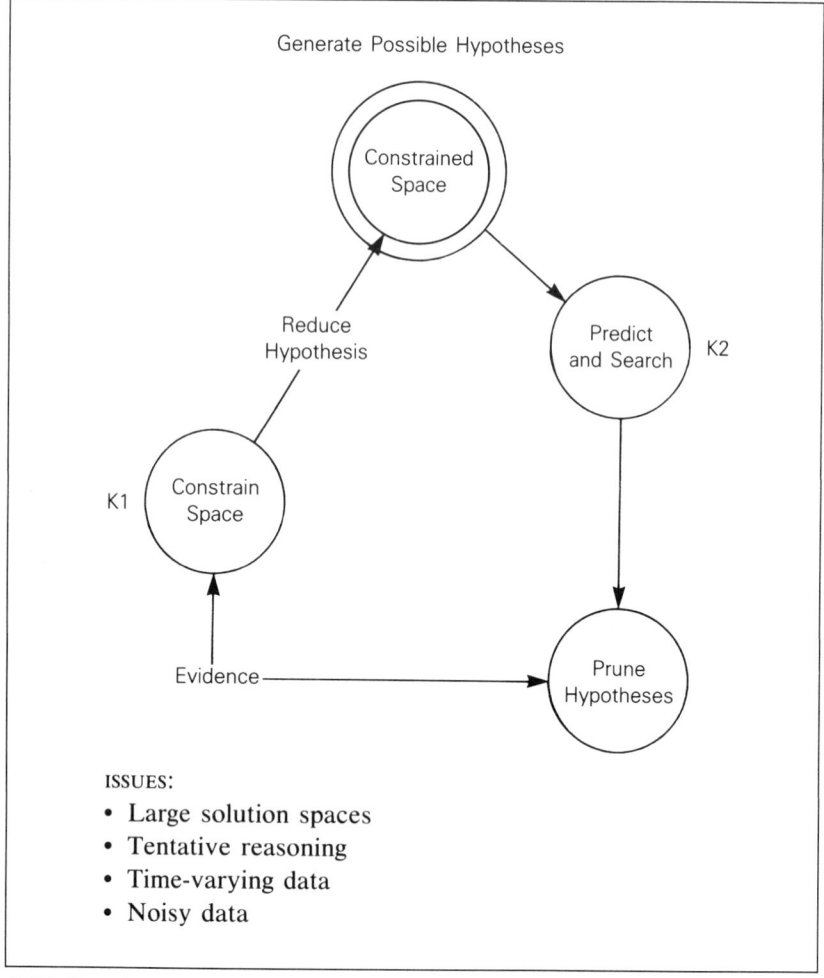

```
                    Generate Possible Hypotheses

                         ┌─────────────┐
                         │ Constrained │
                         │    Space    │
                         └─────────────┘
                        ↗               ↘
              Reduce                      Predict
              Hypothesis                  and Search     K2
                        
                    Constrain
              K1     Space
                        ↑
              Evidence ─────────────→  Prune
                                       Hypotheses
```

ISSUES:
- Large solution spaces
- Tentative reasoning
- Time-varying data
- Noisy data

2-18. Search constraints.

resonance (NMR) data. It uses a special procedure to generate the molecular structure candidates, and it refers to tables of production rules in searching an *and/or* tree (controlled by forward chaining) to derive necessary constraints and to prune, filter, test, and evaluate the candidates. Initially, the data base describes no chemical structure, but merely a chemical formula. At the end of the process of searching the tree, however, the data base possesses a representation of the entire structure of the compound. During the search process, the global data base is a partially structured chemical compound.

This strategy is called plan-generate-test. The planning phase creates lists of recommended and contraindicated substructures. Each list is kept to reasonably small, manageable proportions through the use of constraints based on rules and knowledge of chemistry that eliminate many candidate substructures; if a substructure violates a constraint, it is eliminated. The planning phase typically reduces the set from possibly millions of candidates to a few hundred. The generate-and-test phase then explores a limited number of structures based on this reduced list. Only a very small subset of this list actually receives complete substructure testing (typically, a few tens) because the generate-and-test procedure makes use of heuristics to prune many of the paths in the search tree. The generate procedure systematically generates partial molecular structures consistent with the data and then elaborates them in all plausible ways.

Integrating the use of constraints with plan-generate-test techniques produces a powerful system that overcomes the weaknesses of each component technique. By rapidly eliminating implausible structures, DENDRAL avoids an otherwise exponential search; and by systematically generating all plausible structures, it finds candidates that human experts may occasionally overlook.

■ PLANNING

Planning—thinking about and deciding on a course of action before acting—is used to reduce the amount of a search, to resolve goal conflicts, and to provide a basis for error recovery. Planning is particularly important when steps taken to solve the problem are irreversible, as in a game of chess or in controlling a manufacturing process. Plans can be used to monitor problem-solving progress and to correct errors before they do too much harm. For example, we can compare feedback about the state of the world with results predicted from our planning model; if we find discrepancies, we must modify our planning process accordingly.

A plan usually includes an implicit ordering of goals, such as getting dressed and going out to a show—although it may consist of an unordered list, such as a list of items to buy at the grocery. Often a plan is hierarchically structured or ordered so that it is decomposed into a set of simpler subproblems. Problem reduction of this type is shown in the problem-reduction tree (*and/or* graphs) depicted in figure 2-19. The root of the tree represents a goal, and the interior nodes represent subgoals whose achievement will result in the goal's being achieved. The subgoals

> Decomposition into set of simpler subproblems.
> Typical examples:
> - Theorem proving
> - Program synthesis
> - Robot planning
>
> Problem reduction can be depicted by problem reduction tree (and/or graphs).
>
> Ancestor ↕ Descendents
> Root, Interior Node, Leaves
>
> Develop plan for a goal:
> - Set of subgoals whose achievements will achieve goal
> - Subgoals should be simpler than main goal
> - Plan for subgoal should not conflict with other plans

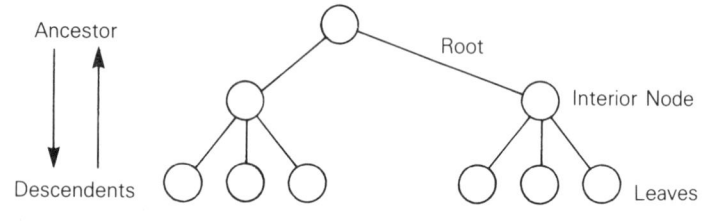

2-19. Problem reduction.

may in turn be subdivided into smaller subgoals. All subgoals should be simpler to plan for and achieve than their parent goals; the various subgoal plans should not conflict with each other.

Top-down refinement, or hierarchical planning, generates a hierarchy of representations in which the highest levels provide a simplification or abstraction of the plan and the lowest levels a plan sufficiently detailed to solve the problem. All other forms are called nonhierarchical planning. A nonhierarchical planner can generate plans with hierarchical subgoal structures. It may reduce its goals to simpler subgoals, or it may use means-ends analysis to reduce the differences between the current world state and the desired goal state. Examples of nonhierarchical planners are STRIPS, HACKER, and INTERPLAN.

STRIPS, for instance, compares the starting state with the goal state and finds a difference. It then looks for an operator capable of eliminating part of this difference. If more than one operator has such a capability, STRIPS must choose between them. Each operator has a set of preconditions that must be satisfied before the operator can be applied to its designated task. The major disadvantage of nonhierarchical planning is that it does not distinguish between critical problem-solving actions and actions involving minor issues; thus plans developed by nonhierarchical planners may get bogged down in unimportant details.

The advantage of top-down refinement (the hierarchical method) is that the plan is first developed at a level at which the details are not computationally overwhelming. Focusing exclusively on critical subgoals before attending to details greatly reduces the search involved. Examples of hierarchical planners include the General Problem Solver (GPS), ABSTRIPS, NOAH, and MOLGEN.

GPS was designed to do its planning in an abstraction space, where all logical connectives are replaced by a single abstract symbol. ABSTRIPS plans in a hierarchy of abstraction spaces. Each operator has preconditions (which are assigned importance levels, called *criticalities*) that must be satisfied before they can be applied. When ABSTRIPS starts planning, it first aims to achieve only preconditions having the maximum criticality. NOAH abstracts problem-solving operators; it plans initially with generalized operators but later refines these into the problem-solving operators given in its problem space. MOLGEN abstracts both the operators and the objects in its problem space.

A third approach to planning makes use of skeleton or stereotype plans that are prestored. The prestored plans contain outlines for solving many different kinds of problems, ranging in detail from extremely specific plans for common individual problems to very general plans for broad classes of problems. The instantiation process—which fills in blank slots in the skeleton—is the mechanism used to refine the planning process. This approach has much in common with R.C. Schank's use of scripts in natural language processing, discussed in chapter 4.

A fourth approach to planning, called opportunistic planning, was devised by F. Hayes-Roth. Based on the blackboard control structure (described in more detail later in this book), it is more flexible than the methods described earlier. It uses the blackboard as a clearinghouse for suggestions about plan steps that are made by planning specialists (specialists do not operate in any particular order). The asynchrony of planning decisions, which are made only when a reason exists for doing so, is what gave rise to the term *opportunistic*. The ordering of the operators is developed piecewise, and this method can develop islands of planning actions within a general plan independently.

Interacting subproblems present a key difficulty to planning systems. They arise in situations involving conjunctive goals, where more than one condition has to be satisfied and the order may be critical to finding a solution. For example, if Abner needs to paint both a ladder and a ceiling, then—since the ladder is needed to paint the ceiling—the ceiling should be painted first. If Abner instead decided to paint the ladder first, when he discovered in the plan that he could not paint the ceiling after painting the ladder, he would have to backtrack and change the plan. Some early planners, such as HACKER, INTERPLAN, and Waldinger's system, worked in this way. These systems applied a heuristic called a *linear assumption*—namely, that subgoals are independent and thus can be sequentially achieved in an arbitrary order (Sussman 1973). The linear assumption is used when no a priori reason exists for ordering one operator ahead of another.

Interactions between subgoals have been called *constraints*. Constraints can often be inferred from the preconditions of operators and are used to establish partial orderings of the problem-solving operators. Such ordering, however, should not be done lightly. Applying constraints according to the principle that it is better not to order operators than to order them arbitrarily is called the *least-commitment approach*. For example, NOAH establishes partial orderings of problem-solving operators by considering their preconditions, but it orders operators only to eliminate problems that might arise from picking an arbitrary ordering. MOLGEN also does not order operators until constraints are available to guide it.

Sometimes we find problems in which the subgoals interact so tightly that we find ourselves stymied; we can proceed no further because several subgoals need each other's results in order to satisfy their own goals, leaving us in a deadlocked situation. Suppose, for example, that we wish to determine the voltage across two points in an electronic circuit. In order to compute the voltage, we need to determine the current flowing through the electronic elements in question. But since one of the elements is a transistor, we cannot determine the current unless we know the bias state of the transistor, which we cannot determine until we know the voltage. To solve this problem, we must guess at a likely bias state for the transistor, then determine the results implied by the guess, and then adjust our guess if the results are found to conflict with the original guess. This method is called *guessing* or *plausible reasoning*. It was used in just the manner described above by the program EL.

The planning methods discussed in this section are summarized in figure 2-20, which shows each of the methods and various programs that have employed each.

Current research in planning systems addresses such issues as:

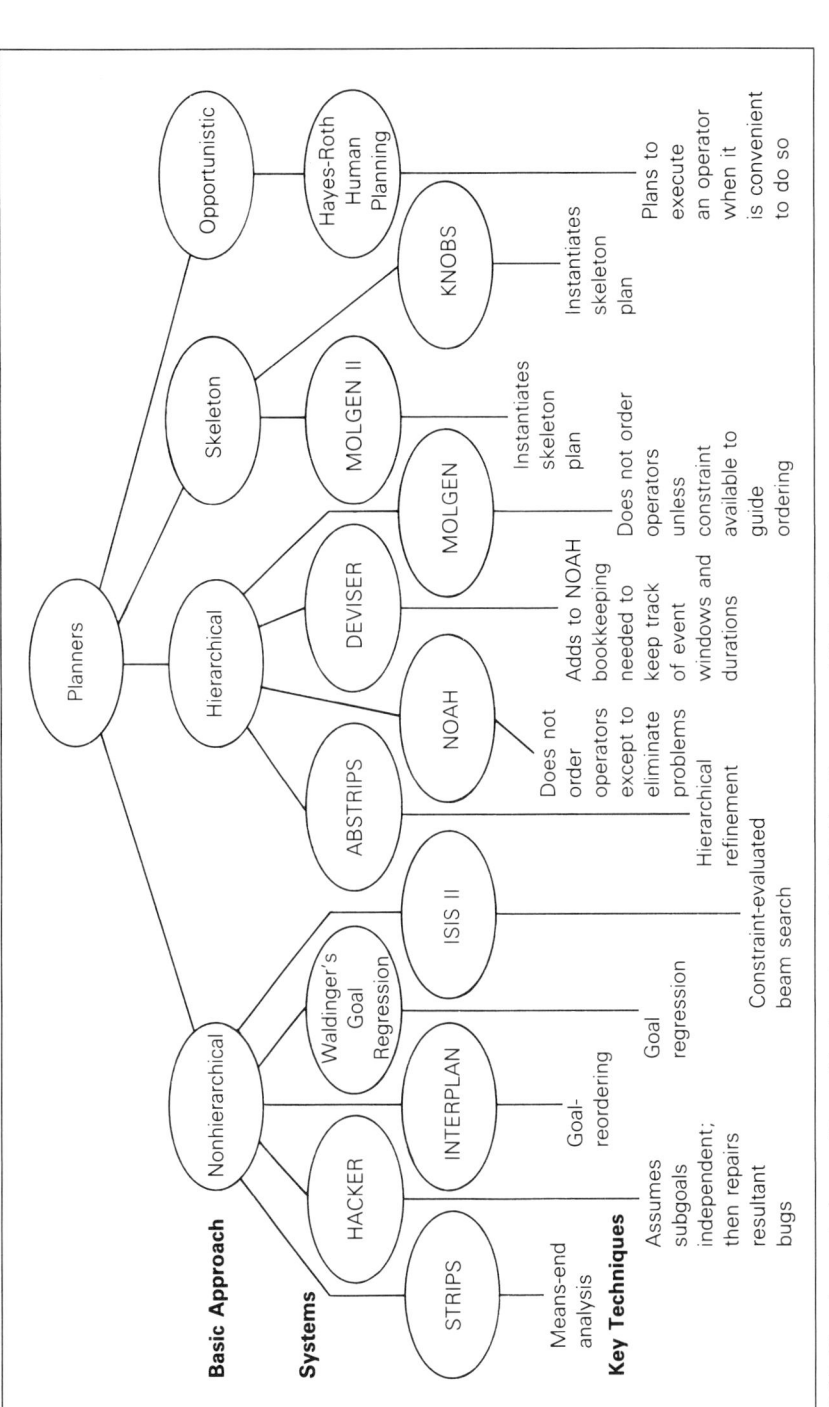

2-20. Planning techniques. (From "An Overview of Artificial Intelligence and Robots" [NASA Technical Memo 85838], by William Gevarter. Reprinted with permission.)

- Techniques for dealing with problems and situations that change over time (such as space shuttle flight planning)
- Techniques for dealing with situations in which the need to handle contingencies is excessive (such as in complex manufacturing operations planning)
- Automatic monitoring and correction, particularly when this must be done in support of a real-time process
- Plan monitoring and repair
- Adaptation and learning

■ LEARNING

The process of learning has occupied the attention of researchers from as early as Plato's time. Philosophers and psychologists have long been interested in improving their understanding of knowledge and how people acquire it. Artificial intelligence is only the most recent field of study to pick up the banner of research into learning. Before the current work on learning in artificial intelligence appeared on the scene, most systems work concerned with learning was centered on the theme of self-organizing and adaptive systems (Yovits, Jacobi, and Goldstein 1962). This included the implementation of various computational analogs of neurons, one of the best known of which was the perceptron (Rosenblatt 1958).

Of course, A.I. research into learning includes a desire not only to understand how people learn, but to provide computers with the ability to learn and to be taught rather than having to be programmed. A strong motivation toward this goal can be found in the burgeoning field of expert systems. The process of developing an expert system is very time-consuming and requires the participation of many talented people, who are in high demand and short supply. Some of the larger expert systems designed in academic settings (admittedly, without any pressing timetables) have taken forty to fifty man-years to develop over six to seven actual years. Simpler systems, predictably, have been built in much shorter periods of time—a year or less in some instances, for the first operational version.

It has been speculated that an expert system can be built in approximately 1 to 1½ times the time period required to train an expert in the field. Some expert system shells in the marketplace today, with their interactive, natural language interfaces, their explanation facilities, and their built-in rule-consistency checking and inferencing, claim to be capable of producing expert systems in an even shorter time. Nonetheless, the inability of computers to learn is one of the great bottlenecks in the computer industry today. Whether the application envisioned is for A.I. or for some more commonplace purpose, the biggest obstacle we face today is programming time and cost.

Conferring on computer systems the ability to learn is still a research topic. Only limited success and commercial offerings exist in this area. This chapter, therefore, is confined to reviewing some of the more popular current research ideas in the field. Five basic learning situations have been identified: rote learning, learning by being told, learning from examples, learning by analogy, and learning by self-sufficient discovery.

Rote learning consists of learning by being programmed. In this situation, knowledge is supplied in a form that can be used directly, without any interpretation or translation required. The exact rules, procedures, and data structure necessary for problem solving are presented to the system. One example is Samuel's checkers-playing program (Samuel 1959), which uses previously memorized board positions to improve the speed and depth of the program's look-ahead search during subsequent games.

Learning by being told, or advice-taking, occurs when high-level knowledge is supplied in a form that is vague and general-purpose and must be interpreted and transformed into a more specific and detailed form to be useful. This transformation, called *operationalization,* corresponds to the situation where an algebra teacher tells a student that solving an algebraic equation requires placing all the unknowns on the same side of the equation; the teacher has still left the student a substantial amount of strategizing, planning, and filling in of details to do before the specific problem is solved. Mostow's work on getting advice on playing the game of hearts (Mostow 1981) and Davis's work on the TEIRESIAS program, as part of the MYCIN project (R. Davis 1976), are examples of research in this area.

Mostow's system uses basic domain concepts and rules, coupled with techniques such as heuristic search, historical reasoning, and filling in additional information, through instantiation of variables, to restructure the original advice into simpler expressions that are amenable to further analysis; in the course of simplification, expressions are ultimately reached that may be directly applied.

Learning from examples involves induction. In this situation, the system is presented with examples—some positive and some negative. A key process here is to generalize the specific pieces of knowledge into higher-level rules, patterns, or concepts that can serve more purposes than can a list of memorized examples. For instance, if we are told that a blue jay can fly, a robin can fly, a sparrow can fly, and a crow can fly, we might infer that all birds can fly.

Winston's work on learning the meaning of structural descriptions, such as *arch*, from examples illustrates this situation (Winston 1975a). We start with some basic concepts of blocks and their shapes, as well as such basic structural facts as that blocks can support each other and touch each other. Then the concept of arch is taught to the system through the presentation of a series of examples; the positive examples cause the system to generalize, and the negative examples cause the system to specialize (see figure 2-21). From these examples, a semantic network description of an arch is constructed and modified until it becomes sufficiently robust to manage the assignment of all future examples accurately.

In the first instance, after being shown the first example in figure 2-21, the system draws the semantic network shown in the upper drawing of figure 2-22. Here we see three nodes, one for each block, with one of the blocks being supported by the other two blocks, and with all three blocks being of rectangular shape. Then the next example of an arch is shown, and the semantic network is generalized to permit the supported block to be of any general shape. Then the negative example of an arch is shown, causing a specialization of the semantic definition of an arch such that the two supporting blocks not be touching.

Winston further speculates that the concept of an arch can be made still more robust if it is understood and represented in terms of its function (for things to pass through, for example) as well as its structure.

A similar type of approach is proposed for a production rule–based system, using a structured rule set that is successively generalized by means of a generate-and-test scheme for handling all of the training instances, followed by pruning with a candidate-elimination algorithm (Michalski and Chilansky 1980; Dietterich and Michalski, 1981).

Quinlan (1979) proposed a decision tree–based algorithm for learning concepts and classification rules. It is based upon Hunt's CLS (Concept Learning System), in which a decision tree is gradually refined and extended by adding decision nodes until the tree can correctly classify all of the training instances. A criterion is used to select the feature that most effectively discriminates between positive and negative instances. New conditions are iteratively added, using the same criterion, until all of the training instances are correctly classified. The criterion is to choose the feature F (with values $V_1, V_2, \ldots V_n$) that minimizes

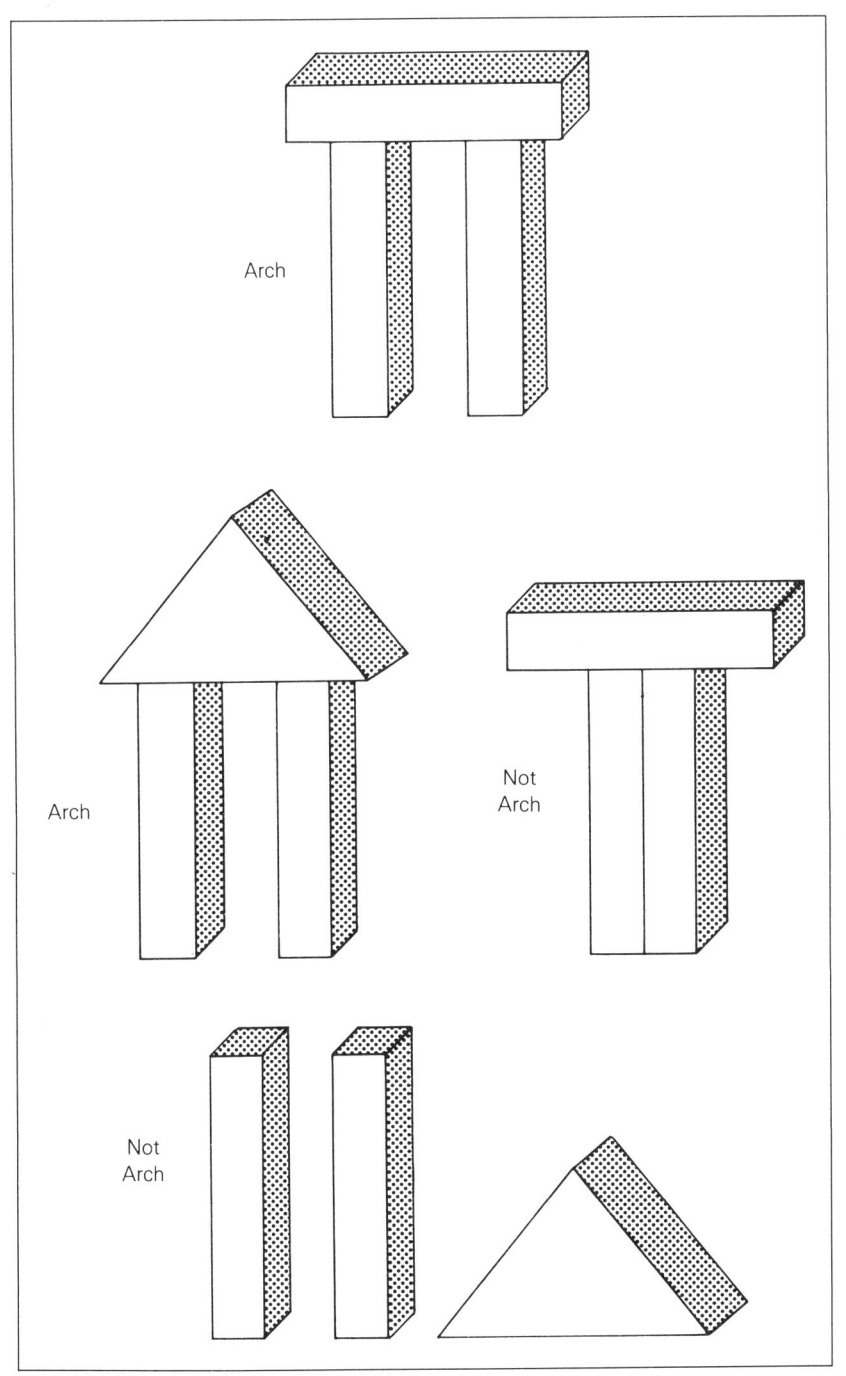

2-21. Examples presented to a learning-concept program. (From *The Thinking Computer: Mind inside Matter,* by Bertram Raphael. Published by W.H. Freeman and Company, New York, 1976. Reprinted with permission.)

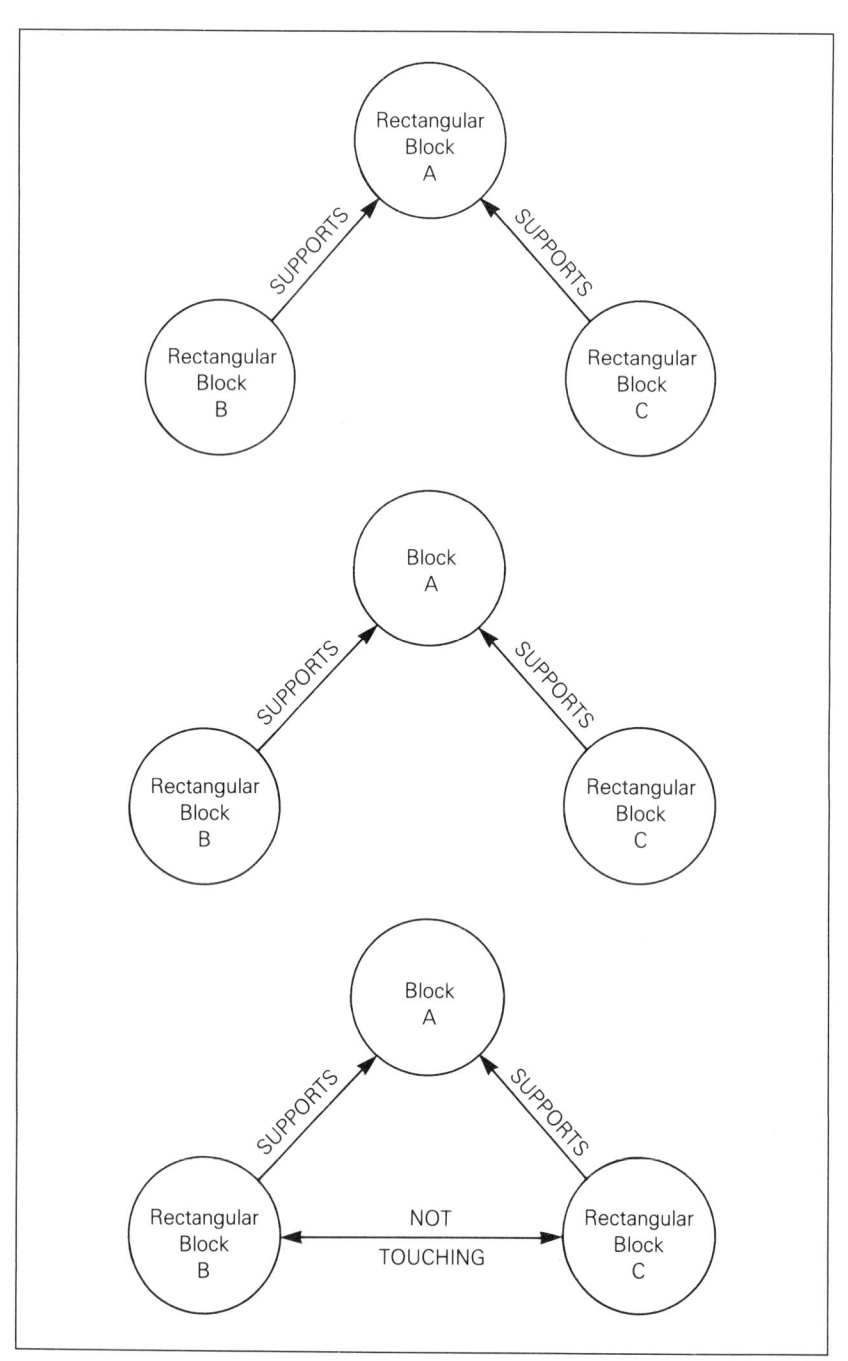

2-22. Semantic network description of an arch.

$$\sum_i \left[-V_i^+ \log_2\left(\frac{V_i^+}{V_i^+ + V_i^-}\right) - V_i^- \log_2\left(\frac{V_i^-}{V_i^+ + V_i^-}\right) \right],$$

where V_i^+ is the number of positive training instances and V_i^- is the number of negative training instances with $F = V_i$.

This approach requires identifying all of the attributes associated with a concept. A product based on some of these ideas is EXPERT-EASE, which is produced by Don Michie's company.

Learning by analogy requires a system to be able to improve its performance by recognizing analogies and thereupon transferring and using the knowledge from the other data base. This is a relatively new area of research, in which some work has been reported (Winston 1980).

Learning by self-sufficient discovery involves the ability of the system to bring all other forms of learning together to formulate, test, and validate new theories and hypotheses. Lenat's work (Lenat 1983a,b) is an example of research in this area. He uses frames to represent concepts; these are filled and modified in accordance with heuristic searches guided by rules representing hints about activities and results that are likely to lead to (for example) interesting new discoveries. In the field of mathematics, Lenat's discovery program AM uses the following rules:

- If f is a function from A to B, and B is ordered, then consider the elements of A that are mapped into the extreme elements of B. Create a new concept representing this subset of A.
- If some (but not most) examples of some concept X are also examples of another concept Y, create a new concept representing the intersection of X and Y.
- If very few examples of a concept X are found, then add to the agenda the task of finding a generalization of X.

Lenat's work can be thought of as applying artificial intelligence concepts toward the problem of discovering new and interesting relationships in a particular field of study.

All A.I.-centered learning research is based on the belief that intelligence and learning are computable functions that can be modeled by symbol-manipulating processes, and that the highest form of learning, self-discovery, can ultimately be understood in terms of rules, plans, and heuristic search strategies expressible through symbol-manipulating activities. Among the most important unresolved research issues are:

- When and how should rules, algorithms, and strategies be adapted on the basis of past performance? Should they be changed whenever an error occurs, when errors exceed a priori tolerable levels, or only under supervision?
- How do we detect when the world has changed in such a way as to make stored information invalid? (This is known as the "frame problem.")
- How do we determine when it becomes cheaper to store memorized information than to compute or infer it from more basic principles?
- How do we structure stored knowledge for most efficient problem solving?
- When do we decide to forget information (*selective forgetting*)?
- How do we best integrate new rules and algorithms into an existing knowledge base when we have more than one concept to learn? (This is known as the "integration problem.") How can we consider all of the possible interactions between a new rule and previous rules in order to avoid having the new rule cause existing rules to be ignored or applied incorrectly?
- How can we diagnose incorrect rules? (This is known as the "credit-assignment problem" [Minsky 1963].) How can we correctly assign credit or blame to the individual decisions that led to some overall result?

Before we can learn a new concept, we must have some basic knowledge about the topic to build on. People try to learn about new things by making use of past learning. New concepts typically are expressed in terms of old concepts, at least initially. For example, to appreciate that the angular force on a balance is equal to the product of the weight times the distance of the weight from the fulcrum, we must first understand the concepts of force, weight, and distance.

Furthermore, if we are being instructed through advice and examples, the order in which the advice and examples are presented is very important. For instance, the lesson that the balance will tilt in favor of a 10-pound weight placed 1 foot from the fulcrum, as against a 2-pound weight placed 4 feet from the fulcrum, will completely go over the head of a child who only has an appreciation for the importance of weight on a balance; the child will simply assume that the 10-pound weight tilts the scale in its favor because it weighs more than the 2-pound weight. The child must first learn (for example) that the balance will tilt in favor of a 2-pound weight placed 6 feet from the fulcrum, as against a 10-pound weight placed 1 foot from the fulcrum.

Learning involves incorporating large amounts of domain knowledge through application of the simple learning concepts and situations described above, in successive stages and in the proper sequence. Negative examples, the exceptions, are often more important in the learning process than positive, reinforcing examples; for example, once we have learned that bigger weights provide larger angular forces than smaller weights, we are ready to learn (by negative examples) under what circumstances a smaller weight can exert a greater angular force than an opposing larger weight can.

3 · Tools and Techniques

*A*rtificial intelligence systems are centrally concerned with representing and manipulating knowledge. Some knowledge, particularly in mathematics and the sciences, is expressed as numbers and formulas—expressions that consist of collections of numbers and arithmetic operations. Most human endeavor, however, requires expression in a richer, more general language. Even mathematics, when it involves more abstract reasoning processes (such as theorem-proving, algebraic transformations, and the symbolic solution of integro-differential equations), requires this more general and powerful language, which must be expressed in concepts and relationships represented by symbols and strings of symbols.

In fact, numbers and formulas are really just a collection of special symbols. Numbers are symbols whose properties are defined over the set of arithmetic operations, and arithmetic operations are represented by symbols or strings of symbols (such as $+$, $-$, $/$, and $\times$). Thus the tools of artificial intelligence consist of the languages, processes, and constructs that allow the acquisition, representation, storing, transformation, and other manipulation of concepts and relationships by information processing machines. In this respect, the field of artificial intelligence is closely allied with the study of language theory, including higher-order computer languages and computer compiler theory.

This chapter provides an introduction to tools in common use today for supporting current artificial intelligence work. Included are sections on symbolic processing languages, logic programming languages, and other languages—many based upon such popular knowledge representation schemes as production rules, frames, scripts, and semantic networks. The chapter also discusses the special hardware and computer systems available to improve the ease and efficiency of A.I. programming.

■ LISP

LISP is currently the most popular computer language used in artificial intelligence programming. It is designed for supporting symbolic manipulation and the interactive, trial-and-error style of programming employed by many A.I. researchers. LISP is, of course, not the only language that can be used to program A.I. applications on a computer; in principle, such applications could even be programmed in machine or assembly language. LISP is just more convenient to use. And with the recent introduction of improved LISP compilers and computers, the efficiency of LISP in comparison to other computer languages has greatly improved.

LISP is not a new language. It was invented by John McCarthy in 1958, and many of its key ideas are derived from IPL, a now-obsolete language developed in the 1950s at Carnegie-Mellon University by Allen Newell, J.C. Shaw, and H.A. Simon. The many dialects of LISP tend to fall into one of two main camps: INTERLISP, which was developed at BBN and originally used primarily (though not exclusively) at Stanford, SRI, and Xerox PARC; and MACLISP and its variants (including FRANZLISP and ZETALISP), which were originally used primarily (though not exclusively) at MIT, Symbolics, and LISP Machine, Inc.

INTERLISP versions tend to have more features and a more integrated environment than the MACLISP versions, but they also tend to run slower.

Although significant incompatibilities exist between these two camps, some compatibility packages have been developed. For example, Symbolics computers have a compatibility package that can run INTERLISP subsets on its ZETALISP compiler.

Recently, in the interest of standardization, Common LISP was developed (Steele 1984). Common LISP is not yet an official standard but was created at the initiative of many vendors and is increasingly becoming the preferred version. Common LISP compilers now exist for several mainframe computers, minicomputers, and microcomputers.

HOW LISP WORKS

LISP programs are rarely compiled; that is, users rarely take a file of LISP source code, convert it into a file of machine code instructions, and then run the machine code. Instead, as the user types a line of LISP code (a LISP expression), the interpreter immediately evaluates it and displays the result back in the form of more LISP code. The

LISP interpreter first reads the typed line of LISP code (the LISP expression), then evaluates that expression by performing any substitutions and operations called for by the LISP expression, and finally displays or prints the result or value. LISP compilers are needed, however, to run many production-version programs more efficiently. LISP characteristics are summarized in figure 3-1.

LISP expressions are called S-expressions, where the S stands for *symbolic*. An S-expression can be a number (an optional plus or minus sign, followed by a digit, followed by zero or more digits), a literal atom or symbol (a letter, followed by zero or more letter or digits), a string (a double quotation mark ["], followed by zero or more characters, followed by another double quotation mark), or a list of S-expressions (a left parenthesis, followed by zero or more S-expressions, followed by a right parenthesis).

The rules for evaluation are:

1. If the expression is a number, or a Boolean variable—T (true) or NIL (false)—then its value is itself.

- Fundamental things formed from bits are word-like objects called <u>atoms</u>.
- Groups of atoms form <u>lists</u>.
- Lists can be grouped to form higher-level lists.
- Atoms and lists are called <u>symbolic expressions</u>.
- LISP is interactive.
- LISP has excellent environmental support tools (editing, debugging).
- LISP functions and data have same form.

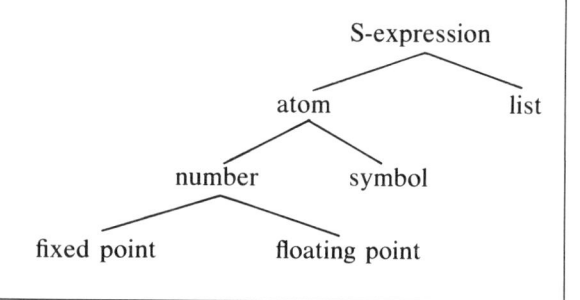

```
                        S-expression
                         /        \
                      atom         list
                     /    \
                number    symbol
               /     \
          fixed point  floating point
```

3-1. LISP. (From *LISP,* by P.H. Winston and B. Horn. Published by Addison-Wesley, Reading, MA, © 1984. Reprinted with permission.)

2. If the expression is an atom, then its value is the last value assigned to it. If no value has been previously assigned, an error results.
3. If the expression is a list in the form of (Function Argument-1 ... Argument-k), then the value is found by first evaluating each *Argument* and then calling *Function* with these values. For example, (PLUS 2 3) evaluates to 2 + 3, or 5. This form is known as *polish notation*, where the operator or function is shown at the head of the list (*prefix*) rather than in-between (*infix*).
4. If the expression is a list in the form of (Reserved-word Argument-1 ... Argument-k), then the value depends completely on the *Reserved-word* term (this can usually be thought of as an operator). The *Argument* terms may or may not be evaluated.

In LISP, almost all operations involve passing values between functions. There is no main program with subroutines; rather the user defines a set of functions that represent an appropriate language in which to describe and solve the particular problem or class of problems being addressed. These functions are defined in terms of S-expressions and LISP reserved words (or operators).

Once these fundamental concepts are understood, learning LISP becomes a matter of learning the reserved words and built-in functions and mastering the appropriate programming techniques. Some of the key operators and functions are reviewed in the sections that follow. A more complete treatment can be found in Winston and Horn (1984).

BASIC FUNCTIONS AND OPERATORS

SET and SETQ

The SET function associates a list with an atom. For example:

$$\text{(SET 'FRIENDS '(DICK JANE))} \quad [3.1]$$

associates the atom FRIENDS with the list (DICK JANE), where the single quotation mark (') prevents LISP from concluding that the S-expressions are associated with some other operators or S-expressions. In equation 3.1, for example, the quotation marks prevent FRIENDS from being associated with some other S-expression and prevent (DICK JANE) from being interpreted as DICK being some sort of operator or S-expression and JANE belonging with some other S-expression.

The SETQ function is like SET except that SETQ makes no attempt to evaluate the first argument.

CAR, CDR, APPEND, LIST, and CONS

Among the basic functions used to manipulate, take apart, and construct lists are CAR, CDR, APPEND, LIST, and CONS. They are best explained by example:

$$(CAR \ '(A \ B \ C)) = A, \qquad [3.2]$$

$$(CDR \ '(A \ B \ C)) = (B \ C), \qquad [3.3]$$

$$(CAR \ FRIENDS \ ) = DICK, \qquad [3.4]$$

$$(CDR \ FRIENDS \ ) = (JANE). \qquad [3.5]$$

Equations 3.2–3.5 illustrate that CAR takes a list and returns the first atom of that list, and that CDR takes a list and returns the rest of the list minus the first atom. CAR and CDR are called the *head* and *tail*, respectively. The names *CAR* and *CDR* are acronyms derived from their early implementations; they stand for *Contents of the Address Register* and *Contents of the Destination Register,* respectively. Equations 3.2 and 3.3 illustrate the inhibitive effect of using the quotation mark; equations 3.4 and 3.5 illustrate that, in the absence of the quotation mark, the S-expression is associated with the list (DICK JANE) to which it was set in equation 3.1.

CAR and CDR can be strung together, and when they are, the redundant C and R can be dropped; for example:

$$(CAR \ (CDR \ '(A \ B \ C))) = (CADR \ '(A \ B \ C)) = B. \qquad [3.6]$$

The functions APPEND, LIST, and CONS are illustrated in the following three equations:

(APPEND FRIENDS FRIENDS) = (DICK JANE DICK JANE). [3.7]

(LIST FRIENDS FRIENDS) = ((DICK JANE) (DICK JANE)). [3.8]

(CONS 'CAROL FRIENDS) = (CAROL DICK JANE). [3.9]

where APPEND takes two or more arguments, each of which should be a list, and returns a list built from the elements of each; LIST takes one or more arguments and makes a list that uses them as elements; and CONS takes an atom and a list and adds the atom to the head of the list.

LIST STRUCTURES

The way LISP represents atoms and lists in a computer is best explained by the abstract data structure called a *dotted pair*, or *CONS cell*. A CONS cell is a pair of pointers that can be graphically illustrated as a rectangle divided into righthand and lefthand boxes (see figure 3-2). Each pointer is shown as an arrow drawn from the appropriate box to its associated CONS cell. The first pointer, coming from the lefthand box, is called the CAR of the pair; the second is called the CDR. If the righthand box represents the end of the list, it has a null pointer (pointing to NIL) and is written as a diagonal slash in the appropriate box of the rectangle.

An atom is written by putting its name in the appropriate box. Of course, the elements composing a list may themselves be lists rather

Cell Address	Cell Contents
2001	9100/2002
2002	9025/2004
2003	9001/0000
2004	9050/2003
	Left-Hand Pointers | Right-Hand Pointers

Atoms and lists are represented as collections of memory cells consisting mainly of pointers to other memory cells. For example, memory cells may be threaded together by right-hand pointers, while left-hand pointers specify list elements.

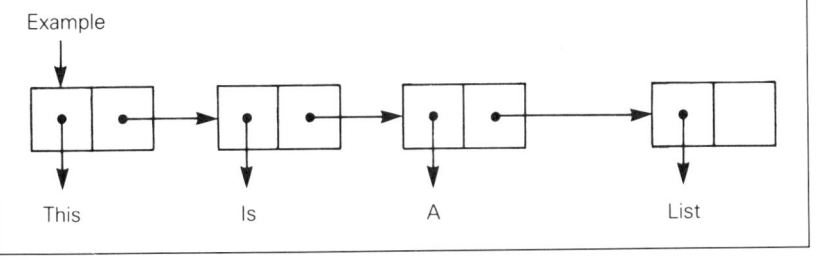

Example

This   Is   A   List

3-2. List storage. (From *LISP,* by P.H. Winston and B. Horn. Published by Addison-Wesley, Reading, MA, © 1984. Reprinted with permission.)

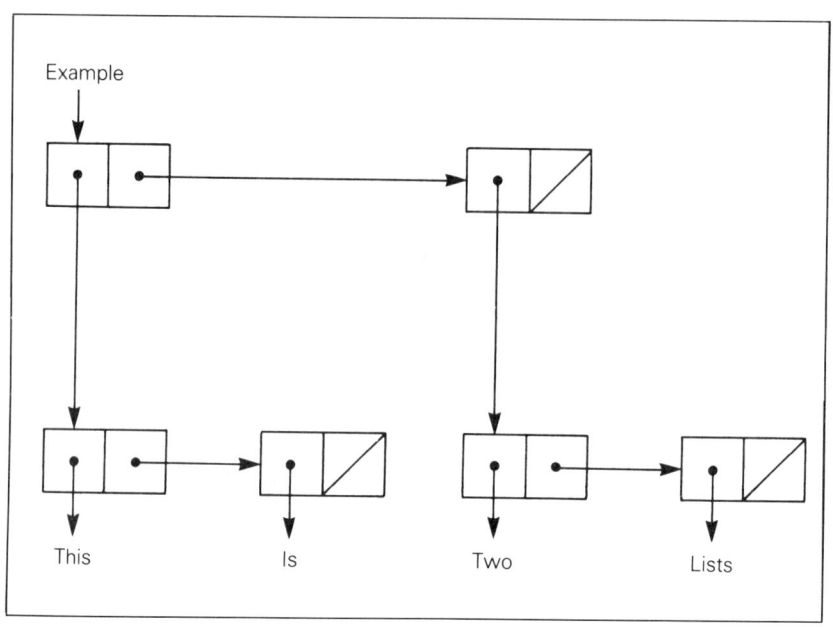

```
┌─────────────────────────────────────────────────────────┐
│   Example                                                │
│      │                                                   │
│      ▼                                                   │
│   ┌──┬──┐                      ┌──┬──┐                   │
│   │ •│ •┼─────────────────────▶│ •│ ╱│                   │
│   └┬─┴──┘                      └┬─┴──┘                   │
│    │                            │                        │
│    ▼                            ▼                        │
│   ┌──┬──┐    ┌──┬──┐          ┌──┬──┐    ┌──┬──┐        │
│   │ •│ •┼───▶│ •│ ╱│          │ •│ •┼───▶│ •│ ╱│        │
│   └┬─┴──┘    └┬─┴──┘          └┬─┴──┘    └┬─┴──┘        │
│    │          │                 │          │             │
│    ▼          ▼                 ▼          ▼             │
│   This        Is               Two        Lists          │
└─────────────────────────────────────────────────────────┘
```

3-3. List structure. (From *LISP,* by P.H. Winston and B. Horn. Published by Addison-Wesley, Reading, MA, © 1984. Reprinted with permission.)

than atoms. Thus, multiple list structures of arbitrary complexity may be represented. An example of a two-list structure is shown in figure 3-3. Here the first box consists of two arrows—the first pointing to the first atom in the first list (the *head*), and the second pointing to the first atom in the second list (the *tail*). More generally, the second arrow would point to the first member of an S-expression that is the CDR of the original S-expression. This might correspond to the first atom in the second list of a list of two lists, as in the example illustrated in figure 3-3, but it might also correspond to an arrow pointing to the first atom of the first list in a list of lists.

DEFINING FUNCTIONS IN LISP

Several different types of functions exist in LISP, and thus several different types of definition functions also exist. The two most basic types of functions in LISP are called EXPR and FEXPR, of which the more common is EXPR. EXPR takes a fixed number of arguments and evaluates them before the function is evaluated. The DE function, which is used to define EXPR functions, has the following syntax:

(DE ⟨function name⟩ ⟨parameter 1⟩...⟨parameter *n*⟩ ⟨process description⟩).

The angle brackets delineate descriptions denoting atoms, lists, or even fragments, as appropriate. DE does not evaluate its arguments; it simply looks at them and establishes a function definition that can be referred to later by having the function name appear as the first element of a list to be evaluated. For example:

(DE EXCHANGE (PAIR)
 (LIST (CADR PAIR) (CAR PAIR)))

defines a function that takes a list and returns a new list consisting of the second element of the original list followed by the first element of the original list. For example, if the expression SINNERS had been set equal to the list (ADAM EVE), evaluation of the list (EXCHANGE SINNERS) would yield the result (EVE ADAM).

The less common FEXPR function starts with an arbitrary number of arguments that are not evaluated before the function is called. It differs from the EXPR function in taking exactly one formal local variable; and when the FEXPR function is called, its formal variable is bound to the list of arguments as they appeared and not to their values. The syntax for the FEXPR definition function, DF, is:

(DF ⟨function⟩ ⟨atom⟩ ⟨expressions⟩).

Consider the following example, where we define QUOTE-LIST as a FEXPR function that just returns the binding of the formal variable. Here the definition is given as:

(DF QUOTE-LIST (*L*) *L*).

The following input/output would occur when QUOTE-LIST is called and evaluated:

(QUOTE-LIST *A*) = (*A*)

(QUOTE-LIST *A B C*) = (*A B C*).

Notice that none of the arguments is evaluated and that QUOTE-LIST can take on an arbitrary number of arguments.

Many of the reserved words we have already seen could be defined as FEXPR functions. For example:

(DF QUOTE(*L*) (CAR *L*))

(DF SETQ(*L*) (SET (CAR *L*) (EVAL (CADR *L*))))

DE and DF are used to create functions that can be recalled later using their names. It is also desirable (and possible) to use a function description in places where a function name would usually be. One need for such a capability involves the use of the LISP mapping functions.

MAPCAR is a mapping function. Starting with two arguments, a function, and a list, it returns a new list consisting of the values of the function applied to the elements of the old list. For example, the S-expression (MAPCAR (SQUARE *L*)) creates a list consisting of the squares of all of the elements of list *L*. Other mapping functions include MAPC, MAPCAN, EVERY, SOME, and SUBSET.

Consider a problem in which we wish to apply to a list a mapping function that we will never have occasion to reuse. For example, suppose that we wish to check which elements in a list named FRUITS are apples. We could start by defining the function APPLEP:

(DE APPLEP (*X*) (EQUAL *X* 'APPLE)).

Then we could write:

(SETQ FRUITS '(ORANGE APPLE APPLE)).

And then we could apply MAPCAR to the list FRUITS, using the APPLEP function, as follows:

(MAPCAR 'APPLEP FRUITS).

Alternatively, we could lay out the function at the spot where it is to be used:

(MAPCAR (DE APPLEP (*X*) (EQUAL *X* 'APPLE)) FRUITS).

To avoid the overhead of defining and storing functions for which we will have no further use and to prevent the proliferation of useless names, LISP provides an anonymous function called the *lambda function*.

We can solve our illustrative example by using the lambda function as follows:

(MAPCAR '(LAMBDA (X) (EQUAL X 'APPLE)) FRUITS).

When called, lambda is evaluated just like a function; first the atoms are bound to the arguments, and then the expressions in the body of the lambda are evaluated. Although especially useful inside the mapping functions, lambda forms can be used anywhere a function can. It involves no overhead and can be reused repeatedly.

OTHER LISP COMMANDS

Although many other LISP commands exist, only a few are listed below, to give a more complete sense of the language.

LENGTH. This command counts the number of elements in a list:

(LENGTH '(A B)) = 2.

REVERSE. This command turns a list around:

(REVERSE '(A B)) = (B A).

SUBSTITUTE. This command replaces an old S-expression with a new S-expression within a larger S-expression:

(SUBST ⟨new S-expression⟩ ⟨old S-expression⟩ ⟨larger S-expression⟩).

For example:

(SUBST 'A 'B '(A B C)) = (A A C).

LAST. This command returns a list that gives only the last element of the list identified as the argument:

(LAST '(A B C)) = (C).

EVAL. This command causes an extra evaluation:

If   (SETQ A 'B),
And   (SETQ B 'C),
Then   (EVAL A) = C.

PREDICATES. LISP also handles predicates. A predicate is a function that returns either T or NIL, where T corresponds to the logical true and NIL corresponds to the logical false (in other situations NIL corresponds to the empty or null set). Representative predicates are:

- *Atom*, which tests to see if the S-expression is an atom
- *Boundp*, which tests to see if an argument has a value
- *Equal*, which returns T if the two arguments are equal, but otherwise returns NIL
- *Member*, which tests to see if one S-expression is an element of another
- *Null*, which checks to see if the argument is an empty list

Of course, among many others are the logical predicates *and, or,* and *not*.

CONDITIONALS. The predicates are often used to determine which of several possible expressions should be evaluated. This choice is often made in conjunction with the branching function COND. COND is defined below as:

$$(COND\ (\langle test\ 1\rangle\ \cdots\ \langle result\ 1\rangle)$$
$$\vdots \qquad \vdots$$
$$(\langle test\ n\rangle\ \cdots\ \langle result\ n\rangle))$$

If no successful clause is found, COND returns NIL; if a successful clause is evaluated, the last thing evaluated is returned as the value of COND. For example, the following expression adds up the integers from 1 to N (the reserved words used are PROG, SETQ, COND, RETURN, and GO, and the functions used are EQUAL, PLUS, and DIFFERENCE):

```
(PROG (SUM)
    (SETQ SUM 0)
LOOP (COND (( EQUAL N 0)(RETURN SUM))
           (T (SETQ SUM (PLUS SUM N))
              (SETQ N (DIFFERENCE N 1))))
    (GO LOOP)).
```

PROG expressions are treated the same way begin-end blocks are in Algol.

PROPERTIES. Besides values and function definitions, we can attach properties to atoms. The value of a property can be any S-expression; and we can store, retrieve, or remove properties. For example:

(PUTPROP 'DOG 4 'LEGS)

gives the atom DOG a property called LEGS with a value 4. This information can be retrieved by writing:

(GET 'DOG 'LEGS),

which provides the number 4. If we wanted to remove this property, we would write:

(REMPROP 'DOG 'LEGS).

The reserved word DEFPROP is like PUTPROP, except the arguments do not require quotation marks.

ASSOCIATION LISTS. Association lists, or A-lists, are lists of pairs. For example, CHART is an A-list in which:

(SETQ CHART '((TEMPERATURE 103)
 (PRESSURE 120 60)(PULSE 70))).

ASSOC, which operates on A-lists, is a function of two arguments. The first argument is called the key; ASSOC looks for its key in the A-list supplied as the second argument, moving down the A-list until it finds a list element whose CAR is equal to the key. It then returns as its value the entire element discovered, key and all:

(ASSOC 'TEMPERATURE CHART) = (TEMPERATURE 103)

SYMBOLIC MATCHING WITH LISP

Having advanced through the preceding quick introduction to LISP, we will now investigate how to do pattern matching in LISP. Pattern matching is fundamental to symbolic processing and has been proposed by Allen Newell as one of the basic processes of human intelligence. The firing of a neuron when its inputs reach some threshold condition bears a strong resemblance to the pattern-matching model.

Many A.I. programs operate by attempting to find matches between one structure and another. Examples include:

- Recognition of key words and phrases in constructing man-machine dialogues
- Looking for a match between an element on the condition side of a set of production rules and some piece of input data in forward chaining
- Looking for a match between an element on the conclusion side of a set of production rules and a desired goal
- Identifying clauses that match in applying the resolution principle to theorem-proving

In exploring how to implement a program that searches for a match between two arbitrary strings of symbols, let us first consider what we wish the end result of the program to look like. This is illustrated below in equations 3.10 and 3.11, with the function MATCH:

(MATCH '(LOVES JOHN MARY) '(LOVES JOHN MARY)) = T, [3.10]

(MATCH '(LOVES JOHN MARY) '(LOVES JOHN SUSAN)) = NIL. [3.11]

In these two examples, the atoms in the first list are compared atom by atom with corresponding atoms in the second list. If all of the atoms match, a *T* for true is returned (as happens in equation 3.10). If a mismatch occurs between one or more of the corresponding atoms, a *NIL* for false is returned (as happens in equation 3.11).

Often we want the MATCH operator to go beyond merely comparing two strings of known symbols—to attempt to match a general pattern (with variables or "don't care" positions) against an arbitrary string of symbols and to identify whether or not the string is a specific instance of this generic pattern. This extension of the use of the operator MATCH is illustrated in equations 3.12 and 3.13:

(MATCH '(LOVES JOHN ?) '(LOVES JOHN MARY)) = T, [3.12]

(MATCH '(LOVES ? MARY) '(LOVES JOHN MARY)) = T. [3.13]

In both of these cases, the prefix ? causes the two strings to match.

Similarly, the prefix + expands the flexibility of the match by allowing it to ignore arbitrary-length strings of atoms. This is illustrated in equation 3.14:

(MATCH '(+ JOHN LOVES +) '(I KNOW THAT JOHN LOVES
            MARY VERY MUCH)) = T.   [3.14]

In this case, the matcher only looks for the two atoms JOHN and MARY and ignores all preceding and succeeding atoms. The matcher tests only for form (or syntax), however, not for meaning.

The function MATCH can be directed to match two lists, atom by atom, as follows:[1]

(DEFUN MATCH (P D)
    (COND ((AND (NULL P) (NULL D)) T)
          ((OR (NULL P) (NULL D)) NIL)
          ((EQUAL (CAR P) (CAR D))
           (MATCH (CDR P) (CDR D))))).   [3.15]

In the first line, this LISP program identifies the name of the defined function as MATCH and identifies the two lists on which it operates as P and D. The function's operation proceeds through a sequence of tests. The first test checks whether both of the lists are empty; if they are, we exit this program with a *T* for true. We also check to see if one of the two lists is shorter than the other; if one is, we exit the program with a *NIL*. If not, the next clause checks to see whether the first atom from each of the lists is equal; if it is not, we exit the program with a *NIL*. If the first atom is equal in each list, the program calls itself recursively on the two lists with the first atoms deleted (the CDR of the two lists). This technique of defining a function recursively in terms of itself is used quite frequently in LISP.

The generalization for allowing for the "don't care" atom, ?, is accomplished by adding an additional line, as follows:

(DEFUN MATCH (P D)
    (COND ((AND (NULL P) (NULL D)) T)
          ((OR (NULL P) (NULL D)) NIL)
          ((OR (EQUAL (CAR P) '?X)
               (EQUAL (CAR P) (CAR D)))
           (MATCH (CDR P) (CDR D))))).   [3.16]

---

1. From *LISP*, by P.H. Winston and B. Horn (Reading, MA: Addison-Wesley, 1984). Reprinted with permission.

We check to see if the first atom of list *P* has the special character ?, or—if it does not—whether the first atom in each of the two lists is equal. If either is true, we continue; if both fail, we exit the program with a *NIL*. Otherwise, the program operates exactly as does that represented in equation 3.15.

Finally, to incorporate the + feature, we add the last three lines shown in equation 3.17 below, which enable the program to check for the special symbol +. If this symbol is found, the MATCH is applied recursively—first for the CDR of the two lists as before, but then (if this test fails) to list *P* and the CDR of list *D*. In brief, the program first checks to see if + matches one atom; if not, it checks to see if + matches two atoms; if not, three; and so forth until a match is finally found.

```
(DEFUN MATCH (P D)
     (COND ((AND (NULL P) (NULL D)) T)
           ((OR (NULL P) (NULL D)) NIL)
           ((OR (EQUAL (CAR P) '?)
                (EQUAL (CAR P) (CAR D)))
            (MATCH (CDR P) (CDR D)))
           ((EQUAL (CAR P) '+)
            (OR ((MATCH (CDR P) (CDR D)))
                ((MATCH P (CDR D))))))).       [3.17]
```

Usually more is involved in the matching problem than what is described above. If a pattern with either single atom variables (?*X*) or arbitrary-length strings of atoms (+ *Y*) does match another reference pattern, we usually wish to assign these variables the values that would make the match successful. This would be quite useful in production rule systems, for example, where the inference engine needs to identify rules that apply to the facts and to the current state of the problem under study, as well as having to associate values with variables in the applicable rule that make these rules relevant to the current problem. This process of binding values to the variables is called *instantiation*. To see more concretely what the desired effect is, let us reconsider equations 3.12, 3.13, and 3.14 as modified in equations 3.12′, 3.13′, and 3.14′ to accommodate these variables:

(MATCH '(LOVES JOHN ?X1) '(LOVES JOHN MARY)) = T,   [3.12′]

(MATCH '(LOVES ?X2 MARY) '(LOVES JOHN MARY)) = T,   [3.13′]

(MATCH '(+Y JOHN LOVES +Z) '(I KNOW THAT JOHN LOVES MARY VERY MUCH)) = T. [3.14']

When equation 3.12 is now applied, we wish to be able to type $X1$ afterward and have LISP interpret this variable as MARY. Likewise, when the matching operation is applied to equation 3.13, we wish LISP to evaluate the variable $X2$ as JOHN; and when the matching operation is applied to equation 3.14, we wish LISP to evaluate the variable Y to the list (I KNOW THAT), and the variable Z to the list (MARY VERY MUCH).

This added capability can be achieved in several ways. We could use two new functions, ATOMCAR and ATOMCDR—ATOMCAR to return the first character in an atom, and ATOMCDR to return an atom with its first character deleted. This could be implemented by means of the EXPLODE and IMPLODE operators found in most LISP processors, which operate as follows:

(EXPLODE 'ATOM) = (A T O M) [3.18]

(IMPLODE '(A B A N)) = ABAN. [3.19]

EXPLODE separates the characters in an atom into individual atoms, whereas IMPLODE collapses a set of atoms into characters of an individual atom. ATOMCAR and ATOMCDR can now be defined as:

(DEFINE (ATOMCAR X) (CAR (EXPLODE X))) [3.20]

(DEFINE (ATOMCDR X) (IMPLODE (CDR (EXPLODE X)))). [3.21]

To implement a MATCH operator with the desired properties, we must rewrite equation 3.16, substituting for the clause (EQUAL (CAR P) '?) the new clause:

((AND (EQUAL (ATOMCAR (CAR P)) '?)
 (MATCH (CDR P) (CDR D)))
 (SET (ATOMCDR (CAR P)) (CAR D)) T). [3.22]

We test to see whether the first character is equal to ?, and then—only after all recursions are completed and the match is successful—we set the variables (minus the special character ?) equal to their matching values.

Likewise, we would modify equation 3.17 by making the substitution just noted and, additionally, by substituting for the clause ((EQUAL (CAR *P*) '+) the new clause:

((EQUAL (ATOMCAR (CAR *P*)) '+)
 (COND ((MATCH (CDR *P*) (CDR *D*))
        (SET (ATOMCDR (CAR *P*) (LIST (CAR *D*))))
        T)
       ((MATCH *P* (CDR *D*))
        (SET (ATOMCDR (CAR *P*))
             (CONS (CAR *D*) (EVAL (ATOMCDR (CAR *P*)))))
        T))).   [3.23]

Once again, no binding takes place and no SET is executed until all recursions have taken place and the match has definitely succeeded.

LOGIC PROGRAMMING AND PROLOG

The close association between logic and artificial intelligence has made the idea of programming A.I. applications in a language designed around logic an appealing one to many A.I. researchers. Such a language would allow programs to be written as hypotheses about the world; our questions would then be treated as theorems that we would like to have proved.

In procedural languages, such as FORTRAN and LISP, tasks must be specified clearly in terms of what the computer should do, and when. By contrast, a logic programming language does not so much tell a computer what to do and when to do it, as tell the computer what is true and ask it to try and draw conclusions. In this sense, logic programming is similar to the nonprocedural, fourth-generation languages RAMIS, FOCUS, and ADABAS, which have been gaining popularity in the business world. Such languages are easier to read because they are not cluttered up with details about how things are to be done, but instead focus on specifications of the desired end product. This brings the programming language closer to the end user—or in the case of PROLOG, closer to language used in the problem-solving domain. Moreover, since the language is expressed much like a series of specifications, it should be easier to check and verify.

PROLOG is a candidate logic programming language. In fact, its name is derived from the phrase "programming in logic." PROLOG has a few built-in practical features that prevent it from being purely a logic programming language, but it can support the logic programming style.

PROLOG, a relatively recent addition to the list of A.I. programming languages, has been receiving increasing attention of late as a tool in such areas as expert system development and natural language processing. PROLOG was invented in 1972 by Alain Colmerauer and his associates at the University of Marseilles, who wrote the first PROLOG interpreter in the ALGOL-W language. In 1975, P. Roussel, a colleague of Colmerauer, implemented a more efficient interpreter in FORTRAN. PROLOG only began to attract widespread attention, however, when David Warren produced his very efficient implementation in 1979 at the University of Edinburgh. This implementation, known as DEC-10 PROLOG or Edinburgh PROLOG, included the first PROLOG compiler. PROLOG was first used most extensively in Europe—particularly in France, England, and Hungary—but it was propelled into international prominence in 1982, when Japan launched its fifth-generation program and named PROLOG as the basis for development of its new programming language, KL (kernel language).

HOW PROLOG WORKS

Computer programming in PROLOG consists of declaring facts, defining rules, and asking questions about objects and their relationships. For example, suppose we told PROLOG that a boy named Tom was the son of Mary; and suppose that we also told PROLOG a rule that related sons to a mother and father who were associated with each other as husband and wife. We could then ask the question, "Who is Tom's father?" PROLOG would then search its knowledge base for what we had told it about Tom, specifically looking for a fact about Tom's father (or Mary's husband) in order to answer our question. Either it would come back with the answer *no,* meaning that no father for Tom had been found, or it would supply us with the name of Tom's father.

Thus, programming in PROLOG means supplying facts and rules and then asking PROLOG questions about them. PROLOG uses the syntax of predicate logic in searching the knowledge base of facts and rules and making the necessary inferences to answer questions in a manner that is transparent to the user. The logic, which is supplied by the user programmer, is kept completely separate from the control, which is built in to the PROLOG interpreter/compiler; the programmer can only influence the inferencing in exceptional cases. PROLOG's built-in inference method is based on the resolution theory discussed in chapter 2.

Like LISP, PROLOG is primarily designed to be used in a conversational language, with the user sitting at a terminal and typing in the questions. Given the right kind of questions, PROLOG will work out the answers and display these on the computer screen.

BASIC FUNCTIONS AND OPERATIONS

Because PROLOG is based upon predicate calculus logic (discussed in chapter 2), we have already considered the logical underpinnings of the language of PROLOG. The syntax used by PROLOG, however, is in some respects unique.

In most versions of PROLOG, the name of a relationship is written first, followed by the names of the objects, which are separated by commas and enclosed by a pair of parentheses. All relationships and facts must end with a period. The names of all relationships and objects must begin in lowercase letters. Variables must begin with uppercase letters. Consider the following relationship facts, expressed in PROLOG's syntax:

likes(john,flowers).

likes(john,mary).

likes(paul,mary).

likes(susan,wine).

likes(susan,food).

These correspond to the facts that John likes flowers, John likes Mary, Paul likes Mary, Susan likes wine, and Susan likes food. We could now ask the following series of questions, in response to which PROLOG would give the answer that appears on the line immediately following the question:

```
?- likes(john,flowers).
yes
?- likes(john,paul).
no
?- likes(paul,flowers).
no
?- likes(john,mary).
yes
```

PROLOG searches its knowledge base—in this case a knowledge base composed exclusively of facts—and provides a *yes* where a match is found and a *no* where no match is found.

We could also ask PROLOG who John likes, by using the variable X as shown below:

> ?- likes(john,X).
> X = flowers

In this case, PROLOG searches for an instantiation of the variable X, which would result in a match. Because it searches in top-to-bottom, left-to-right order, the first match it finds is that John likes flowers, which it provides as the answer.

Some versions of PROLOG search exhaustively, providing all possible instantiations and matches. Our version of PROLOG, however, asks us if we wish to ask the question again; if we reply *yes,* it resumes its search where it left off and provides a second reply, X = mary. PROLOG then asks us if we wish to try the question again; if we again reply *yes,* PROLOG would resume its search but find no further qualifying candidates in the knowledge base, and so would provide the reply *no.* In this sense, operations such as the matching operation we investigated in our discussion of LISP are built in to PROLOG. The essence of the PROLOG inferencing mechanism is to search for matches and to instantiate any variables to the values for which the matches succeed.

We can also ask more complicated compound questions, such as "Do Mary and John like each other?"—which, from the knowledge base given above, would be answered *no.* We can express this question in the syntax of PROLOG as follows:

> ?- likes(john,mary), likes(mary,john).

The comma between *likes(john,mary)* and *likes(mary,john)* is pronounced *and* and serves as the logical conjunction, separating a sequence of goals that must all be satisfied in order to constitute an affirmative answer to the question.

Likewise, a semicolon is pronounced *or* and stands for the logical disjunction. For example, the compound question, "Does either John like Mary or Mary like John?" can be expressed as:

> ?- likes(john,mary);likes(mary,john).

Suppose we wished to state a fact about the kinds of people John liked without explicitly identifying all the people John liked and writing down all the separate facts known about these people. To accomplish this, we could use a rule. In PROLOG, rules are applied when the user wants to say that a fact depends on a group of other facts. In English, we can use the word *if* to express such a rule. PROLOG states the conclusion first and then the *if* conditions—the facts that are necessary to make the conclusion true. For example, consider the rule that John likes a person if that person likes wine and likes food. This rule can be expressed in the syntax of PROLOG as:

likes(john,X) :- likes(X,wine), likes(X,food).

In PROLOG, a rule consists of a head (the conclusion) and a body (the *if* condition). The head and the body are connected by a compound colon/hyphen symbol, which is pronounced *if*.

Adding a rule, such as the one immediately above, to our original knowledge base of facts fundamentally enhances this knowledge base. Now when we ask a question, PROLOG does not merely scan for variable substitutions that allow one of our facts to match the question, it also tries to apply our rule to the known facts in order to make inferences that may help answer our question. Hence, given our earlier question:

?- likes(john,X).

the system will first respond X=flowers and then respond X=mary, as before; but then, applying our introduced rule to the last two facts in the original knowledge base, the system will discover that John likes Susan and will respond X=susan.

LISTS IN PROLOG

Lists in PROLOG are manipulated by being split into a head and a tail. The head of a list is the first argument of the set that is used to construct lists. The term *head* thus means different things depending on whether we are referring to the head of a list or to the head of a rule. The tail of a list is the second argument of the set. The head and tail are separated by the first comma that appears within the set. When a list appears in square bracket notation, the head of the list is the first element of the set, and the tail of the list consists of every element except the first. For example:

- In set [a,b,c,d], a is the head, and b,c,d is the tail
- In set [a], a is the head, and the null set [ ] is the tail
- In null set [ ], there is neither head nor tail

A special notation is used in PROLOG to represent a list with head X and tail Y. This is written [X|Y], where the symbol separating the head X from the tail Y is a vertical bar. The anonymous variable (symbolized by a hyphen) is often used to stand for a member of the list— for example, the tail or the head of the list—when we are expressing a rule or fact for the list that does not use any information about that member.

Suppose we wish to write a predicate, member(X, Y) expression that is true if the object represented by the variable X is a member of the list represented by the variable Y. To implement this predicate in PROLOG, all we need do is define it. In this case, we define the predicate, member(X, Y) as being true if it satisfies either of two conditions. The first condition states that "X is a member of a list if X is the same as the head of the list"; or in PROLOG:[2]

member(X,[X|-]).

The second condition states that "X is a member of the list if X is a member of the tail of the list." In PROLOG, this condition must be stated recursively:

member(X,[-|Y]) :- member(X, Y).

Thus in PROLOG, we can define the predicate, member(X, Y) expression by storing in the knowledge base its definition, consisting of one fact (the first condition above), expressed in terms of the variable X, and one rule (the second condition above), expressed recursively in terms of the predicate, member(X, Y) and the variables X and Y.

Now observe how this PROLOG predicate operates on the question,

---

2. From *Programming in PROLOG*, by W.F. Clocksin and C.S. Mellish (Berlin: Springer-Verlag, 1981). Reprinted with permission.

"Is *d* a member of the set [*a,b,c,d,e,f,g*]?"—stated in the syntax of PROLOG as:

?- member(*d*,[*a,b,c,d,e,f,g*]).

In attempting to answer this question, PROLOG first tries to match the first condition, "Is *d* the head of the set [*a,b,c,d,e,f,g*]?" Since this condition is not true, PROLOG moves on to the second condition, "Is *d* a member of the tail of the set [*a,b,c,d,e,f,g*]?"—that is, is *d* a member of the set [*b,c,d,e,f,g*]? This question causes reinvocation of the entire PROLOG member predicate, this time to test whether *d* is a member of the tail of the original set. Again, the first condition is found not to apply (since *d* is not equal to *b*), so the second condition is tried again. This time the predicate is invoked to test whether *d* is a member of the set [*c,d,e,f,g*]. Again, the first condition is found not to apply (since *d* is not equal to *c*), so again the second condition is applied. Once more, the full member predicate is invoked, this time to test whether *d* is a member of the set [*d,e,f,g*]. This time, the first condition is satisfied: *d* equals the head of the set, and PROLOG responds by answering the initial question *yes*. If no *d* had been present in the set, the program wuld have kept reapplying itself until no tail remained, and then it would have responded *no* to the initial question.

PREDICATES THAT AFFECT THE CONTROL STRATEGY

Another type of predicate function, called a *cut,* allows the programmer to tell PROLOG which previous choices it need not reconsider when it backtracks through a chain of satisfied goals. The cut thus moves PROLOG away from being a pure nonprocedural logic programming language toward being a procedural language in which the programmer can influence not only the problem PROLOG works on, but the way PROLOG goes about solving it. The cut function also allows the programmer to alter the goal-based resolution theorem-proving inferencing that is built into PROLOG.

A cut function can be useful primarily for three reasons. First, the cut operator keeps the program from wasting time trying to satisfy goals that the user knows beforehand will never contribute to a solution. Second, more economical use can be made of memory if backtracking points do not have to be recorded for later examination. Third, importantly, using the cut makes the difference in some cases between a program that will run and one that will not.

Syntactically, the cut function is invoked by means of an exclamation point placed without any arguments. The ! is interpreted by PROLOG as a goal that succeeds immediately and cannot be resatisfied. The system thus becomes committed to all choices made since the parent goal was invoked. All other alternatives are discarded, and an attempt to satisfy any goal between the parent goal and the cut (!) goal will fail.

For example, consider the predicate *sum-*,[3] where the goal:

$$?- \text{sum-to}(N, X)$$

causes X to be instantiated with the sum of the numbers from 1 to N (where N is an integer). For example, the predicate sum-to(5,X) would cause X to be set to 15. The following program in PROLOG to implement this predicate is a recursive definition that includes the use of the cut:

sum-to(N,1) :- $N \leq 1$, !.   (rule 1)
sum-to(N,Res) :-   (rule 2)
    $N1$ is $N-1$,
    sum-to($N1$,Res1),
    Res is Res1 + N.

This definition states that, if the first number is less than or equal to 1, the answer is 1. The second clause introduces the recursive use of the predicate sum-to goal, where *sum-to* is applied to a new goal that is 1 less than the original. Each time the predicate sum-to is recursively applied, the answer is increased by the current value of the first argument; and each time the sum-to is recursively applied, the first argument is decreased by 1. Eventually the first clause will be reached, and the program will terminate.

The control logic of this program is fairly simple. First the program tests to see if the first argument is less than or equal to 1. It only tries the second rule if the first rule fails—that is, if the first argument is greater than 1. In the absence of the cut function, if PROLOG ever backtracks and reconsiders which rule to choose and apply to the number 1, it will find the second rule applicable. The cut prevents this

3. From *Programming in PROLOG,* by W.F. Clocksin and C.S. Mellish (Berlin: Springer-Verlag, 1981). Reprinted with permission.

from happening, by specifying that on no account is the second rule ever to be tried if the number is equal to or less than 1. It instructs PROLOG that, once the program gets this far in the first rule, it must never remake the decision about which rule to use for the sum-to goal.

This same program could be written using the *not* function rather than the cut. The function not(X) is a built-in PROLOG predicate specifying that X is not satisfiable as a PROLOG goal. The not(X) function only succeeds if X fails as a PROLOG goal. In this case, the sum-to definition can be rewritten as

$$\text{sum-to}(N,1) :- N \leq 1. \quad \text{(rule 1)}$$
$$\text{sum-to}(N,R) :- \text{not}(N \leq 1), \quad \text{(rule 2)}$$
$$N1 \text{ is } N-1,$$
$$\text{sum-to}(N1,R1),$$
$$R \text{ is } N1+R1.$$

The program using the *not* predicate is probably easier to read than the program using the cut function, but it involves the additional step of trying to show that the goal stated can be satisfied.

Similarly, the *append* function operates on two lists and creates a new list consisting of the first list prefixed to the second list. The following PROLOG program uses recursion and the cut function:[4]

$$\text{append}([\,],X,X) :- !. \quad \text{(rule 1)}$$
$$\text{append}([A|B],C,[A|D]) :- \text{append}(B,C,D). \quad \text{(rule 2)}$$

This definition states that an empty list appended to a list X results in list X, and that otherwise the list consisting of head A and tail B, when appended to list C, results in a new list with head A and tail D (where D is the list that results when list B is appended to list C). When backtracking occurred (absent the cut), the program would try to use the second rule on a predicate such as append($[\,],[a,b,c],X$) even though the attempt would be bound to fail. We know that, if the first list is $[\,]$, the first rule is the only possible correct rule; in this case, therefore, use of the cut prevents the fruitless application of the second rule and increases the space and time efficiency of the program.

Finally, consider an example that uses a combination of the cut function and the *fail* predicate (a popular combination for many appli-

---

4. From *Programming in PROLOG,* by W.F. Clocksin and C.S. Mellish (Berlin: Springer-Verlag, 1981). Reprinted with permission.

cations). Suppose we wish to write a program that computes how much tax a person should pay. One thing we might want to determine is whether a particular person qualifies as an average taxpayer. The calculations here are relatively simple, and we can avoid considering numerous special cases. One way we might consider defining an *average taxpayer* is by enumerating some common circumstances that would exclude someone from that status. For instance, we might include a rule that checks whether the person is a citizen of another country. Foreigners would not be classified as average taxpayers because they are specially treated. This would involve a rule such as:

average-taxpayer(X) :- foreigner(X), fail.   (rule 1)

followed by a series of other tests consisting of rules such as:

average-taxpayer(X) :- gross-income(X,Inc), Inc > 5000,
                        Inc < 50000.   (rule 2)

Rule 1 above makes use of the *fail* predicate, which is a built-in predicate like the *not* predicate. It has no arguments, so its success does not depend on what any variables stand for; in fact, *fail* always fails and causes backtracking. Thus rule 1 states that the goal average-taxpayer(X) should fail if X is a foreigner. Use of the *fail* predicate in rule 1 without a cut function, however, leads to difficulties. If we ask the question:

?- average-taxpayer(schmidt).

about a German citizen named Schmidt, the first rule would match and the foreigner goal would succeed. Next, the *fail* goal would initiate backtracking. The problem here is that, when PROLOG attempts to apply the second rule to Schmidt, it is quite likely to let Schmidt pass and be mistakingly classified as an average taxpayer. The first rule is thus rendered completely ineffective as a means of rejecting Schmidt as an average taxpayer. To remedy this problem, we rewrite the rule, using the cut, as follows:

average-taxpayer(X) :- foreigner(X), !, fail.   (rule 1')

The effect of the cut is to freeze the decision that X is a foreigner and is not an average taxpayer before the fail goal is reached, preventing any backtracking that involves reconsideration of the decision as to whether X is an average taxpayer.

PROLOG AND THE RESOLUTION PRINCIPLE

PROLOG is based on the idea of theorem-proving and the resolution principle, although the syntax does differ. As was discussed in chapter 2, resolution in predicate calculus is designed to work on logical propositions in clause form; for example:

$$((a \text{ or } b \text{ or } c) \text{ and } (d \text{ or } e \text{ or } f)).$$

In PROLOG, the same expression would be written:

$$((a; b; c),(d; e; f)).$$

In predicate calculus, implications or rules are written:

$$(a \text{ and } b \text{ and } c) \rightarrow (d \text{ or } e \text{ or } f).$$

By applying the appropriate transformations, we can express the same rule equivalently as:

$$((d \text{ or } e \text{ or } f) \text{ or not}(a \text{ and } b \text{ and } c))$$

In PROLOG, these rules are equivalently written as:

$$d;e;f :\text{-} a,b,c.$$

Given two clauses that can be appropriately related, predicate calculus can point to a third clause that is a consequence of them. Specifically, if an atomic formula on the lefthand side of one rule can (with appropriate values assigned to any variables in the formula) be made to match an atomic formula on the righthand side of the other rule, these two atomic formulas are said to resolve, and they can be eliminated to form a new rule. Suppose, for example, that the following two clauses must both be true:

sad(merle); angry(merle) :- workday(today), raining(today).   (rule 1)

unpleasant(X) :- angry(X), tired(X).   (rule 2)

In this case, the atomic formula angry(merle) on the left side of the first rule matches the formula angry(X) on the right side of the second rule, when the variable X is assigned the value *merle*. Therefore, this atomic formula can be resolved (eliminated), and the two rules can be combined to produce the following third rule:

sad(merle);unpleasant(merle) :-
workday(today),raining(today),tired(merle).   (rule 3)

As was discussed earlier, the process of assigning values to variables so that atomic formulas match is called *instantiating,* and the process of matching clauses is called *unification.* All computable functions can be transformed into Horn Clause form. A Horn Clause is a clause that has at most one unnegated literal, the lefthand side of a PROLOG formula. For example, the goal:

:- loves(john,X).

which has no unnegated literal and is therefore called *headless,* is a valid Horn Clause. So is the rule:

loves(john,X) :- loves(X,tennis), unmarried(X).

which has a single unnegated literal and is called *headed.* So also is the fact:

loves(john,mary):- .

or more simply:

loves(john,mary).

which has a single unnegated literal and therefore is a headed clause, too.

In fact, any solvable problem that is expressable in Horn Clauses can be expressed in such a way that all the clauses are headed. This constraint is added in PROLOG: we view the headless clause as the goal and the rest of the clauses as hypotheses and facts, and we write the headless clause as a PROLOG question. For example, the headless clause:

:- loves(john,X).

is written as the PROLOG question:

?- loves(john, X).

In PROLOG, we base our inferencing on a resolution-prover for Horn Clauses. We start with the goal statement, or question, and resolve it with one of the hypotheses, or facts, yielding a new clause; then we resolve that clause with another of the hypotheses, yielding another new clause; and so on.

In PROLOG, we always select these clauses in the order in which they appear, top to bottom. Likewise, when a literal is to be matched, the one selected is always the first one in the goal clause. The new goals derived from the use of a clause are placed at the front of the goal clause; thus PROLOG finishes satisfying a subgoal before it tries anything else. In accordance with its depth-first strategy, PROLOG only considers one alternative at a time, following up the implications under the assumption that the choice is correct. Of course, this strategy can be modified through such special functions as *cut* and *fail*. The capacity to handle these special functions and others such as *print* are included in PROLOG for efficiency and other practical reasons (including the need for an input/output capability). Thus, although PROLOG should be used primarily to program logic functions, it can also be used to program procedural functions and certain not strictly logical functions.

■ OTHER LANGUAGES AND HIGHER-ORDER SOFTWARE TOOLS

In principle, any language can be used to implement A.I. programs, and despite the popularity of LISP and PROLOG, other languages have been used in A.I. development. More conventional languages such as C, FORTRAN, and PASCAL have occasionally been used in A.I. work. Languages other than LISP and PROLOG that have been identified as especially suitable for A.I. programming include:

- SAIL. Stanford A.I. Language, which is used mostly in vision-processing work. It is ALGOL-like and is built around a structure similar to LISP's CONs cell except that a single cell, or record, can point to more than two addresses.
- FUZZY. Developed in 1977; based upon fuzzy set theory.
- LOGLISP. Developed in the early 1980s at Syracuse University; combines features of both LISP- and PROLOG-like logic programming.

- FORTH. Combines many of the symbol manipulation features of LISP with the compactness and efficiency of lower-level assembler languages. It cannot support recursion.
- POP-2, POPLER, and POPLOG. A family of languages used in Great Britain. POP-2 is similar to LISP. POPLER is based upon PLANNER, a pattern-directed inferencing language developed at MIT. POPLOG is similar to PROLOG.
- APL2. An enhancement of APL. It applies functions in parallel to arrays of data. It has recently been shown to be capable in handling problems traditionally programmed in LISP and of being used as a possible implementation language for PROLOG-like languages (Brown, Eusebi, Cook, and Groner 1986).

In the late 1960s and early 1970s, an effort was made to extend LISP to support a generic inferencing capability. This resulted in QLISP, an extension to INTER-LISP, and in the development of the programming languages PLANNER and CONNIVER, which were built on top of MACLISP at MIT.

With the introduction of PROLOG and the emphasis on expert systems and natural language processing systems, these early language extension efforts were subsumed by a new family of software tools, namely, the expert system shells, discussed in more detail in chapter 4, and the natural language interface packages, also discussed in chapter 4.

Those tools were outgrowths of early research efforts. Research systems developed for a specific application were generalized and expanded until they could be adapted for use across a much larger class of problems, thus eliminating the need for continual redevelopment of the same software modules for each new application. These tools were refined and improved with use, incorporating a growing collection of time-saving software aids for the knowledge acquisition and maintenance phases of a project. These tools are covered much more extensively in chapter 4 and the appendixes.

■ LISP MACHINES AND OTHER SPECIAL HARDWARE

Several classes of work stations can be used to support A.I. work. One significant group consists of LISP machines, an outgrowth of government-sponsored research at MIT (the first LISP machine built at MIT was called the CADR machine) and research at Xerox Park aimed at building a personal work station optimized for a symbolic computing–development environment. These LISP machines have several unique features:

- Tagged architecture for run-time data-type checking
- Hardware-assisted garbage collection
- Stack-oriented architecture with a large stack buffer (one high-speed stack buffer)
- Wide (36-bit) internal data paths
- Microprogrammed processor designed for LISP
- Parallelism in certain operations such as garbage collection

In addition they usually have a second conventional processor to handle peripherals, high-resolution bit-mapped graphics to support the windowing/mouse interaction paradigm, networking hardware and software, and high-speed disk storage.

LISP machines range in price from $20,000 to over $100,000, with scaled-down delivery versions being offered by Xerox for as little as $9,000. Current LISP machines, their capabilities, and representative A.I. software supported on these machines are summarized in figures 3-4 and 3-5. In response to growing interest in PROLOG, the manufacturers have adapted all of these machines to support PROLOG. Symbolics and LISP Machine (LMI) are two MIT spinoffs resulting from the early CADR work. Explorer, by Texas Instruments (which has a financial and licensing interest in LMI), is based on the LMI design. Several LISP machine companies are producing special LISP processing attachments for some of the current crop of conventional mainframes. In addition, all are building bridges for increased networking and interfacing with more conventional computer hardware and software systems.

At the same time, the scientific work station community, originally targeted for engineering design and CAD/CAM, but having similar man-machine interface (for example, high-resolution bit-mapped graphics, windows, and mouse) and networking capabilities, is beginning to offer a complement of A.I.-based software; these offer a lower-cost (albeit less powerful) alternative to LISP machines. Some of the more popular scientific work stations—and the A.I. software they support—are:

- Apollo: I-LISP and COMMON LISP, SMALLTALK
- Perq: LISP, OPS-5
- Sun: LISP
- Tektronix 4404: SMALLTALK-80, LISP, PROLOG
- Hewlett Packard: LISP

LISP Machines and Other Special Hardware ■ 125

Special architecture to support symbolic processing
Large 64-Mbyte address space

High-resolution, memory-mapped display

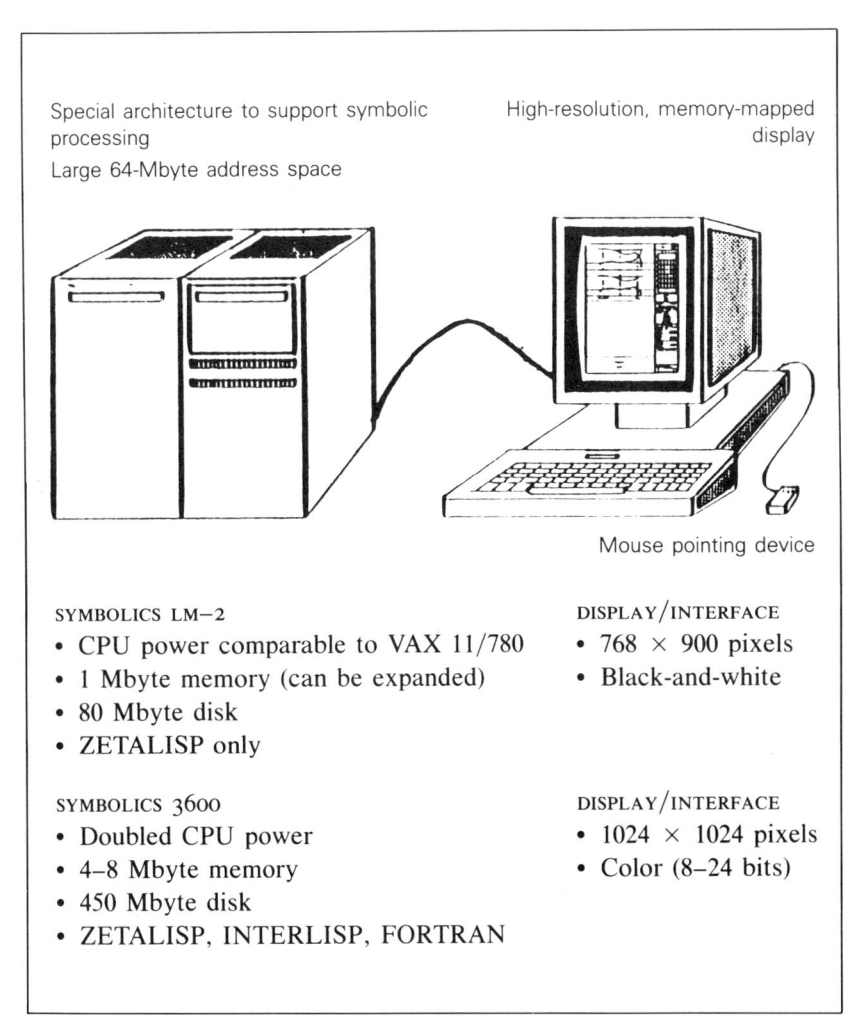

Mouse pointing device

SYMBOLICS LM-2
- CPU power comparable to VAX 11/780
- 1 Mbyte memory (can be expanded)
- 80 Mbyte disk
- ZETALISP only

DISPLAY/INTERFACE
- 768 × 900 pixels
- Black-and-white

SYMBOLICS 3600
- Doubled CPU power
- 4–8 Mbyte memory
- 450 Mbyte disk
- ZETALISP, INTERLISP, FORTRAN

DISPLAY/INTERFACE
- 1024 × 1024 pixels
- Color (8–24 bits)

3-4. Advanced personal computer hardware.

Even the traditional mainframe and super minicomputer manufacturers are now offering an array of A.I.-based software on their computers. Before the advent of the LISP machines, DEC was the preferred computer for A.I. research. The company has built several expert systems for in-house use, and it offers an extremely wide variety of A.I. software capable of running on DEC computers. The company has also introduced a special A.I. work station for approximately $20,000 based on their micro-Vax technology. These mainframe and minicomputer offerings are summarized in figure 3-6.

Specifically designed or microcoded for LISP, graphics display with bit map integrated with memory.

XEROX
- 1100 Dolphin
- 1108 Dandelion
- 1132 Dorado
- Dandetiger
- 1186
- 1187
- Software includes: INTERLISP D and COMMONLISP; LOOPS; KEE

SYMBOLICS
- 3600, 3640, 3670
- Software includes: ZETALISP and COMMONLISP; PROLOG; ART; OPS; KEE; ACRONYM; TEAM; DUCK; KBASE

LISP MACHINE, INC.
- Lambda, 2×2, 4×4
- Software includes: ZETALISP PLUS and COMMONLISP; LM PROLOG (University of Sweden); PICON (Carnegie Group); KEE

TEXAS INSTRUMENTS
- Explorer, LISP Machine
- Software includes: COMMONLISP; PROLOG; productivity tool kits (graphics, natural language interface, knowledge engineering)

FUJITSU
- Facom Alpha, high-speed LISP processor, also attaches to GP processor
- Relational Table Manager, command interface, knowledge engineering
- Software includes: COMMONLISP; PROLOG

MITSUBISHI
- SIM/1, outgrowth of ICOT's PSIM (Personal Sequential Inference Machine)
- Software includes; ESHELL, expert system shell; LISP; PROLOG

NEC, Toshiba, and Hitachi have LISP machines under development.

3-5. LISP machines.

DEC (VAX AND MICRO-VAX WORK STATIONS)
Software includes:
- COMMONLISP (Gold Hill Computers)
- OPS (CMU)
- KNOWLEDGE CRAFT and SRL+ (Carnegie Group)
- LANGUAGE CRAFT and PLUME (Carnegie Group)
- INTELLECT (A.I.C, soon to be offered)
- PROLOG II (Prologia, Marseilles)
- INTERLISP (USC-ISI)
- DEC LISP
- COMMONLISP
- MACLISP
- TEAM
- KEE
- KES
- DUCK
- ART
- S-1

IBM (370 ARCHITECTURE, E.G., 43XX, 30XX)
- LISP-VM
- INTELLECT
- PROLOG-VM
- EXPERT SYSTEMS ENVIRONMENT-VM

DATA GENERAL (MV SERIES)
- COMMONLISP

SPERRY (1100 SERIES AND TI LISP MACHINES)
- LISP
- Industry-targeted expert systems

HEWLETT PACKARD (9800 SERIES)
- LISP

GOULD (SEL SERIES)
- FRANZ LISP

PRIME
- LISP
- PROLOG
- Working on a special LISP processor that attaches to Prime mainframe

3-6. Minicomputers and mainframes.

IBM, too, is actively building expert systems and natural language systems for its own use and extending its selection of A.I. software that runs on its machines. IBM is concentrating most of its current crop of A.I. software offerings on mainframes (see figure 3-7).

Finally, more and more A.I. products are being offered on IBM and IBM-compatible personal computers and on the Apple Macintosh. As the memory and the processing capacity of these machines grow, the machines' viability as A.I. delivery vehicles—particularly when networked with larger A.I. computers—increases too (figure 3-8).

As relatively conventional computers enter the A.I. field in greater numbers, the LISP machines continue to upgrade their product lines, offering higher performance at lower cost, and to build bridges for interfacing with the large existing base of conventional hardware/software. The future of these various hardware products is unclear. The LISP machines currently represent the Cadillac of A.I. computer hardware. Whether they can stay in front or not remains to be seen. What will be the impact of new, more advanced computer designs, such as the RISC technology? Will they supplant the current crop of LISP machines

---

- PRISM—prototype inference system
- ESPIRIT MEMBERSHIP
- DOD and university research in parallel processing: NYU, MIT, Stanford, Syracuse, Columbia
- PEACH—rumored LISP machine
- EPISTLE—natural language, critiques texts and summarizes letters
- DART—computer diagnosis expert system
- PSC PROLOG
- YES/MVS
- SCRATCHPAD II—symbolic algebra
- HANDY—educational appliances
- INTELLECT—licensed from Artificial Intelligence Corp. (A.I.C.)
- LISP-VM
- TQA (Transformational Question-Answering—natural language front end to System R relational data base (DB2 is subset of System R)
- Version of OPS-5 implemented on 370 architecture
- IBM researchers designing new algorithms for symbolic computation

3-7. A.I. software for IBM mainframes.

Motorola 6800, 68010, 68020
IBM and IBM-compatible

LANGUAGES INCLUDE:
- COMMONLISP, Gold Hill
- Integral Quality LISP
- Soft Warehouse, LISP
- Norell Data System LISP
- Metacomco, Cambridge LISP
- PROLOG-1, Expert Systems International
- PROLOG-86
- Arity PROLOG
- TLC LISP
- Q'NIAL (APL & LISP combination)

EXPERT SYSTEM SHELLS INCLUDE:
- M1, Teknowledge
- Expert-Ease, Expert Software
- TIMM, General Research
- ES/P Advisor, Expert Systems International
- Personal Consultant, Texas Instruments
- EXSYS
- XSYS
- INSIGHT
- REVEAL
- KES

NATURAL LANGUAGE SYSTEMS INCLUDE:
- Intellect, Artificial Intelligence Corp.
- Clout, Microrim
- Natural Link, Texas Instruments

3-8. Personal computers.

and scientific work stations? What will emerge from the parallel processing research coming out of Japan's fifth-generation program and DARPA's strategic computer program? Will they produce a new A.I. computer architecture that will render obsolete all of the current crop of offerings? Only time will tell.

4 · Current Applications

At this point it should be clear that A.I. is a young, evolving field. Basic concepts and theories are still incomplete, and important research issues need to be resolved before A.I. can reach its full potential. Nevertheless, A.I. can be successfully applied right now, provided one is fully cognizant of and attentive to its current shortcomings and limitations.

These applications are primarily in the areas of expert systems and natural language processing systems. These two important applications areas help make the automation of many previously manpower-intensive tasks practical, cost-effective, and reliable. They are defined and discussed in this chapter, and systems techniques and architectures employed in the design of working applications in these areas are reviewed.

A.I. holds the promise for better human being–machine interaction, with the machine adapting more to the natural human modes of communication—speech and vision, and multiple senses. Machine perception applications are just beginning to emerge in the commercial world; speech synthesis and speech recognition devices are already in the marketplace, as are, to a lesser extent, vision-processing modules. Current systems approaches and architectures, including their present limitations and difficulties, are reviewed.

Finally, no discussion of A.I. applications would be complete without a discussion of robotics: intelligent machines that can manufacture, assemble, paint, clean, and entertain, including the friendly, human-style robot that has been romanticized in books, movies, and television as the ultimate in A.I. Although still mostly in the realm of fiction, real, intelligent robots, albeit still quite limited in contrast to their Hollywood brothers and sisters, are already entering the marketplace. The design and uses of these robots are discussed herein.

■ EXPERT SYSTEMS

An expert is someone who is recognized as being able to solve a particular class of complex, often ill-defined problems especially well and efficiently. An expert also usually knows the limits of his or her expertise. One way to think about problem solving is in terms of the problem space, which consists of a set of knowledge states and a selection of operators that can be used to transform states. A problem is defined in terms of an initial state and a goal (a state or set of states). Solving the problem involves finding a sequence of operators—a *path*—by which to transform the initial state into the goal state. Thus problem solving is a matter of searching the problem space on the basis of partial knowledge of how to proceed (what operator to select); this *search control knowledge* guides the search through the space. The difficulty of performance in the space can be assessed according to the extent to which the search control knowledge available constrains behavior.

In gaining expertise, the problem solver amasses search control knowledge; this, when compiled into integrated procedures or packages of operators structured for efficient performance, suffices in most particular situations to enable the problem solver to go straight to the desired goal, with relatively few false steps and relatively little need for backtracking (Card, Moran, and Newell 1983). If a class of problems can ultimately be solved by a control strategy composed of fixed procedures requiring no search at all, we generally describe the solver's ability as a cognitive skill rather than as an expertise.

Once a cognitive skill or expertise is learned, the expert devotes little conscious attention to the search control strategy and therefore is usually poorly prepared to explain the control strategy to others.

Several reasons motivate us to want to build an expert system rather than just hiring experts when we need them: productivity, profitability, education, customer service, and competitive advantage.

Productivity. By automating expertise we can clone scarce resources and provide more advice, often with faster turnaround time. Computers commonly work faster than a human expert can, and certainly they work longer and at odder hours without fatigue.

Profitability. Once automated, an expert system can be run on a computer at far less expense than would be required for a high-priced expert. Furthermore, using the computer to do more tasks faster saves additional cost.

Education. Often when an expert system is implemented, it renders the expert knowledge clearer and more explicit. Studying the organization and content of the expert system and using the system as a trusted advisor provide excellent training and testing opportunities for apprentices. The medical expert system Caduceus, for example, not only provides expert consultation advice, but acts as a training aid for younger physicians. Similarly, the expert system DENDRAL has been used for checking chemists' papers.

Customer service. An expert system can be operated in many locations at once, serving a much larger, more widely scattered audience than a handful of experts could. An expert investment advisor, for example, would be available to many more potential investors, both large and small, than would any individual human advisor or firm. Moreover, this expertise can be made available in the remotest of places (such as at the site of oil wells in jungles) or in locations unsafe or uninhabitable (such as inside a defective nuclear plant or thousands of feet under the sea). This allows a company to provide service faster, to more people, at more diverse locations than would otherwise be possible or profitable.

Competitive advantage. Being able to offer scarce expertise to a wider audience, being able to apply scarce expertise to a broader range of problems, and being able to devote more time to identifying the best solution to a given problem—these are but one side of the coin. By setting a computerized expert to work on these subjects, we free the talents of our scarce human experts to concentrate on especially complex, difficult problems, without having to attend to the demanding but more routine assignments now handled by their computerized research assistant.

The areas of expertise addressed by expert systems are concerned with problems that cannot be reduced to a series of algorithms or formulas, or that require skills for which a person can be easily and inexpensively trained. The class of problems for which expert systems are most ideally suited are those that require a fairly large degree of judgment and intuition, acquired through a relatively long and difficult apprenticeship. For many real classes of problems, both people and machines must apply problem-solving methodology to find satisfactory, approximate solutions. Some of the factors and characteristics of these problems are described below.

Tight time constraints. Although a more structured, algorithmic, and complete treatment exists, it requires a greater amount of time than is available. One example would be the traveling salesman problem discussed earlier. As the number of cities to be visited grows to ten or more, the processing time, which increases exponentially, becomes prohibitively long. Other examples include a military fire control system or a Star

Wars defensive shield that has only seconds to minutes to discover, identify, track, and fire upon enemy targets.

Lack of sufficient information. Proper or complete information is required for a more complete or algorithmic solution but is not available. Furthermore, much of the information is suspect or uncertain, requiring the expert to determine what information to believe. Finally, insufficient domain knowledge is available regarding how to judge a situation with sparse or uncertain information. How does one weight and combine the knowledge one does have? How does one compensate for missing information?

Complexity and magnitude of the task. Often the job at hand has too many factors to coordinate and/or too much data to absorb easily.

Confusion and misunderstanding. A conceptual overview of the problem objectives, status, and alternatives is lacking. The required methodology may be novel and unfamiliar. Many conflicting objectives with unclear trade-offs may be involved.

Lack of perseverance. The task is too overwhelming, too boring, or too tiring; or other things simply have a higher priority.

To be entirely satisfactory, an expert system, like a trusted human expert, should be able:

- To explain its reasoning process (its assumptions and its premises)
- To explain and substantiate its results (its conclusions and its recommendations)
- To guide the user and to catch user misunderstandings and errors
- To communicate with the user in the language and terms natural to the user (in the semantics of the problem domain)
- To reflect the domain knowledge as deeply and flexibly as possible, by mathematical models and algorithms and by subjective and factual reasoning
- To treat the problem domain broadly, preferably from several perspectives

Today, expert systems are being applied in such areas as:

- Decision support—for example, financial advisor
- Diagnostics and maintenance—for example, computer repair systems by DEC, IBM, Prime, and Sperry-Rand; telephone cable repair systems by AT&T; and electronic trouble-shooting systems by Tektronics
- Factory rationalization—for example, configuring computers by DEC;

134 ■ CURRENT APPLICATIONS

circuit assembly systems by Hazeltine; manufacturing planning and layout systems by Westinghouse; and intelligent robotics by GM
- Military—for example, strategic computing initiative (Command and Control, smart autonomous weapons, pilot's assistant)

Among the specific systems already in use are:

- Medicine—MYCIN and PUFF from Stanford
- Structural analysis—SACON from Stanford
- Chemistry—DENDRAL and MOLGEN from Stanford
- Geology—PROSPECTOR from SRI
- Programming—PHI NAUGHT from Schlumberger
- Military—in multisensor integration/correlation/fusion, SIAP from Stanford and SCI; in air mission planning, KNOBS from Mitre; in battlefield management, BATTLE from Naval Research Lab
- Math—MACSYMA from MIT
- Maintenance—in locomotive maintenance, CATS from GE; in telephone cable trouble-shooting, ACE from Bell Labs
- Oil drilling/signal interpretation—DIPMETER ADVISOR from Schlumberger
- Finance—loan classification from Syntelligence; financial planning from Apex
- Business—strategic product planning from A. D. Little
- Computers—XCON/R1 from DEC and Carnegie-Mellon
- VLSI design—PALLEDO
- Circuit board layout and assembly—OPGEN from Hazeltine

A more extensive list of expert system applications is provided in Appendixes A and B.

Many expert system shells are currently being offered commercially to assist users in developing expert systems. A comprehensive list of many of such expert system shells is provided in Appendix B. Some of the more popular system shells and their developers are:

    OPS—DEC
    OPS-83—Production Systems; Technologies Corp.
    M1 (for PCs) and SI—Teknowledge
    KEE—Intellicorp
    ART—Inference
    LOOPS—Xerox
    EXPERT-EASE (for PCs) and EXTRAN—Expert Software
    TIMM—General Research

SRL+—Carnegie Group
DUCK—Smart Systems
JEN-X—General Electric
ES/P ADVISOR—Expert Systems
RULEMASTER—Radian Corp.
KES—Software A & E
REVEAL—InfoTym (a subsidiary of McDonnell Douglas)
PICON and AIBASE—LMI
PERSONAL CONSULTANT—Texas Instruments
EXPERT EDGE—Human Edge Software Corp.
KDS (Knowledge Delivery System)—KDS Corp.
KNOWLEDGE CRAFT—Carnegie Group Inc.
EXPLICIT—Quantum Development Corp.
ESCE/ESDE (The Expert System Consultant/Development Environment)—IBM
INSIGHT—Level 5 Research Inc.
1ST CLASS—Programs in Motion Inc.
XSYS—California Intelligence
EXSYS—EXSYS Inc.
ESHELL—Mitsubishi

An expert system shell consists of a collection of expert system building tools that are designed to assist the developer by minimizing the amount of specialized knowledge and engineering and programming skills required to build an expert system. For example, most expert system shells have a user-friendly interface that, in the building mode, accepts knowledge in the form of English-like rules and/or frame structures. Some systems allow the knowledge base to be built with rules, frames, and procedures written in LISP or some other computer language.

An object-oriented paradigm such as Smalltalk is generally employed as the means for integrating these various knowledge bases. Rules, frames, and procedures can be combined to form a single object, or they can be defined as separate objects that are interrelated through user-defined links, relationships, or messages. Typically, the user is assisted in designing these interrelated object structures by a highly interactive, user-friendly interface that relies heavily on graphics employing the icon, mouse (cursor/pointer), windowing style of user interaction developed at Xerox Park and made popular by the Apple Macintosh and the scientific work station community.

Most expert system shells have a default search control strategy so that the designer need not be concerned with the control strategy except by choice. Production rule–based system shells generally employ either backward chaining or forward chaining as their default mode. Often the user is permitted to tailor the control strategy by means of parameters, user-specified control strategy procedures, or rule sets (metarules) and by structuring the knowledge base rules into related rule sets, applicable contexts, or hierarchical subgoals.

Frame-based shells generally do require the user to define links and relationships between the various frames, but this is usually done with the assistance of a highly interactive, user-friendly interface in high-level natural language statements and graphics input. The system can usually be run immediately, once an initial knowledge base has been defined, without regard to the inference search control process.

The normal run mode of the system is a dialogue in which the machine prompts the user for more information as it is needed. The prompts differ in the various expert system shells on the market, but commonly the user can interrupt the system at any time to ask it why the question is being asked, why the information is being requested, what aspect of the problem the system is currently working on, what tentative conclusions and deductions the system has already made, or on what grounds the system has reached its conclusions and deductions. These user-initiated questions are usually answered in natural language responses, sometimes augmented with graphics displays. At any time, the user can also require the system to make the best decision it can without receiving any further information from the user. The explanation facilities of expert systems are still quite limited in scope, however, particularly when compared to the abilities of a human expert advisor. Much remains to be learned about explanation.

The run-time dialogue feature is usually built in to the expert system shell, with a default dialogue generated by the system in response to knowledge previously entered during the design phase and information entered by the user during the current run in response to the system's questioning. In design mode, most systems allow the user to modify and customize this dialogue to suit personal style preferences. For example, more verbose replies can be directly input by the user (with word processing support) to replace the default replies.

Each expert system shell handles uncertainty differently, but most currently employ certainty measures based on the MYCIN approach (described earlier in this book) to deal with uncertainty in information and knowledge (rules) or do not provide any facility for handling uncertainty at all. For systems in the latter group, the user is responsible for developing an appropriate structure, without any system support.

A few systems on the market employ more formal probabilistic measures and statistical inferencing methodologies to deal with uncertainty.

The expert system shells run on computers ranging from personal computers (generally IBM, IBM-compatibles, and Macintosh) to scientific work stations (APOLLO, SUN, PERQ) to large minicomputers and mainframes (VAX, IBM) to specialized LISP machines (Symbolics, Xerox, LMI, Texas Instruments). Some shells have versions that run on several of these machines. Clearly, the more powerful the machine is, the more powerful the expert system can be with respect to such features as the maximum supportable size of the knowledge base, the run-time efficiency, and the speed of execution.

Expert systems have been variously categorized in efforts to gain insight into the best methodologies and tools to use in developing a particular expert systems application. One approach is to categorize expert systems according to the type of problem they confront; for example:

- Interpretation
- Diagnosis
- Prediction
- Planning
- Design

This approach would allow us to select a methodology or tool that has been successfully employed in the past to solve other problems in the same category. Rule-based systems have typically been employed successfully in solving problems of interpretation and diagnosis and have had some success in handling prediction problems. Far fewer planning and design applications have been developed; these two problem categories are less well understood and have generally required more powerful knowledge representation and control strategy schemes—often involving a mixture of rules, frames, and procedures.

Another way of thinking about the categorization of expert systems is illustrated in figure 4-1, where expert systems are categorized according to the complexity of the problem. We use problem-descriptive attributes such as the search space's size and factorability (whether the problem can be decomposed into smaller subproblems, and the degree to which these subproblems are interrelated), the data's reliability and certainty, and the extent to which the applicable rules and data vary with time.

Under this categorization scheme, problems of increasing complexity appear in descending order. The current collection of expert system

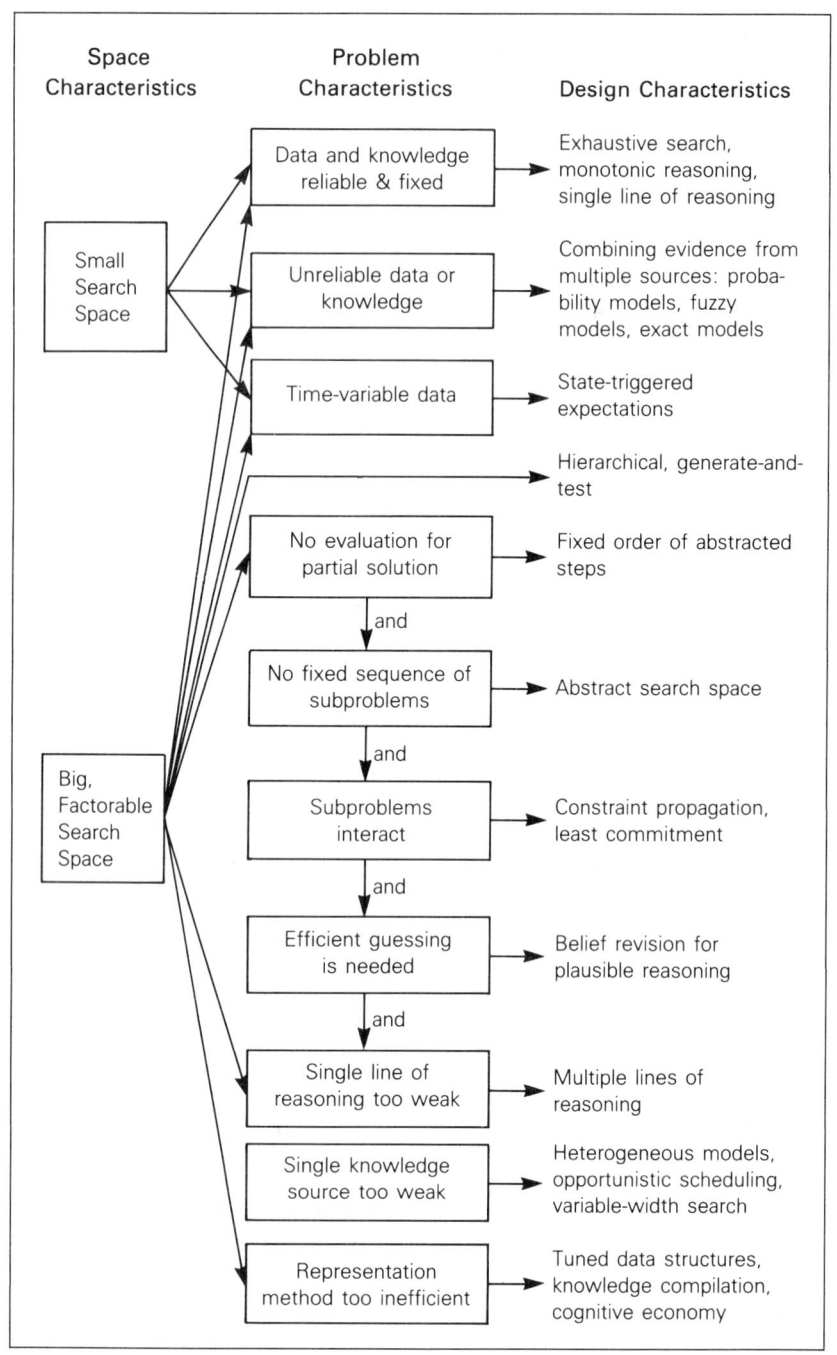

4-1. Architectural prescriptions for building knowledge systems. (From "The Knowledge-based Expert System: A Tutorial," by Frederick Hayes-Roth. In *Computer,* vol. 17, no. 9, © 1984 IEEE. Reprinted with permission.)

shells are typically powerful enough to handle only the first four or five levels of complexity; indeed, most can handle only the first two levels. A few powerful mixed-representation systems have, with the addition of special user-supplied procedures, been able to solve problems of greater complexity. Typically, attempting to solve a problem of complexity level six (or greater) involves more research than development. Furthermore, state-of-the-art expert systems are still rather brittle because the scope of their competence is narrow. When applied outside their domain of expertise, they tend to give silly answers because they do not know that they do not know. Today's expert systems are generally quite limited in size and scope; for example, rule-based systems tend to be limited to a few thousand rules, and most PC-based systems are restricted to under 500.

The following table illustrates some typical sizes for current expert systems.

CURRENT APPLICATION DOMAINS

Application	# rules	# facts
Communications		
satellite comm. link	70	523
Planning		
space shuttle hazard analysis	70	1010
Monitoring		
identify aircraft	14	110
battle management	90	600
Guiding		
navigation of autonomous vehicle	12	900
Electronic Maintenance (baseband distribution system)		
HP digital voltage source	91	1200
eight-channel console	365	1600
diagnosis of missile batteries	70	237
Design Checking		
DECKES—design checking and verification	66	200
DECGUIDE—design checking tutor	171	320
CCBACS—bucking analysis consultant	42	34
Surveillance		
photo interpretation aid	25	11000

AN EXAMPLE OF EXPERT SYSTEM DESIGN

To understand better the issues underlying the design of an expert system, consider the following example taken from the work of Morik and Rollinger (1985). The example deals with the design of a system that can provide advice to a user on the selection of a suitable apartment. Finding something suitable for the user requires knowledge about his or her requirements. The advisor's task is to compare the requirements of the user with the system's knowledge about the available objects.

This comparison is generally not straightforward. It is often not possible for the system to reach a clear decision about an apartment's suitability because no one apartment will likely meet all the requirements of the user in every respect. Furthermore, many of the facts about apartments are incomplete (for example, the statement "The apartment is in a quiet area" does not guarantee the apartment is quiet, since the neighbors could be noisy), uncertain (for example, "The apartment will presumably be free on January 1, 1984"), and/or vague ("The apartment has an area of about 100 square meters").

The system considers all the arguments for and against an apartment and selects those apartments that merit consideration. Since the information can be incomplete, uncertain, or vague, they are weighted using an approach based upon Shafer's mathematics of evidential reasoning. The system can make strong or weak recommendations, indicating which criteria are fulfilled and which are not, leaving the final decision to the user. The system may, however, also point out positive features of the apartment that were not explicitly required by the user but which the system has deduced will be attractive to the user. The system may also call the user's unfulfilled requirements into question. In this way the system enables the user to assess more fully the system selections; the system does not simply decide yes or no and make a positive or negative recommendation. The system therefore exhibits some "intelligence" and begins to behave like an expert real-estate agent.

The system must develop an internal representation of the user's value judgments—the criteria that the user sets and the conditions for fulfilling a criterion. To do this, the system requests the user to supply pertinent information about himself or herself. For this example, these user facts include: price range, number of persons who will occupy the apartment, the presence of children and their age(s), and any special conveniences requested by the user, such as a fireplace. These user-supplied facts are assigned a high evidence value, such as (1,0), indicating that certain evidence supports the fact and no evidence contradicts it.

The criteria for an apartment satisfying a user requirement are used to select a set of rules of application to be used in examining the list of available apartments. A rule of application consists of conditions necessary for the fulfillment of a criterion or a list of premises with the associated criterion as the conclusion. Since there may be one or more alternative rules of application, the appropriate rules are selected based upon the user characteristics. Consider for example the two rules:

1. An apartment is large if it has as many rooms of a standard size as it has occupants.
2. An apartment is large if it has more rooms of at least standard size than it has occupants.

For this example, rule 1 is applied to a user who has specified a low price range, whereas rule 2 is applied to a user who has specified a high price range.

Conditions that an apartment fulfills with a certain degree of certainty represent arguments for the suitability of the apartment. Conditions that are not fulfilled with an adequate degree of certainty represent arguments against the apartment. If more arguments speak for the fulfillment of a criterion than against, the apartment is more suitable to the user.

The conditions correspond to possible characteristics of apartments. Knowledge about apartments is represented in the form of SRL statements with evidence points, a frame-based language. In order to determine a suitable apartment for a particular individual, the metarule SUITABILITY is called. This rule attempts to verify the important and very important criteria for the user with the largest possible amount of evidence. If this procedure is not successful for any of the apartments, the important criteria are eliminated and the very important criteria are checked again with a weaker grade of evidence required for an apartment to pass.

If an apartment is found to be suitable with a high degree of positive evidence, a point close to (1,0), then an unqualified recommendation of the apartment is given.

If the criteria are fulfilled with a lesser degree of positive evidence, a point in the neighborhood of (0.6,0), a weaker, but still unqualified recommendation of the apartment is given. A qualified recommendation is given if there are explicitly unfulfilled criteria—if there are arguments that speak against the apartment that are outweighed by arguments that speak in favor of the apartment, a point close to (0.6,0.3).

If there is as much evidence for as against the apartment, a point around (0.5,0.5), then the user is in need of additional information. In this case, the system searches for "extras" offered by the apartment. These are features not determined by the criteria set by the user but which are generally considered to be desirable. An example might be a view of the river.

Finally, if none of the available apartments meets enough of the user's criteria to be recommended, even with qualifications, then the user is so informed and the system outputs the conditions and criteria set by the user, permitting the user to modify them.

An initial system was implemented in PROLOG and SRL. It consisted of twenty-seven rules with forty-three entry points and fifty-four evidence-evaluated SRL statements. It required 1-megabyte storage. Answering a decision question or an additional information question formulated as an SRL expression requires, on the average, 2.7 seconds CPU time. This processing time is progressively reduced, since, after being checked for consistency, all derived statements, including intermediate steps, are incorporated by the system into the knowledge base.

■ MACHINE PERCEPTION

Perception is a basic process of intelligence, tying the raw signals we receive through our senses (vision, hearing, and touch, for example) to the concepts and knowledge we have previously acquired and stored in our cognitive processor. Perception is thus at bottom a classification process.

Classification problems come in many varieties. What distinguishes a simple pattern detection problem (such as identifying the presence of a transmitted communications signal) from a pattern recognition problem (such as determining the class of wave a received radar signal belongs to) from perception (such as recognizing and reacting to a spoken word) or logical reasoning (such as when a physician diagnoses a patient's complaint) is the size of the population from which the objects must be classified and the degree of overlap and similarity between objects. In some cases, we do not even know in advance what classes the objects are to be sorted into (or even how many classes there are), and yet we must decide on an appropriate definition of the classes.

Traditionally the simpler classification problems have been handled by parallel statistical techniques such as analysis of variance, maximum likelihood estimation, Bayesian decision theory, and statistical clustering. This methodology involves observing one or more estimates of an object's attributes and applying a decision rule on the observed results to determine the most likely classification. Consider the simple one-dimensional example using Bayes' rule, discussed in chapter 2 in the section dealing with uncertainty. An observer notes evidence, Ej, such as the amplitude of a communications signal. He must select from which class, Hk, the observation comes when there are two possible, mutually exclusive classifications, $H0$ and $H1$, from which to select. Since the possible classifications, or hypotheses, are mutually exclusive, the probability of both classifications being true simultaneously is zero, or:

$$\Pr(H0, H1) = 0$$

Applying Bayes' rule, we find that:

$$\Pr(H1/Ej) = \frac{\Pr(Ej/H1) \times \Pr(H1)}{\sum_{a=1}^{2} \Pr(Ej, H0)}$$

where $\Pr(H1/Ej)$ is the probability of hypothesis $H1$, given that event Ej is observed, $\Pr(Ej/H1)$ is the probability of Ej given $H1$ is true, and $\Pr(Ej/H0)$ is the joint probability of Ej being observed and $H0$ being true. We can experimentally determine the conditional probability $\Pr(Ej/H1)$ and the a priori probability $\Pr(H1)$; then we can use Bayes' rule to select the hypothesis $H1$, given the observation Ej, that minimizes the likelihood of misclassification.

Bayes' rule can now be used as the basis of a decision rule according to which we choose $H1$ if Ej is greater than a given value and we choose $H0$ if Ej is less than a given value (see figure 4-2).

This same approach can of course be extended to allow selection from among an arbitrarily large number of hypotheses, using an arbitrarily large number of measurable attributes (figure 4-3). As the number of objects to be classified increases and the object classes grow more similar, there is a greater overlap among the decision regions and the probability of misclassification increases. A greater number of object attributes must be measured in order to distinguish less ambiguously among classes and to associate an object with its proper class. The main distinction of this technique is that all the measurements are obtained and manipulated in parallel.

The above approach is fundamentally limited by the fact that the percentage of correct classifications is determined by the relative size of the measurement errors with respect to the separation between the objects in multidimensional measurement space. Moreover, the technique works best as a relatively local classification approach, and it tends to break down when the observation space is smaller than the object space

144 ■ CURRENT APPLICATIONS

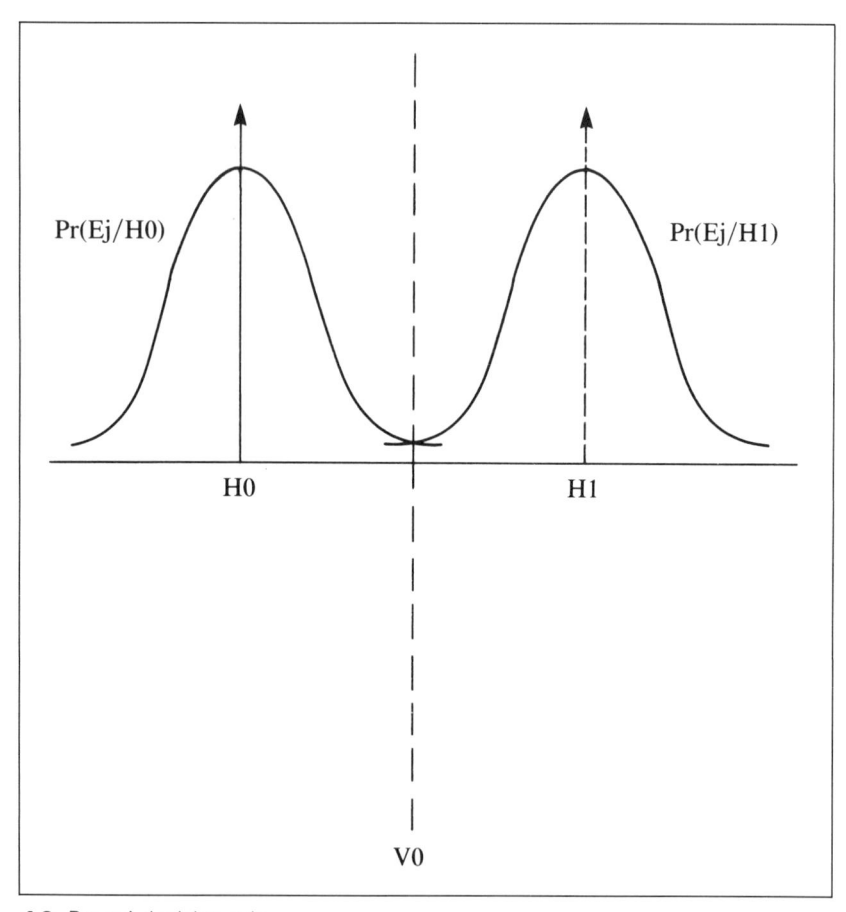

4-2. Bayes' decision rule.

or when many of the objects can be present simultaneously and can obstruct and interfere with each other.

Inspired by analogies to what was then known of the human neural system, researchers in the late 1950s and the 1960s extended the parallel discrimination approach into adaptive classification techniques that can "learn" how to discriminate between objects. One of the better-known adaptive classification designs was known as the *Perceptron* (Rosenblatt 1957, 1958, 1962). It was studied and analyzed to a great extent. Many researchers who wrote on the Perceptron are now active and well known in the A.I. field, including N.J. Nilsson, who published a mathematical theory for Perceptrons (1965), and M. Minsky and S. Papert, whose book *Perceptrons* (1969) showed that the Perceptron (in particular) and

Machine Perception ■ **145**

Fundamental limitations: perception

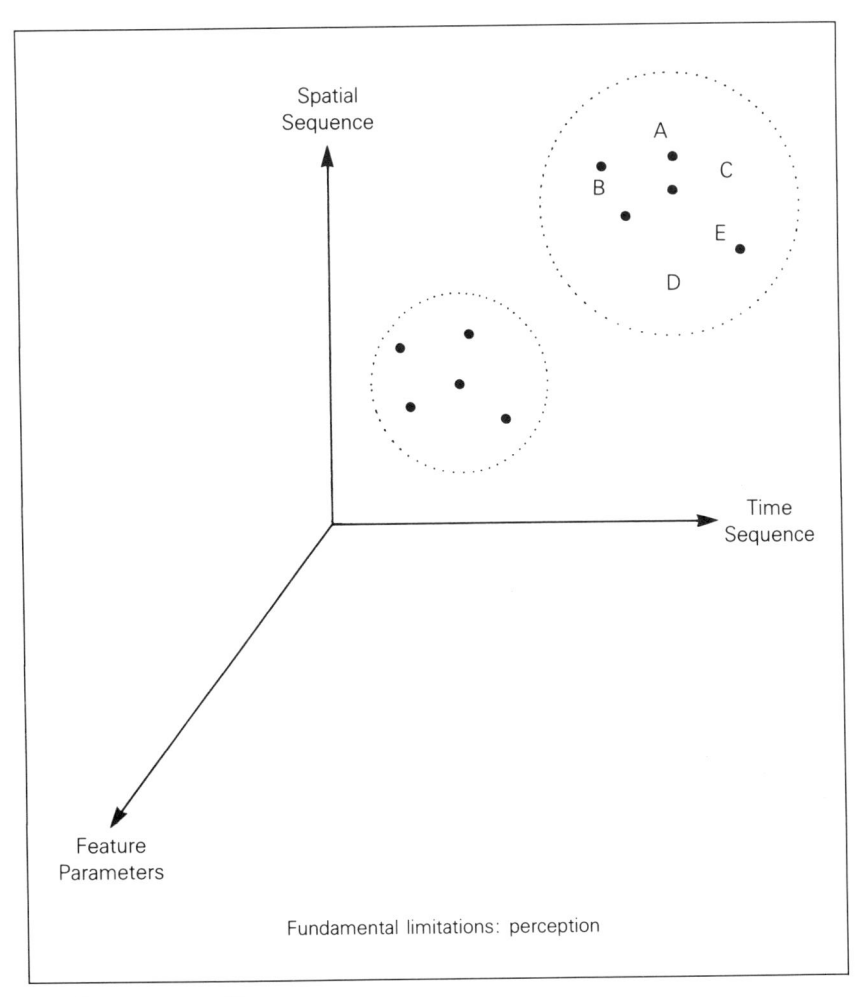

4-3. Pattern recognition.

its single parallel-decision algorithm (in general) have many important and fundamental limitations, although they remain perfectly adequate for a large class of important pattern-recognition problems.

The Perceptron was inadequate for many of the more complex, variable, and ill-structured situations typically presented to human perception. This led researchers toward a different methodology—one more characteristic of what we now can describe as the artificial intelligence paradigm. It is a decision process represented by a sequence of decision-classification rules (illustrated by the discrimination network shown in figure 4-4).

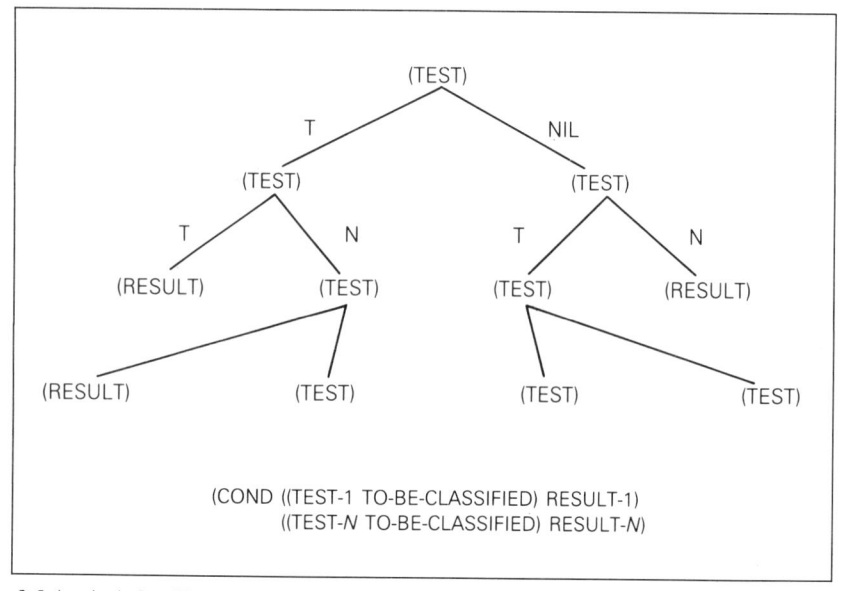

```
                        (TEST)
                T  /          \  NIL
                (TEST)          (TEST)
            T /      \ N      T /      \ N
      (RESULT)    (TEST)   (TEST)    (RESULT)
        /    \      |        |        /    \
  (RESULT)      (TEST)    (TEST)         (TEST)
```

(COND ((TEST-1 TO-BE-CLASSIFIED) RESULT-1)
      ((TEST-N TO-BE-CLASSIFIED) RESULT-N))

4-4. Logical classification discrimination nets. (From *Artificial Intelligence Programming*, by E. Charniak, C.K. Riesback, and D. McDermott. Published by Lawrence Erlbaum Associates, Inc., Hillsdale, NJ, 1980. Reprinted with permission.)

Discrimination networks are often quite complex and too large to define or examine completely. The actual decision test sequence, therefore, is determined dynamically; on the basis of the outcome of the first set of tests, a second set of tests to be taken and examined is determined, and so on down the line. This indeed is the underlying methodology of much current-day machine perception work.

■ NATURAL LANGUAGE PROCESSING

The goal of designing a computer system capable of conversing with people in their own natural language has been an aspiration of A.I. research almost since the inception of digital computers in the 1940s (Bott 1970). McCarthy was working on computer systems that could participate in question-answer dialogues as early as 1958. To be able to converse in human language is a basic prerequisite of any intelligent assistant. After all, language serves as our basic vehicle for thought and communication. By actively engaging people in conversation, the intelligent machine can infer their wants. It was for this reason that Turing first proposed his now-famous test of intelligence: if a person conversing by typewriter with an entity hidden behind a curtain is unable to determine whether the entity is a person or a machine, then the machine (if that is what the entity is) is intelligent (1963). Attempts were also made, in the early 1950s, to use the computer to design automatic language translators. In 1949, Warren Weaver proposed that computers might be useful for "the solution of worldwide translation problems" (Weaver 1955). These efforts are closely associated with the problem of replicating natural language.

These early attempts were highly optimistic and confident of early successes. After all, natural language processing seemed to involve the simplest of machine perceptions; the conversations were printed rather than spoken, and the computer responses could be canned, so the environment seemed easy to control; and the physical signal detection problem is virtually eliminated, so the probability of misclassifying the input signal is negligible. Consequently it was thought that all the computer needed was to store a few rules of grammar and the meaning of a lot of words, and it could perform as a natural language processing system.

The problem, however, proved much more difficult, and it has still not been completely solved. Natural language—any language people use to converse among themselves, such as English, French, or Russian—is much more ambiguous and ill-structured than the artificial languages that have been invented to deal with machines and specialized fields of study, such as FORTRAN, COBOL, LISP, algebra, and music; therefore, although it is much richer and more concise, natural language is far more difficult to understand and requires considerable cognitive activity and background context to be properly interpreted.

Ambiguity pervades natural language, helping to make it rich, expressive, and interesting. Ambiguity exists in word meanings, in adjective modifiers, in possible sentence structures, and even in overall sentence meaning after all of these other areas have been resolved (for example, is "List the flights on Tuesday" a request for a list of all flights that are scheduled to arrive or depart during a particular Tuesday, or is it a request to see, on Tuesday, a list of the airline's entire weekly flight schedule?).

Many amusing anecdotes describe one or another ill-fated attempt to design a computer system capable of understanding natural language. One such story concerns a Russian translation system (one way to test a translation system is to translate a phrase from the source language into the target language and then to retranslate the phrase into the source language, after which the new creation is compared to the original phrase). This incident concerns the phrase "The spirit is willing, but

148 ■ *CURRENT APPLICATIONS*

the flesh is weak,'' which, when translated from English into Russian and then from Russian back into English, produced the phrase "The wine is sour and the meat is rotten."

Some of the potential applications for natural language processing systems include:

- Question-answering systems, including: natural language interface systems, such as data base query systems, expert systems, simulation or analysis models, and operating-system help facilities; and computer-aided instruction front ends
- Machine translation
- General discourse systems
- Remote supervisory control and high-level robotics programming
- System-building tools, such as user-interactive automatic programming
- Text generation
- Text understanding, browsing, and summarizing

Of these potential applications, only a few have been achieved in the form of practical commercial applications; the rest remain research and development challenges.

The commercial offerings currently available are summarized in Appendix C. They consist mostly of natural language interfaces to data bases and machine translators.

Natural language interfaces to data bases were the first commercial offerings, with AIC's INTELLECT appearing in 1981. These front ends commonly must be customized by the user to match their data base management system's syntax and the specific natural language subset suitable for the problem domain. Today's state-of-the-art machine translators typically work in a semiautomated fashion, where the machine does its best job of translation and then a human translator is required to take the machine input as an intermediate result from which a finished product is produced. Alternately, the system interactively displays a tentative translation or translations, sometimes with particular words missing, to the human for resolution; then the system continues on with the translation.

SRI's TEAM presents a typical design for a natural language interface to data bases (see figure 4-5). TEAM's design consists of two main modules: DIAMOND (the user interface), and SODA (the interface to the system data bases). The system operates in two primary modes: build mode, and query or use mode. In build mode, the user customizes the data base and the natural language subset by inputting the task-

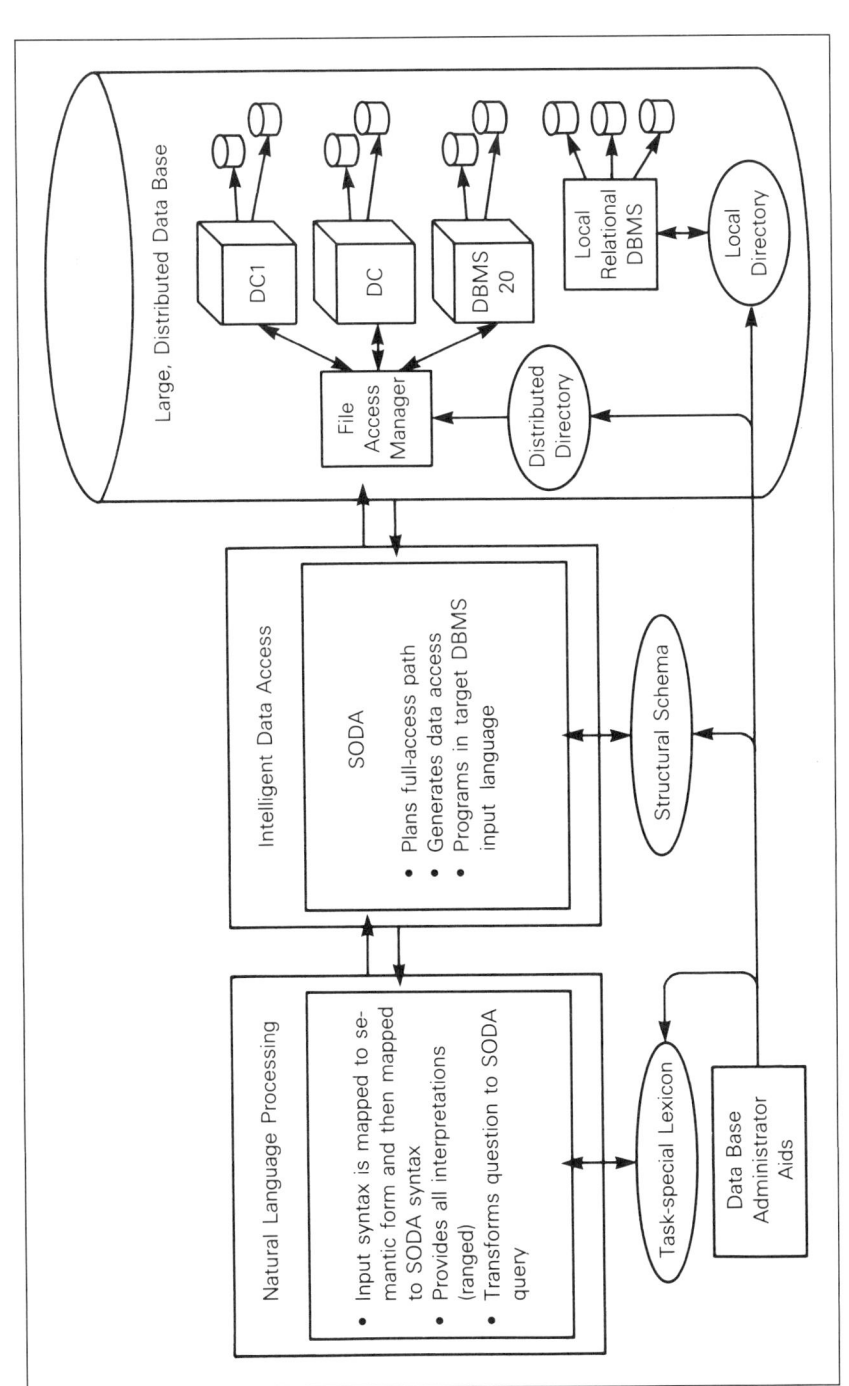

4-5. Functional elements of TEAM.

specific lexicon (the problem domain–specific vocabulary and grammar) and the current structural schema for the system data bases. TEAM already has a built-in minimal subset consisting of some of the more commonly used English words, as well as knowledge of several common data base query languages. The build input can either be loaded in batch fashion or updated interactively by the user.

When being interactively updated, the system asks the user questions about the natural language words being used, such as sentences in which they are used, the part of speech they are, and so on. The system uses these answers to construct a natural language interpreter that performs efficiently.

In query or use mode, the user types in a natural language query (as illustrated in figure 4-6), and the system module, DIAMOND, interprets the query and translates it into a standard internal format, which it then passes to the SODA module. The SODA module locates the data base or bases that contain the requested information, determines what data base queries and data manipulations are required, and formulates the necessary statements. When SODA obtains the retrieved data in properly manipulated form, it returns it to DIAMOND, which presents it to the user. Many natural language interfaces generate a natural language response to the user.

The natural language interface is only one of a number of competitive means of querying and interacting with a computer system. Menus and pointers, function keys, artificial command languages, and data request templates are but some of the alternatives. Many of these alternative methods are likely to be preferred by the frequent user because they generally require fewer keystrokes, run faster and more efficiently, and

---

What ships are in British ports?
What U.S. ships are within 500 miles of Wilmington?
What U.S. ships faster that the *Gridley* are in Norfolk?
What is the fastest ship in the Mediterranean Sea?
How close is that ship to Naples?
What is its home port?
Print the American cruisers' current positions and states of readiness
How is the *Los Angeles* powered?

4-6. Example queries handled by TEAM.

are less likely to misinterpret the user's request. On the other hand, they generally require more user training and assume greater familiarity of the user with the data base's content and structure. The design of these alternative technologies involves a trade-off between training time and flexibility. A system designed for a few fixed queries and reports will require relatively little user training; but as system flexibility increases, allowing the user more latitude in making data requests, the system input becomes more complex and more user training will be required.

Natural language front ends typically require a lot of computer memory and processing time—a significant percent of a large mainframe's memory, and several seconds to minutes in response time. And because natural language is ambiguous, a natural language interface must often resolve choices among multiple interpretations by coming back to the user with questions to narrow down the possibilities, by asking for confirmation or correction of a restated version of the query, or by presenting all interpretations (possibly with rankings) and/or offering more information than was requested in order to cover most of the possible interpretations of the user's request. Clearly, the smaller the computer is, the less capable the natural language processing system will be. PC-based natural language processing systems are considerably slower than larger mainframe-based ones, and they are much more limited as to the vocabulary they can handle and the ambiguities and language complexities they can successfully resolve.

Thus the natural language front end is probably best for the relatively casual user who has little or no training on the system but who makes diverse, ad hoc demands on the system data. Probably the best thing to do for such a user is to design a front end that integrates natural language interfacing with one or more of the alternative technologies, allowing the user to combine efficiency, power, and user-friendliness in optimum proportions. Such integrated front-end designs are becoming more commonplace.

One pitfall in using natural language interfaces is failure to match user expectations. Users conversing with a system in their own natural language may begin to believe that the system possesses a reasonably high level of intelligence only to be disappointed in the system when it can only retrieve information that is explicitly stored in the form requested. For example, if the user asks the system for John's mother's name, but the system only stores such data under the classification *women* and the subclassification *sons*, the user will not obtain the information sought because the system will not be able to determine

152 ■ *CURRENT APPLICATIONS*

the relationship between boys and their mothers from a relationship between women and their sons.

Consider the TEAM query "Where is the fastest U.S. carrier within 500 miles of Naples?" (illustrated in figure 4-7). Here we have a situation where more is required of the system than simply to access the data

---

Question:
Where is the fastest U.S. carrier within 500 miles of Naples?

Answer:
(Date 17Jan79, 1200 Position 4000N00600E Ship *CONSTELLATION*)
(Date 17Jan79, 1200 Position 3700N01700E Ship *KITTY HAWK*)

Question:
What is the steaming time for the ship *Kennedy* from Naples to Norfolk?

Answer:
The shortest great circle route From (NOSPD 16.0 #HRS 272 MXSPD 36.0 #HRS 124 Position 4445W01430E) To (Position 3700N07600W) Is 4355.0 Nautical Miles.

From (Lat/Long)	To (Lat/Long)	Distance (nm)	Comment
44.45N/14.3E	36N/9W	1149	Strait of Gibraltar
38N/8W	37N/76W	3206	

This answer states that the *Kennedy* will take 272 hours at a speed of 16 knots, and 124 hours at a speed of 36 knots. Moreover, she must go through the Strait of Gibraltar.

Question:
Who commands the U.S. carriers with an operational air search radar?

Answer:
Ship	**Rank/Name**
Constellation	Capt/Ellison J
Kennedy JF	Capt/Moffett P
America	Capt/Halsey W
Saratoga	Capt/Brown A
Independence	Capt/Jackson S

4-7. Sample TEAM dialogue.

base for a particular item of stored information. The system must search among the collection of U.S. carriers, considering both their current location and speed, find the location of Naples, and calculate which carriers can get to Naples the fastest. This program is not trivial: the equivalent FORTRAN code and data base queries necessary to perform this task are illustrated in figure 4-8 for the relational data base Datacomputer and for the more traditional data base DBMS-20.

A natural language system that can handle this sort of query on the fly is effectively providing a kind of automated programming capability, albeit a severely restricted one. In its absence, fulfilling this one-time request would involve having programmers interview the user, write the program, and then return a day (or perhaps a week) later with the answer, perhaps too late to help the commander come to a decision regarding ship allocations. A natural language system that can take the user's request and automatically provide an answer ten seconds or even fifteen minutes later is certainly cost-effective and worthwhile.

The A.I. approach to natural language processing is to represent and use knowledge of the subject matter to help resolve ambiguities in interpretation and understanding. This is typified by Winograd's seminal work, SHRDLU, which could converse about toy blocks on a table (Winograd 1972).

Natural language processing can be hierarchically subdivided as shown in figure 4-9. The typewritten characters are combined to form morphemic words or word phrases—the smallest unit that has meaning (for example, *cat, will be, home*). These words can then be parsed; that is, the sentence is broken down into its constituent grammatical parts (noun, verb, adverb, and so on).

Parsing is the process of going from words to syntactic structures. These syntactic structures are commonly represented by means of sentence diagrams—for example, (it (is getting) cold (in here))—where the syntactics are encoded as a list structure, or parse tree, such as that shown in figure 4-10.

Ambiguities in word meanings, pronoun substitutions, and modifiers can often be resolved or reduced as an outcome of this parsing activity. Once parsed, the sentence's meaning can be determined and transformed into an internal system representation, from which, in turn, the system can determine the pragmatic—the desired function, use, or action—implied by the sentence. For a data base query front end, the pragmatic is implicitly obvious, since the retrieval and presentation of information is always requested. For other, more complex applications, the pragmatic is not necessarily so obvious.

154 ■ *CURRENT APPLICATIONS*

DATACOMPUTER

Question:
Where is the fastest U.S. carrier within 500 miles of Naples?

Query:
For NSTDPORT1 , XX1 in port with (XX1.DEP EQ 'Naples')Strings1 = XX1.PTP ;

Begin Declare Y1 String (,100) ,D=')'
    Declare Y2 String (,100) ,D=') Y2 = '00.0'
    For Y3 Integer Y3 = 0.
    For XX1 in ship with (XX1.TYPE2 EQ 'V')
                  And (XX1.TYPE1 EQ 'C')
                  And (XX1.NAT EQ 'US')
    For XX2 in trackhist with (
GCDIST(XX2.PTPX , XX2.PTPNS , XX2.PTPY , XX2.PTPEW , 4446 , 'N' , 1430 , 'E') LE 500) And (XX2.VICVCM EQ XX1.UIICVCN)
  Begin Y1 = XX1.MC5F
        Of Y1 LE '99.9'
        And Y2 LT Y1
      Then begin Y2 = Y1
            Y2 = 1

                    End

  End if Y3 EQ 1
      Then for XX3 in ship with (XX3.TYPE2 EQ 'V')
                    And (XX3.TYPE1 EQ 'C')
                    And (XX3.NAT EQ 'US')
                    And (XX3.MCSF EQ Y2)
    For NSTDPORT1 , XX4 in trackhist with (
GCDIST(XX4.PTPX , XX4.PTPNS , XX4.PTPY , XX4.PTPEW , 4446 , 'N' , 1430 , 'E') LE 500) And (XX4.ICVCM EQ XX3.UIICVCN)
    Begin String1 = XX4.PTD
    Begin String2 = XX4.PTP
    Begin String3 = XXE.NAM

                    End
End:

4-8 (a). Sample Datacomputer dialogue.

DBMS-20

Question:

Where is the fastest U.S. carrier within 500 miles of Naples?

Query:
  Open Green $
  Set Port-Dep to 'Naples' $
  Find Port Record $
10 If Error Status = 326 Goto 11 $
  Print Port-PTP $
12 Find Duplicate Port Record $
  Goto 10 $
11 = $
  Goto XT $
  "End"

  Open Green $
  Compute XSTRX11 = '00.0' $
  Compute XY10 = 0 $
  Find First Ship Record of Greenarea Area $
13 If Error-Status = 397 Goto 14 $
  Compute Xand16 = 0 $
  If Ship-Type2 NE 'V' Goto 17 $
  If Ship-Type1 NE 'C' Goto 17 $
  If Ship-Nat NE 'US' Goto 17 $
  Compute Xand16 = 1 $
17 If Xand16 = 0 Goto 15 $
  Compute XSTR22 = Ship-MCSF $
  PUSHLP $
  Find First Trackhist Record of Shipdata Set $
19 If Error-Status <> 0 Goto 18 $
  Compute XAND21 = 0 $
  Compute XNUM24 = Trackhist-PTPX $
  Compute XSTR25 = Trackhist-PTPNS $
  Compute XNUM26 = Trackhist-PTPY $
  Compute XSTR27 = Trackhist-PTPEW $
  Compute XNUM28 = 4446 $
  Compute XSTR29 = 'N' $
  Compute XNUM30 = 1430 $
  Compute XSTR31 = 'E' $

4-8 (b). Sample DBMS dialogue.

156 ■ *CURRENT APPLICATIONS*

```
    GEDIST XNUM24 XSTR25 XNUM26 XSTR27 XNUM28 XSTR29
    XNUM30 XSTR31 XARG23 $
    If XARG23 GT 500 Goto 22 $
    Compute Xand21 = 1 $
 33 If Xand21 = 0 Goto 20 $
    Compute XSTRZ12 = XSTR32 $
    If XSTRZ12 GT '99.9' OR XSTRX11, XSTRZ12 Goto 20 $
 20 Find Next Trackhist Record of Shipdata Set $
    Goto 19 $
 18 = $
    POPLP $
 15 Find Next Ship Record of Greenarea Area $
    Goto 13 $
 14 = $
    If XY10 = 0 Goto XT $
    First Find Ship Record of Greenarea Area $
 33 If Error-Status = 307 Goto 34 $
    Compute Xand36 = $
    If Ship-Type2 NE 'V' Goto 37 $
    If Ship-Type1 NE 'C' Goto 37 $
    If Ship-NAT NE 'US' Goto 37 $
    If Ship-MCSF NE XSTR32 Goto 37 $
    Compute Xand36 = 1 $
 37 If Xand36 = 0 Goto 35 $
    Compute XSTR52 = Ship Nam $
    PUSHLP $
    Find First Trackhist Record of Shipdata Set $
 39 If Error-Status <> = Goto 38 $
    Compute XAND41 = 0 $
    Compute XNUM44 = Trackhist-PTPX $
    Compute XSTR45 = Trackhist-PTPNS $
    Compute XNUM46 = Trackhist-PTPY $
    Compute XSTR47 = Trackhist-PTPEW $
    Compute XNUM48 = 4446 $
    Compute XSTR49 = 'N' $
    Compute XNUM50 = 1430 $
    Compute XSTR51 = 'E' $
    GCDIST XNUM44 XSTR45 XNUM46 XSTR47 XNUM48 XSTR49
```

4-8 (b), *continued.*

```
    XNUM50
    XSTR51 XARG43 $
    If XARG43 GT 500 Goto 48 $
    Compute Xand41 = 1 $
 42 If Xand41 = 0 Goto 40 $
    Print XSTR52 $
 40 Find Next Trackhist Record of Shipdata Set $
    Goto 39 $
 33 = $
    POPLP $
 35 Find Next Ship Record of Greenarea Area $
    Goto 33 $
 34 = $
    Goto XT $
    " "End" "
```

4-8 (b), *continued.*

Ultimately, we would wish our system to be able to determine from interactive conversation with us, our real goals or wants, independent of the actual requests being made, and to satisfy these wants. Consider the example of a user querying the natural language front end of a word processor help module. The user asks for information about a print command, but from the nature of his questions and the ensuing dialogue, the system deduces that what the user really wants to do is to format his word processor file in a particular way. Once this goal is discovered, the system can volunteer to the user its best guess as to the information the user actually wants, even though he has failed to articulate the proper words to request this information.

Most parsing approaches are based on the theories of formal languages and grammar introduced by Noam Chomsky (1956). Chomsky delineated four types of grammars, which he numbered 0 through 3. A grammar is defined in terms of its terminal and nonterminal symbols, a start symbol, and a set of legitimate transformations or productions. The four grammars identified by Chomsky are summarized below.

Type 0 has no restrictions.

Type 1, also called a context-sensitive grammar, has only one restriction: after a transformation, the resultant string must contain at least as many

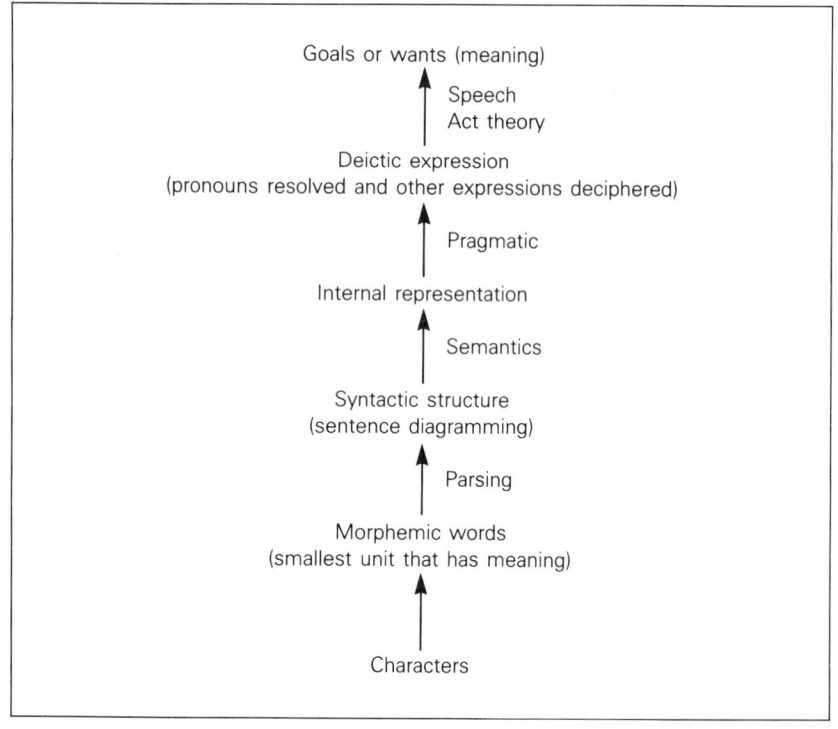

```
Goals or wants (meaning)
            ↑
          Speech
         Act theory
    Deictic expression
(pronouns resolved and other expressions deciphered)
            ↑
         Pragmatic
            |
   Internal representation
            ↑
         Semantics
            |
     Syntactic structure
     (sentence diagramming)
            ↑
          Parsing
            |
       Morphemic words
  (smallest unit that has meaning)
            ↑
         Characters
```

4-9. Hierarchy of abstraction.

symbols as the original string. An equivalent way of stating this restriction is that an input string must be rewritten as a new string within the context of the symbol strings immediately preceding and following the string to be transformed.

Type 2, also known as a context-free grammar, is characterized by the fact that a string to be transformed must have only a single nonterminal symbol. Another important property is that every derivation can be represented as a tree.

Type 3, also known as a regular grammar, can only transform a single variable to a single terminal symbol or to a single terminal symbol followed by another single variable.

For regular and context-free grammars, practical parsing algorithms that are free of ambiguity can be used. Most programming languages are context-free grammars. The simplest formal languages (types 2 and 3) are generally inadequate for describing the complexities of human languages. Context-sensitive grammars, like context-free grammars, can use derivation trees and both types are often called phrase-structure

```
                         S
              ┌──────────┼──────────┐
             NP         VERB        NP
            ╱  ╲         │         ╱  ╲
          DET  NOUN     saw      DET  NOUN
           │    │                 │    │
          the  boy                a   box
```

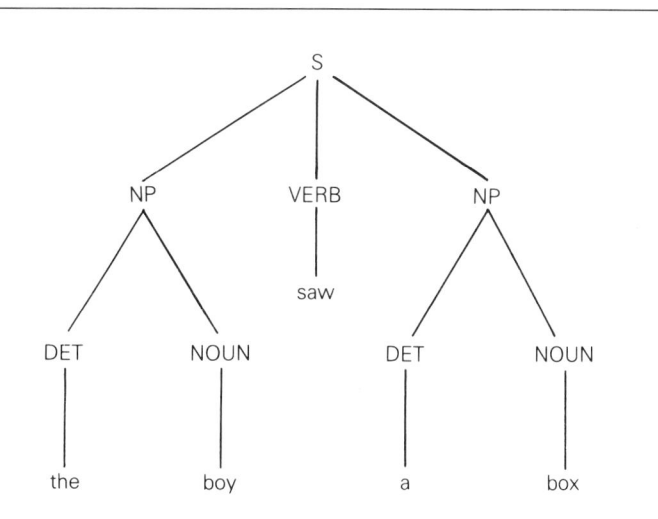

Phrase marker for "The boy saw a box."

- Augmented transition net—augments basic net with ability to use registers.
- Net can store intermediate results in registers.
- Nodes are written in registers.
- Registers are represented as properties of the corresponding node.

4-10. Augmented transition network (ATN). (From *Artificial Intelligence Programming,* by E. Charniak, C.K. Riesback, and D. McDermott. Published by Lawrence Erlbaum Associates, Inc., Hillsdale, NJ, 1980. Reprinted with permission.)

grammars. Many of the parsing algorithms used for context-free grammars can be augmented or extended to handle context-sensitive grammars.

One such parsing technique, the augmented transition network (ATN), is a method for analyzing natural language by building syntactic derivation tree structures, based on the use of finite state-transition networks and subnetworks. Typically, the subset of natural language to be analyzed can be expressed through a collection of interrelated state-transition networks, where the nodes represent states and the arcs represent tests. Subnetworks are used to represent node groupings that are responsible for parsing one type of construction.

A simplified augmented transition network is shown in figure 4-11. It represents one of several possible ways a sentence might be con-

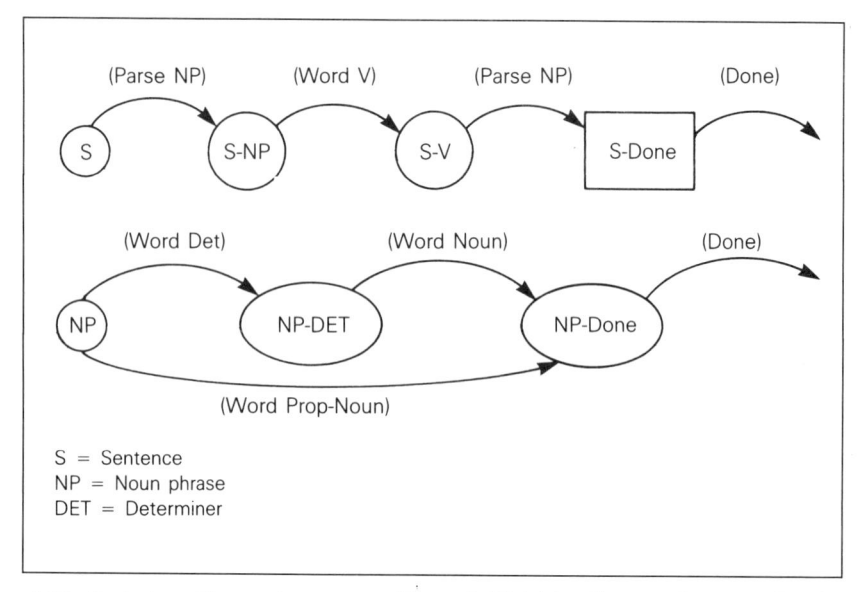

```
                (Parse NP)       (Word V)        (Parse NP)         (Done)
         ( S ) ─────────▶ ( S-NP ) ──────▶ ( S-V ) ──────▶ [ S-Done ] ──────▶

                (Word Det)              (Word Noun)           (Done)
         ( NP ) ─────────▶ ( NP-DET ) ──────▶ ( NP-Done ) ──────▶
              └──────────────(Word Prop-Noun)─────────▶

         S   = Sentence
         NP  = Noun phrase
         DET = Determiner
```

4-11. Basic transition net grammar. (From *Artificial Intelligence Programming*, by E. Charniak, C.K. Riesback, and D. McDermott. Published by Lawrence Erlbaum Associates, Inc., Hillsdale, NJ, 1980. Reprinted with permission.)

structed—namely, as a noun phrase followed by a verb followed by a noun phrase (a noun phrase is defined as either a determiner followed by a noun or a proper noun). The sentence derivation tree for the sentence "The boy saw a box" (see figure 4-10), is a result of testing each word, in turn, with the augmented transition network shown. In this case, the augmented network results in a correct parsing because a path through the network is found that passes all the tests. If the sentence fails all the networks, other networks must be tried.

The sentence above is simple enough that the parsing can probably be interpreted unambiguously as correct. More complex sentences might have more than one potentially correct parsing associated with them. In these more complex cases, the problem reduces to a search through the space for possible parsings, where the transition networks nodes represent permissible successor states and the links represent tests for evaluating the acceptability of the state.

An example of a technique for transforming the meaning of a natural language statement into some consistent internal representation is the one developed by R.C. Schank and his colleagues at Yale (Schank 1972). The technique is called *conceptual dependency* and involves associating a collection of semantic primitives with fixed templates into which the semantic meanings are encoded. Implicit in this approach is a belief that all human experience can be expressed through a nested hierarchy of a finite number of primitives representing all actions, states, and entities. To date, Schank has introduced between twenty and fifty of these primitives; a few are shown below, to illustrate the approach:

BASIC ACTIONS
    PTRANS: Physical transfer, change of location
    MTRANS: Mental transfer, transfer of information
    INGEST: Ingest object, eating of food or drink

BASIC STATES
    HAS: Character owns something
    AT: Indicates where character is
    GOAL: Goal of character
    KNOW: Character knows something
    HOME-OF: Where character lives

Examples of how sentences are encoded into internal representations using templates based upon these primitives are shown below:

1. Sentence: John ate an apple.
   Internal representation: (INGEST JOHN APPLE)
2. Sentence: John went from Boston to New York.
   Internal representation: (PTRANS JOHN JOHN NEW-YORK BOSTON)
3. Sentence: John told Mary that Bill ate an apple.
   Internal representation: (MTRANS JOHN MARY (INGEST BILL APPLE))
4. Sentence: John is next to Mary.
   Internal representation: (AT JOHN MARY)
5. Sentence: John knows that Bill has an apple.
   Internal representation: (KNOW JOHN (HAS BILL APPLE))
6. Sentence: John wants to have an apple.
   Internal representation: (GOAL JOHN (HAS JOHN APPLE))

Schank does not go through a formal parsing, or syntactic analysis; rather, he attempts to encode the natural language statements directly into their internal semantic representations, parsing only when necessary— for example, in order to resolve ambiguities in pronoun substitutions. He also uses higher-level structures, such as scripts, to help resolve ambiguities in the determination of the internal semantic representations.

The scripts define stereotypical situations representative of the subject being read about. The proper template is chosen and its parameters are filled through a combination of finding key words in the sentence and attempting to fill empty slots in the script. Previous sentences would already contain filled slots that could be used to interpret and anticipate the sentences that follow. If enough inconsistencies are found in the course of trying to match empty slots in the script with new templates, a story monitor is called in to resolve the conflict and perhaps to summon and try a different script.

Some conflict situations trigger demons—procedures embedded in the script and activated by the conflict situation that suggest alternative courses of action, such as modifying the value of a slot that was filled earlier or trying another script. Switching scripts or changing slot values involves backtracking to undo tentative goals and story fragments that had been assumed until the conflict/story failure was detected.

Spanning the entire process are story goals, plans, and themes. Plans represent the means by which goals are accomplished. A plan must discern the goals of the actor and conceive actions to accomplish these goals. This involves determining the actor's main goal, establishing subgoals that lead to the main goal, and matching the actor's actions with these plan boxes. Routinized plans become scripts, with standardized players, props, and events. Goals and themes must remain consistent throughout the process; otherwise, some backtracking is probably in order.

Many other techniques have been developed to assist in natural language processing. They include:

- *Simple phrase structure grammars.* These are useful only for context-sensitive grammars that span a very limited domain.
- *Case grammars.* These involve semantically relevant syntactic relationships, where different verbs are assumed to be associated with certain fundamental templates that identify what is called the deep structure (as opposed to the surface structure) of the sentence (Fillmore 1971). Although a sentence can have many different semantically equivalent surface structures, it can have only one deep structure.
- *Semantic grammars.* These involve modification of the phrase-structure grammar technique to allow use of the semantic categories of the particular problem domain. An example is LIFER (Hendrix 1977).
- *Systemic grammars.* These are grammars whose linguistic structure is related to the pragmatics (the function or use) of the language (Halliday 1961).

Despite the large number of successful natural language processing systems commercially available, many important research issues remain unresolved. One is the problem of how to scale up the current generation of systems to handle broader, more diverse problem domains; this would mean, for example, not just being able to answer queries concerning Company ABC's data base of accounts receivable and the sales performance of their XYZ widget. As more natural language processing applications are implemented, perhaps this scaling-up can be accomplished through the design of a big switch that can determine which modules to call up and when. If we keep building up our natural language processing memory of words, concepts, scripts, and so on, other issues arise: how do we clean up the memory to prevent clutter and to keep response time acceptable? Many other issues must also be detailed with respect to this approach, and much debate continues as to the best approach or mix of approaches: whether syntax processing is required as a necessary step before semantic processing; whether these two steps can be integrated and done in parallel; whether both need to be done or only one or the other is necessary.

No natural language processor exists that can perfectly interpret all possible statements. In fact, few human beings can read a natural language without ever making a mistake of interpretation, even if the context is known. We can classify current natural language processing systems by the degree to which they can successfully overcome the following sorts of difficulties:

- Multiple word senses
- Modified attachment
- Noun-noun modification (for example, fruit fly: is it a kind of fly or a kind of fruit?)
- Pronouns
- Ellipsis and substitution (such as for incomplete sentences; for example: What is the fastest carrier to Naples? And to New York?)
- Anaphoric reference (where a sentence or word makes a reference that can be interpreted only in terms of earlier sentences, phrases, or words)
- Ambiguous noun groups
- Incorrect usage/grammar

The sudden, recent surge of interest in artificial intelligence, and in the fifth-generation model in particular, has led to renewed interest in accelerating the level of research in natural language processing. The amount of research money devoted to natural language processing has increased significantly, and the establishment of a center of natural language processing and computational linguistics at Stanford represents another major commitment.

■ SPEECH UNDERSTANDING

Speech understanding is much more difficult than natural language understanding. It has all of the difficulties of the latter, and in addition it must cope with speech recognition at the acoustic level. Many words and word groups sound the same. Words are often spoken in a run-on manner that makes it difficult to recognize where one word ends and another begins. Great variations in pronunciation exist among people: regional accents can involve extreme differences in pronunciation; women generally have higher pitched voices than men; some people slur their words or drop endings; stress and intonation patterns vary; even the same person's speech may vary from day to day as a result of a cold, stress, or something else.

A speech-understanding system must be able to separate linguistically significant variations in speech signals from insignificant variations such as variations in word pronunciation. Background noise can contribute to aural confusion and to the likelihood of misclassification of speech sounds, as well.

The two main errors made by speech recognizers are substitution and rejection; less common errors include insertion. These difficulties combine to create considerable ambiguity even at the lowest level of a speech-understanding problem. Nevertheless, speech remains the most natural form of human communications, and some early studies have shown that speech can be the most efficient form of communications for handling many problems. One experiment, for example, showed that speech was the single most effective medium to use in explaining to someone how to assemble a bicycle.

Speech has important advantages as an input medium. Casual users with relatively little training could access a computer that was capable of receiving speech input. Speech is our fastest mode of communication (about twice as fast as the average typist). And a speech input allows users free use of their hands for pointing, manipulating a display, flying an aircraft, controlling a device, or making a repair. Among the many speech recognition and understanding applications are:

- Manufacturing processes and control: quality-control data entry into computers; shipping and receiving; record entry; package sorting; maintenance and repair orders; part availability; work needed or underway
- Office automation: executive work stations; word processing; data entry; control functions
- Technical data gathering: cartography inputs for working with maps

or blueprints; medical applications (dental records, pathology, services for the handicapped, operating room logging, command/control of medical instrumentation)
- Security applications: building access; computer file access; communications security; speaker verification/identification
- Consumer products applications: control functions; status queries
- Equipment subsystem operation: aircraft; spacecraft; military equipment

The current state-of-the-art systems possess capabilities that are a far cry from true speech understanding. They are essentially pattern recognizers that can detect prestored speech patterns. Most of these systems have the following characteristics:

- **Speaker dependence.** Each speaker must go through a training session in which he or she repeats the words the system must recognize.
- **Discrete speech.** The word phrases to be recognized must be separated by a few seconds' pause
- **Limited vocabularies.** Typically a few hundred words/word phrases are the maximum allowable, although some systems can handle several sets of vocabularies, resulting in a total vocabulary of about 1,000 words
- **Expensiveness.** Prices average a few thousand dollars

Figure 4-12 illustrates some currently available commercial speech recognizers. The first two systems, priced at $65,000 each, are capable of recognizing connected speech with small vocabularies with reasonable success rates. One major problem is that no standards yet exist for testing and evaluating these systems, so it is difficult to compare them with respect to relative price performance.

The approach to speech understanding parallels the approach to natural language understanding in its hierarchical decomposition of the processing steps. The processing steps in speech understanding are:

- Acoustic phonetics—characteristics of speech sound
- Lexicon—sound patterns of words
- Syntax—grammatical structure of language
- Semantics—meaning of words and sentences
- Pragmatics—context of the conversation

The reason speech understanding is so much harder than natural language understanding is that error and ambiguity permeate the speech

Manufacturer	Model*	Nominal Price in 1981	Nominal Price for Comparable 1983 Model	% Substitutions
Verbex	1800	$65K	$19.6K	0.2
Nippon Electric	DP-100	$65K	$27K	1.2
Threshold Technology	T-500	$12K	$5K	1.4
Interstate Electronics	VRM	$2.4K	$2.4K	2.9
Heuristics	7000	$3.3K	NA	5.9
Centigram	MIKE 4725	$3.5K	NA	7.1
Scott Instruments	VET/1 (home computer peripheral)	$.5K	$.9K	12.6
Kurzweil Applied Intelligence**	KVS 3000 (speech recognition)	$3K		
Sindex Speech Tech, Ltd.***	Part of Alvey, Britain's 5th-generation program			

*First two systems are capable of connected speech. Verbex is the only system having speaker-independent capability.

**1,000-word recognition under 250 msec/word. Forerunner to Kurzweil Voicewriter, a 10,000-word speech-to-text voice-activated typewriter (VAT). Being readied for Beta text, early 1986.

***Under research is a machine able to listen and talk in Chinese. Reportedly whatever one says in Chinese will appear on screen in Chinese characters.
After Doddington and Schalk (1981).

4-12. Texas Instruments's test of speech recognizers on individual words. (From "An Overview of Artificial Intelligence and Robots" [NASA Technical Memo 85838], by William Gevarter. Reprinted with permission.)

understanding problem at all levels; the speech sound exhibits variability in both pronunciation (phonology) and stress and intonation patterns (prosodics).

In the early 1970s, the Department of Defense Advanced Research

Projects Agency (DARPA) funded a five-year program in speech-understanding research (SUR). The systems to be designed and built were to accept normally spoken sentences (connected speech) in a constrained domain with a 1,000-word vocabulary and were to respond reasonably quickly with less than 10 percent error. The programs funded included HWIM (Hear What I Mean) built by BBN, HARPY and HEARSAY built by Carnegie-Mellon, and a system developed jointly by SRI and Systems Development Corp (SDC). The HEARSAY and HARPY systems applications were concerned with retrieval of A.I. computer literature documents; HWIM was concerned with answering questions from a data base.

The HEARSAY architecture is pictured in figures 4-13 and 4-14. Its architecture is particularly interesting in view of current interest in fifth-generation parallel processing architectures. The planners envisioned multiple PDP 11s connected to each other and to a common memory through a switch. Unfortunately, the 16-bit PDP 11s proved to be too small, and the system was actually run on a DEC 20 (and later was transported to a VAX).

Although implemented on a single processor, the distributed processing principles remain intact. The central idea behind the HEARSAY architecture is the *blackboard,* which serves as a communications vehicle between a collection of cooperating expert systems, each one being expert in some aspect of the problem. Each expert system posts hypotheses on the blackboard, so that it represents an evolving three-dimensional picture shared by the various cooperating systems of the current state of knowledge about the problem. The horizontal axis of the representation tracks time. The vertical axis records the hypotheses, structured along hierarchical lines: the likely phonemes uttered at each time interval are represented first, then the words or word phrases made up of these phonemes, then the likely sentence fragments, and finally the likely requests. The third dimension is used for the representation of probabilities associated with each of the candidate phonemes, words, and sentences.

The expert systems exchange messages by placing them on the blackboard; a blackboard monitor continuously oversees the various expert systems—scheduling the work flows and queues, resolving conflicts between the experts, and maintaining a focused effort toward interpreting the speech input and determining the appropriate response. The scheduling is opportunistic, with the highest-ranking hypotheses being expanded first. The blackboard monitor also evaluates how to combine estimates

168 ■ CURRENT APPLICATIONS

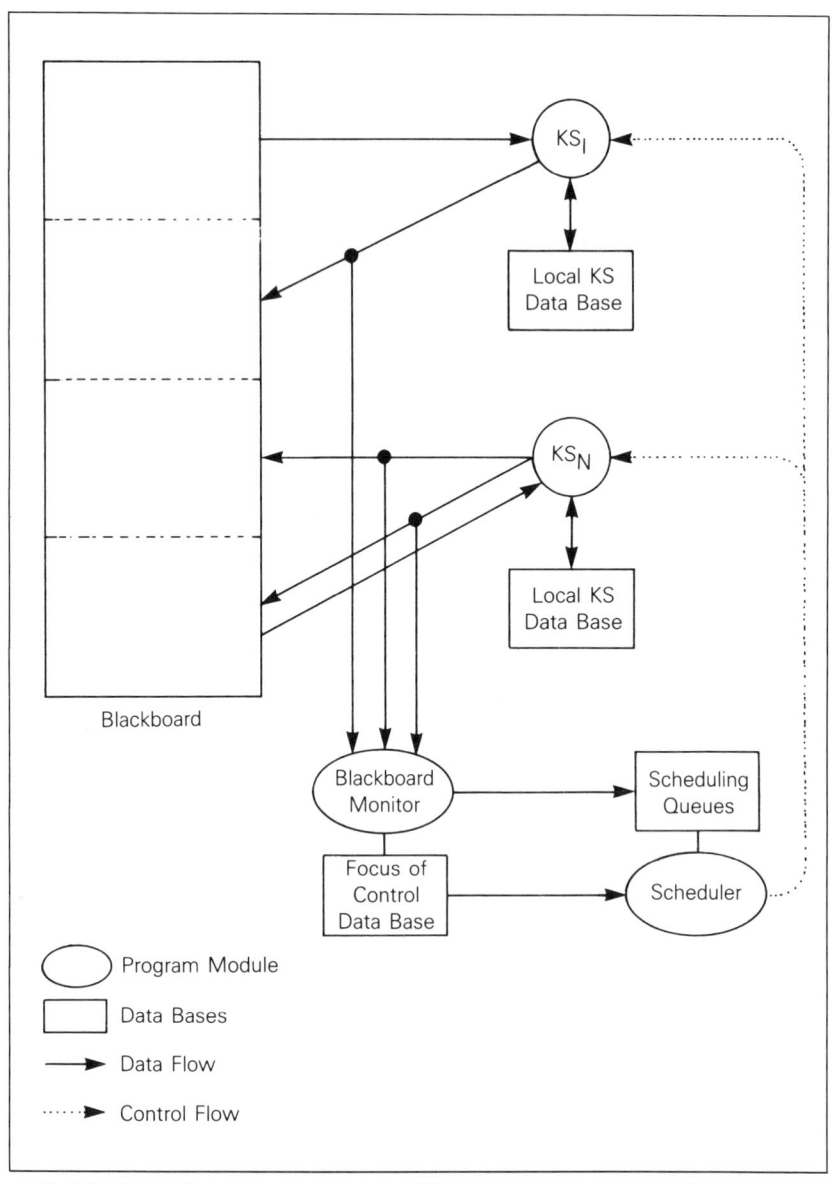

4-13. HEARSAY II system architecture. (From *Knowledge Engineering in Speech Understanding Systems,* ONR Series in AI, by D.R. Reddy. Reprinted with permission.)

and assessments from these various experts. For example, if two experts each assign a probability of likelihood to a given hypothesis, can these probability estimates be weighted equally or is one estimate more conservative than the other?

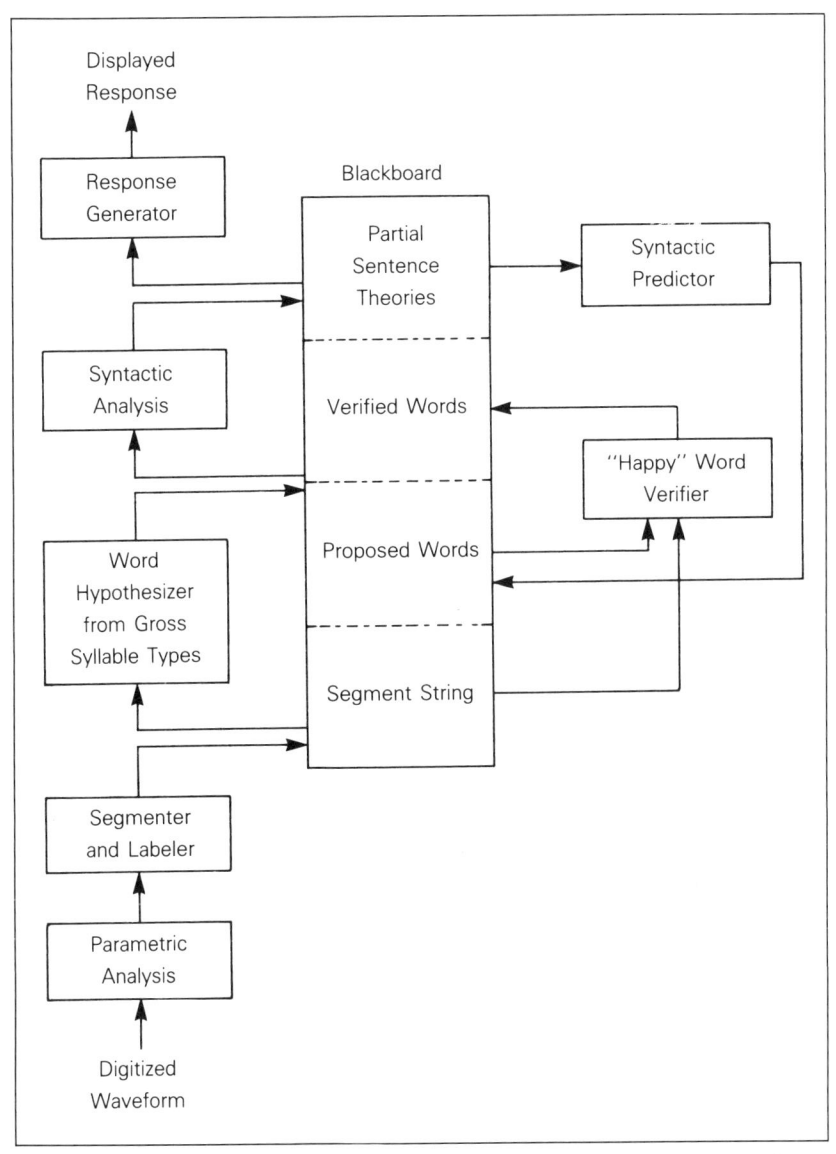

4-14. Block diagram of the Carnegie-Mellon HEARSAY II system organization. (From "An Overview of Artificial Intelligence and Robots" [NASA Technical Memo 85838], by William Gevarter. Reprinted with permission.)

HEARSAY's expert systems are event-driven. Thus, when a new sound is uttered, the experts on phoneme detection are called; when they are finished, the experts on proposing words from gross syllables are called; when they are finished, expert systems are called in to verify the words and to perform syntactic analyses on the partial sentences so as to decide between likely sentence meanings, resolve ambiguities, and predict future words. These predictions, in turn, trigger the phoneme detectors and word-hypothesizing experts to reexamine earlier assessments and to use the most recent predictions in their current hypotheses. The systems could also be described as island-driven, however, since they expanded about recognized and verified hypotheses. Analysis proceeds at all levels, top-to-bottom, bottom-to-top, and at the middle hierarchical levels.

The expert systems include SEG (which digitizes the raw acoustic signals), WORD-SEG (which forms word/sequence hypotheses), WORD-SEQ-CTL (which proposes goal hypotheses), PARSE (which parses sentences and partial sentences), PREDICT (which predicts words), VERIFY (which verifies or rejects predicted words), CONCAT (which creates new and longer phrases), and STOP (which detects when the system has found a valid interpretation). Most of these systems are production rule–based and pattern-invoked. Many of the systems compete; for example, the expert systems POW, MOW, and WORD-CTL all form bottom-to-top word hypotheses, and SEMANT and DISCO both provide semantic interpretations to the partial sentences (although in these cases each uses a different approach).

The HEARSAY system worked with 90 percent accuracy for a single speaker uttering continuous speech, using approximately a 1,000-word vocabulary, and with twenty to thirty training utterances required. The system was run at a speed slower than real time; it would have had to perform 200–500 million operations per second to keep up with speech in real time—a processing speed at current supercomputer levels! Between four and ten top-of-the-line IBM Sierras would be needed to keep up with this processing requirement. HEARSAY also had focus-of-attention problems, stopping problems, monitoring problems, and sharing knowledge source problems.

HARPY uses a precompiled network in which each node is a template of *allophones* (representations of sounds as they actually occur in words, as opposed to *phonemes*—more abstract representations that capture the common characteristics of a class of allophones); when linked, the allophones form acoustic representatives of every possible pronunciation of words in the domain. Thus HARPY's designers had to compile a network of all the possible sentences; the paths through the network are called *sentence templates*.

HARPY's semantic, syntactic, lexical, and word juncture processes are integrated to drive its network search algorithm. A beam search algorithm (an optimum network path selection algorithm) is used to generate the most promising states and to prune the unlikely states from future consideration. A state is expanded by hypothesizing and testing the successor states; backtracking is not permitted. The HARPY system approach is illustrated in figure 4-15.

HARPY, like HEARSAY, was designed for a single speaker using a 1,000-word vocabulary in continuous speech. It had superior performance: 95 percent accuracy and only 28 million operations per second required to keep up with speech in real time (versus 200–500 million

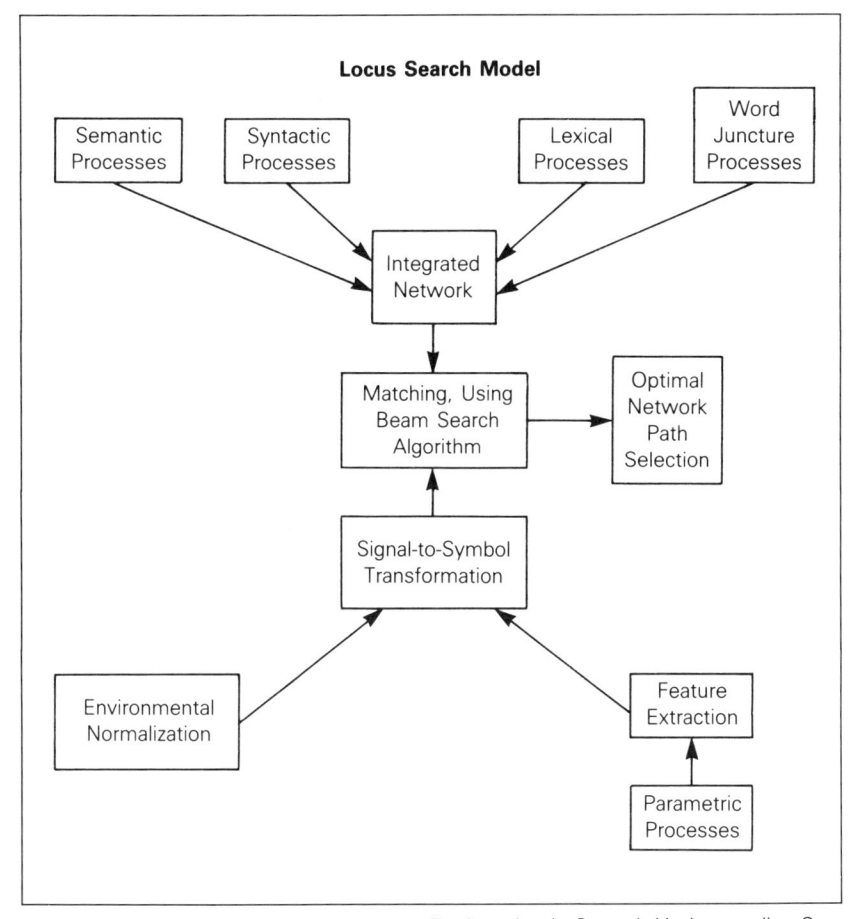

4-15. HARPY system. (From *Knowledge Engineering in Speech Understanding Systems,* ONR Series in AI, by D.R. Reddy. Reprinted with permission.)

operations per second for HEARSAY), although in today's technology maintaining that speed would require an IBM Sierra mainframe. On the negative side, however, HARPY had some very serious deficiencies:

- It lacked generality and extensibility
- It required excessive cost and time for knowledge integration
- It needed an extremely large memory
- It was sensitive to missing acoustical segments and missing words

The HWIM system answers questions from a travel management data base (see figure 4-16). The system extends bottom-to-top word theories using top-to-bottom syntactic components. It verifies hypothesized words by generating a parameter representation and comparing this with the representation from the actual speech input. HWIM uses an augmented transition network semantic grammar; a centralized control makes use of specialized knowledge systems as subroutines, expanding sentences about the first recognized word in the sentence (island driving).

This system represented the most difficult domain in the SUR project. Its average branching factor (the average number of words that might come after each word in each legal sentence) was 196 (in contrast to 33 for HARPY and HEARSAY), and it was designed for speaker-independent, continuous speech. It performed with only 44 percent accuracy and was very slow in comparison with HEARSAY and HARPY.

From examining these systems, we can appreciate just how difficult a problem speech understanding is. Given today's thrust toward new fifth-generation computer architectures, with ambitious goals being addressed through advanced-device technology and novel non–Von Neumann parallel-processing structures, renewed hope has sprung up regarding a near-term solution to the speech understanding problem; DARPA funding has also reappeared.

Japan has targeted speech understanding as one of the objectives of its fifth-generation program. Japanese speech-understanding systems may well appear before English systems. The Japanese language has only about 500 syllables compared to the 10,000 syllables in the English languages. Moreover, the Japanese-Chinese *kanji* written character set is quite complex and in the past has proved difficult to computerize completely, adding impetus to the Japanese speech-understanding program as a much-needed alternate input/output mode.

Other efforts include an ambitious project headed by Kurzweil, who developed reading machines for the blind and electronic music syn-

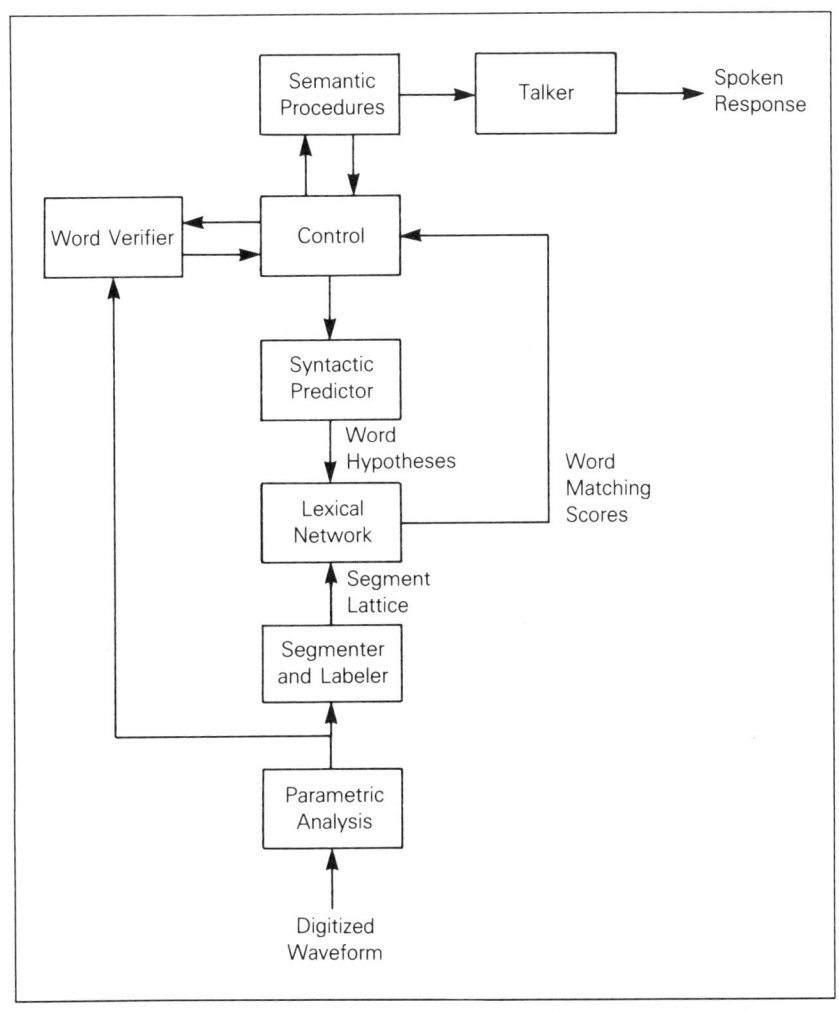

4-16. Block diagram of the BBN HWIM system organization. (From "An Overview of Artificial Intelligence and Robots" [NASA Technical Memo 85838], by William Gevarter. Reprinted with permission.)

thesizers; he predicts that 10,000-word continuous-speech recognizers will be available at affordable prices by 1987. Kurzweil Applied Intelligence has recently introduced the KVS-3000, a speech-recognition product.

IBM is also said to be developing a listening typewriter for automatic dictation that will be capable of recognizing 10,000 words in connected speech and will be on the market by the end of the 1980s. A listening typewriter would not have to recognize speech in real time. The input speech could be recorded, then recognized and transcribed onto a word processor some hours later, and the system would still be attractive. The 10,000-word goal is based on IBM studies of potential users' evaluations of simulated listening typewriters, which concluded that 10,000 words would be the minimum acceptable vocabulary size. A pocket dictionary contains over 50,000 different words; 10,000 words represents an average elementary school child's vocabulary.

Researchers have discovered that there is relatively little variability among speakers with respect to the pronunciation of stressed syllables (Zue and Schwartz 1982). Furthermore, most words in the English language can be represented by fairly unique sequences of stressed syllables; most stressed syllable sequences are unique to one or two possible words, and only a handful of stressed syllable sequences could be associated with more than five words. These results and activities give promise of a solution, perhaps by the 1990s. Once words can be recognized with high accuracy, the same technology currently used for natural language processing can be used for speech understanding with the same success. By 1990, speech recognition and understanding is expected to be a billion-dollar industry.

Speech synthesis is not an A.I. problem, but it represents a companion technology for speech recognition, just as text generation represents a companion capability for text understanding. Speech synthesis is an easier problem to solve, and the technology is much further along in its development. Many such systems are already embedded in toys, incorporated in computers, or sold as stand-alone products. Appendix D lists some of the currently available commercial synthesizers and their characteristics. The quality of the speech generated depends on the coding scheme; these always involve a tradeoff between output rate and memory requirements (see figure 4-17). The numerous uses of speech synthesizers are reviewed in Appendix D.

VISION AND IMAGE UNDERSTANDING

Many important potential applications exist for vision processing technology. Some of these can be satisfied merely by sophisticated signal-processing techniques, such as image enhancement; others require classification techniques, such as character recognition; and still others

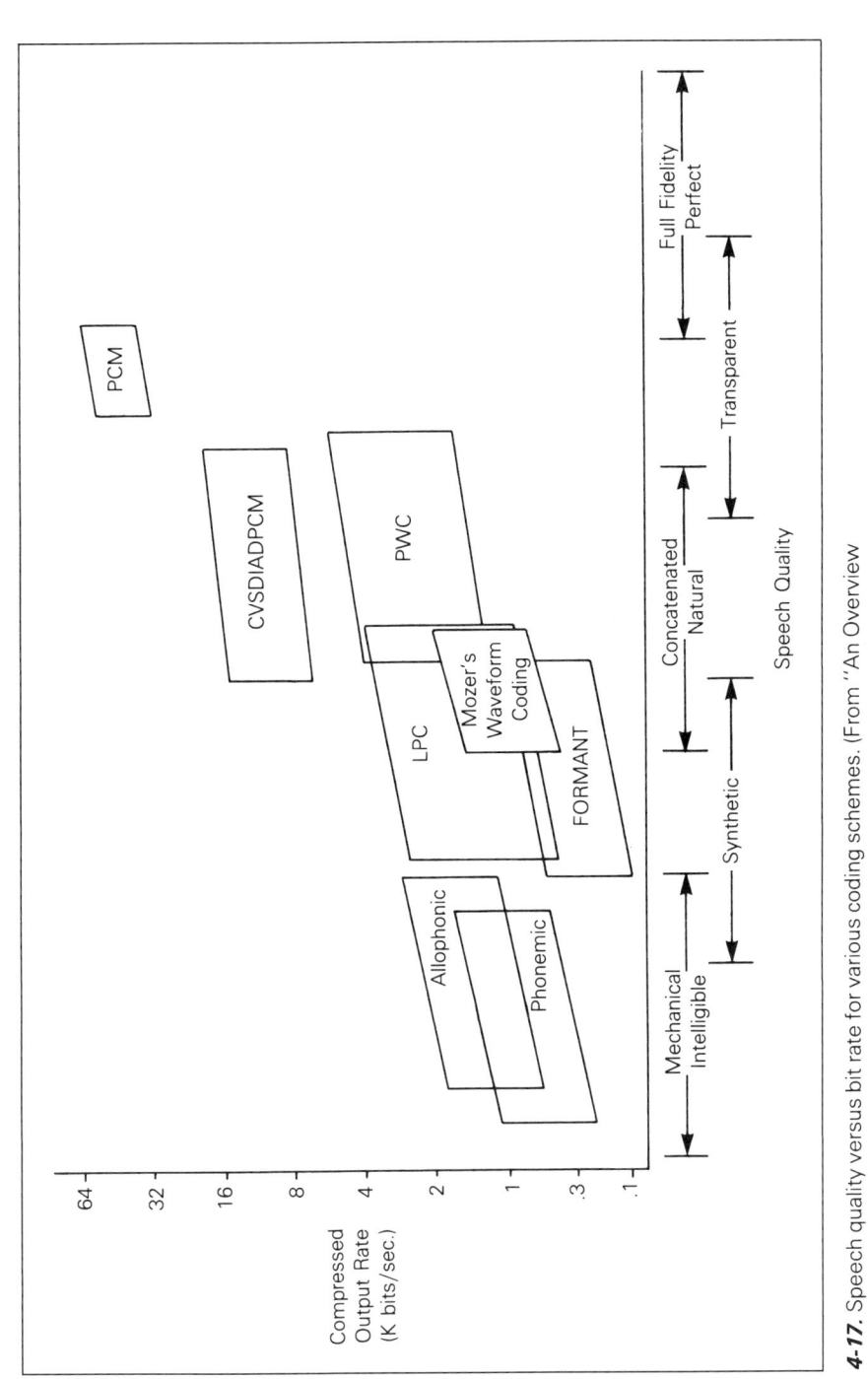

4-17. Speech quality versus bit rate for various coding schemes. (From "An Overview of Artificial Intelligence and Robots" [NASA Technical Memo 85838], by William Gevarter. Reprinted with permission.)

require true image understanding. An image-understanding program builds a description of the scene and of the image. Image understanding requires knowledge about the problem domain in addition to sophisticated image-processing techniques.

This hierarchy of vision-processing tasks is illustrated in figure 4-18. It closely parallels the hierarchies that are used in natural language processing and speech understanding. Figure 4-18 depicts an automated forward observer—a relatively easy task for a human being, but a very difficult task for a machine.

The image is recorded by a smart sensor—possibly a light-sensitive CCD (charge-coupled diode) array that transforms the image into small picture elements called *pixels* (the smallest resolvable picture elements, coded in terms of light intensity)—and an image processor for transforming the image into a sketch that retains only the higher-level features of the image (such as lines, regions, and possibly shape information such as surface orientation and occlusion). From this sketch, the system identifies *iconics*, individual image segments that can be associated with physical objects such as vehicles, trees, roads, rivers, and bridges. These objects can then be associated with symbols, which—taken in context with where and under what conditions the image is being observed—enable the lookout to understand the scene sufficiently to compose the message shown in figure 4-18, describing the scene as representing a tank convoy approaching the bridge over the Elbe River.

Among the many potential applications for this kind of capability are:

AUTOMATION OF INDUSTRIAL PROCESSES
- Object acquisition by robot arms (for example) for sorting or packing items arriving on conveyor belts
- Automatic guidance of seam-welders and cutting tools
- Guidance of VLSI-related processes, such as lead bonding, chip alignment, and packaging
- Monitoring, filtering, and containing of the flood of data from oil-drilling sites or from seismographs
- Visual feedback for automatic assembly and repair

INSPECTION TASKS
- Inspection of printed circuit boards for spurs, shorts, and bad connections
- Checking the results of casting processes for impurities and fractures

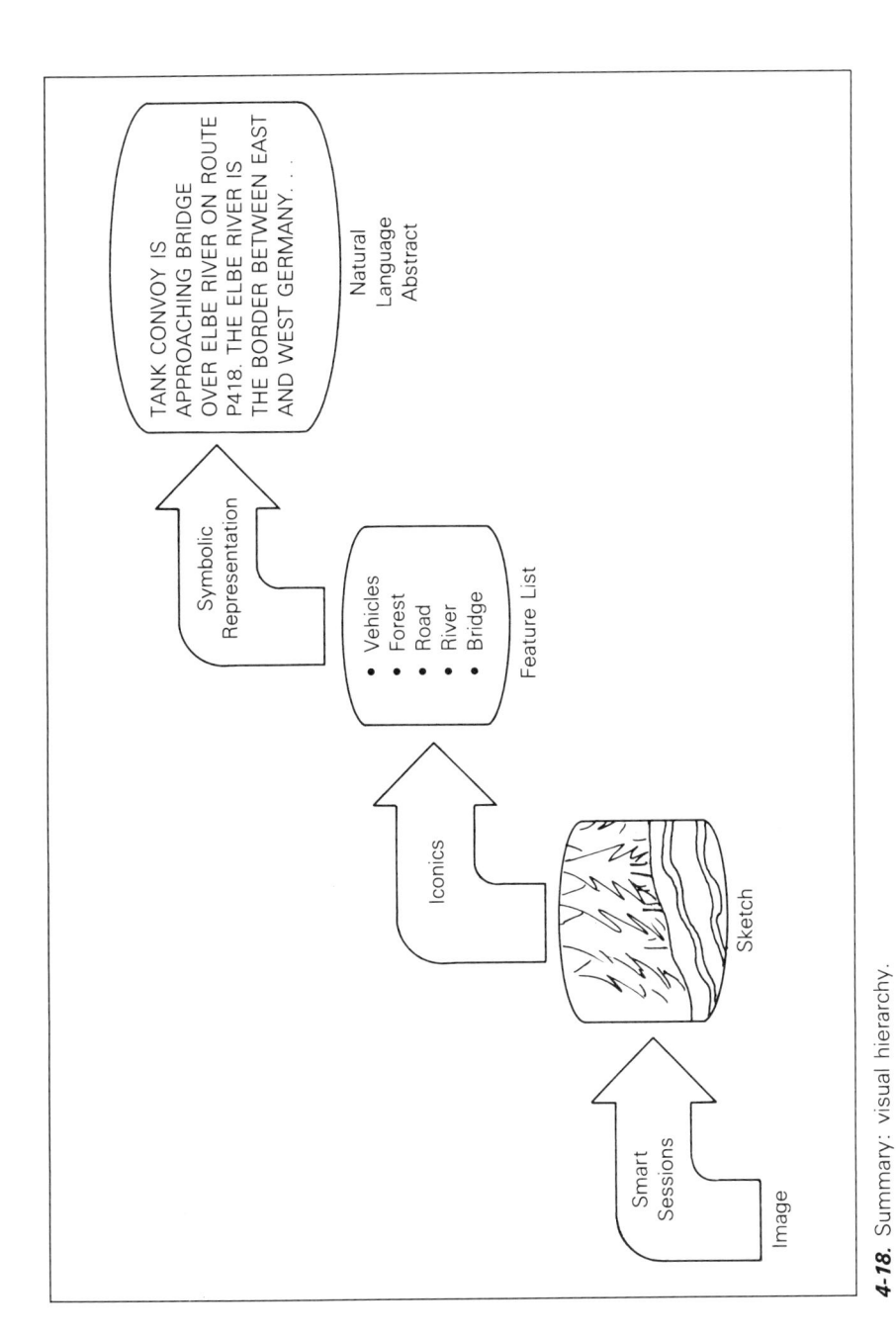

TANK CONVOY IS APPROACHING BRIDGE OVER ELBE RIVER ON ROUTE P418. THE ELBE RIVER IS THE BORDER BETWEEN EAST AND WEST GERMANY. . . .

Natural Language Abstract

↑ Symbolic Representation

Feature List
- Vehicles
- Forest
- Road
- River
- Bridge

↑ Iconics

Sketch

↑ Smart Sessions

Image

4-18. Summary: visual hierarchy.

- Screening medical images such as chromosome slides, cancer smears, X-ray and ultrasound images, and tomography
- Routine screening of plant samples
- Inspection of alphanumerics on labels and manufactured items
- Checking packaging and contents in pharmaceutical and food industries
- Inspection of glass items for cracks, bubbles, and the like

REMOTE SENSING
- Cartography, automatic generation of hill-shaded maps, and registration of satellite images with terrain maps
- Monitoring traffic along roads, on docks, and at airfields
- Management of land resources, including water conservation, forestry maintenance, soil erosion prevention, and crop growth
- Detecting mineral ore deposits

MAKING COMPUTER POWER MORE ACCESSIBLE
- Management information systems that have considerably wider human–machine communication channels than do current systems addressed by typing or pointing
- Document readers (for people who still use paper)
- Design aids for architects and mechanical engineers
- Strategies for indexing into data bases of models

MILITARY APPLICATIONS
- Guidance for obstacle avoidance
- Ranging
- Object recognition
- Target detection and identification
- Detecting changes in scenes
- Remote lookout
- Indicators and warning detection
- Photo analysis/interpretation aids

Many research and engineering obstacles must be overcome before we can realize most of these potential applications. First we do not really understand how human beings see—that is, how a person represents an image, what features are extracted by the eye, which features are important for which human vision-processing tasks, and what constraints are imposed during vision processing to resolve ambiguities. Consider the questions that follow.

How does a human being compensate for underconstrained images? A two-dimensional image underconstrains a scene because it does not provide enough information by itself to recover the scene. For this reason, we lose depth information when we collapse a three-dimensional scene into a two-dimensional one.

How does a systems designer compensate for perturbations in the image due to surface material, atmospheric conditions, angle of light from the light source, ambient light, and camera angle?

How does a systems designer overcome the engineering problem of processing the enormous amount of information associated with even the simplest image-processing task? For example, an aerial photograph, digitized into 3,000 × 3,000 pixels with the amplitude encoded at 8 bits per pixel, requires 9 Mbytes of operating space per image. A simple edge detector that performs, say, 10 operations per pixel would require 90 million operations per image.

A typically organized vision system is pictured in figure 4-19. The products currently offered by commercial vision processing companies still are predominantly at lower image-processing levels and are focused in the manufacturing area, although some more advanced development is being undertaken for military applications. Such systems serve as vision modules for one-armed robots and as manufacturing inspection units. Generally, the image processing is limited to two-dimensional silhouettes (binary black/white intensity scale) and is capable of distinguishing only about ten different classes. Some industrial vision systems, however, are already employing structured light and building three-dimensional sensing systems. Examples of these product offerings include:

- Machine Intelligence Corporation's vision unit (selling for approximately $35,000) can be combined with the one-armed Unimation (a Westinghouse subsidiary) robot, which is capable of lifting 22 pounds, to provide that robot with vision feedback. So equipped, the robot sells for about $100,000.
- General Motors's Consight system is used for sorting parts.
- Westinghouse's APAS system is used in assembly and mixed production.
- Automatix's Autovision Artificial Vision System is used for inspecting, sorting, and robot guidance.

Companies in the field include:

- Machine Intelligence Corporation; Sunnyvale, CA
- Automatix; Burlington, MA

- Octek; Burlington, MA
- Robotic Vision Systems; Melville, NY
- Control Automation; Princeton, NJ
- General Motors
- Westinghouse
- General Electric
- IBM
- Lockheed
- Hughes
- Texas Instruments
- PAR; Rome, NY
- AI & DS; Los Altos, CA

DARPA's image-understanding program has sponsored such research projects as: stereo image-processing and image segmentation techniques with Carnegie-Mellon University; relaxation transform image-processing algorithms with the University of Maryland; Hough transform image-processing techniques with the University of Rochester; Marr stereo image-processing techniques with MIT; a camera model reconstruction system, called Ransac, with Stanford Research Institute (SRI); and linear feature and texture extraction techniques with the University of Southern California. With the exception of the MIT work (which uses a LISP machine) and the SRI Ransac project (which was coded in MAIN SAIL), all work is in C because of its numerical processing orientation. DARPA and DMA (Defense Mapping Agency) sponsored a joint test bed, run by SRI, for testing and evaluating these vision-processing projects.

A few of the projects were more comprehensive, addressing the higher vision-processing levels. For example, SRI developed a road expert, coded in MAIN SAIL, that uses its understanding of the properties of roads to pick out and follow roads in overhead photographs. Rod Brooks and Tom Binford of Stanford developed a highly comprehensive vision-processing system called ACRONYM (Brooks 1981). Its original applications were to classify aircraft from overhead aerial photographs at an airport and to aid in low-angle viewing of automated assembly work stations with a wide range of industrial parts.

Recently, image understanding has been propelled into the limelight. Military research spending in the area has increased, and many joint government/university/industrial centers of research have been established; for example:

Vision and Image Understanding ■ **181**

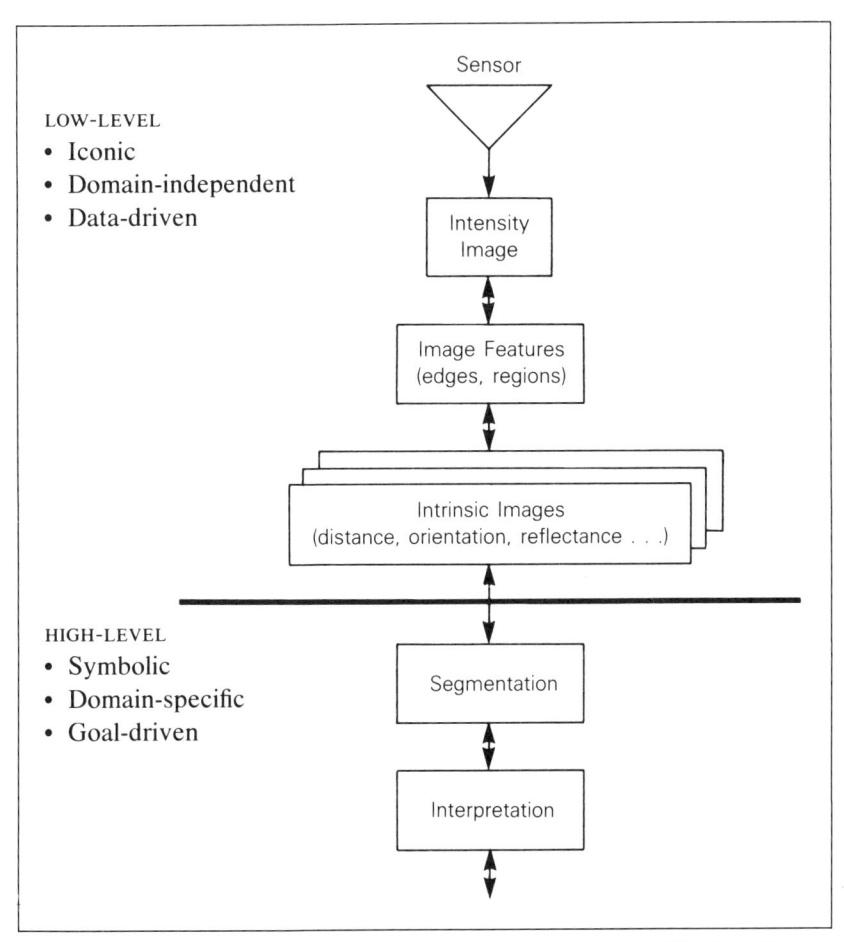

```
LOW-LEVEL
 • Iconic
 • Domain-independent
 • Data-driven

                    Sensor
                      ▽
                      ↓
               ┌──────────────┐
               │  Intensity   │
               │    Image     │
               └──────────────┘
                      ↕
               ┌──────────────┐
               │Image Features│
               │(edges, regions)│
               └──────────────┘
                      ↕
               ┌──────────────┐
               │Intrinsic Images│
               │(distance, orientation, reflectance ...)│
               └──────────────┘
                      ↕
━━━━━━━━━━━━━━━━━━━━━━━━━━━━━━━━━━━━━━━━━

HIGH-LEVEL
 • Symbolic
 • Domain-specific
 • Goal-driven
               ┌──────────────┐
               │ Segmentation │
               └──────────────┘
                      ↕
               ┌──────────────┐
               │Interpretation│
               └──────────────┘
                      ↕
```

4-19. Organization of a visual system. (From "An Overview of Artificial Intelligence and Robots" [NASA Technical Memo 85838], by William Gevarter. Reprinted with permission.)

- Carnegie-Mellon and Westinghouse
- Stanford and Lockheed
- University of Maryland and Westinghouse
- University of Rochester
- Stanford Research Institute
- MIT
- USC and Hughes

The ACRONYM system is illustrated in figure 4-20. ACRONYM does both top-to-bottom and bottom-to-top processing, based on a vision

182 ■ *CURRENT APPLICATIONS*

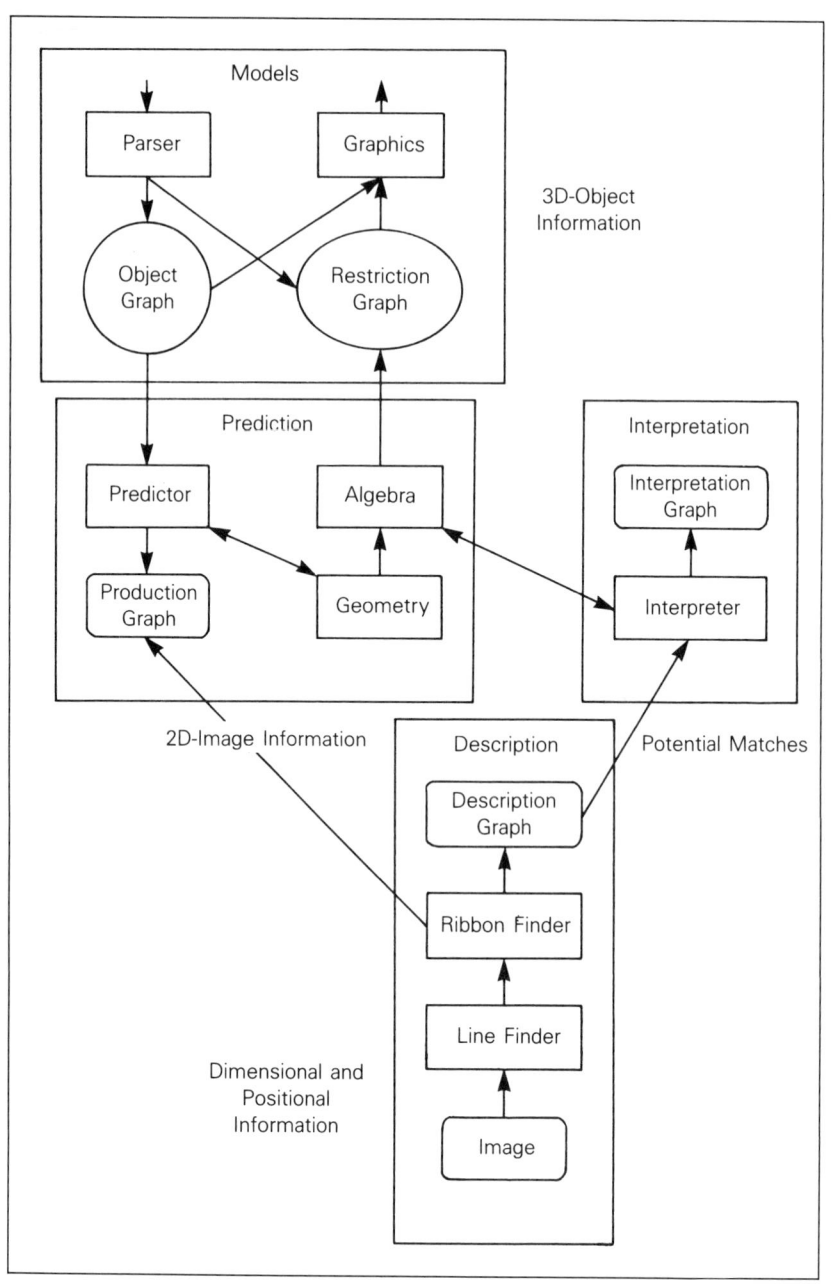

4-20. ACRONYM. (From *The Handbook of Artificial Intelligence,* edited by A. Barr and E. Feigenbaum. Published by William Kaufmann, Inc., Los Altos, CA, 1981. Reprinted with permission.)

model. Its vision processing is divided into four parts: modeling, prediction, description, and interpretation. At the bottom level, a two-dimensional image is digitized into a pixel map—a coding of intensity levels of the lowest resolvable two-dimensional cells or pixels. The resulting pixel map is then processed to produce an elementary sketch or line drawing. This is accomplished through the application of edge detectors and ribbon finders. First, sharp changes in intensity (edges) are detected by means of the Nevatia/Babu edge detector; this involves a convolution of the pixel map with various window masks of dimension n by n, representing lines at different orientations. Whenever the output of a convolution exceeds the threshold, an edge is assumed. Then the resulting collection of edges is processed, adding edges, deleting edges, and reorienting edges according to a set of heuristic rules that include:

- Producer rules, which select the best edge segments to form a contour
- Reaper rules, which reject segments that do not contribute to convex closure
- Culler rules, which eliminate unlikely contours
- Follow supersegment rules, which designate special segments to be followed
- Continuation rules, which bridge gaps in contour data
- Nearby vertex rules, which select nearby segment endpoints

The successful use of constraints to identify and associate ribbons and regions with objects was first successfully applied by D.L. Waltz (1972) to the world of blocks. Here an ingenious labeling convention was developed for labeling boundary lines and junctions; when applied to the world of blocks, the convention strongly constrained possible alternatives and rapidly converged to the single correct interpretation. Figure 4-21 illustrates how this worked.

In ACRONYM's initial implementation, the photograph of interest was assumed to be already centered and scaled so that it effectively framed the object of interest. In general, a preliminary step involved determining the area of interest within a larger scene. This could generally be done using state-of-the-art image processing techniques such as energy detectors and special feature extractions.

The lower-level image processing associated with obtaining a primitive sketch abstraction from the actual image was not done in real time and was performed on a large computer. Today, more efficient algorithms and special image-processing VLSI and VHSIC devices can be embedded

184 ■ *CURRENT APPLICATIONS*

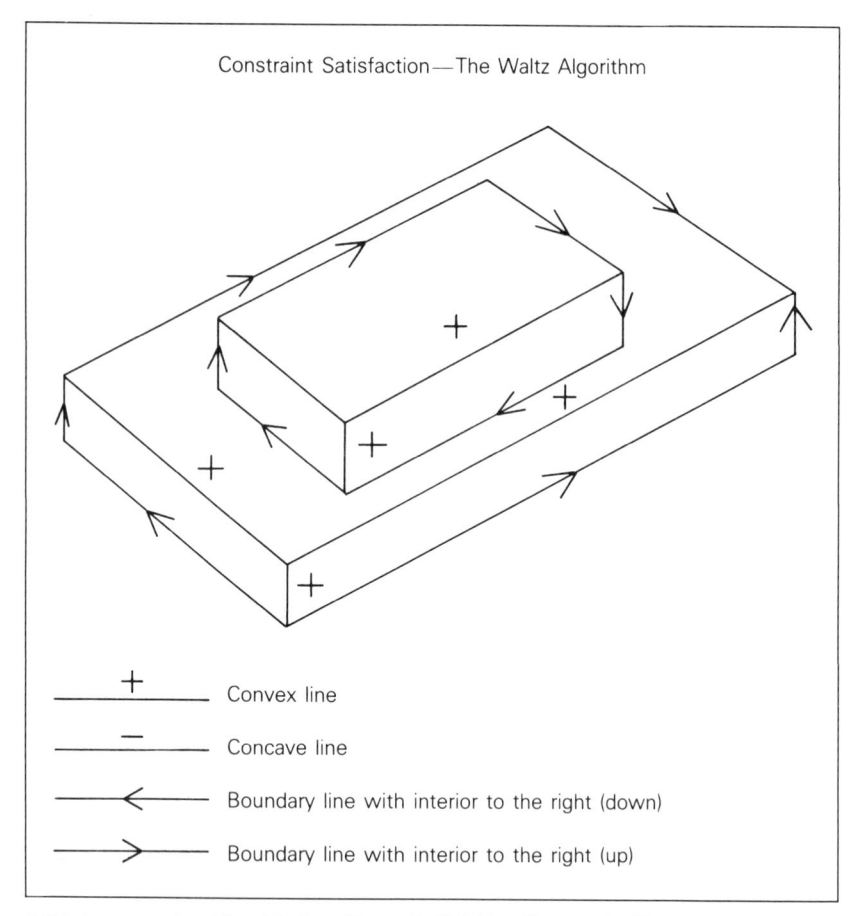

```
             Constraint Satisfaction—The Waltz Algorithm
```

———+——— Convex line

———−——— Concave line

———<——— Boundary line with interior to the right (down)

———>——— Boundary line with interior to the right (up)

4-21. An example of line labeling. (From *Artificial Intelligence,* by Elaine Rich. Published by McGraw-Hill, New York, 1983. Reprinted with permission.)

into the sensors, enabling the sensors to perform the processing more rapidly, efficiently, and effectively.

Some advanced algorithms can help in image-understanding applications where clutter, clouds, haze, or snow/ice could obscure the picture, increase the background noise, reduce the contrast, and otherwise hamper performance of this lower-level processing task. These advanced techniques include texture regional analysis, prominence feature detection, shape-from-shading analysis, spectral analysis, and superior edge detectors such as those developed by Marr, Poggia, and Hildreth, which make use of the zero crossings of nondirectional Laplacian, and the Sobol edge detector.

The resulting ribbons are then combined to grow regions, whose forms are then analyzed and represented by a high-level, geometrically based scheme called a *description graph*.

Some current research activity centers on issues of how to represent these processed images. For example, figure 4-22 illustrates a two-and-one-half-dimensional sketch that shows the curvature of the surfaces by means of lines whose orientation is normal to the surface and whose length corresponds to the amount of curvature in the surface, as well as by means of an outline of the object.

Other relevant research involves stereo processing techniques such as calculating zero crossings taken in front of, on, or behind the focal plane. Such computations have been used at MIT to process a 1,000-pixel-squared image in two seconds, using a LISP machine. Another current area of research involves moving objects. Here, optical flow processing techniques are being investigated that involve consideration of the following effects:

- Distribution of velocities of apparent movement caused by smoothly changing brightness patterns
- Motion detected from temporal changes in zero crossings
- Position of a zero crossing interpolated precisely by linear interpolation for static images (such interpolation improves the spatial-temporal resolution over the physical limit of the detectors)
- Incorporation of constraints such as constant velocity directly into the interpolation computation for time-varying images

At the top level of ACRONYM, the entire collection of possible objects is represented in terms of three-dimensional models. These models were based upon a concept called *generalized cylinders* (Agin and Binford 1973)—cylinders that are obtained by generalizing the definition of a cylinder. An ordinary cylinder is defined as the volume swept out by a circle moving along a straight line that runs through its center at right angles to the plane of the circle. In a generalized cylinder, the spline (or axis) of the cylinder may be curved, the cross-sectional radius may change as a function of its position along the spline, the cross section itself may be some planar figure other than a circle, and it may be oriented at a nonperpendicular angle to the spline. An object can then be represented as a collection of these generalized cylinders placed relative to one another.

186 ■ *CURRENT APPLICATIONS*

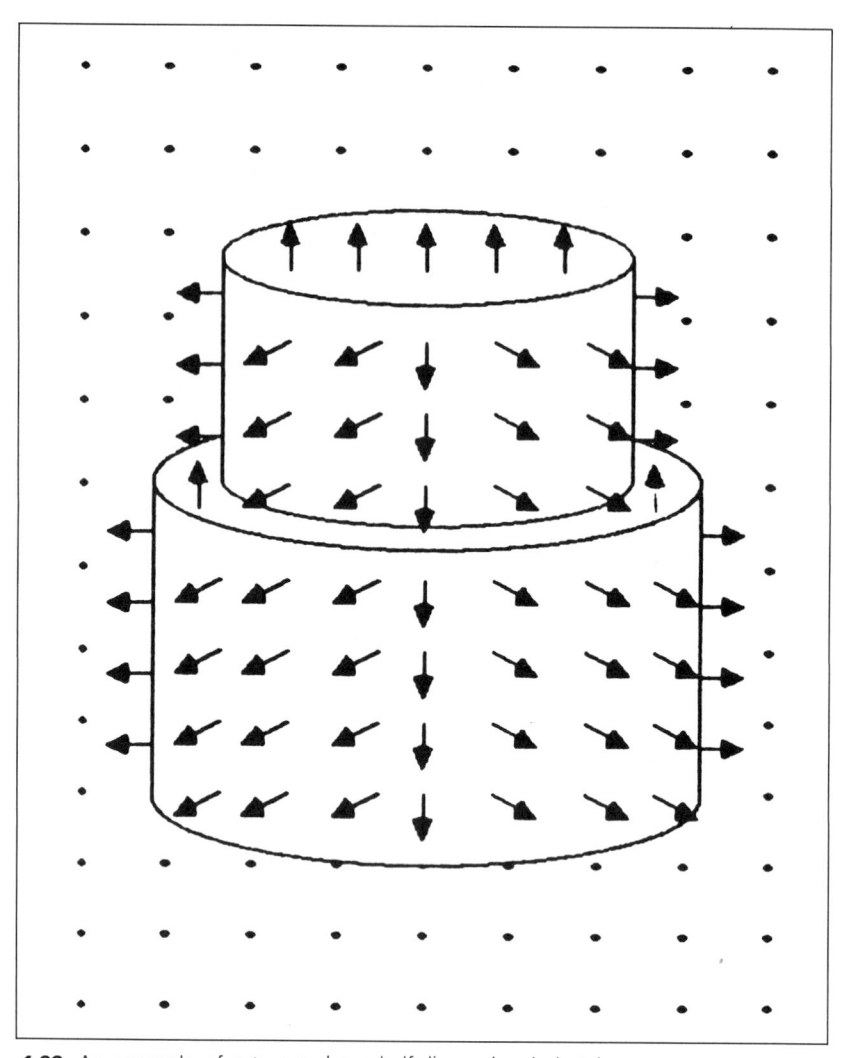

4-22. An example of a two-and-one-half-dimensional sketch.

This representation has been shown to be quite rich and can adequately represent most man-made objects if the object is decomposed into a sufficiently large number of small, generalized cylinders. For example, even a collection of Grecian urns has been satisfactorily modeled in terms of generalized cylinders. Thus a man-made object can be represented quite compactly by means of a collection of generalized cylinders, each completely specified according to its spline (straight or of a given curvature), its cross section (circle, square, or other), its cross-sectional sweep rate (its cross-sectional growth as a function of the cross section's position down the spline; for example, constant or linear), and the relative position of each generalized cylinder (the subparts) to a main piece called the *main code* (or in the case of an aircraft, the hull). This representation is called an object graph.

An entire scene can be represented with a collection of objects all represented by their object graphs. The object graph, taken together with a restriction graph (whose nodes denote constraints on the position, orientation, and dimension affixment rules governing the connected subparts associated with the particular objects and environments of interest, plus rules associated with camera views and background illumination), can be developed through some elegant mathematics based on theories of geometric reasoning concerning the relationship of shapes and contours under rotations and special views to predict possible two-dimensional projections of the objects. These parametric prediction rules can then be used to build a predicted geometrical representation of the expected two-dimensional view of the hypothesized object, called a *production graph*.

The production graph is then compared to the description graph derived by the actual processed image, to interpret whether the viewed object could possibly be the hypothesized three-dimensional object— perhaps rotated, tilted, or the like. If a poor match is found between a hypothesized object and the actual processed image, another object must be hypothesized and compared. The image is interpreted as the object that produces the best match.

In the original work, various large-bodied commercial aircraft were correctly classified by this model. Of course the model was extremely slow, taking many hours to run.

The work has since been extended to include more complex multiobject scenes by using scripts like those used by Schank in natural language processing to predict or eliminate from consideration various objects and object relationships, based on previous knowledge and stereotyping of the likely scene variations (Bullock et al. 1982). Other extensions involved the use of three-dimensional modeling techniques, largely from CAD/CAM technology (wire models, fractals, and so on), to model more complex shapes and more amorphous objects, such as trees and terrain. Other relevant research involves illumination models (shading and surface properties) and volumetric models (prediction and interpretation at the level of volumes).

188 ■ CURRENT APPLICATIONS

■ ROBOTICS

The field of robotics is predicted to grow to a multibillion-dollar industry. Japan paved the way for the large-scale use of robots to decrease production costs, reduce inventories of parts, and improve the quality and speed of production—both at start-up and during later execution. As early as 1981, Japan reportedly had over 70 percent of the world's robots.

Manufacturing is, of course, the most obvious use of robots, but they have many other uses. In medicine, the PUMA robot provides assistance during neurosurgery. Seeing-eye robots the size of small Volkswagens guide the blind in Japan. In prisons, over 200 robots are already deployed in the United States as security guards. They are equipped with smell sensors to detect people by their ammonia smell. For the military, a large United States military research program is aimed toward developing intelligent autonomous vehicles. For hazardous environments (such as nuclear plants, mining, space, and undersea), robots are being developed and used to repair and operate machines and systems.

Robots in the home have, perhaps, attracted the most interest from the general public. The following toy robots are currently available commercially: Heath Electronics' Hero I; Androbot's B.O.B. ("Brains on Board"); Sandhu Machine Design's Rhino XR2; Microbot's Teachmover; and Tomy Toys' Armatron. These robots currently are limited to serving drinks, reciting stories, and the like, but their sophistication and usefulness will grow with the technology. A robot was even registered as a candidate for the 1984 presidential election; "Rebecca the Robot" was entered and backed by four women from Baltimore.

The generation of robots used today is not very intelligent, and does not involve much in the way of A.I. technology. Robot attributes now available include:

- Teaching and playback facilities, with local and library memories
- Random program selection by external stimuli
- Repositioning accuracy, repeatable to within 0.3 millimeters
- Weight handling to 150 kilograms
- Point-to-point and continuous path control
- Synchronization with moving work pieces
- Interface with computers
- Palletizing capability
- Reliability of better than 400 hours MTBF

More intelligent robots will be needed in the future: robots that can be directed to perform operations with just a few high-level problem-domain-oriented commands (for example, tighten the bolt holding the steering wheel to the shaft), thus allowing rapid reprogramming and remote supervision of robots in environments that do not support direct microcontrol because of limited communications band width (under the sea) or unacceptable time delays (deep space); robots that can use their senses to direct their operations with less costly control systems; robots that possess the intelligence to overcome unexpected, unplanned contingencies; robots that possess the maneuverability to climb inside large structures (such as ships) and weld seams, or to navigate over difficult terrain in military operations; robots that can be trusted to perform in less-structured environments, such as in the home—where objects can be moved and where the robot must be careful not to hurt the family dog, run over a favorite plant, or crush the eggs while preparing breakfast—or in a military setting, where the enemy actions cannot be preplanned and where the environment is hostile and unpredictable.

In manufacturing situations, an intelligent robot could perform more delicate and complex operations less expensively through the use of senses such as sight and touch to direct its motion.

An intelligent robot is capable of:

- Receiving high-level communications
- Understanding its environment through the use of models
- Formulating plans
- Executing plans
- Monitoring its own operation

The components of an intelligent robot are pictured in figure 4-23. The robot is capable of:

- Reasoning, learning, and adapting
- Seeing, touching (skinlike membranes have been designed at MIT that have an array of pressure sensitive sensors embedded in it; the result is a sensor output much like the two-dimensional pixel map found in many vision sensors), hearing, and speaking
- Manipulation
- Mobility, perhaps including free walking
- Spatial management
- Coordinating multiple operations (for example, the coordinated use of two arms, or actual mobile robot operations)

One year after it launched its fifth-generation computer project, Japan launched a next-generation robot project. As pictured in figure 4-24,

190 ■ CURRENT APPLICATIONS

CAPABLE OF
- Receiving communication
- Understanding its environment by the use of models
- Formulating plans
- Executing plans
- Monitoring its operation

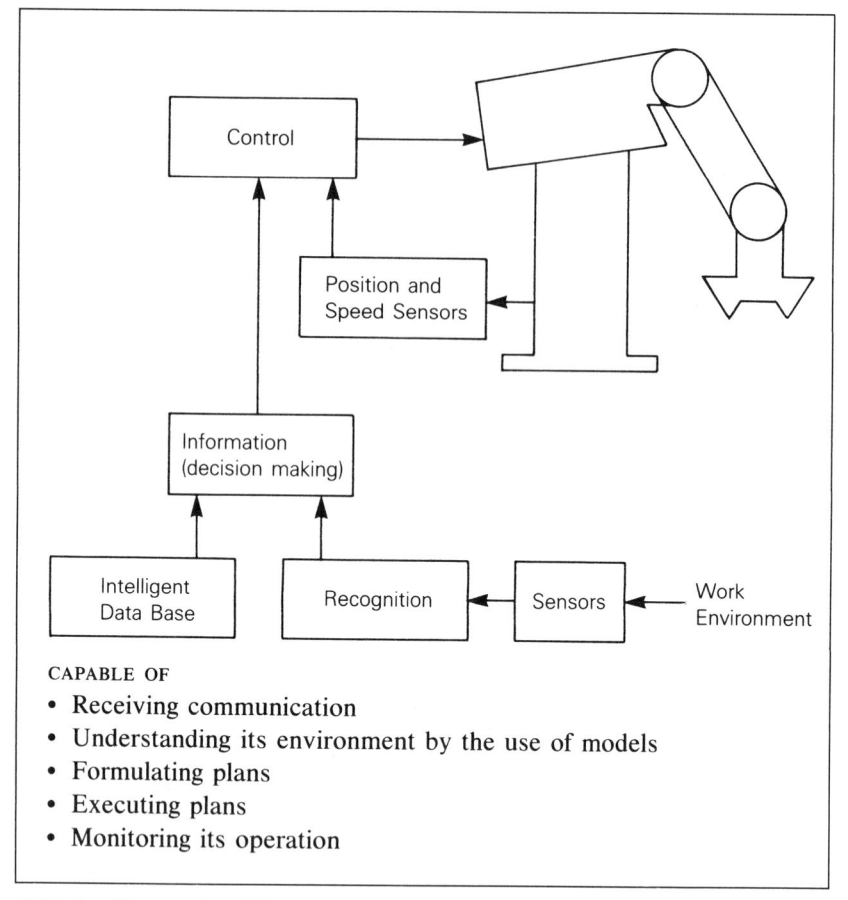

4-23. Intelligent robot. (From "Next Generation Robot Project," by Masaki Togai. In *Computer,* vol. 17, no. 3. © 1984 IEEE. Reprinted with permission.)

the idea for the project came from a JIRA study and is sponsored by MITI. It plans to capitalize on the results of earlier projects—namely, the pattern information process systems project sponsored by ETL, the fifth-generation computer project sponsored by MITI, and the next-generation production technology development project sponsored by MCL. Figure 4-25 depicts the technologies targeted by Japan's next-generation robot project; the initial applications are planned for nuclear plants, undersea work, and rescue operations.

The planned capabilities of the third-generation robots currently under development are contrasted with the capabilities of the first-generation robots and of the current, second-generation robots in figure 4-26. The current state of the art is represented by the following capabilities:

Robotics ■ 191

```
                    ┌─────────────────┐
                    │ Fifth-generation│
                    │ Computer Project│
                    │      MITI       │
                    └────────┬────────┘
                             │
                             ▼
┌──────────────────┐  ┌─────────────────┐  ┌──────────────────┐
│ Pattern-information│  │  Next-generation│  │ Research & Study │
│  Process Systems │─▶│   Robot Project │◀─│  Committee for   │
│     Projects     │  │      MITI       │  │  Next-generation │
│       ETL        │  │                 │  │      Robots      │
└──────────────────┘  └────────▲────────┘  │       JIRA       │
                               │           └──────────────────┘
                      ┌────────┴────────┐
                      │ Next-generation │
                      │   Production   │
                      │   Technology    │
                      │   Development   │
                      │    Project      │
                      │      MCL        │
                      └─────────────────┘
```

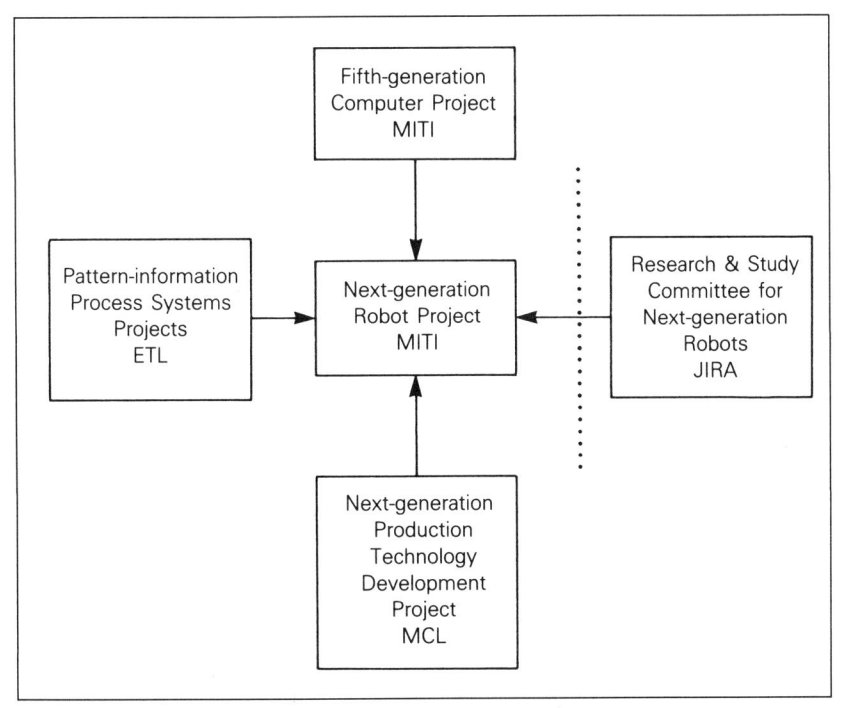

4-24. Next-generation robot. (From "Next Generation Robot Project," by Masaki Togai. In *Computer,* vol. 17, no. 3. © 1984 IEEE. Reprinted with permission.)

- Assembly (for example, Automatix's Cypervision system)
- Arc welding (typical price is $100,000; without such a machine, a worker can productively spend only about 20 percent of a workday actually welding; with the aid of these robotic machines, this figure expands to 70 to 90 percent)
- Welding seam tracking (in 30 percent of cases, the weld location needs to vary from part to part)
- CAD/CAM link (computer vision module on system linked to Automatix Robovision II arc welding system)
- Flexible manufacturing systems (FMS)—IBM 7535 manufacturing system and the IBM RS1

Among the leading American companies involved in producing robots are General Motors (with interests in seven vision companies: Automatix Inc., Applied Intelligence System Inc., Diffracto Ltd., Robotic Vision Systems Inc., View Engineering Inc., GMF Robotics, and Teknowledge; they also own EDS and Hughes), Westinghouse (which bought out

192 ■ CURRENT APPLICATIONS

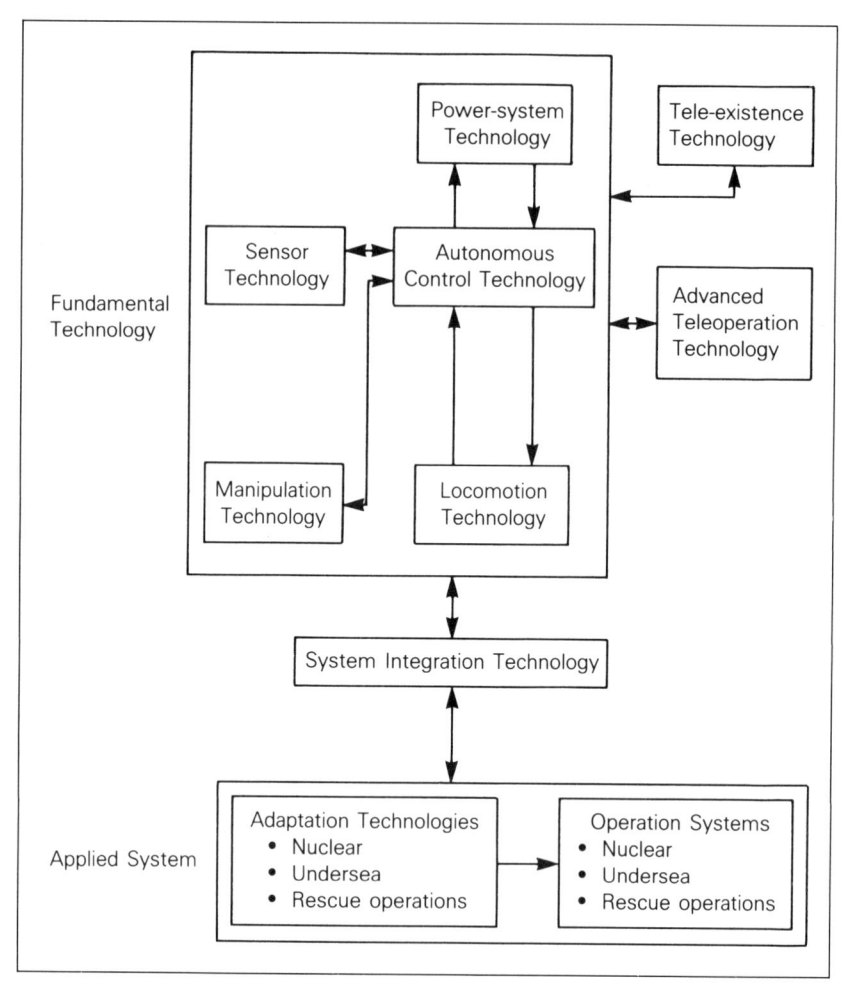

4-25. Technologies of intelligent robotics. (From "Next Generation Robot Project," by Masaki Togai. In *Computer,* vol. 17, no. 3. © 1984 IEEE. Reprinted with permission.)

Unimation), General Electric, IBM, Cincinnati Milacron, United Technologies, Allied-Signal, Machine Intelligence Corporation, Automatix, Octek, Advanced Robotics, and ASEA (U.S. branch of a Swedish electrical manufacturer).

A key feature for the intelligent industrial robot is its ability to be programmed at the task level (at which the user specifies operations according to their desired effect on objects, rather than specifying detailed prestored motions or motions computed as functions of sensory inputs). It is the capability of a robot to receive high-level instructions that will

First Generation (1960–70s)	Second Generation (1980s)	Third Generation (1990s)
Playback robot	Perception and problem solving	Learning, interface
Link and CAM Teaching/playback	Feedback sensors (visual, tactile, ultrasound, chemical)	High-level decision making
Conventional Mobile Systems	Omnidirectional	Walking
Paint spraying Spot welding Pick-and-place	Arc welding Assembly Medical/nursing Remote operation	Automated assembling Independent, autonomous operation Advance inspection Domestic

4-26. Generational trends in industrial robots. (From "Next Generation Robot Project," by Masaki Togai. In *Computer,* vol. 17, no. 3. © 1984 IEEE. Reprinted with permission.)

give it the flexibility to be programmed rapidly enough to undertake new tasks under a time-sharing arrangement that involves many operations in a day; this, in turn, will enable it to be economically used for many short production runs, rather than for a few longer-duration production runs, including the manufacture of individually customized items.

Today's robots can only be programmed either by guiding the system (where the user leads the robot through the motions), or by robot-level programming (where the user writes a program that specifies all of the detailed motion and sensing operations). Robot-level programming allows more flexibility and conditional operation than the guiding system approach, but it is still far less flexible and requires more costly and timely programming efforts than task-level programming would. S-macro, a recently proposed NBS standard robot-level programming language, is a hierarchical table-driven system, written in FORTH. Each table consists typically of 50–100 lines of code and runs at a 28-millisecond cycle time on the 8086.

The key requirements for any robot programming system include the capabilities for:

- Sensing
- World modeling (includes geometric and physical descriptions of objects, kinematic descriptions of all linkages, and descriptions of robot characteristics)
- Motion specification
- Flow of control
- Appropriate programming support tools

Task-level programming remains the subject of research and development in CAD/CAM, computer-integrated manufacturing, and A.I. It involves conferring to the robot the capabilities of spatial reasoning, planning, modeling, task specifying, and robot program synthesizing. Appendix E summarizes many currently available robot programming systems, including extended guiding, robot-level languages, and some research prototype task-level programming languages.

5 · Systems Implications

This chapter summarizes what we have learned and discusses the system implications to keep in mind when applying artificial intelligence techniques to a system design.

A.I. techniques are best used in problems involving:

1. No well-defined algorithmic solution
2. Some decision-making information available (for example, that the problem can at least be solved by a human being)
3. Large amounts of uncertainty
4. Missing and incorrect information

A.I. technology is concerned with organizing complex problem-solving systems, with representing knowledge efficiently, with flexible and efficient decision making that makes use of symbolic processing and both heuristic and (where applicable) algorithmic analysis, with informal knowledge (heuristics) and formal knowledge (algorithms), and with using metarules (generalized control rules) to direct the flow of tasks leading to the problem solution.

Many different A.I. system architectures may be designed to tackle a problem, including:

- Goal-directed or data-directed systems; for example, backward-chaining and forward-chaining production rule systems
- Inference network model; for example, the HARPY speech-understanding system design
- Template-driven; for example, the conceptual dependency templates used by Schank in his work on natural language understanding
- Model-driven; for example, the ACRONYM model-driven design
- Cooperative knowledge sources sharing a common blackboard; for example, the HEARSAY speech-understanding system design

196 ■ *SYSTEMS IMPLICATIONS*

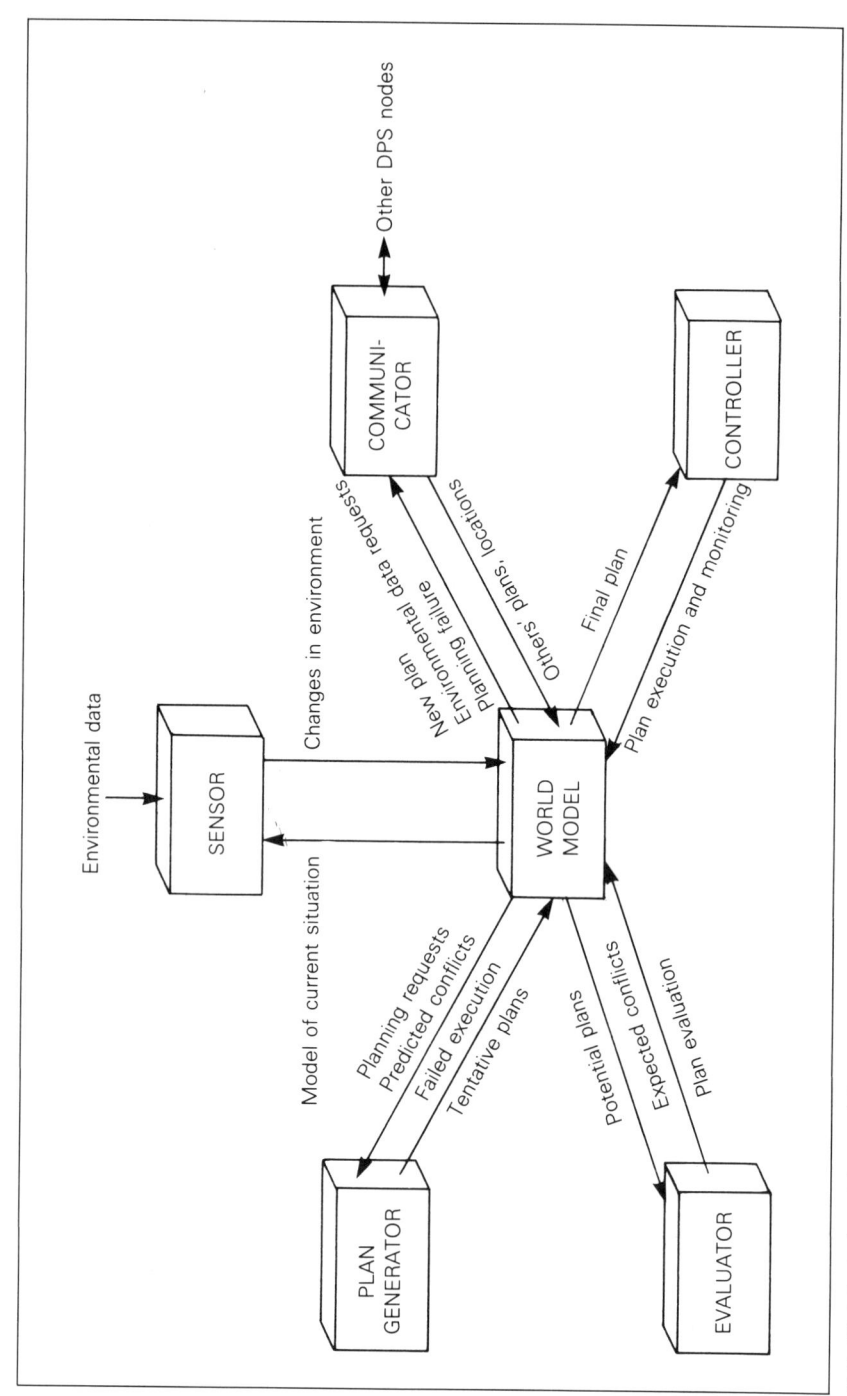

5-1. Distributed problem solving.

- Distributed problem solving; similar in concept to the HEARSAY system except that not only the tasks, but the control and even some of the detailed knowledge of the problem state are distributed across systems functionally and spatially. This is illustrated in figure 5-1, showing a pilot's assistant application.

No single system approach or technique works best in all cases; often a trade-off must be made between the generality of the problem solution and the performance achieved on a specific problem (the required processing and memory capacity). Figure 5-2 illustrates this trade-off for an application called TATR (Tactical Air Targeting and Reconnaissance) developed by Rand for the air force. The application was directed toward planning an aircraft's flight path and deployment of jammers and decoys to maximize its likelihood of surviving and completing its mission in the face of enemy opposition, most notably SAM (Surface-to-Air Missiles) sites. This application was written using the expert system shell ROSIE, developed by Rand. ROSIE was written in INTERLISP, a dialogue of LISP. The entire program was written, compiled, and run under the auspices of the general-purpose DEC-20 operating system, TOPS-20. If the program had been written in INTERLISP rather than ROSIE, it would probably have run much faster. ROSIE is a particularly inefficient system, using very large amounts of computer resources. INTERLISP also offers the designer the opportunity to take advantage of that language's increased flexibility to custom-design more efficient knowledge representation and control procedures for the problem

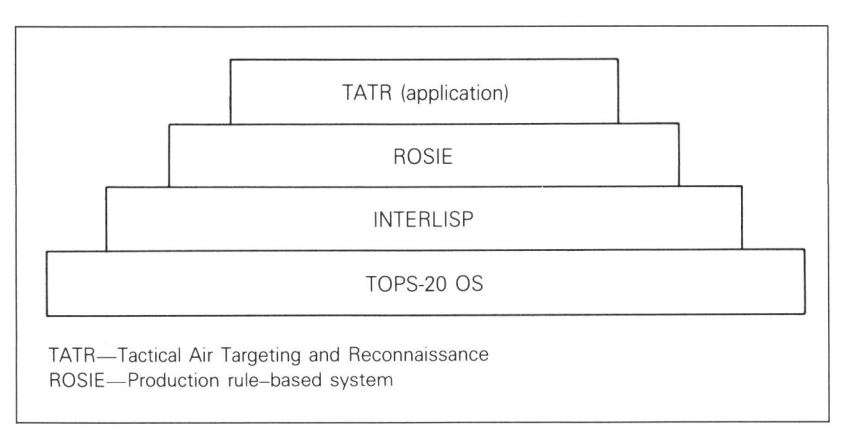

```
              TATR (application)
          ROSIE
      INTERLISP
   TOPS-20 OS
```

TATR—Tactical Air Targeting and Reconnaissance
ROSIE—Production rule–based system

5-2. Tool hierarchy.

at hand. Likewise, if the program had been written in C or ASSEMBLER, it would have run still faster and consumed far less resources. Unfortunately, it would also have taken much longer to design and program and would be harder to maintain or modify. Finally, use of the general-purpose operating system itself involves a great deal of overhead when contrasted with a more specialized operating system customized to the particular application, but using the general-purpose system allows for considerable savings in development time and convenience to the designer. These sorts of trade-offs will always be available to the system designer. In this case, speed of implementation of a prototype system, for minimum development cost, that would be easy to modify, were the overriding considerations.

Many of the system issues are not new. The choice of software tools is still influenced by:

- The maturity of the products
- The state of the documentation
- The user's familiarity with the product
- The compatibility of the product with existing hardware and software facilities and standards (for example, it would be desirable that selected software be compatible with existing hardware and software such as data bases, applications, operating systems, etc.)

Currently, LISP and PROLOG are still the most mature of the special A.I. tools. LISP is the more established, currently has better graphics and I/O capabilities, and has a more comprehensive systems environment, including interfaces with other software systems. A fairly extensive library of applications has been written in LISP, which, because of LISP's flexibility and adaptability, are easily shared and reused. Shapiro (1979) and Winston (1984) give examples of many of these programs. LISP, however, is being challenged by other higher-order tools, such as the expert system shells. The expert system shells OPS, S-1, and KEE have been around longest and have had the greatest use. ART, LOOPS, and KNOWLEDGE CRAFT are also frequently used.

The hardware and software selected must meet constraints on cost and performance. Unfortunately, the current crop of A.I. products are particularly deficient in this area. They still tend to be less efficient than more conventional computer products. There are no satisfactory performance standards or comparative evaluation tools for A.I. software, only some limited benchmarks prepared for some of the more popular computers used in A.I. applications development. One of the more well-known is the Stanford University benchmark series compiled by Richard Gabriel for DARPA, in which he compared several computers (VAX 780, Xerox Dandelion, Xerox Dolphin, Xerox Dorado, Symbolics 3600, Cray, Perq, LISP Machine, DEC 10, 68000) using twenty-four different programs, each exercising a different aspect of the LISP environment.

In addition, A.I. applications must be concerned with other, more specialized issues and features. Does the product have an explanation facility? Is there a natural language interface? What knowledge representation schemes are supported—production rules, semantic networks, frames, and the like?

Many currently available A.I. software products remain relatively immature. They are primarily an outgrowth of stand-alone academic prototypes designed to be used in a man-machine consultation mode that is not suitable for all commercial applications. Most have not adequately considered how to interface with the huge invested software base that already exists in industry. Many have not been completely validated and debugged. Only a handful of A.I. software tools are capable of handling continuous signal streams, real-time processing, multiple input-output events, and space/time models. In order for many A.I. applications to be successful, they will have to be designed as add-ons to existing systems.

Despite the tremendous progress being made, most A.I. software tools are slower than more conventional software, and specialized A.I. hardware is often relatively expensive and unnecessarily large for many of the applications. Figure 5-3 compares several A.I. software tools with respect to many of the criteria just discussed.

Applying A.I. involves learning many new skills and approaching old problems in new ways; this must be taken into account before an A.I. project is initiated. On the other hand, many traditional design approaches may be improved by incorporating techniques and lessons learned from A.I. For example, the traditional software engineering approach is to perform a top-level requirements analysis, followed by a top-level functional design, followed by a detailed design, followed by implementation, followed by a test-and-evaluation phase; A.I. technology, however, generally involves rapid prototyping and early fielding of a preliminary operational system, whose design is verified through actual trial and use rather than through review and sign-off of paper documents. The

	ART	EXPERT	KEE	KES	OPS5	TIMM
Knowledge representation	O.H., P.R.	P.R.	O.H., P.R., Frames	P.R., Frames, Stat.	P.R.	P.R.
Inference techniques	INH., forward/backward pattern match	Forward chaining	INH., forward/backward chaining	Backward chaining, Bayesian	Forward chaining	Forward
Explanation	yes	yes	yes	yes	no	?
KE support	Medium	Medium	Medium	Medium	Low	Low
Edit and debug	?	Trace	Comp.	Trace	LISP-like	Rule-consist.
Machine/languages	Symbolics, LMI, VAX, LISP	FORTRAN	LISP machines	VAX, Symbolics, LISP	VAX, Symbolics, LISP	FORTRAN
Externals	LISP	?	LISP	Yes	LISP	?
Cost	$45,000–60,000	N/A	$60,000	$4,000–23,000	$5,000–10,000	$40,000
Support	Yes	None	Yes	Yes	Depends on source	Yes

5-3. Comparison of software tool chart (as of July 1984).

requirements and design can thus evolve together in an evaluative environment much closer to the actual operational environment.

In fact, A.I. allows the user to task the system directly with an application requirement, rather than through an intermediary programmer or systems analyst. The system can communicate directly with the user in human language and terminology at the problem-domain, task-oriented level, developing in hours or days new application designs and outputs that would have taken a programmer weeks or months to implement and run successfully. This is clearly a preferred design mode for highly interactive man-machine systems and for new systems that have little historical precedence. It may also prove useful in the design or upgrading of more standard systems applications.

Environments in which this rapid prototyping is possible were first developed in A.I. and in computer graphics because these areas are particularly prone to specification instability. Dynamic typing of data is one of the features typical of A.I. and is available in LISP. The freedom to defer deciding the value until run-time is important, allowing the programmer to experiment with the type structure itself. As experience with the application evolves, the distinctions that determine type structure are selected after experimentation and so are usually the last to evolve. Dynamic typing makes it easy for the programmer to write a code that allows these decisions to be delayed as long as possible. This is one of the key reasons that LISP was recommended by Stanford Research Institute to the Department of Defense as the preferred research development language for A.I.

One characteristic of LISP that is particularly important for A.I. work is that the programs are represented in the same data structure as all other data, namely in a list structure. This simple device is of great importance to A.I. programs, whose purpose is often to manipulate other programs. For example, a program that is to explain its line of reasoning must examine its operation in reaching a conclusion. In most other programming languages, the executing program does not have access to the actual code, whereas any procedure in LISP can manipulate another procedure as easily as it can manipulate other data. Finally, because of their simple structure, LISP programs that produce other programs or high-level problem-solving languages as their output need not express their results in a complex format.

Figure 5-4 reviews some of the typical ways different organizations have prepared themselves for starting an A.I. program. Most importantly, top management should be honestly apprised of the magnitude of the

202 ■ SYSTEMS IMPLICATIONS

---

1. Flying start
   - Hire team of 4–8 competent A.I. practitioners
   - Buy several LISP machines with applications software
   - Create A.I. products quickly without outside help
2. Buy and build
   - Retain consultants to develop first applications
   - Build staff concurrently with system development
   - Buy LISP machines and applications software either as soon as possible or when staff is ready
   - Prepare to develop all systems in-house ultimately
3. Build from within
   - Build A.I. capabilities by training existing staff
   - Buy LISP machines and applications software to build expertise to develop products
   - Develop products slowly
4. Test the waters
   - Start small in-house A.I. group, train 1–2 people
   - Buy LISP machine when A.I. staff is competent and when specific need is manifest
   - Initial activities: R&D, with real applications further down the road

5-4. Examples of models for starting A.I. programs.

---

investment with respect to time, people, money, and training before any project is initiated. The resources required to launch a typical A.I. project are not insignificant and should not be understated. Success depends on the efforts of a team that has adequate A.I. expertise (still a relatively scarce commodity), full cooperation from top management, and adequate computer/software resources.

It is generally a good idea to have some near-term output, since a good demonstration goes a long way toward educating management. The application chosen should be an appropriate one for A.I.—one that has a reasonable chance of succeeding, that is unfeasible through more traditional approaches, and that offers a significant payoff. Figure 5-5 illustrates a typical five-phase program; figures 5-6, 5-7, and 5-8 illustrate the skills required of the team that will build this system, the training time the team will need (this varies according to the makeup, numbers, and background of the team), and typical budgets involved. Depending

> 1. Develop a demonstration system—three months, 2-3 FTEs
>   - Small system on A.I. machine
>   - Shows feasibility and relevance
> 2. Develop a preprototype—four months, 3-4 FTEs
>   - Larger system on A.I. machine
>   - Only operable by developers
> 3. Build prototype—five months, 4-5 FTEs
>   - Use fully large system, still on A.I. machines
>   - Operable by trained users in the field
> 4. Complete deployable system—twelve months, 6-8 FTEs
>   - Full-scale system, tested on target medium
>   - Fully integrated with users and MIS
>   - Fully designed systems and procedures for exploiting system
> 5. Deploy system—six months, large team
>   - Build and install networks and work stations
>   - Train users
>   - Charge business to take advance of system
> 6. Maintain and expand—indefinitely, 1-3 FTEs
>   - Expand knowledge base
>   - Find and correct undesirable aspects
>
> Total to build a KBS: twenty-four calendar months—11-person team Expectations are that these requirements may be halved within next five years.

5-5. How do we build KBS?

> - A.I. project management
> - Domain expertise
> - Work function analysis
> - Knowledge acquisition
> - Knowledge representation
> - A.I. programming
> - A.I. methodology and technology expertise
> - A.I. system maintenance and development
> - MIS integration
> - A.I. business analysis
> - Supporting communication services skills (secretarial, video technician, librarian)

5-6. Skills required to build KBS.

	Months to Reach Competence to:		
Skill	Work as Apprentice	Work as Team	Work Alone
Knowledge acquisition	1	2	3
Knowledge representation	2	3	5
KBS design	3	6	12
A.I. programming	3	6	12
General A.I. theories and techniques	6	9	12
Expert A.I. practitioner	12	24	60
A.I. systems maintenance	1	3	6

It is assumed that professionals to be trained in A.I. have no previous A.I. expertise but have a broad, solid background (Masters degree or Ph.D.) in some relevant area such as computer sciences, experimental psychology, mathematical logic, etc., and spend full time (40- to 60-hour week) in preparation.

5-7. Time required to prepare to do A.I. work.

Internal manpower
 First year: 2–4 FTE = salaries of $35K $200K
 Second year: 3–6 FTE $350K
Equipment budget: $200K–$400K
 1–2 LISP machines $150K
 File server $ 60K
 Network host $ 20K
 (1 LISP machine per 1.5–2 FTE) $230K
 Outside assistance (depends upon scope and urgency) $50–500K

Typical budget commitments for two years are above $1 million.

5-8. Typical budgets for starting A.I. groups.

on the complexity of the problem addressed and the similarity of the proposed system to an existing system, some of these steps may be skipped or accelerated, but in general these figures are representative of the kind of commitment required today.

6 ▪ *Future Prospects*

The future should see a dramatic increase in the number of A.I. applications. This is due to many factors.

First, the capability of the hardware has increased dramatically, while its cost has decreased. Figures 6-1 and 6-2 show some projections of future hardware trends. Hardware that used to cost millions of dollars and occupy an entire room in the early days of A.I. research can now fit on a desk top and cost a few thousand dollars.

Second, industry is more aware of the technology. Knowledge of the techniques is more widespread, and A.I. expertise is more readily available. Third, the underlying principles of the technology are better understood and appreciated. Fourth, the necessary tools are improving in capability, dropping in cost, and increasing in availability. Fifth, the number of successful applications and offerings is growing, stimulating more applications and encouraging further development. Sixth, more specialized hardware and software are being developed for A.I. applications, making them easier and more cost-effective to implement.

Finally, several important major new architectural thrusts are aimed toward making A.I. more practical and affordable. Japan's fifth-generation project (figures 6-3, 6-4, and 6-5) has, since its inception in 1982, already produced a personal sequential inference machine (PSIM) that is optimized to run KL-0 (kernel language zero), a variant of PROLOG. PSIM is capable of 30K logical inferences per second (lips), 16M words, and 32-bit logical address. One lips, which can be thought of as the matching and instantiation of a single condition in a logical clause, has been equated to approximately 1,000 computer operations per second, and 30K lips represent the kind of processing power found at the high end of current commercially available LISP machines.

Fujitsu's LISP machine, ALPHA, is an outgrowth of the fifth-generation project, as is a relational data base machine, DELTA. The project's long-term goals include producing a parallel-processing inference engine

206 ■ FUTURE PROSPECTS

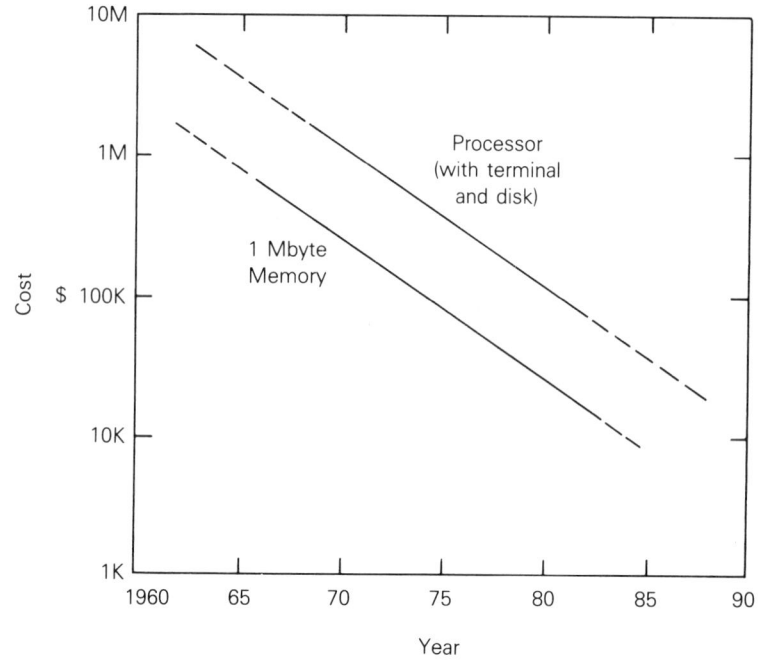

6-1. A.I. equipment trends.

that consists of over 1,000 processing elements optimized around a parallel version of KL-0 called KL-1, which can process 100M–1G lips and store over 100M facts and 20K rules. The data-flow architecture, based upon MIT research, is the preferred architecture under investigation for this inference engine. Also targeted in the project is an intelligent interface system with natural language speech, highly interactive graphics interfaces, and a knowledge base management system for intelligent information retrieval.

The Microelectronics and Computer Technology Corporation (MCC) is American industry's answer to this fifth-generation program. It consists of a research group investigating research in VLSI design, artificial intelligence, and other high-technology fields related to the computer industry. It is supported through the contributions of many of the leading U.S. companies in the electronics industry (IBM is not a member). The participating members will share in the fruits of the research. The current minimum contribution is $1 million.

The U.S. Department of Defense has also launched an ambitious project to accelerate A.I. research in support of the military. The main program is the DARPA Strategic Computing Program (outlined in figure

Future Prospects ■ 207

	1983	1985	1990	2000
Processors	One 16/32-bit Two 8-bitters	Three 32-bitters Many 8-bitters	Many 32-bitters	Many Parallel Processors
Main Memory	1 Mbyte	4 Mbytes	16 Mbytes	64 Mbytes
Local Bulk Memory	50 Mbytes	450 Mbytes	5 Gbytes	50 Gbytes
Display	1,000 × 1,000, b&w	1,000 × 1,000, color	2,000 × 2,000, color	4,000 × 4,000, color
Speech Recognition	No	No	Limited vocabulary	Very large vocabulary
Network	10 Mbytes/sec.	10 Mbytes/sec.	100 Mbytes/sec.	1,000 Mbytes/sec.
Imbedded Knowledge-based Systems	None	None	4/6	10/20
Total Price	$18K	$16K	$14K	$12K
Price in 1984 $	$18K	$15K	$10K	$5K

6-2. What will top-of-the-line work stations be?

Goal: To develop by the 1990s a supercomputer with 10^{12} bytes of main memory and capable of 10^9 logical inferences per second (lips)

Themes and Subthemes:

Basic application systems	1	1-1) Machine translation system 1-2) Question-answering system 1-3) Applied speech-understanding system 1-4) Applied picture- and image-understanding system 1-5) Applied problem-solving system
Basic software systems	2	2-1) Knowledge base management system 2-2) Problem-solving and inference system 2-3) Intelligent interface system
New advanced architecture	3	3-1) Logic programming machine 3-2) Functional machine 3-3) Relational algebra machine 3-4) Abstract data-type support machine 3-5) Data-flow machine 3-6) Innovative von Neumann machine
Distributed functional architecture	4	4-1) Distributed function architecture 4-2) Network architecture 4-3) Data base machine 4-4) High-speed numerical computation machine 4-5) High-level man-machine communication machine
VLSI technology	5	5-1) VLSI architecture 5-2) Intelligent VLSI CAD system
Systematization technology	6	6-1) Intelligent programming system 6-2) Knowledge base design system 6-3) Systematization technology for computer architecture 6-4) Data base and distributed data base system
Development supporting technology	7	7-1) Development support system

6-3. ICOT's fifth-generation project. (From A.I. Symposium: Intelligence Applications of A.I.—The Japanese Fifth Generation Computing Project, by J. Robinson. 1983. Reprinted with permission.)

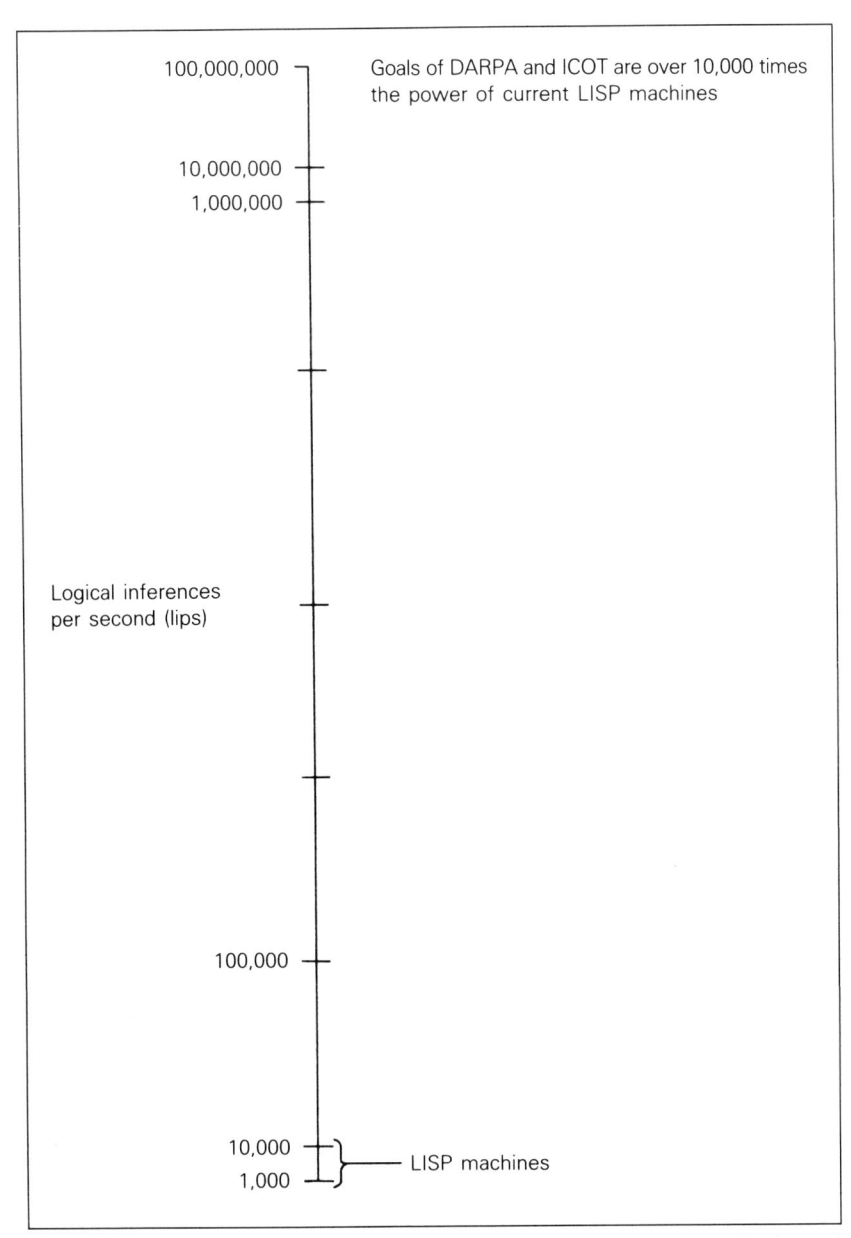

Future Prospects ■ 209

```
100,000,000 ─┐  Goals of DARPA and ICOT are over 10,000 times
              the power of current LISP machines
 10,000,000 ─┤
  1,000,000 ─┤




Logical inferences
per second (lips)




    100,000 ─┤




     10,000 ─┤⎫
      1,000 ─┘⎭── LISP machines
```

6-4. Symbolic processing goals. (From A.I. Symposium: Intelligence Applications of A.I.—DARPA Strategic Computing Program, by R. Kahn. 1983. Reprinted with permission.)

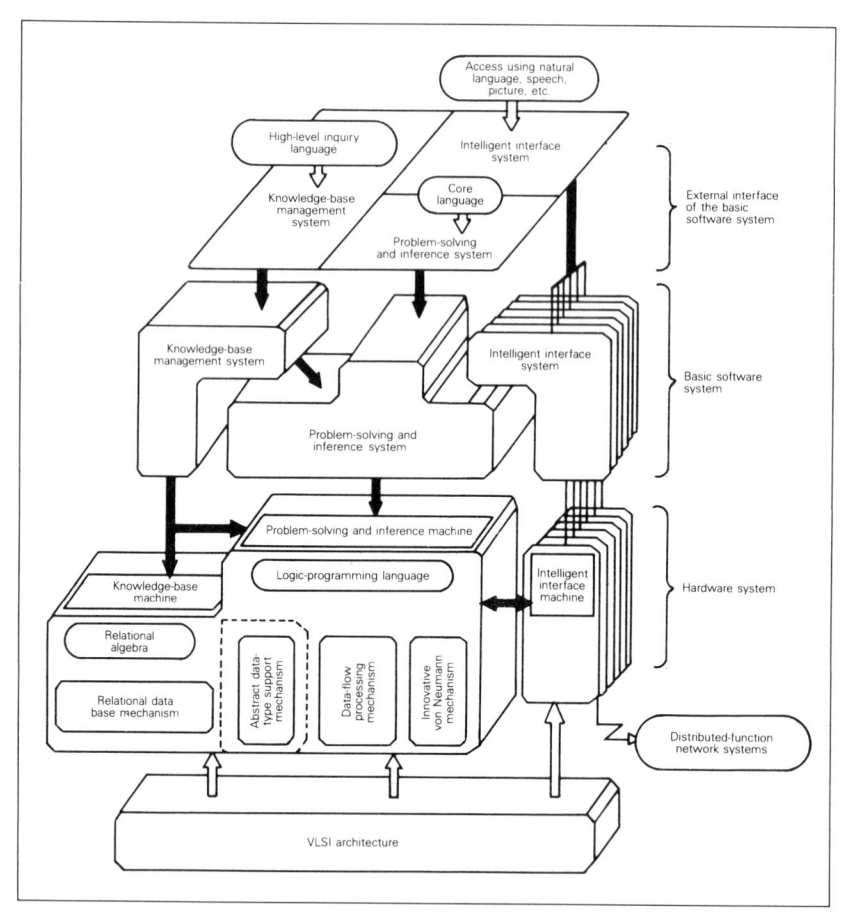

6-5. Basic configuration of fifth-generation systems.

6-6), but many other important research efforts are being independently sponsored by the army, the navy, and the air force, as well as by NASA, DOE, and the National Science Foundation. The goal of the strategic computing program is to produce an advanced A.I. computer capable of 10^8 lips by 1990–94, with an initial stand-alone system in the near term capable of 4–12K lips.

DARPA is sponsoring several applications of this technology, as shown in figure 6-7, the main three being an autonomous land vehicle for the army, a pilot's associate for the air force, and a battle management system for the navy. DARPA is also funding Intellicorp and Teknowledge to develop advanced A.I. software tools. The A.I. system capabilities being developed are needed for each of these three major military

Pyramid Diagram

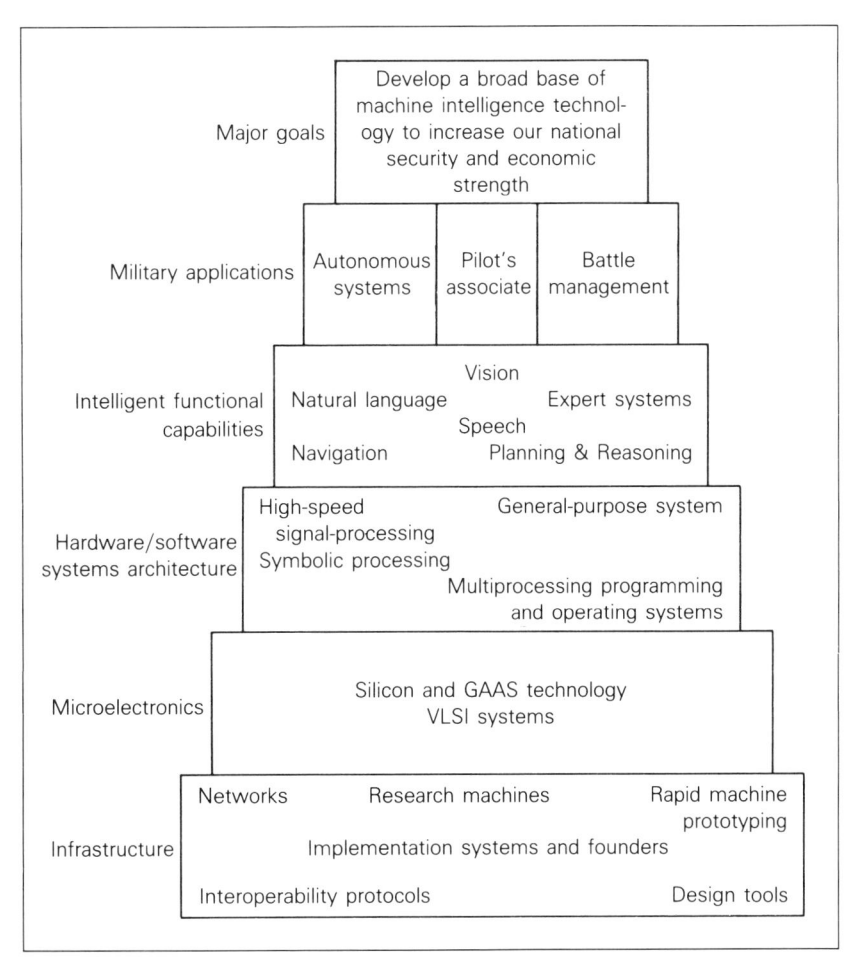

Major goals: Develop a broad base of machine intelligence technology to increase our national security and economic strength

Military applications: Autonomous systems | Pilot's associate | Battle management

Intelligent functional capabilities: Natural language, Vision, Expert systems, Speech, Navigation, Planning & Reasoning

Hardware/software systems architecture: High-speed signal-processing, General-purpose system, Symbolic processing, Multiprocessing programming and operating systems

Microelectronics: Silicon and GAAS technology, VLSI systems

Infrastructure: Networks, Research machines, Rapid machine prototyping, Implementation systems and founders, Interoperability protocols, Design tools

6-6. Outline of DARPA strategic computing program. (From A.I. Symposium: Intelligence Applications of A.I.—DARPA Strategic Computing Program, by R. Kahn. 1983. Reprinted with permission.)

applications, as well as for such uses as terminal homing, automated design and analysis, and war games.

Other U.S. government–sponsored programs are summarized in figure 6-8. They include such programs as the NSF-sponsored supercomputer project, and a navy contract with Texas Instruments to develop a custom LISP processor chip using 2 micron CMOS technology.

Great Britain is working on its own program, the ALVEY program. It involves the design of a parallel computing machine and has four demonstration projects: an automated factory that integrates design and

	Autonomous vehicle	Battle management & assessment	Pilot's assistant	Terminal homing	Automated design & analysis	Wargaming
Vision	R	O		R		
Speech		O	R			
Natural language	R	R			O	R
Information fusion	R	R	R			
Planning & reasoning	R	R	R		R	R
Signal interpretation	R	R	R			
Navigation	R			R		
Simulation/modeling	R	R			R	R
Graphics/display		R	R		R	R
DS/IM/KS	R	R	R	R	R	R
Dist. communication	R	R	R			R
System control	R	O	R	R		

R = Required capability
O = Optional capability

6-7. Matrix of systems capabilities versus military applications. (From A.I. Symposium: Intelligence Applications of A.I.—DARPA Strategic Computing Program, by R. Kahn. 1983. Reprinted with permission.)

Research area	Types of applications	Number of projects Army	Number of projects Navy	Number of projects Air Force	FY '83 funding ($100K)
Knowledge presentation and display	Expert systems Decisions aids Knowledge representation Information presentation	5	22	14	5,464
Knowledge acquisition and information fusion	Knowledge acquisition Information fusion Intelligence fusion	0	11	6	1,138
Planning and problem solving	Problem solving Distributed problem solving Reasoning, evaluation, and choosing Logistical planning support	0	11	1	935
Target classification and recognition	Signal recognition Pattern recognition	1	14	5	1,444
Speech and natural language understanding	Voice recognition Voice control Natural language C	1	15	4	1,999
Image understanding	Image understanding	2	2	3	1,500
Robotics	Robotics	8	0	2	2,200
Equipment maintenance	Very reliable electronics maintenance, diagnosis, and repair	0	4	2	455
Programming and software development	Programming aids software production	0	2	8	1,267
Training and simulation	Training and simulation	0	7	2	1,320

6-8. Ongoing research in applying artificial intelligence technology to military problems.

production systems; an expert system for interpreting rules that govern welfare payments; a voice-driven typewriter; and an intelligent system that would provide route guidance to drivers in vehicles equipped with electronic maps.

Britain also belongs to the European Common Market program called ESPRIT (European Strategic Program for Research in Information Technologies), a $1.3 billion European Common Market program with over 104 projects spread over 265 separate organizations, including IBM Germany; DEC Germany; AT&T teamed with N.V. Phillips, ITT's Belgian subsidiary; and Bell Telephone Labs.

France and Germany have their own national programs, in addition to belonging to ESPRIT. The Scandinavian countries also have their own national programs; for example, Sweden launched a national microelectronics program in 1984, and in 1985 she founded the Institute of Applied Computer Science and its fifth-generation computer development program.

Even the Soviet Union has launched its own version of a national research program in A.I. Part of the Soviets' third five-year program for computing highlights fifth-generation technologies. This program, which will run until the end of 1989, involves a strong collaboration between the U.S.S.R. and its six East European partners in the Council for Economic Mutual Assistance (CEMA). The Moscow Academy of Sciences will coordinate the program, which will cover five strategic design areas:

1. Design and manufacture of VLSI microprocessors
2. Development of parallel and multiprocessor architectures
3. Design of operating systems to increase support of logic programming
4. Creation of problem-solving software
5. Development of expert systems and user-responsive applications

The performance goals of these programs are orders of magnitude greater than the capabilities of today's systems, but they still fall short of human performance levels in all respects except individual processing element speeds. These goals represent the kind of processing performance and capacity believed necessary to achieve a minimum level of human-style intelligence. Human experts are believed to apply as many as 50,000 chunks (rules) to solve a typical problem. Even to master a minimum 10,000-word vocabulary (comparable to an elementary school student's vocabulary) requires over 1 Gbyte of knowledge. These facts are summarized in figure 6-9.

> CURRENT A.I. PROGRAMS
> - 1–2M words
> - 30 rules/sec., 600–1000 matches/sec.
> - 1,000 instructions/sec. = 1 lips
>
> STANDARD HUMAN VOCABULARY
> - 10K words
> - 150 bytes/word definition
> - 10–100X semantic relationships
> - 11.5×10^8 bytes
>
> HUMAN BRAIN
> - 10 billion neurons, 10–30% useful for intelligent functions
> - 10–30 billion bytes
> - 10 miles/hr.
> - 1,000–10,000 inputs/neuron
> - 100 trillion interconnections

6-9. Comparisons between human and artificial intelligence.

In order to achieve the kind of impressive performance goals set by the above programs, some kind of parallel-processing, non–Von Neumann architecture will probably be required. The signal transmission speed in silicon is less than 3×10^7 meters/sec. Today's chips are about 3 centimeters (slightly over an inch) in diameter, so they can produce signals in 10^{-9} seconds. They are therefore capable of about 10^9 floating point operations per second, or approximately 1G flops. Current supercomputers are within a factor of ten of this limit. Furthermore, the speed of light, which is 183×10^8 meters/second, represents an upper limit to the speed of any single processing element. These limits cause us to look at parallelism as a means of breaking through processing barriers. After all, the human processor is a highly parallel associative processor. Some of the more promising research directions include the following (IJCAA 1985):

- CMU's semantic network computer, the Boltzman machine
- CMU's production machine (tree-type interconnections)
- Cal Tech's hypercube
- MIT's connection and Mega machines
- MIT's data flow machine—MIT researchers Dennis and Arvind originated much of the work on the data-flow model of computation. This model discovers opportunities for concurrent execution of fine-grain tasks by requiring the user to employ a functional language. A data-

flow computer is not a sequential program; any instruction becomes enabled (ready to execute) as soon as all input values (tokens) become available at the outputs of some execution unit. A data-flow computer has multiple execution units of various types, with outputs that can be interconnected to any of their inputs via a switchable interconnecting machine.
- Columbia's Non-Von and DADO architectures (Shaw and Stolfo)—These architectural approaches are based upon a tree type of interconnection, a very efficient VLSI interconnection to manufacture. This research takes advantage of its tree-type interconnection architecture by compiling a rule set into a decision tree, where the leaves are the rules corresponding to that particular sequence of object-attribute condition tests. The OPS compiler operates on this principle (Forgy 1979).
- NYU's ultra-computer, which involves distributed processing, where the memory is treated as a global shared resource
- University of Tokyo's associative data base machine, Paralog
- Fermi Lab's Advanced Computer Project (tree-type interconnections)
- Teradata's data base machine (tree-type interconnections)

Commercial startups, such as Minsky's Thinking Machine Inc., are independently pursuing the design of these advanced parallel inference machines. Thinking Machines Inc. has developed a 64,000-processor parallel system called the connection machine, based on MIT research.

In addition, Intel, Ametek Computer, and N Cube have designs based on Cal Tech's hypercube concept. Bolt Beranek and Newman (BBN) has developed the Butterfly system with global memory and distributed processing. Goodyear Aerospace has its Massively Parallel Processor, with single-instruction multiple data stream architecture. Goodyear has delivered a 16,384-processor version of this machine for NASA, which has been in operation since mid-1983. IBM has its twelve-node Research Parallel Processor System, called RP3. It is based partially on NYU's ultra machine. IBM is also sponsoring six other experiments in variants of parallel-processing architectures. Electrotechnical Lab of Japan's NTT is building SIGMA1, a data-flow machine.

Many difficulties must be overcome. For tasks with heavy I/O demands, set-up time (time to read in data from disk or tape) creates a problem. Moreover, some portion of a problem must always remain serial, and this represents an absolute upper limit on performance. Many of the currently proposed parallel-processing systems are awkward to program, requiring recognition of the presence of multiple processors. Often the parallel processor cannot act independently and must be attached to a conventional host computer to distribute the data and programs to the multiple-processing nodes and to collect the results. By far the key problem preventing the acceptance of parallel systems is the lack of effective applications software development tools and parallel debugging tools.

Regardless of the ultimate success of these programs, the next generation of computers will certainly be much more efficient at performing A.I. functions than current systems are, and we will most likely see the emergence of A.I. as a major force in the computer industry. A.I. technology, however, will merge with and become an integrated part of numerous product offerings. Figure 6-10 illustrates the categories of A.I. applications we are likely to find in the future; these categories will include many products with embedded knowledge-based systems.

COMMODITY SYSTEMS

Systems that are widely used in a single manifestation. Examples:
- Expert systems included in automobiles
- Expert systems in home appliances and in office machines such as copiers

GENERIC SYSTEMS

Systems marketed to many customers for access by many users. Examples:
- Natural language data base advisory and access systems
- Tax advisory systems provided by financial institutions
- Medical knowledge-based systems

CORPORATE SYSTEMS

Systems developed for a single corporation for broad in-house use. Examples:
- Customer services advisory system for banks
- Product configuration advisory system
- Planning and budgeting expert system

PERSONALIZED SYSTEMS

Systems developed for dedicated use by one or a few highly specialized workers. Examples:
- Shop floor scheduling knowledge-based systems
- Strategic management of technology expert systems
- Traffic manager advisory system

6-10. Categories of A.I. applications.

218 ■ *FUTURE PROSPECTS*

Some of the more likely areas for embedded knowledge-based systems are shown in figure 6-11.

The A.I. industry will grow and merge with the general computer industry so that future "conventional" computer systems, development tools, building blocks, and computer-based applications will be steeped in A.I. technology. Figure 6-12 summarizes the A.I. products that are likely to be traded in the future. The functionality of a typical work station of the future is depicted in figure 6-13. These will likely revolutionize offices by offering such capabilities as direct entry of correspondence or documents, grammatical structuring, and synonym substitution; a restructuring of the office work force is a predictable consequence of these innovations. They will make possible a new form of knowledge industry that includes intelligent textbooks and manuals capable of capturing the corporate knowledge asset and the active

---

IN WORK STATIONS
- Speech recognition and synthesis
- Natural language recognition
- Text creation aids ("writer workbench")
- Text management

IN INSTRUMENTS
- Medical instruments to provide diagnoses
- Physical measurement guidance (CRTs, NMR scanners)
- Test devices

IN APPLIANCES
- Copiers (recirculating copiers)
- Microwave ovens to dishwashers for operator guidance and appliance control

IN INDUSTRY
- Intelligent robotics
- Visual inspection systems
- Process sensors and inferential control

IN VEHICLES (CARS, AIRPLANES)
- Operations control on first and supervisory levels
- Collision avoidance
- Communication, including recognizing incoming messages

MILITARY APPLICATIONS

6-11. Where will we find embedded knowledge-based systems?

COMPUTERS
- Large development systems
- Small development systems
- Work stations
- Large central A.I. processors
- Imbedded and portable systems

A.I. DEVELOPMENTS—TOOLS AND BUILDING BLOCKS
- A.I. languages (LISP, PROLOG, etc.)
- Specialized building blocks—graphics systems, inference engines, DBMS, etc.
- Knowledge-based systems development environments
- Knowledge bases (Lexica, Tax Laws, etc.)

APPLICATION SYSTEMS
- Knowledge-based systems
- Natural language systems
- Computer-aided instructions
- Vision systems
- Robotics
- Software development environments

6-12. A.I. products that may eventually be incorporated into "conventional" computer systems.

knowledge product, a system that alerts the user to new and unusual information situations it encounters as it reports and maintains data. This new industry will make automated expert advice available and affordable to everyone, changing the roles of many traditional professionals (Schutzer 1985).

Many social and legal issues surround these likely changes, and a great contrast in opinion regarding the nature and future of this new technology can be found. For example, consider the following two contrasting quotes:

> *Business Week* (July 9, 1984)—That dramatic feat [referring to PROSPECTOR] was the first demonstration that revolutionary kinds of computerized helpers called expert systems could have vast commercial potential.
>
> *Fortune* (August 20, 1984)—Why Computers Can't Outthink the Experts: Programs called expert systems are being ballyhooed as the hottest technology around. While useful for some tasks, the systems

220 ■ *FUTURE PROSPECTS*

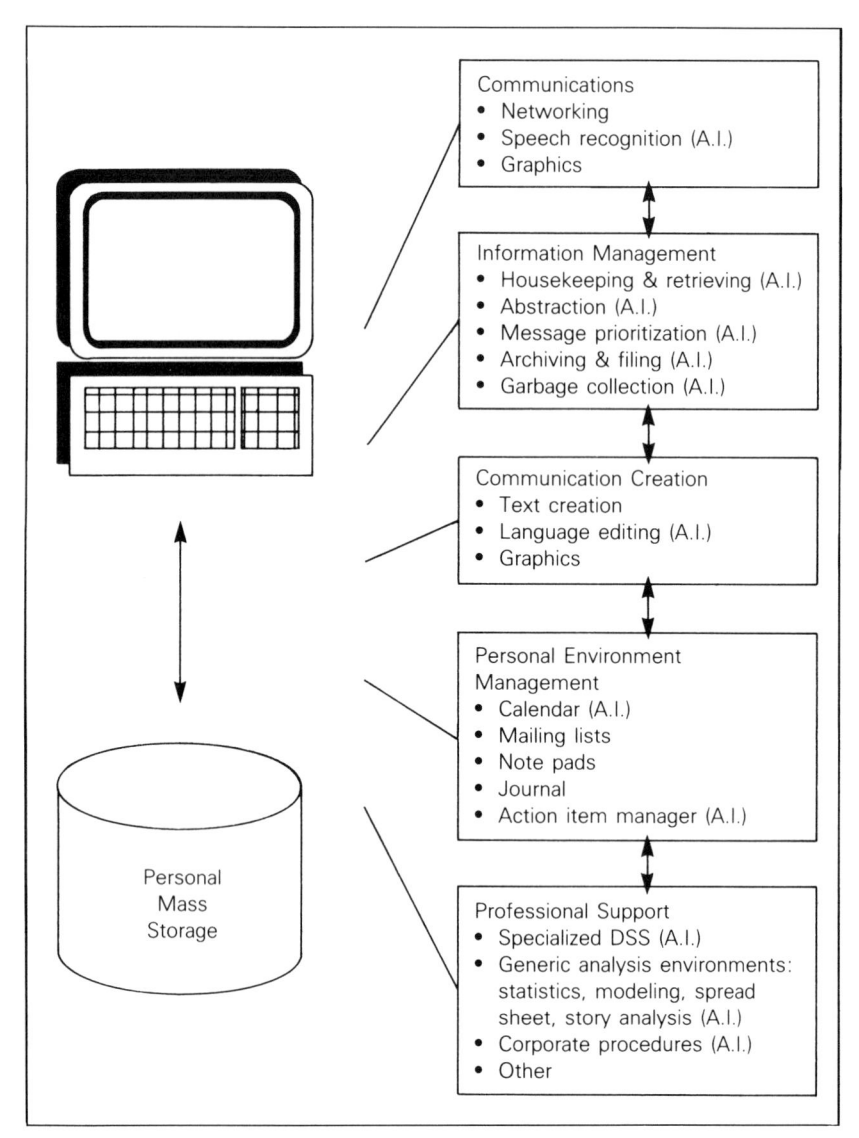

Communications
- Networking
- Speech recognition (A.I.)
- Graphics

Information Management
- Housekeeping & retrieving (A.I.)
- Abstraction (A.I.)
- Message prioritization (A.I.)
- Archiving & filing (A.I.)
- Garbage collection (A.I.)

Communication Creation
- Text creation
- Language editing (A.I.)
- Graphics

Personal Environment Management
- Calendar (A.I.)
- Mailing lists
- Note pads
- Journal
- Action item manager (A.I.)

Professional Support
- Specialized DSS (A.I.)
- Generic analysis environments: statistics, modeling, spread sheet, story analysis (A.I.)
- Corporate procedures (A.I.)
- Other

Personal Mass Storage

6-13. Selected work-station tasks.

aren't as smart as they sound. We'll keep needing old-fashioned specialists whose intelligence isn't artificial.

The truth lies somewhere in the middle. The problems being tackled by A.I. are difficult and will not be solved overnight. Moreover, people are slow to accept revolutionary changes; they prefer the familiar to the new, even when the new is superior. This phenomenon, known as historical precedence, represents a strong force in people for maintaining the status quo. For example, why switch to a new word processor and have to learn a new set of commands—even if the new word processor is better—when the old word processor is adequate? Because some useful capabilities that A.I. technology offers cannot be achieved with more conventional computer technology, however, progress is likely. Still, the progress will be evolutionary, not abrupt, and we will probably talk less about A.I. and instead simply begin describing powerful new applications.

Appendix A.
Summary of A.I. Research

This summary is organized into the following application-area categories:

Programming and computing
Medicine
Engineering and science
Military command and control, correlation and fusion
Education
Computer systems
Mathematics
Business, economics
Machine perception: natural language, speech, and image understanding
Knowledge engineering

■ APPLICATION: COMPUTING

SYSTEM	RESEARCHERS	DESCRIPTION
PSI	Cordell Green, et al. (Kestrel Institute and Stanford)	Autoprogramming through natural language dialogue
LIBRA	E. Kant (CMU)	Efficiency-analysis component of PSI
PECOS	D.R. Barstow (Schlumberger)	Knowledge-based program synthesizer for PSI
AURA	Argonne National Lab and Northern Illinois University	Automated reasoning assistant, automatic programming aid
Programmers Workbench	R.C. Waters, MIT	Smart programmers' library and programmers' interface

■ APPLICATION: MEDICINE

SYSTEM	RESEARCHERS	DESCRIPTION
INTERNIST (CADUCEUS)	J.D. Myers, H.E. Pople (University of Pittsburgh)	Internal medicine diagnostic consultant
MYCIN	E.H. Shortliffe (Stanford)	Diagnoses bacterial infections and prescribes antibiotic treatment
ONCOCIN	E.H. Shortliffe (Stanford)	Assists in treating cancer patients, guides management of complex drug regimens
PUFF and CENTAUR	J.C. Kunz (Stanford)	Helps identify possible lung disorders (derivative of MYCIN)
RX	R.L. Blum (Stanford)	Helps guide statistical analysis of chronic-disease patients' histories
VM (Ventilator Manager)	L.M. Fagan (Stanford)	Uses physiological transfers from patients to help guide when to take a patient off the ventilator
PIP	S.G. Pauker, et al.	Medicine diagnosis
CASNET	S.M. Weiss, et al.	Medicine diagnosis

■ APPLICATION: ENGINEERING & SCIENCE

SYSTEM	RESEARCHERS	DESCRIPTION
SACON	J.S. Bennett, R.S. Engelmore (Stanford)	Structured analysis consultant
AL/X	D. Michie (Univ. of Edinburgh)	Fault diagnosis
META-DENDRAL, DENDRAL	Lederberg, E.A. Feigenbaum, B.G. Buchanan (Stanford)	Uses mass-spectrometry data to induce rules about behavior of fragmented molecules (earlier version DENDRAL had search capability only)

Summary of A.I. Research: Engineering & Science ■ **225**

SYSTEM	RESEARCHERS	DESCRIPTION
MOLGEN	J. Lederberg, M. Stefik (Stanford)	Helps geneticists plan experiments involving structural analysis and synthesis of DNA
SECHS	Wipke	Chemistry data search
SYNCHEM	Gelernter, et al.	Chemistry data search
CRYSALIS (SU/P)	Engelmore, Terry	Chemistry understanding
EL	Stallman, Sussman (MIT)	Electronic circuit analysis, problem solving, and planning
MECHO	Bundy, et al.	Mechanics problem solving and planning
PROSPECTOR	R.E. Hart, R.O. Duda (SRI)	Evaluates sites for potential mineral deposits; based on CBC (computer-based consultant), which diagnoses electromechanical equipment—geology
DIPMETER ADVISOR	Schlumberger	Analyzes information from oil well logs—geology
NOAH	E.D. Sacerdoti	Planning and problem solving—robotics application
BACON	P. Langley	Induces general laws of physics from empirical data
VLSI	Stanford	Research toward designing VLSI circuits
DART	Joint, Stanford and IBM	Uses explicit causal, structural, teleological knowledge about computer systems in diagnosing hardware faults
LOGIN	Joint, Stanford and Schlumberger	Analyzes information from oil well logs

APPLICATION: MILITARY COMMAND AND CONTROL, CORRELATION AND FUSION

SYSTEM	RESEARCHERS	DESCRIPTION
SIAP [formerly SU/X, HASP]	H.P. Nii, E.A. Feigenbaum (SCI/Acoustic Research Center and Stanford)	Identifies and evaluates moving objects (location, velocity, etc.) from primary signal data (primarily acoustic data)
MSIS	Garvey, Fischler	Multisensor integration and interpretation system (early stage of development)
AIPS	BBN	Advanced information presentation system—graphics, maps, tables, window-oriented; built on KL-ONE

APPLICATION: EDUCATION

SYSTEM	RESEARCHERS	DESCRIPTION
GUIDON	W.J. Clancey (Stanford)	Computer-aided instruction, primarily medicine; over 700 rules, based on MYCIN, initial version 1979
SOPHIE	Brown	Computer-aided instruction, primarily electronics

APPLICATION: COMPUTER SYSTEMS

SYSTEM	RESEARCHERS	DESCRIPTION
RI (XCON)	J. McDermott (Carnegie-Mellon University)	Determines relations among computer components for VAX machines primarily; includes sizing

SYSTEM	RESEARCHERS	DESCRIPTION
XSEL	J. McDermott (Carnegie-Mellon University)	Extension to RI—assists computer sales personnel
DART	Joint, Stanford and IBM	Computer-assisted fault diagnostic assistance
PALLADEO	Joint, Xerox, Stanford, and Fairchild	Chip-design system

■ APPLICATION: MATHEMATICS

SYSTEM	RESEARCHERS	DESCRIPTION
MACSYMA	W. Martin, J. Moses, C. Engleman (MIT)	Symbolic manipulations, algebraic computations, integrations, etc.
AM	D. Lenat (Stanford)	Mathematics learning—discovers new concepts

■ APPLICATION: BUSINESS, ECONOMICS

SYSTEM	RESEARCHERS	DESCRIPTION
COMEX	Stansfield	Business
TESTBED	Rosenberg	Operations research
INDUCE	Dietterich, Michalski	Agriculture learning
OIL	Coles, et al. (SRI)	Oil price simulation implemented 1975; uses qualitative rule-based political model of OPEC pricing decisions to derive quantitative, econometric model of global oil demand, supply, and revenue; approximately 90 rules derived from news media; numerical factors weigh credibility of source, importance, and plausibility of rule, re-

APPENDIX A

SYSTEM	RESEARCHERS	DESCRIPTION
		alism of time intervals; primarily feasibility study of general hybrid-system concepts
FOLIO	Cohen	Investment portfolio manager

APPLICATION: MACHINE PERCEPTION—NATURAL LANGUAGE, SPEECH, AND IMAGE UNDERSTANDING

SYSTEM	RESEARCHERS	DESCRIPTION
ACRONYM	Brooks, Binford (Stanford)	Image understanding
HEARSAY II	Reddy, et al. (Carnegie-Mellon University)	Speech understanding
HARPY	Reddy, Baker, et al. (Carnegie-Mellon University)	Speech understanding
SHRDLU	T. Winograd	Natural language, front end for block world; sentences analogous to programs to carry out various block tasks
PHLIQA 1	Phillips Research Labs	Natural language question answering system
FRUMP	Yale	Can read story, extract and store concepts in symbolic form, and generate summary story
LUNAR	Woods (BBN)	Natural language front end for moon rock sample data base
LADDER/ LIFER	Hendrix (SRI)	Natural language front end; user interface to external data systems (used, among others, as 1,000-rule Navy data base)

Summary of A.I. Research: Machine Perception

SYSTEM	RESEARCHERS	DESCRIPTION
PLANES	University of Illinois, David Walls	Natural language front end for aircraft maintenance data base
NLPQ	G. Heidorn	Natural language front end to a simulation model generator
MARGIE	R. Schank (Yale)	Natural language data base front end—introduced "primitives of conceptual dependency" idea
REL	Thompson, et al. (Cal Tech)	Natural language front end to data base
REQUEST	Plath	Natural language front end to data base
ROBOT	Harris	Natural language front end to data base
INTELLECT	Artificial Intelligence Corp. (AIC)	Calls up data by typing memolike requests; natural language front end based on ROBOT
EPISTLE	IBM	Reads mail and informs recipient of important parts
TEAM	SRI	Learns about new subjects by asking user questions; natural language data base front end based on LADDER

APPLICATION: KNOWLEDGE ENGINEERING

SYSTEM	RESEARCHERS	DESCRIPTION
KAS	R. Reboh (SRI)	Knowledge acquisition system—uses existing systems to design other systems; part of PROSPECTOR

SYSTEM	RESEARCHERS	DESCRIPTION
AGE	H.P. Nii, N. Aiello (Stanford)	System building—"Attempt to generalize"; guides building of expert systems; used in building PUFF
EMYCIN (Essential MYCIN)	Randy Davis, W. Van Melle, et al. (Stanford)	Knowledge acquisition—rule-based consultant; derived from MYCIN; assumes backward chaining
RLL	R. Greiner, D.B. Lenat (Stanford)	Knowledge representation language, frame based
TEIRESIAS	R. Davis (Stanford)	Knowledge acquisition—transfers knowledge from a human expert to a system and guides acquisition of new inference rules (part of MYCIN)
EXPERT	Weiss and Kulikowski	Knowledge acquisition, in Fortran
SEEK	P. Politakis (Rutgers University)	Knowledge acquisition—provides assistance in rule refinement during the design of expert systems
ROSIE	Waterman (Rand)	Knowledge representation—rule-based (no explanation system); forward chaining and backward chaining, in InterLISP, English-like syntax, three-value logic system (true, false, indeterminate)
OPS	CMU	Knowledge representation, rule-based, forward chaining, implemented in LISP, BLISS, PASCAL
HEARSAY III	Erman (CMU)	System building
KL-ONE	BBN	Knowledge representation, semantic net–based
FRL	Roberts, Goldstein (MIT)	Knowledge representation, frame-based

SYSTEM	RESEARCHERS	DESCRIPTION
UNITS	Stanford	Knowledge representation, frame-based; part of MOLGEN project
SYNAPSE	Buffalo	Knowledge representation, network-based
EURISKO	Lenat (Stanford)	System building—develops own theories and ideas once given the principles of a discipline
KLAUS	SRI	Under development; can learn and coordinate various tools

Appendix B. Commercially Offered Expert Systems

ADVANCED COMPUTER TUTORING INC., PITTSBURGH, PA
  A.I. tutorial systems

ADVANCED INFORMATION AND DECISION SYSTEMS (AI & DS)
  IPE (Intelligent Program Editor): works on ADA and CMS-2; three major parts: knowledge of program structures, understand user's intent, semantics analysis and manipulation tools
  INSFAMS (Inertial Navigation System Fault Analysis and Management System)

AION CORPORATION, PALO ALTO, CA
  Expert system shell

ALCOA
  Expert system: for configuration of aluminum alloys, developed by Carnegie-Mellon, used OPS-5 (being reimplemented with KNOWL-EDGE CRAFT)
  Industrial automation

ALLOY COMPUTER PRODUCTS, FRAMINGHAM, MA
  FORMULA/ONE: expert system shell for equation solving

AMERICAN INTERNATIONAL GROUP
  Expert system: provides risk assessment for commercial insurance companies developed by Syntelligence

AMERICAN MICROSYSTEMS
  CAD/CAE Design

ANALOG DEVICES
  CAD/CAE Design

APPLIED EXPERT SYSTEMS, INC. (APEX), CAMBRIDGE, MA
  PLAN-POWER: runs on Xerox 1186 LISP machines, uses LOOPS, financial advisor—does net worth, cash management, tax strategies, retirement and estate planning

ARCO CORPORATION
  A.I. research and development

ARITY CORPORATION, CONCORD, MA
: LOTUS spin-off
: Arity PROLOG: for PC

ARTELLIGENCE, INC., DALLAS, TX
: OPS-5+ for IBM PC and Apple Macintosh

ARTHUR ANDERSON
: Expert system to help auditors plan audits and choose audit techniques

ARTHUR D. LITTLE
: Using A.I. as an aid for strategic product planning for client companies
: Developing a stock-traders' work station

AT&T
: Expert systems to teach A.I.

AUTOMATED DESIGN ASSOCIATES
: PROLOG

AUTOMATED REASONING, NEW YORK, NY
: IN-ATE Shell: for CAD/CAM

AUTOMATIC DESIGN ASSOCIATES, DRESHER, PA
: FS PROLOG
: VMS PROLOG
: VML PROLOG
: VMA PROLOG

BABCOCK AND WILCOX
: Expert system: acts as welding scheduler, used KEE

BAROID
: Expert system, diagnoses drilling problems, developed by Carnegie-Mellon, used OPS-5

BATELLE MEMORIAL INSTITUTE
: Workshops on A.I. and expert systems

BBN (BOLT BERANEK AND NEWMAN, INC.)
: Steamer: Trainer for navy personnel on ships' steam plants
: KL-TWO: Successor to KL-ONE, semantic network tool

BECKMAN INSTRUMENTS
: SPIN PRO: expert system, provides advice about use of ultra-centrifuge, implemented in Gold Hill COMMON LISP on PC.

BELL TELEPHONE LABS
: ACE (Automated Cable Expertise): expert system, diagnoses and troubleshoots telephone cables, implemented in OPS-4
: REX (Regression Expert): 50–100 frames, intelligent front end for statistical package

BOEING
: Expert system, helps design airplane parts, performs weights risk assessment
: Used S-1 and PERSONAL CONSULTANT

BOEING COMPUTER SERVICES
: Plant scheduling program, uses KNOWLEDGE CRAFT on VAX

BRATTLE RESEARCH, CAMBRIDGE, MA
: Expert systems and natural language interface financial systems software

BULL, LONVECIENNES, FRANCE
: Expert system shell

BYNAS DIVISION, UNY COMPANY LTD., NAGOYA, JAPAN
: Kyoto COMMON LISP
: PROLOG—KABA, runs on SUN, APOLLO

CALIFORNIA INTELLIGENCE, SAN FRANCISCO, CA
: XSYS: expert system shell for PC

CAMPBELL SOUP
: Expert system to diagnose soup-cooking machinery, uses TI's PERSONAL CONSULTANT

CARNEGIE GROUP, PITTSBURGH, PA
: KNOWLEDGE CRAFT: expert system shell derived from SRL+, supports multiple representations
: LANGUAGE CRAFT: natural language interface derived from PLUME
: Application shells in: CAE, software engineering, project management, knowledge-based simulation, production management, process control and diagnostics, MORE—an expert system to help select and build expert systems
: Stakes sold to: DEC, Boeing, Texas Instruments, GSI, and Ford

CARNEGIE-MELLON UNIVERSITY, PITTSBURGH, PA
: OPS: expert system shell, rule based, forward chaining
: IRIS: expert system for factory scheduling, done in conjunction with Westinghouse
: RI (predecessor of XCON): expert system, configures computers, done for DEC

CCA UNIWORKS, INC., WELLESLEY, MA
: MPROLOG

CENTRE DE RECHERCHE, FRANCE
: KOOL: expert system shell

CHALCEDONY SOFTWARE, LA JOLLA, CA
: PROLOG V-PLUS
: PROLOG V

CITICORP
: Expert system to train personnel
: Expert system to read natural language messages, implemented on LMI LISP machine in LISP

COGNITECH SA, PARIS, FRANCE
: TIGRE-1: tool for developing diagnostic expert systems

Developing expert systems for farming applications for French government

COGNITIVE SYSTEMS

Advisory systems for banks: consumer investment advisors (for example, COURTIER, a stock-portfolio management system), automated teller machine, automated will writer, estate planner, tax assistance

Intelligent natural language front end to Standard & Poor's data base, oil well industry data base

Marketeer: NL front end for ACCESS, a market analysis program developed by Dialog, Inc., which provides access to internal data and syndicate sources such as Nielsen

COMPOSITION SYSTEMS, INC., ELMSFORD, NY

Expert systems for newspaper composition

COMPUTER THOUGHT CORPORATION, PLANO, TX

Educational: ADA teaching aid

COOPERS AND LYBRAND

Expert system to help health-care organizations select computer systems; implemented using KDS

Expert system tax auditor

DAISY SYSTEMS, SUNNYVALE, CA

Logician Gatemaster: VLSI circuit and computer design front end to modules in PASCAL, frame-based, used for querying and extracting information

DEC (DIGITAL EQUIPMENT CORPORATION)

XCON: computer configuration selection, started as 750 rules, now about 4,000 rules, runs at rate of 500 rules/minute; man required 25 minutes; used OPS

XSEL: interactive, provides sales assistance in equipment selection and configuration, used OPS

XSITE: helps to make site selections for computers

Knowledge network with six systems, including manufacturer, customer order schedules, materials, and floor capacity; used OPS

SPEAR: diagnoses tape drive faults, used OPS

KBS: assembly of printed circuit boards, used OPS

CALLISTO: management and control of large projects, used OPS

PTRANS: assists with manufacturing plant management, used OPS

INET: supports corporate distribution, used OPS

Consults about long-range planning, used SRL

Performs strategic analysis of organization structure, used SRL

Manages large design projects, used SRL (reimplemented with KNOWLEDGE CRAFT)

DELCO PRODUCTS
: Expert system, designs brushes for motors; used S-1

DYNAMIC MASTER SYSTEMS INC., ATLANTA, GA
: TOPSI: OPS-5 implementation for PCs; MS-DOS and CP/M systems

DYNAQUEST CONSULTING GROUPS, LTD.
: Helps consumers choose computer systems at local retail stores

EDF
: ALOVETTE 85: expert system shell

EDWARD REASOR, TAMPA, FL
: ESIE (Expert System Inference Engine): expert system shell, backward chaining, runs on PC, distributed under Shareware concept

ELECTRICAL POWER RESEARCH INSTITUTE
: Expert system that interfaces with control instrumentation in a nuclear power plant and performs maintenance and diagnostics, implemented by Intellicorp using KEE

EPS MANAGEMENT SOFTWARE
: Financial expert systems

ESL (SUBSIDIARY OF TRW)
: ACES (A Cartographic Expert System): aids cartographers in placing point, areal, and lineal feature labels when preparing maps

EVANS AND SUTHERLAND
: Software design

EXPERTELLIGENCE, BELLEVUE, WA
: LISP machine environment: on Macintosh, LISP, and OPS-5; used to develop expert medical diagnosis system for a patient to use at home after discharge

EXPERT-KNOWLEDGE SYSTEMS, INC., MCLEAN, VA
: Training in knowledge engineering

EXPERT SOFTWARE INTERNATIONAL, EDINBURGH, SCOTLAND
: EXPERT-EASE: expert system shell in spreadsheet form, written in PASCAL, induces rules, runs under UCSD PASCAL, IBM-PC based; used to test electronic systems and to identify dangerous drugs

: EXTRAN: written in FORTRAN, based upon EXPERT-EASE, runs under PC DOS, interfaces with FORTRAN

: Don Michie, developer; distributed by Jeffrey Perrone & Associates, Human Edge, Expert Systems Inc.

EXPERT SYSTEMS INC., HOUSTON, TX
: CLASS: expert system shell for PCs and mainframes (IBM VM/CMS, VAX, VMS, and UNIX)

EXPERT SYSTEMS INTERNATIONAL, KING OF PRUSSIA, PA
: ESP ADVISOR: expert system shell

PROLOG-1 and PROLOG-2: 2,500 lips on IBM PC, 16,000 lips on PC/AT

EXSYS, INC., ALBUQUERQUE, NM

EXSYS: expert system shell, probabilistic, backward chaining, 700 rules for memory over 192K

FAIRCHILD CAMERA

Expert system that accepts and interprets sensor data for manufacturing

FIRST NATIONAL BANK OF CHICAGO

Expert systems for internal auditing, corporate credit reviews, and training; uses IBM PC and M1

FORD AEROSPACE

Developing a planning system for a space flight control center for NASA

FORMATIVE TECHNOLOGY, PITTSBURGH, PA

Helps architects write specifications; runs on Apple Lisa

FRANZ INC., ALAMEDA, CA

Franz LISP

COMMON LISP

GENERAL ELECTRIC

CATS-1 (Computer-Aided Trouble Shooting): expert locomotive diagnosis system; programmed in FORTH on PDP 11/23, 10M-byte Winchester disc

GETREE: expert system shell, graphically represents rules as sets of and/or assumptions; interactive graphics, runs on VAX/VMS with VT100 terminal

GENERAL MOTORS

Expert systems to: design quiet fans to cool car engines, diagnose engine transmission faults, identify faults and recommend corrective action for car-engine and electronic-control systems; all implemented using KS300

GENERAL RESEARCH CORP

TIMM/TIMM PC general-purpose expert system shells, both written in FORTRAN, statistically based, can induce rules

GENERAL TELEPHONE AND ELECTRONICS

Designs least-cost telecommunications networks

Used M-1

Also using A.I. for software design

GEORGIA INSTITUTE OF TECHNOLOGY

SPILLMAP: advises on how to deal with a "spill crisis" involving hazardous materials on an industrial park site

GOLD HILL COMPUTERS

COMMON LISP, CGLISP: can address full 16M bytes of AT memory; can add HALO graphics package, which has more than 150 graphics primitives; can add CGLISP network, allows LISP programs on PC and Symbolics to interconnect and interact with each other

GOULD, INC.
Factory floor management and diagnostics

GRUMMAN-CTEC, INC., MCLEAN, VA
A.I. consulting

HARMON ASSOCIATES, SAN FRANCISCO, CA
Training in expert systems

HARRIS CORPORATION
Developing expert systems to aid in automatic chip design and design of large-scale digital systems

HAZELTINE
OPGEN (formerly HAIL-1): configures printed circuit boards, programmed in OPS; can form new rules based on dialogue with user-specific information
Authoring systems
Training systems

HELIX EXPERT SYSTEM LTD., ENGLAND
TESS (The Expert System Shell): expert system for banking and finance, PC based

HEWLETT PACKARD
Smart instruments and work stations
Sortware robots, programs that act as a computer user's secretary, or accountant; e.g., would actively advise, search for relevant data, plan airline routes, screen messages
Expert systems in manufacturing and fabrication
Photolithography advisor, expert system for IC manufacturing
Integration of IR & mass spectrometer information in chemical research

HONEYWELL
Planning, diagnostics
MENTOR: assists in preventative maintenance of large central-air-conditioning units in commercial buildings

HUGHES AIRCRAFT
Expert system to assist in assembly of printed circuit boards

HUMAN EDGE SOFTWARE, PALO ALTO, CA
EXPERT EDGE: expert system shell, backward and forward chaining, developed in England by Alvey committee, written in C
Also markets other IBM PC–based business strategy products, such as EXPERT-EASE

HYPER TECH ASSOCIATES, DALLAS, TX
A.I. software tools

IMPEDIMENT INC., DUXBURY, MA
LISP

INFERENCE CORPORATION, CULVER CITY, CA (FORMERLY SYSTEMS COGNITION)
    Built VLSI-design software for control data
    SMP (Symbols Manipulation Program)
    ART (Advanced Reasoning Tool): expert system shell, supports multiple knowledge representations, runs on mini- and mainframes, highly interactive

INFOLOGIC, SWEDEN
    PC-PROLOG

INFOTYM (SUBSIDIARY OF MCDONNELL-DOUGLAS)
    REVEAL: expert system shell that reasons with fuzzy or approximate quantities

INRIA, VALBONNE, FRANCE
    CRIQUET: expert system shell

INSTITUTE FOR ARTIFICIAL INTELLIGENCE, LOS ANGELES, CA
    Training in expert systems

INTEGRAL QUALITY, SEATTLE, WA
    IQ LISP

INTELLICORP, PALO ALTO, CA (FORMERLY INTELLIGENETICS)
    KEE (Knowledge Engineering Environment): expert system shell, supports multiple representations, runs on mini- and mainframes, delivery version runs on PCs, highly interactive
    Marketing agreement with Hewlett Packard

INTELLIGENT COMPUTER SYSTEMS RESEARCH INSTITUTE
    A.I. research and development
    Publishes *Applied Artificial Intelligence Reporter*

INTELLIWARE, INC., MARINA DEL REY, CA
    Training in expert systems (EXPERTEACH)

INTERFACE COMPUTER, MUNICH, GERMANY
    IF/PROLOG: runs under UNIX and PC DOS

INTERNAL REVENUE SERVICE
    Looks for suspicious tax returns and SEC filings

IBM
    Computer systems fault diagnosis; e.g., DART, disc control unit fault analysis
    EPISTLE: reads mail and informs recipient of important parts
    YES/MVS: answers questions, provides help, and exerts interactive control on MVS
    PRISM (Prototype Inference System)
    SCRATCHPAD II: symbolic algebra
    HANDY: educational appliances
    PROLOG-VM
    LISP-VM

EXPERT SYSTEMS ENVIRONMENT/VM: expert system shell written in PASCAL, based on PRISM
COBOL/SF (structured facility): restructures old COBOL programs

ITT
Next-generation communications switch, fault diagnosis of telecommunications networks

JEN-X (GENERAL EXPERT SYSTEM)
A.I. development tool

JET PROPULSION LABS
Mission planning on the Voyager Uranus mission

KDS CORPORATIONS, WILMETTE, IL
KDS (Knowledge Delivery System): expert shell that generates rules

KESTREL INSTITUTE, CHICAGO, IL
CHI: knowledge-based programming environment

KNOWLEDGE ANALYSIS, INC., RIDGEFIELD, CT
Consulting

LANGUAGE TECHNOLOGY
COBOL REGIMENTER

LAWRENCE LIVERMORE LABS
Tunes triple quadripole mass spectrometer
Used KEE

LEVEL FIVE RESEARCH INC., MELBOURNE, FL
INSIGHT and INSIGHT 2: expert system shells; INSIGHT 2 interfaces with dB II

LEXEME CORPORATION, PITTSBURGH, PA
Intelligence software translators from FORTRAN, PL/1, BLISS SPL, COBOL BASIC, ALGOL, JOVIAL, CMS-2 to ADA and C; written LISP

LICID, INC., PALO ALTO, CA
COMMON LISPS

LISP MACHINES INC.
IKE: expert system shell, menu driven, supports rules and predicates
AIBASE: menu-driven natural language interface and knowledge base construction
RTIME: links any LISP program to real-time program
PICON (Process Control Language)

LITHP SYSTEMS BV, THE NETHERLANDS
DAISY: expert system shell for PC

LITTON INDUSTRIES
Provides real-time analysis and advice on simulated flow of factory materials
Schedules testing of instruments used in inertial navigation systems

LOCKHEED
> LES (LOCKHEED'S EXPERT SYSTEM): expert system shell written in ADA, frame based and object oriented, implemented using case grammar, already used in: hazard analysis, autonomous vehicle, IC design checking

LOGICWARE, TORONTO, CANADA
> M PROLOG: runs on PC, mini-, and mainframe

LOGO SYSTEMS, INC.
> Educational software

MCC
> CAD/CAE design

MCGRAW-HILL
> MICRO EXPERT: expert system shell

MATCHWARE COMPUTER SERVICES, INDIANAPOLIS, IN
> Expert system for software selection

MEDX SYSTEMS, LTD., DOVER, MA
> Expert systems for medical diagnosis

METALOGIC, INC.
> CAD/CAE design, using Symbolics to develop a silicon compiler

METROPOLITAN LIFE INSURANCE COMPANY
> Expert system that designs pensions, runs on IBM 3083 in M PROLOG

MICRO DATABASE SYSTEMS, LAFAYETTE, IN
> GURU: Knowledge-base system

MICROFORMATIC, PARIS, FRANCE
> GOLEM: expert system shell

MIRROR SYSTEMS
> Legal aids

MIT
> MACSYMA: simplifies and solves algebra and calculus problems; offered by computer vendors, is on ARPANET and various computers (such as Symbolics and VAX)

NASA
> Interprets radar-tracking data
> Space shuttle planning
> Both use ART

NEURON DATA CORPORATION, PALO ALTO, CA
> Expert system for Apple's Macintosh

NIXDORF COMPUTER AG, MUNICH, GERMANY
> FAULTFINDER, REPLANT: expert systems

NORTHWEST COMPUTER ALGORITHMS, LONG BEACH, CA
> LISP for PCs

NORTHWEST ORIENT AIRLINES, SEATTLE, WA
> Custom Sperry-designed expert system, optimizes seat revenues, on UNIVAC 1100

OPTISOFT, BERKELEY, CA
  Expert system for equation solving
PALLADIAN SOFTWARE, INC., CAMBRIDGE, MA
  Financial advisor expert system: supports corporate cost-benefit analysis
PANGARO, INC.
  Training and simulation
PEAT MARWICK
  Program that restructures old COBOL
PERCEPTRONIC, INC., WOODLAND HILLS, CA
  A.I. training devices
PERSOFT, INC., WOBURN, MA
  MORE: expert system that provides advice for direct-mail marketeers; mainframe based
PLANNING RESEARCH CORPORATION, MCLEAN, VA
  A.I. consulting
PRIME COMPUTER
  DOC: diagnoses annoyance problems in Prime hardware
PRO CODE INTERNATIONAL, PORTLAND, OR
  WALTZ LISP
  CLOG PROLOG
  Runs on micros under MS DOS, PC DOS, and CP/M
PRODUCTION SYSTEMS TECHNOLOGIES, INC., PITTSBURGH, PA
  OPS-83, expert system shell, very fast running, updated version of OPS-5
PROGRAMMING LOGIC SYSTEM INC., MILFORD, CT
  MICRO PROLOG: for IBM PCs
  SIGMA PROLOG: for mainframes
  MAC PROLOG: for Apple's Macintosh
PROGRAMS IN MOTION, INC., WAYLAND, MA
  1ST CLASS: PC-based, rule-based expert system shell
PULSETRAIN, NEW YORK, NY
  APES (Augmented PROLOG for Expert Systems)
QUANTUM DEVELOPMENT CORPORATION, DENVER, CO
  EXPLICIT: expert system for litigation support, based on company's fourth-generation Knowledge Management System (KMS)
  AiSOP: expert system for customer service
QUINTUS COMPUTER SYSTEM, INC., PALO ALTO, CA
  Quintus PROLOG: runs 20K lips on SUN-2, 23K lips on VAX 11/780
R/L GROUP, EL CERRITO, CA
  LISP for PCs
RADIAN CORPORATION, AUSTIN, TX
  RULEMASTER: expert system shell, rule based, can induce rules
ROHM AND HAAS COMPANY, SPRING HOUSE, PA
  Expert systems for chemical formulations

SAN MARCO SMARTWARE
  LISP tutor
SCHLUMBERGER, LTD.
  DIPMETER ADVISOR: interprets data from oil well logging devices
  PHI NAUGHT: assists in creation of software that analyzes oil well logging data
SCHONFELD AND ASSOCIATES, INC., EVANSTON, IL
  INGOT: intelligent business modeling
SCIENCE APPLICATIONS INTERNATIONAL
  GESBT: Generic Expert Building Tool, production-rule based
SEMANTIC MICROSYSTEMS, SAUSALITO, CA
  MACSCHEME: LISP for Apple's Macintosh
SERVIO LOGIC DEVELOPMENT CORPORATION, PORTLAND
  Object-oriented data base
SHEARSON LEHMAN/AMERICAN EXPRESS, INC.
  MERCURY: advises on interest rate swaps
  Provides portfolio management advice
SILOGIC, LOS ANGELES, CA
  KNOWLEDGE WORKBENCH: A.I. knowledge tool
SMART SYSTEMS, FALLS CHURCH, VA
  Consulting, courses on DUCK expert system shell
SOFTWARE ARCHITECTURE AND ENGINEERING, ARLINGTON, VA
  KES (Knowledge Engineering System): expert system shell, supports multiple representations—KES.PC (production rules), KES.BAYES (statistical), KES.HT (hypothesize test, frame); runs on mini- and mainframes and PCs, micro version originally written in IQ LISP, now has C version
SOFT WAREHOUSE, HONOLULU, HI
  MU LISP
  MU MATH
  Runs on PCs
SOLUTION SYSTEMS, NORWOOD, CA
  PROLOG and LISP for PCs
SPERRY-RAND
  Expert system for configuring computer communications systems
  UNIVAC is developing many industry-specific expert systems, for example, in airline reservations
STANFORD RESEARCH INSTITUTE (SRI)
  PROSPECTOR: predicts mineral deposits; under development since 1976; U.S. Geological Survey now financing
STANFORD UNIVERSITY
  DENDRAL: analyzes chemical compounds, molecular structure, using mass spectrometry data; available over COMPUSERVE

PUFF: in use at Pacific Medical Center; respiratory medical diagnosis system; runs on Apple

MACSYMA: simplifies and solves algebra and calculus problems; offered by computer vendors and available on ARPANET

STARWOOD CORPORATION, SAN ANTONIO, TX

A.I. programming language

STEWART HUGHES, SOUTHAMPTON, UNITED KINGDOM

Expert system for gas turbine management

STOCHOS, INC., SCHENECTADY, NY

A.I.-based process simulation program

SU INFOLOGICS AB, STOCKHOLM, SWEDEN

PC—PROLOG

SYNTELLIGENCE, MENLO PARK, CA

Expert systems for financial companies, purchasing, distribution, and construction, including loan and credit advisors

SYSTEM DESIGNERS SOFTWARE INC., WOBURN, MA

POPLOG: includes following languages: POP-11 (LISP-like), PROLOG, LISP; runs on VAX, SUN, APOLLO, HP 9000/200

SYSTEM DEVELOPMENT CORPORATION (SDC)

DADM (Deductively Augmented Data Management): can access multiple data bases

SYSTEM INTELLIGENCE LABS, NEW YORK, NY

WIZDOM: expert system shell, semantic network based

SYSTEMS RESEARCH LAB, INC., DAYTON, OH

DEXPERT: expert system shell

LISP to ADA translator

LISP to FORTRAN translator

LISP tutor

TASC (THE ANALYTICAL SCIENCES CORPORATION), BOSTON, MA

ACRONYM: version that runs on Symbolics

Expert systems for tank and truck image classification

Icing expert for FAA

MSIAS: classifies surface materials in satellite multispectral imagery (LANDSAT thematic mapper)

TEKNOWLEDGE, PALO ALTO, CA

Expert system shells: S-1 for mini- and mainframes, written in LISP and C, version in ADA is planned; M-1 for microprocessors, versions written in PROLOG and C, used to train junior bank loan officers, in automobile engine maintenance advice, in oil drill sticking problems, to help insurance companies calculate individual dividends, to help select and assign personnel; M-1 and S-1 derived from EMYCIN, then KS-300

DRILLING ADVISOR, for ELF, rule-based oil exploration front end to statistical package

Computer order entry and configuration system for NCR

Fault-diagnosis expert systems

Intelligent front end for LOTUS spreadsheet

Companies that have purchased a share in Teknowledge include General Motors, Proctor & Gamble, NYNEX, Framatome of Geneva and Monaco, CIE, FMC Corp, and ELF Acquitaine

TEXAS INSTRUMENTS

EXPLORER: LISP machine

PERSONNEL CONSULTANT: expert system shell for PC; used to develop diagnostic system for epi-reactors, for Dallas INFO MART system to analyze needs of user and to direct user to appropriate showrooms

Developing seismic interpretation system

THINKING MACHINES CORPORATION, WALTHAM, MA

Builds connection machine and jointly develops products

THOUGHTWARE, INC., COCONUT GROVE, FL

A.I. software

TRAVELERS INSURANCE

Advises agents about insurance and financial services; implemented by Index Systems

U.S. DEPARTMENT OF AGRICULTURE

COMAX: Cotton Management Expert System, PC-based expert system that determines when cotton crops need irrigation, fertilization, and pesticide treatment and when to harvest

UNITED TECHNOLOGIES

Vancouver, Canada, expert strategist, designed for accountants, interprets financial statements

UNIVERSITY OF ILLINOIS

KBPA (Knowledge Based Programming Assistant): partially supported by IBM's Palo Alto scientific center

VERAC, SAN DIEGO, CA

OPS-5E: an enhanced version of OPS that runs on Symbolics

Developing signal interpretation and military correlation systems

WESTCOMP SOFTWARE ENGINEERING GROUP, UPLAND, CA

LISP and PROLOG

WESTINGHOUSE

IMS (Integrated Manufacturing System): about 300 rules, uses shell, PDS (Process Diagnostic System), based on direct sensor readings

Expert system to help engineers select material in construction of nuclear generators

Expert system for metallurgical engineering advice, implemented using TI PERSONAL CONSULTANT

Expert system that configures elevators, implemented by Carnegie-Mellon, used OPS-5

Expert system that diagnoses malfunctions in steam turbines and generators, used SRL

Expert system that does job shop scheduling, used SRL (being reimplemented with KNOWLEDGE CRAFT)

Appendix C. Commercially Offered Natural Language Systems

INTELLECT, BY ARTIFICIAL INTELLIGENCE CORPORATION, WALTHAM, MA
- Derivative of ROBOT
- Distributed as: ON-LINE ENGLISH for Culliane; GRS EXECUTIVE for Information Sciences; licensed by IBM; now also available on VAX; has a PC version as well as mainframe
- Natural language interface for data-base retrieval
- Several hundred systems sold
- Takes about two weeks to implement on new data base
- Originally written in PL/1
- Available since 1980
- Costs about $50,000/system

COGNITIVE SYSTEMS, NEW HAVEN, CT
- Custom natural language interfaces
- Also builds advisory (expert) systems
- Based on PEARL (an outgrowth of SAM and PAM)
- Costs about $250,000/system
- Large start-up cost in building knowledge base
- Several systems have been built, e.g., EXPLORER, an interface to mainframe geological data base, which draws maps upon request
- Written in LISP

THEMIS, BY FREY ASSOCIATES, AMHERST, MA
- Natural language interface for data-base retrieval
- Interactively learns new words
- Written mostly in INTERLISP, some FORTRAN and PL/1
- Runs on VAX, with plans to transport to IBM 4300 and PCs

TEAM (TRANSPORTABLE ENGLISH ACCESS MANAGER), STANFORD RESEARCH INSTITUTE
- Interfaces with multiple data bases
- Written in LISP
- Runs on VAX and LISP machines, e.g., Symbolics
- SRI has also built other natural language front ends and related projects,

e.g., worked on text-understanding system for the Library of Congress, handcoded logic formulas that depict content of paragraph

ENGLISH, MATHEMATICA, PRINCETON, NJ

Natural language interface to RAMIS II, fourth-generation programming and data-base language

SUPERNATURAL, SOFTWARE AG, RESTON, VA

Natural language interface to NATURAL, fourth-generation language

ADR (APPLIED DATA RESEARCH)

Natural language product integrated with office automation

THE KNOWLEDGE WORKBENCH, SIGLOGIC

Natural language–based expert system environment for external data base

Runs under UNIX

ROSIE, RAND

Natural language–based expert system environment

Production rules and relational data base

XCALIBUR, DEC

Natural language front end to expert systems and data bases

LANGUAGE CRAFT (BASED ON PLUME), CARNEGIE GROUP

Natural language interface to expert system, KNOWLEDGE CRAFT, and to data bases

Runs on VAX and LISP machines

NAT PACK (ALSO CALLED THE LANGUAGE WORKBENCH), BRODIE ASSOCIATES, BOSTON, MA

Natural language tool kit

Allows user to build natural language capability into any software

SAVVY, EXCALIBUR TECHNOLOGIES

Natural language interface for IBM PC and Apple

Not linguistic; uses adaptive (best-fit) pattern-matching to strings of characters, plus some heuristic rules

Interfaces to dB II and company's own relational data base

User customized

Costs about $950

NLMENU, TEXAS INSTRUMENTS

Menu-driven natural language query system, all queries constructed from menu fall within linguistic and conceptual coverage of the system; therefore all queries are successful

Semantic grammars, context-free

Producing an interface to any arbitrary set of relations is automated

Takes 15–30 minutes of interaction to produce

Runs on TI personal computer

Also built NATURAL LINK, front end to Dow Jones

CLOUT, MICRORIM, BELLEVUE, WA
: Natural language front end to R Base
  ATN plus production rule expert system approach
  Runs on PCs

PARADOX, ANSA, INC, BELMONT, CA
: Intelligent data-base management system
  IBM PC-based

HAL, GNP DEVELOPMENT CORPORATION, PASADENA, CA
: Natural language front end for LOTUS

Q&A, SYMANTEC, SUNNYVALE, CA
: Natural language package
  Interface to object-oriented data base and word processor on PC
  Learns new words during query session
  Also offers: NOTE IT, add-on for LOTUS; STRAIGHT TALK (derivative of LIFER), available through Dictaphone on System 6000 word processor, written in PASCAL, front end for data bases

WEIDNER SYSTEM, WEIDNER COMMUNICATIONS CORPORATION, PROVO, UT
: Semiautomatic natural language translation
  Linguistic approach
  Written in FORTRAN IV
  Performs translation with human editing
  Approximately 100 words/hour, eight times as fast as a human alone
  Over twenty sold by end of 1982, mainly to large corporations
  Costs about $16/language

ALPS, ALPS, PROVO, UT
: Interactive natural language translation
  Linguistic approach
  Uses dictionary that provides the various translations for technical words as a display to a human translator who then selects among the displayed words

BROWN UNIVERSITY
: Developed experimental natural language problem-solving system for warehouse management problems

Appendix D.
Speech Synthesis Systems

■ AVAILABLE COMMERCIAL SYNTHESIZER SYSTEMS

MANUFACTURER	MODEL	COST	TYPE	COMMENTS
Kurzweil Computer Products (Cambridge, MA)	Reading machine for the blind	$30,000	Formant	Uses Speech Plus Prose 2000 synthesizer
American Microsystems (Santa Clara, CA)	53610 53620	* *	LPC LPC	
General Instruments (Hicksville, NY)	Allophone Synthesis Module		LPC	Enunciates 64 Allophones
	SP250 SP256	* *	Formant Formant	Single-channel synthesizer Single-channel synthesizer with microprocessor control
Hitachi	HD 38880	*	PARCOR	Uses partial autocorrelation (closely related to LPC)
Nippon Electric Corp.			PARCOR	
Sanyo	LC 1800		PARCOR	
Mitsubishi	M58817	*	PARCOR	
Matsushita (Japan)		*	LPC	
Master Specialties (Costa Mesa, CA)	1650	$500+ vocab. @ $50/word	Word Synthesis	

Company	Product	Price	Text-to-Speech Synthesizer	Description
Intex Micro Systems (Troy, NY)	Intex-Talker			Uses a text-to-phoneme algorithm and a Votrax SC-01 chip
Motorola			CVSD	Encoder and decoder chips
Phillips/Signetics	MEA 8000	*	Formant	
	MEA 1000	*	Formant	
OKI Semiconductor			ADPCM	Encoder and decoder chips
Votrax (Troy, MI)	VSM/1	$995	Formant	A single-board complete system incorporating a programmable memory
	SVA		Formant	Single-board synthesizer for unlimited text to speech (no internal word storage)
	SC-02		Formant	Synthesizer chip with phoneme library
Speech Plus, Inc. (Mountain View, CA)	Prose 2000	$3500	Formant	Single-board system achieving an unlimited vocabulary capability by using 400 rules and a 3,000-word exceptions lexicon, for use with text
	Speech 1000	$1200	LPC	Synthesizer board with up to 6 minutes stored vocabulary
Texas Instruments (Dallas, TX)	TMS 5220	$5	LPC	Single-chip voice synthesizer processor
	TMS 6100	$5	LPC	Single-chip voice synthesizer memory
	Speech synthesizer for TI 99/4A Personal Computer	$100	LPC	Text to speech implemented in 99/4A.

MANUFACTURER	MODEL	COST	TYPE	COMMENTS
National Semiconductor (Santa Clara, CA)	TM 990/306		LPC	Speech module (does not have unlimited vocabulary capability of Formant systems)
	Digitalker MM 54104		Mozer's Waveform Digitizer	Single chip with 256 possible addressable expressions
Centigram (Sunnyvale, CA)	GIM	$350	Formant	An SBX module using the G1250 synthesizer chip
	SYBIL	$495	Formant	A single-channel synthesizer for the IBM PC

*Chip prices range from $3 to $15, depending on model and quantity. Speech Plus provides custom vocabulary generation services for speech synthesizer chips at $100/word.

SOURCE: "An Overview of Artificial Intelligence and Robots" (NASA Technical Memo 85838), by William Gerarter, 1983.

DARPA'S SPEECH-UNDERSTANDING SYSTEMS

NAME	DOMAIN/ PURPOSE	APPROACH	KNOWLEDGE REP.	CONTROL	ABF	ACCURACY	COMMENTS
HEARSAY II (CMU)	A.I. publications; Document retrieval	Utilizes cooperating independent systems experts (knowledge sources) that communicate via posting hypotheses on a blackboard	Independent KSs composed of production rules	Asynchronous pattern-invoked knowledge sources; opportunistic scheduling by first expanding the highest scoring hypothesis	33	90%	Development of blackboard architecture and use of independent cooperating knowledge sources most significant; a parallel processor version has been built to exploit KS modularity
HARPY (CMU)	A.I. publications; Document retrieval	Compiled a network of all possible sentences; paths through network are "sentence templates"	Precompiled network; each node is a template of allophones, which, when linked, form acoustic representatives of every possible pronunciation of words in the domain	"Beam search"; no backtracking	33	95%	Approach cannot easily accommodate pragmatics; needs a large memory; sensitive to missing acoustical segments and missing words

NAME	DOMAIN/ PURPOSE	APPROACH	KNOWLEDGE REP.	CONTROL	ABF	ACCURACY	COMMENTS
HWIM (BBN)	Travel budget management	The system extends bottom-up word theories using top-down syntactic components; verifies hypothesized words by generating a parameter representation that is compared with that from the actual speech input; uses an ATN semantic grammar	Uses networks to represent: trip facts and relations; lexicon; phoneme hypotheses from signal	Centralized control using KSs as subroutines; expands sentences about the first recognized word in sentence (island driving)	196	44%	Speaker-independent; very slow; most difficult domain in SUR project

SOURCE: "An Overview of Artificial Intelligence and Robots" (NASA Technical Memo 85838), by William Gerarter, 1983.

■ APPLICATIONS OF SPEECH SYNTHESIS

MILITARY

- Operation of military equipment
- Warnings
- Reminders
- Service and operation aids
- Trainers and simulators
- Secure communications

COMPUTER

- Communication by computers to users

CONSUMER

- Talking appliances
- Teaching devices
- Toys
- Talking typewriters and calculators
- Talking watches
- Automobile warning devices, reminders, and enunciators for instruments
- Devices for the blind
- Communication for the speech handicapped

TELECOMMUNICATIONS

- Synthesized telephone messages
- Speech compression for "store and forward" to reduce communication costs
- Vocal delivery of electronic mail

INDUSTRIAL

- Speaking instruments
- Speaking cash registers
- Alarm systems
- Automated office equipment
- Industrial process control
- Station and floor announcers for trains, buses, elevators, etc.

- Systems operations where the operators have their visual attention elsewhere
- Emergency warning devices for airplanes, machines, etc.
- Control room enunciators for sensors
- Text readers
- Data entry (with vocal verification)

Appendix E.
Robot Programming Systems

EXTENDED GUIDING

- Robot is taught motions interpreted relative to coordinate frame that may be modified at execution time
- Coordinate frames are determined by sensor that encounters object
- Examples: ASEA, Cincinnati Milacron, IBM
- ASEA and Cincinnati Milacron support simple conditional branching control structures; branch based on test pattern

ROBOT-LEVEL LANGUAGES

- MHI (Mechanical Hand Interpreter): developed for MH-1 robot at MIT, 1960-61; implemented on TX-0 computer; framed primarily around guarded move—move until sensor condition is detected
- WAVE, 1960-75: developed at Stanford; first general-purpose robot programming language; "new" syntax modeled after PDP-10 assembler ran on PDP-10, produced trajectory file executable on-line by dedicated PDP-6; describes positions by Cartesian coordinates of end-effector; coordination of joint motions to achieve continuity in velocities and accelerations; specification of compliance in Cartesian coordinates
- MINI, 1973-74: developed at MIT; extension to existing LISP system; robot joints controlled independently; trajectory planning facility of WAVE was more sophisticated and did not require preplanning
- AL, Stanford, 1974-present: designed to support robot-level and task-level specification; runs on two machines, like WAVE and MINI; one machine compiles to lower-level languages, second machine, real-time interpreter; provides four major capabilities: WAVE manipulation capabilities, concurrent execution of processes, synchronization, and on-conditions; data and control structures of an ALGOL-like language,

including data types for geometric calculations; and support for world-modeling AFFIXMENT mechanism
- VAL, 1975–present: used in Unimation robots, especially PUMA series; provides subset of WAVE capabilities on stand-alone mini; interpreter uses improved trajectory calculations; basic capabilities: point-to-point, joint-interpolated, Cartesian motions; specification and manipulation of Cartesian coordinate frames; integer variables and arithmetic, conditional branching, and procedures; set and test binary signal lines that execute procedure when event detected
- AML (A Manufacturing Language), 1977–present: used in IBM's robot products; "new" language, borrows from designs of LISP and APL; supports operations on data aggregates, joint-space trajectory planning, systems environment where different interfaces may be built; does not support Cartesian motion, compliant motion, affixment of frames, or multiple processes
- TEACH, 1975–78: developed as part of PACS system at Bendix; parallel execution of multiple tasks with multiple devices; robot-independent programs; programs composed of partially ordered statement sequences that could be executed sequentially or in parallel; flexible mapping between logical devices; all motions specified relative to local coordinate frames
- PAL, MIT, 1978–present: consists primarily of sequence of homogeneous coordinate equations involving locations of objects and robots end-effector; still under development
- MCL, McDonnell Douglas, 1979–present: extension of APT languages used for numerically controlled machining includes: data types, control structures, real-time I/O, vision interface
- ML, IBM, 1975: low-level robot language, similar to assembly language; supports two parallel robot tasks; guarded moves
- EMILY, IBM, 1976: off-line assembler for ML
- MAPLE, IBM, 1975: interprets AL-like language; actual manipulation operations carried out using ML
- SIGMA, 1978: developed at Olivetti for SIGMA robots; comparable to ML at syntactic level
- MAL, Milan Polytechnic, Italy, 1979: controls multiple Cartesian robots, supports multiple tasks and task synchronization; BASIC-like
- LAMA-S, Iria, France, 1980: VAL-like
- LM, IMAG, Grenoble, France, 1981: being used for recently announced Scemi, Inc., industrial robot; provides most of manipulation facilities of AL; supports affixment but not multiprocessing
- RAIL, AUTOMATIX, INC., 1982: includes large subset of PASCAL; variety data types; high-level program control mechanisms; interfaces to binary vision and robot welding systems; flexible way of defining

and accessing I/O lines; RAIL statements translated into intermediate representation; comparable to MAL and LM

TASK-LEVEL PROGRAMMING

- Still subject of research
- Outgrowth of R&D in CAD/CAM and A.I.
- Three phases: modeling, task specification, and robot program synthesis

WORLD MODELING

- Geometric description of objects
- Physical description of objects
- Kinematic description of all linkages
- Description of robot characteristics

GEOMETRIC DESCRIPTION TYPES

- Line representation
- Surface representation as set of surfaces
- Solid, combinations of primitive solids

TASK-LEVEL PROGRAMMING

- LAMA, M.I.T., 1976–77: only partially implemented; formulated relationship of task specification, obstacle avoidance, grasping, skeleton-based strategy syntheses, error detection
- AUTOPASS, IBM, 1977: partial implementation, syntax and semantics; PLACE statement implemented
- RAPT, 1978: transforms symbolic specification of geometric goals, with program that specifies direction of motions, but not their length, into sequence of end-effector positions
- LM-GEO, 1982: implemented extension to LM; incorporates symbolic specifications of destinations
- ROBEX, 1981: full-blown ROBEX not yet implemented

COMPANIES AND UNIVERSITIES INVOLVED IN INTELLIGENT ROBOTICS

Adept Technology, Inc.
American Robot Corporation
AMS Engineering Group
ASEA, Inc.
Automation Resources, Inc.
Carnegie-Mellon University
Cincinnati Milacron
Deere and Company
General Electric Corporation
General Motors Corporation
Georgia Institute of Technology
GMF Robotics
IBM
Lehigh University
Lockheed-Georgia
Prab Robotics, Inc.
Unimation, Inc. (a Westinghouse company)
United States Navy
Westinghouse Research and Development Center

Glossary

ARTIFICIAL INTELLIGENCE (A.I.). A discipline devoted to developing and applying computational approaches to intelligent behavior; also referred to as *machine intelligence* or *heuristic programming*.

ATOM. An individual; a proposition in logic that cannot be broken down into other propositions.

BLACKBOARD APPROACH. A problem-solving approach whereby the various system elements communicate with each other via a common working data storage called the blackboard.

BLOCKS WORLD. A small artificial world consisting of blocks and pyramids, used to develop ideas in computer vision, robotics, and natural language interfaces.

COGNITION. An intellectual process by which knowledge is gained about perceptions or ideas.

COMPILE. The act of translating a computer program written in a high-level language (such as LISP) into the machine language that controls the computer's basic operations.

COMPUTATIONAL LOGIC. A science designed to make use of computers in logic calculus.

COMPUTER ARCHITECTURE. The way various computational elements are interconnected to achieve a computational function.

CONCEPTUAL DEPENDENCY. An approach to natural language understanding in which sentences are translated into basic concepts that are expressed as a small set of semantic primitives.

CONTROL STRUCTURE. Reasoning strategy—the strategy for manipulating the domain knowledge to solve a problem.

DATA BASE. An organized collection of data about a subject.

DATA BASE MANAGEMENT SYSTEM. A computer system for storing and retrieving information about some domain.

DATA STRUCTURE. The form in which data are stored in a computer.

DECLARATIVE KNOWLEDGE REPRESENTATION. Representation of facts and assertions.

EDITOR. A software tool to aid in modifying a software program.

EMBED. To write a computer language on top of (embedded in) another computer language (such as LISP).

EXPERT SYSTEM. A computer program that uses knowledge and reasoning techniques to solve problems normally requiring the abilities of human experts.

FIFTH-GENERATION COMPUTER. A non–Von Neumann, intelligent parallel-processing form of computer now being pursued by Japan.

FIRST-ORDER PREDICATE LOGIC. A popular form of logic used by the A.I. community for representing knowledge and performing logical inference. First-order predicate logic permits assertions to be made about variables in a proposition.

GENERAL PROBLEM SOLVER (GPS). The first problem solver (1957) to separate its problem-solving methods from knowledge of the specific task being considered. The GPS problem-solving approach employed was "means-ends analysis."

HEURISTICS. Rules of thumb or empirical knowledge used to help guide a problem solution.

HEURISTIC SEARCH TECHNIQUES. Graph-searching methods that use heuristic knowledge about the domain to help focus the search. They operate by generating and testing intermediate states along potential solution paths.

HIGH-ORDER LANGUAGE (HOL). A computer language (such as FORTRAN or LISP) requiring fewer statements than machine language and usually substantially easier to use and read.

INFERENCE ENGINE. The control structure of an A.I. problem solver in which the control is separate from the knowledge.

INSTANTIATION. Replacing a variable by an instance (an individual) that satisfies the system (or satisfies the statement in which the variable appears).

KNOWLEDGE BASE. An A.I. data base that is made up not merely of files of uniform content, but of facts, inferences, and procedures corresponding to the types of information needed for problem solution.

KNOWLEDGE ENGINEERING. The A.I. approach focusing on the use of knowledge (for instance, in expert systems) to solve problems.

LISP (LIST PROCESSING LANGUAGE). The basic A.I. programming language.

LOGICAL OPERATION. The execution of a single computer instruction.

LOGICAL REPRESENTATION. Knowledge representation by a collection of logical formulas (usually in first-order predicate logic) that provide a partial description of the world.

MEANS-END ANALYSIS. A problem-solving approach (used by GPS) in which problem-solving operators are chosen in an iterative fashion to reduce the difference between the current problem-solving state and the goal state.

NATURAL LANGUAGE PROCESSING. Processing of natural language (English, for example) by a computer to facilitate human communication with the computer—or for other purposes, such as language translation.

OBJECT-ORIENTED PROGRAMMING. A programming approach focused on objects that communicate by message-passing. An object is considered to be a package of information and of descriptions of procedures that can manipulate that information.

PARALLEL PROCESSING. Simultaneous processing, as opposed to the sequential processing in a conventional (Von Neumann) type of computer architecture.

PATTERN RECOGNITION. The process of classifying data into predetermined categories.

PROCEDURAL KNOWLEDGE REPRESENTATION. A representation of knowledge about the world by a set of procedures—small programs that know how to do specific things in well-specified situations.

PRODUCTION RULE. A modular knowledge structure representing a single chunk of knowledge, usually in an if-then or antecedent-consequent form; popular in expert systems.

PROGRAMMING ENVIRONMENT. The total programming setup that includes the interface, the languages, the editors, and other programming tools.

PROLOG (PROGRAMMING IN LOGIC). A logic-oriented A.I. language developed in France and popular in Europe and Japan.

PROPOSITIONAL LOGIC. An elementary logic that uses argument forms to deduce the truth or falsity of a new proposition from known propositions.

RULE INTERPRETER. The control structure for a production rule–based system.

SEARCH SPACE. The implicit graph representing all the possible states of the system that may have to be searched to find a solution. In many cases, the search space is infinite. The term *search space* is also used for nonstate space representations.

SEMANTIC NETWORK. A knowledge representation for describing the properties and relations of objects, events, concepts, situations, or actions, by a directed graph consisting of node and table edges (arcs connecting nodes).

SEMANTIC PRIMITIVES. Basic conceptual units in which concepts, ideas, or events can be represented.

SOLUTION PATH. A successful path through a search space.

STATE GRAPH. A graph in which the nodes represent the system and the connecting arcs represent the operators that can be used to transform the state from which the arcs emanate into the state at which they arrive.

SYLLOGISM. A deductive argument in logic whose conclusion is supported by two premises.

SYMBOLIC. Relating to the substitution of abstract representations (symbols) for concrete objects.

SYNTAX. Order or arrangement (for example, the grammar of a language).

VON NEUMANN ARCHITECTURE. The current standard computer architecture that uses sequential processing.

Bibliography

Agin, G.J., and T.O. Binford. 1973. "Computer Description of Curved Objects." *Proceedings of the 3rd IJCAI,* Stanford, CA: 629–40.

Aikins, J.S. 1979. "Prototypes and Production Rules: An Approach to Knowledge Representation for Hypothesis Formation." *Proceedings of the 6th IJCAI,* Tokyo: 1–3.

———. 1983. "Prototypical Knowledge for Expert Systems." *Artificial Intelligence* 20(2):163–210.

Alexander, Tom. 1982. "Computers on the Road to Self-Improvement." *Fortune,* 14 June 1982, p. 148.

Allen, J. 1978. *Anatomy of Lisp.* New York: McGraw-Hill.

Amarel, S. 1971. "On Representation of Problems of Reasoning about Actions." In *Machine Intelligence* 3, edited by D. Michie. Edinburgh: Edinburgh University Press.

Andriole, S.J. 1985. *Applications in Artificial Intelligence.* Princeton, NJ: Petrocelli Books.

Ano, A.V., and J.D. Ullman. 1972. *Parsing.* The Theory of Parsing, Translating and Compiling, vol. 1. Englewood Cliffs, NJ: Prentice-Hall.

"Applied Computational Linguistics in Perspective." NRL Workshop at Stanford University, 26–27 June 1981. In *American Journal of Computational Linguistics* 8(2):55–83.

Arbob, B., and D. Michie. 1985. "Generating Rules from Examples." *Proceedings of the 9th IJCAI,* vol. 1:631–34.

Arden, B.W., ed. 1980. *What Can Be Automated? (COSERS).* Cambridge, MA: MIT Press.

Asnoy, W.R. 1952. *Design for a Brain.* New York: Wiley.

Baizer, R., L.D. Erman, P.E. London, and C. Williams. 1980. "Hearsay III: A Domain-Independent Framework for Expert Systems." *Proceedings of the 1st AAAI,* Stanford, CA: 108–10.

Barr, A., and E. Feigenbaum. 1981. *The Handbook of Artificial Intelligence.* Vols. 1–3. Los Altos, CA: Kaufmann.

Barrow, H.G. 1979. "Artificial Intelligence: State of the Art." Tech. Note 198. Menlo Park, CA: SRI International.

Bartlett, F.C. 1932. *Remembering: A Study in Experimental and Social Psychology.* Cambridge, England: Cambridge University Press.

Bates, M., and Ingria. 1981. "Controlled Transformational Sentence Generation." *Proceedings of 19th annual meeting of the Association of Computational Linguistics.*

Baudet, G.M. 1978. "On the Branching Factor of the Alpha-Beta Pruning Algorithm." *Artificial Intelligence* 10(2):173–99.

Bawden, A., J. Holloway Greenblatt, T. Knight, D. Moon, and D. Weintraub. 1979. "The LISP Machine." In *Artificial Intelligence: An MIT Perspective,* vol. 2, edited by P.H. Winston and R.H. Brown. Cambridge, MA: MIT Press.

Bennett, J., and C. Hollander. 1981. "DART: An Expert System for Computer Fault Diagnosis." *Proceedings of the 7th IJCAI,* Vancouver, British Columbia: 843–45.

Benson, D.B., B.R. Hilditch, and J.D. Starkey. 1979. "Tree Analysis Techniques in Tsumego." *Proceedings of the 6th IJCAI,* Tokyo.

Bentley, J.L. 1979. "An Introduction to Algorithm Design." *Computer,* February 1979.

Bentley, J.L., and J.B. Saxe. 1980. "An Analysis of Two Heuristics For the Euclidean Traveling Salesman Problem." *Proceedings of 18th Allerton Conference of Communication, Control, and Computing.*

Berliner, H.J. 1977. "Search and Knowledge." *Proceedings of the 5th IJCAI,* Cambridge, MA: 975–79.

———. 1978. "A Chronology of Computer Chess and Its Literature." *Artificial Intelligence* 1(1):201–14.

———. 1979a. "The B* Tree Search Algorithm: A Best-First Proof Procedure." *Artificial Intelligence* 12(1):23–40.

———. 1979b. "On the Construction of Evaluation Functions for Large Domains." *Proceedings of the 6th IJCAI,* Tokyo.

———. 1980a. "The Backgammon Computer Program Beats World Champion." *Artificial Intelligence* 14(1).

———. 1980b. "Computer Backgammon." *Scientific American,* June 1980.

Bernstein, J. 1981. "A.I. (Artificial Intelligence)." *New Yorker,* 14 December 1981, p. 50.

Bledsoe, W.W. 1977. "Non-resolution Theorem Proving." *Artificial Intelligence* 9:1–35.

Bobrow, D.G. 1968. "Natural Language Input for a Computer Problem-solving System." In *Semantic Information Processing,* edited by M. Minsky. Cambridge, MA: MIT Press, pp. 146–226.

———. 1975. "Dimensions of Representation." In *Representation and Understanding: Studies in Computer Science,* edited by D.G. Bobrow and A. Collins. New York: Academic Press, pp. 1–34.

Bobrow, D.G., and A. Collins. 1975. *Representation and Understanding: Studies in Computer Science.* New York: Academic Press.

Bobrow, D.G., R.M. Kaplan, M. Kay, D.A. Norman, H. Thompson, and T. Winograd. 1977. "Gus, a Frame-driven Dialog System." *Artificial Intelligence* 8:155-73.

Bobrow, D.G., and B. Raphael. 1974. "New Programming Languages for Artificial Intelligence Research." *Computing Surveys* 6(3):155.

Bobrow, D.G., and T. Winograd. 1977. "An Overview of KRL, A Knowledge Representation Language." *Cognitive Science* 1(1):3-46.

———. 1979. "KRL: Another Perspective." *Cognitive Science* 3(1):29-42.

Boden, M. 1977. *Artificial Intelligence and Natural Man.* New York: Basic Books.

Booth, A.D. 1967. *Machine Translation.* Amsterdam: North Holland.

Bott, M.F. 1970. "New Horizons in Linguistics." In *Computer Linguistics,* edited by J. Lyons. Harmondsworth, England: Penguin Books, pp. 215-28.

Bowdan, B.V. 1953. *Faster Than Thought.* London: Pitman.

Boyer, R.S., and J.S. Moore. 1979. *A Computational Logic.* New York: Academic Press.

Brachman, R.J. 1979. "On the Epistemological Status of Semantic Networks." In *Associative Networks,* edited by M.V. Findler. New York: Academic Press.

Brachman, R.J., and B.C. Smith. 1980. *SIGART Newsletter* 70 (special issue on knowledge representation).

Brady, J.M. 1981. *Artificial Intelligence* 17 (no. 1-3, special issue on Vision).

Brodie, M.L., and S.N. Ziles, eds. 1980. *Proceedings of the Workshop on Data Abstraction, Databases and Conceptual Modelling.* ACM. (Appeared as *SIGART Newsletter,* January 1981; *SIGMOD Record,* February 1981; and *SIGPLAN Notices,* January 1981.)

Brooks, R.A. 1981a. "Model-based Three Dimensional Interpretations of Two Dimensional Images." *Proceedings of the 7th IJCAI,* Vancouver, British Columbia: 619-24.

———. 1981b. "Symbolic Reasoning among 3-D Objects and 2-D Models." *A.I. Journal* 16:285-348.

Brown, J.S., and R.R. Burton. 1975. "Multiple Representations of Knowledge for Tutorial Reasoning." In *Representation and Understanding,* edited by D.G. Bobrow and A. Collins. New York: Academic Press, pp. 311-49.

———. 1978. "Diagnostic Models for Procedural Bugs in Basic Mathematical Skills." *Cognitive Science:* 155-92.

Brown, J.S., E. Eusebi, J. Cook, and L.H. Groner. 1986. "Algorithms for Artificial Intelligence in APL2." IBM Technical Report TR 03.281.

Bruce, B. 1975. "Case Systems for Natural Language." *Artificial Intelligence* 6:327–60.

Buchanan, B.G. 1982. "New Research on Expert Systems." In *Machine Intelligence,* vol. 10, edited by J.E. Hayes, D. Michie, and Y.H. Pao. Edinburgh: Edinburgh University Press, pp. 269–99.

Bullock, B.L., and D.H. Close. 1982. "Image Understanding Application Project: Status Report."

Burstall, R.W., and J.A. Darlington. 1977. "A Transformation System for Developing Recursive Programs." *Journal of the ACM* 24:44–67.

Burton, R.R. "Semantic Grammar: An Engineering Technique for Constructing Natural Language Understanding Systems." Technical Report 3453 for Bolt Beraneck and Newman.

"Calling 'Dr. SUMEX.' " *Time,* 17 May 1982, p. 71.

Carbonell, J.G., Sr. 1970. "AI in CAI: An Artificial Intelligence Approach to Computer-Aided Instruction." *IEEE Transactions on Man-Machine Systems* 11:190–202.

Carbonell, J.G., Jr. 1980. "POLITICS: An Experiment in Subjective Understanding and Integrated Reasoning." In *Inside Computer Understanding: Five Programs Plus Miniatures,* edited by R.C. Schank and C.K. Riesbeck. Hillsdale, NJ: Erlbaum.

Carbonell, J.G., Jr., R. Cullingford, and A. Gershman. 1981. "Steps Towards Knowledge-based Machine Translation." *IEEE Transactions on Pattern Analysis and Machine Intelligence* 3(4):376–92.

Card, S.K., T.P. Moran, and A. Newell. 1983. *The Psychology of Human–Computer Interaction.* Hillsdale, NJ: Erlbaum.

Chang, C.L., and R.C. Lee. 1973. *Symbolic Logic and Mechanical Theorem Proving.* New York: Academic Press.

Chapin, P.G., and L.M. Norton. 1968. "A Procedure for Morphological Analysis." Information System Language Studies no. 18. Bedford, MA: The MITRE Corp.

Charniak, E. 1978. "With Spoon in Hand This Must Be the Eating Frame." *Proceedings of TINLAP* 2:187–93.

———. 1981. "Six Topics in Search of a Parser: An Overview of AI Language Research." *Proceedings of the 7th IJCAI,* Vancouver, British Columbia: 1079–87.

Charniak, E., C.K. Riesbeck, and D. McDermott. 1980. *Artificial Intelligence Programming.* Hillsdale, NJ: Erlbaum.

Charniak, E., and Y.A. Wilks. 1976. *Computational Semantics: An Introduction to Artificial Intelligence and Natural Language Comprehension.* Amsterdam: North Holland.

Chase, Martyn. 1983. "Expert Warns of U.S. Software Gap: Sees Research Lagging, Especially in Artificial Intelligence." *American Metal Market* 91:9.

Cherry, L.L. 1978. "PARTS—A System for Assigning Word Classes to English Text." Computing Science Tech. Report no. 81. Murray Hill, NJ: Bell Laboratories.

Chomsky, N. 1956. "Three Models for the Description of Language." *IRE Transactions on Information Theory* 2:113–24.

———. 1969. *Syntactic Structures*. The Hague: Mouton.

Clark, K., and R. McCabe. 1982. "PROLOG: A Language for Implementing Expert Systems." *Machine Intelligence* 10:455–70.

Clocksin, W.F., and C.S. Mellish. 1981. *Programming in PROLOG*. Berlin: Springer-Verlag.

Clowes, M.B. 1971. "On Seeing Things." *Artificial Intelligence* 2:79–116.

Cohen, P., A. Davis, D. Day, M. Greenberg, R. Kjeldson, S. Lander, and C. Loiselle. 1985. "Representativeness and Uncertainty in Classification Systems." *AI Magazine* 6(3):136–49.

Cohen, P.R., and C.R. Perrault. 1979. "Elements of a Plan-based Theory of Speech Acts." *Cognitive Science* 3:177–212.

Cohen, R., and M.R. Grinberg. 1983. "A Theory of Heuristic Reasoning about Uncertainty." *A.I. Magazine* 4(2).

Colby, K. 1975. *Artificial Paranoia*. Elmsford, NY: Pergamon Press.

Cullingford, R. 1981. "SAM." In *Inside Computer Understanding*, edited by R.C. Schank and C.K. Riesbeck. Hillsdale, NJ: Erlbaum.

Davis, L.S. 1976. "Shape Matching Using Relaxation Techniques." Tech Report TR-480. Computer Science Center, University of Maryland.

Davis, M., and H. Putnam. 1960. "A Computing Procedure for Quantification Theory." *Journal of the ACM* 7(3):201–15.

Davis, R. 1976. "Applications of Meta Level Knowledge to the Construction, Maintenance and Use of Large Knowledge Bases." Report #STAN-CS-76-564. Computer Science Dept., Stanford University. (Also in *Knowledge-based Systems in Artificial Intelligence*, edited by R. Davis and D.B. Lenat. New York: McGraw-Hill, pp. 229–40.)

———. 1977. "Interactive Transfer of Expertise: Acquisition of New Inference Rules." *Proceedings of the 5th IJCAI*, Cambridge, MA: 321–28.

———. 1982. "Expert Systems: Where Are We?—And Where Do We Go from Here?" *A.I. Magazine* 3(2):3–22.

Davis, R., B.G. Buchanan, and E.H. Shortliffe. 1977. "Productions Rules as a Representation for a Knowledge-based Consultation Program." *Artificial Intelligence* 8(1):15–45.

Davis, R., and J.J. King. 1977. "An Overview of Production Systems." In *Machine Intelligence 8*, edited by E. Elcock and D. Michie. Chichester, England: Horwood.

Davis, R., and D.B. Lenat. 1982. *Knowledge-based Systems in Artificial Intelligence*. New York: McGraw-Hill.

de Champeaux, D., and L. Sint. 1977. "An Improved Bi-Directional Heuristic Search Algorithm." *Journal of the ACM* 24:177–91.

de Groot, A.D. 1966. "Perception and Memory versus Thought: Some Old Ideas and Recent Findings." In *Problem Solving,* edited by B. Kleinmuntz. New York: Wiley.

DeJong, G.F. 1979. "Skimming Stories in Real Time: An Experiment in Integrated Understanding." Research Report #158. Department of Computer Science, Yale University.

———. 1982. "An Overview of the FRUMP System." In *Strategies for Natural Language Processing,* edited by W.G. Lehnert and M.H. Ringle. Hillsdale, NJ: Erlbaum, pp. 149–76.

Dempster, A.P. 1968. "A Generalization of Bayesian Inference." *Journal of the Royal Statistical Society* 30(Series B):205–47.

Denn, N. 1981. "Story Generation after Tale-Spin." *Proceedings of the 7th IJCAI,* Vancouver, British Columbia.

Dietterich, T.G., and R.S. Michalski. 1981. "Inductive Learning of Structural Descriptions: Evaluation Criteria and Comparative Review of Selected Methods." *Artificial Intelligence* 16:257–94.

Dijkstra, E.W. 1972. "Notes on Structured Programming." In *Structured Programming,* edited by O.J., Dahl, E.W. Dijkstra, and C.A. Hoare. New York: Academic Press.

Doyle, J. 1979a. "A Glimpse of Truth Maintenance." In *Artificial Intelligence: An MIT Perspective.* Vol. 1. Cambridge, MA: MIT Press.

———. 1979b. "A Truth Maintenance System." *Artificial Intelligence* 12(3):231–72.

———. 1983a. "Methodological Simplicity in Expert System Constructions: The Case of Judgements and Reasoned Assumptions." *A.I. Magazine* 4(2).

———. 1983b. "Some Theories of Reasoned Assumptions: Essays in Rational Psychology." Carnegie-Mellon University. CMU-CS-83-125.

Dreyfus, H. 1972. *What Computers Can't Do: A Critique of Artificial Reason.* New York: Harper & Row.

Duda, R.O. 1981. "Knowledge-Based Expert Systems Come of Age." *BYTE* 6(9):238–81.

Duda, R.O., J. Gaschnig, and P. Hart. 1979. "Model Design in the PROSPECTOR Consultant System for Mineral Exploration." In *Expert Systems in the Microelectronic Age,* edited by D. Michie. Edinburgh: Edinburgh University Press.

Duda, R.O., P.E. Hart, K. Konolige, and H. Reboh. 1979. "A Computer-based Consultant for Mineral Exploration." Technical Report. Menlo Park, CA: SRI International.

Duda, R.O., P.E. Hart, and N.J. Nilsson. 1976. "Subjective Bayesian

Methods for Rule-based Inference Systems." *Proceedings of the National Computer Conference, AFIPS Proceedings* 45:1075–82.

Earl, L.L. 1970. "Experiments in Automatic Extracting and Indexing." *Information Storage and Retrieval* 6(4):313–34.

Engelberger, J.F. 1980. *Robotics in Practice.* London: Kogan Page.

Erman, L.D., F. Hayes-Roth, V.R. Lesser, and D.R. Reddy. 1980. "The Hearsay-II Speech Understanding System: Integrating Knowledge to Resolve Uncertainty." *Computing Surveys* 12(2):213–53.

Erman, L.D., P.E. London, and S.F. Fikas. 1981. "The Design and an Example Use of Hearsay-III." *Proceedings of the 7th IJCAI,* Vancouver, British Columbia: 409–15.

Ernst, G.W., and A. Newell. 1969. *GPS: A Case Study in Generality and Problem Solving.* New York: Academic Press.

Evans, T.G. 1968. "A Program for the Solution of Geometric-Analogy Intelligence Test Questions." In *Semantic Information Processing,* edited by M. Minsky. Cambridge, MA: MIT Press.

Fahlman, S.E. 1979. *NETL: A System for Representing and Using Real-World Knowledge.* Cambridge, MA: MIT Press.

———. 1980. "Design Sketch for a Million-Element NETL Machine." *Proceedings of the 1st AAAI,* Stanford, CA.

Feigenbaum, E.A. 1963. "The Simulation of Verbal Learning Behavior." In *Computers and Thought,* edited by E.A. Feigenbaum and J. Feldman. New York: McGraw-Hill, pp. 297–309.

———. 1977. "The Art of Artificial Intelligence: Themes and Case Studies in Knowledge Engineering." *Proceedings of the 5th IJCAI,* Cambridge, MA: 1014–29.

———. 1980. "Knowledge Engineering: The Applied Side of Artificial Intelligence." Memo HPP-80-21. Computer Science Department, Stanford University.

———. 1982. "Knowledge Engineering for the 1980's." Computer Science Department, Stanford University.

Feigenbaum, E.A., and J.A. Feldman, eds. 1963. *Computers and Thought.* New York: McGraw-Hill.

Feldman, J.A., and P.D. Rovner. 1969. "An ALGOL-based Associative Language." *Communications of the ACM:* 12(8):439–44.

Fikes, R.E. 1972. "REF-ARF: A System for Solving Problems Stated as Procedures." *Artificial Intelligence* 1(4):251–89.

Fikes, R.E., P.E. Hart, and N.J. Nilsson. 1972. "Learning and Executing Generalized Robot Plans." *Artificial Intelligence* 3(4):251–88.

Fikes, R.E., and T. Kehler. 1985. "The Role of Frame-based Representation in Reasoning." *Communications of the ACM* 28(9):904–20.

Fikes, R.E., and N.J. Nilsson. 1971. "STRIPS: A New Approach to the

Application of Theorem Proving to Problem Solving." *Artificial Intelligence* 2:189–208.

Fillmore, C. 1968. "The Case for Case." In *Universals in Linguistic Theory*, edited by E. Bach and R.T. Harms. New York: Holt.

———. 1971. "Some Problems for Case Grammar." In *Report of the 22nd Round Table Meeting on Linguistics and Language Studies*. Monograph Series on Languages and Linguistics, no. 24, edited by R.J. O'Brien. Washington, DC: Georgetown University Press, pp. 35–56.

Findler, N.V., ed. 1979. *Associative Networks: Representation and Use of Knowledge by Computer*. New York: Academic Press.

Finin, T.W. 1980. "The Semantic Interpretation of Compound Nominals." Ph.D. dissertation, University of Illinois at Urbana.

Flavell, J.H. 1977. *Cognitive Development*. Englewood Cliffs, NJ: Prentice-Hall.

———. 1979. "Meta Cognition and Cognitive Modelling: A New Area for Cognitive-developmental Inquiry." *American Psychologist* 34:906–11.

Forgy, C.L. 1979. "On the Efficient Implementation of Production Systems." Ph.D. dissertation, Carnegie-Mellon University.

Forgy, C.L., and McDermott, J. 1977. "OPS, a Domain-Independent Production System Language." *Proceedings of the 5th IJCAI*, Cambridge, MA, vol. 2: 933–39.

Freiherr, Gregory. 1980. *The Seeds of Artificial Intelligence—SUMEX-AIM*. Washington, DC: Division of Research Resources, NIH; prepared by Research Resource Information Center.

Frey, P.N. 1977. *Chess Skill in Man and Machine*. New York: Springer-Verlag.

Friedberg, R.M. 1958. "A Learning Machine: Part 1." *IBM Journal*, January 1958, pp. 2–13.

Gallaire, H., and J. Minker. 1978. *Logic and Databases*. New York: Plenum.

Gaschnig, J. 1979. "Performance Measurement and Analysis of Certain Search Algorithms." Ph.D. dissertation, Carnegie-Mellon University.

Gawron, J.M. et al., 1982. "Processing English with a Generalized Phrase Structure Grammar." *Proceedings of the 20th Meeting of ACL*, University of Toronto, Canada (16–18 June 1982):74–81.

Gazdar, G. 1981. "Unbounded Dependencies and Coordinate Structure." *Linguistic Inquiry* 12:155–84.

Gelernter, H., J.R. Hansen, and D. Loveland. 1963. "Empirical Explorations of the Geometry Theorem Proving Machine." In *Computers and Thought*, edited by E.A. Feigenbaum and J. Feldman. New York: McGraw-Hill, pp. 153–63.

Gelperin, D. 1977. "On the Optimality of A*." *Artificial Intelligence* 8:69–76.

Gevarter, W.B. 1982. *An Overview of Computer Vision*. Memo NBSIR 82-2582. Washington, DC: National Bureau of Standards.

———. 1983. *An Overview of Artificial Intelligence and Robotics*. Vol. 1. Washington, DC: National Bureau of Standards.

Ginsberg, M.L. 1984. "Monotonic Reasoning Using Dempster's Rule." *Proceedings of the Xth AAAI:* 126–29.

Gloess, P.Y. 1981. *Understanding Artificial Intelligence*. Sherman Oaks, CA: Alfred Publishing.

Goldman, N. 1975. "Conceptual Generation." In *Conceptual Information Processing*, edited by R.C. Schank. Amsterdam: North Holland.

Gordon, D., and G. Lakoff. 1975. "Conversational Postulates." In *Studies in Syntax*, vol. III, edited by P. Cole and J.L. Morgan. New York: Seminar Press.

Graham, N. 1979. *Artificial Intelligence*. Blue Ridge Summit, PA: Tab Books.

Graham, S.L., M.A. Harrison, and W.L. Ruzzo. 1980. "An Improved Context-Free Recognizer." *ACM Transactions on Programming Languages and Systems* 2(3):415–62.

Green, C. 1969. "Application of Theorem Proving to Problem Solving." *Proceedings of the 1st IJCAI*, Washington, DC: 219–37.

Grice, H.P. 1975. "Logic and Conversation." In *Studies in Syntax*, vol. III, edited by P. Cole and J. Morgan. New York: Seminar Press.

Griesmer, J.H., S.J. Hong, M. Karnaugh, J.K. Kastner, M.I. Schor, R.L. Ennis, D.A. Klein, K.R. Milliken, and H.M. Van Woerkom. 1984. "YES/MVS: A Continuous Real Time Expert System." *Proceedings of the Xth AAAI:* 130–36.

Grosz, B.J. 1977a. "The Representation and Use of Focus in a System for Understanding Dialogs." *Proceedings of the 5th IJCAI*, Cambridge, MA.

———. 1977b. "The Representation and Use of Focus in Dialogue Understanding." Tech. Note 151. Menlo Park, CA: Artificial Intelligence Center, SRI International.

Halliday, M.A.K. 1961. "Categories of the Theory of Grammar." *Word* 17:241–92.

Harris, L.R. 1974. "The Heuristic Search Under Conditions of Error." *Artificial Intelligence* 5(3):217–34.

———. 1977. "ROBOT: A High Performance Natural Language Processor for Data Base Query." *SIGART Newsletter* 61:39–40.

———. 1978. "The ROBOT System: Natural Language Processing Applied to Database Query." Conference of the Association for Computing Machines.

Hart, P.E., R.O. Duda, and N.T. Eihaudi. 1978. "A Computer-based Consultation System for Mineral Exploration." Technical Report. Menlo Park, CA: SRI International.

Hart, P.E., N.J. Nilsson, and B. Raphael. 1968. "A Formal Basis for the Heuristic Determination of Minimum Cost Paths." *IEEE Transactions on SSC* 4:100–107.

———. 1972. "Correction to 'A Formal Basis of the Heuristic Determination of Minimum Cost Paths.'" *Sigart Newsletter* 37:28–29.

Hayes, P.J., and G. Mouradian. 1980. "Flexible Parsing." *Proceedings of the 18th Annual Meeting of the Association for Computational Linguistics.*

Hayes-Roth, F. 1981. "AI the New Wave—A Technical Tutorial for R&D Management." AIAA-81-0827. Santa Monica, CA: Rand Corporation.

———. 1984. "The Knowledge-based Expert System: A Tutorial." *Computer* 17(9):11–28.

Hayes-Roth, F., and V.R. Lesser. 1977. "Focus of Attention in the Hearsay-II System." *Proceedings of the 5th IJCAI*, Cambridge, MA.

Hayes-Roth, F., D.A. Waterman, and D.B. Lenat. 1983. *Building Expert Systems.* Reading, MA: Addison-Wesley.

Heitmeyer, C.L., and S.H. Wilson. 1980. "Military Message Systems: Current Status and Future Directions." *IEEE Transactions on Communications* 28(9):1645–54.

Hendrix, G.G. 1977a. "Expanding the Utility of Semantic Networks through Partitioning." *Proceedings of the 5th IJCAI*, Cambridge, MA: 115–21.

———. 1977b. "Human Engineering for Applied Natural Language Processing." *Proceedings of the 5th IJCAI*, Cambridge, MA: 183–91.

———. 1977c. "The LIFER Manual: A Guide to Building Practical Natural Language Interfaces." Technical Report 138. Stanford, CA: Artificial Intelligence Center, SRI International.

———. 1977d. "LIFER: A Natural Language Interface Facility." *Sigart Newsletter* 61:25–26.

Hendrix, G.G., and W.H. Lewis. 1981. "Transportable Natural-Language Interfaces to Databases." *Proceedings of the 19th Annual Meeting of the Association for Computational Linguistics*, Stanford University.

Hendrix, G.G., and Sacerdoti, E.D. 1981. "Natural Language Processing: The Field in Perspective." *BYTE*, September 1981, pp. 304–52.

Hendrix, G.G., E.D. Sacerdoti, D. Sagalowicz, and J. Slocum. 1978. "Developing a Natural Language Interface to Complex Data." *ACM Transactions on Database Systems* 3:105–47.

Henle, P. 1965. *Language, Thought, and Culture.* Ann Arbor, MI: University of Michigan Press.

Heuristic Programming Project 1980. 1980. Computer Science Department, Stanford University.

Hewitt, C. 1971. "Procedural Embedding of Knowledge in PLANNER." *Proceedings of the 2nd IJCAI*, London: 167.

———. 1972. "Description and Theoretical Analysis of PLANNER: A Language for Proving Theorems and Manipulating Models in a Robot."

Tech. Report TR 258. Cambridge, MA: Artificial Intelligence Laboratory, MIT.

Hilgard, E.R., and G.H. Bower. 1975. *Theories of Learning*. Englewood Cliffs, NJ: Prentice-Hall.

Hodge, M.H., and F.M. Pennington. 1973. "Some Studies of Word Abbreviation Behavior." *Journal of Experimental Psychology* 98(2):350–61.

Hofstadter, D.R. 1981. "How Might Analogy, the Core of Human Thinking, Be Understood by Computer?" *Scientific American,* September 1981, p. 18.

Hunt, E. 1975. *Artificial Intelligence*. New York: Academic Press.

"Is this Computer Really Intelligent?" 1981. *Technology Review* 83:82.

Jensen, K., and Heidorn, G.E. 1983. "The Fitted Parse: 100% Parsing Capability in a Syntactic Grammar of English." *Proceedings of the Conference on Applied NLP,* Santa Monica, CA: 93–98.

Johnson, Jan. 1981. "Intellect on Demand. (English Query Language)." *Datamation* 27:73.

Joseph, E.C. 1982. "Defense Computers and Software—What's Ahead for AI?" *Concepts* 5:141.

Josni, A.K., B.L. Webber, and I.A. Sag, eds. 1981. *Elements of Discourse Understanding*. Cambridge, England: Cambridge University Press.

Kahn, G., S. Nowlan, and J. McDermott. 1985. "MORE: An Intelligent Knowledge Acquisition Tool." *Proceedings of the 9th IJCAI,* Los Angeles, CA, vol. 1: 581–85.

Kaplan, S.J. 1981. "Appropriate Responses to Inappropriate Questions." In *Elements of Discourse Understanding,* edited by A.K. Josni, B.L. Webber, and I.A. Sag. Cambridge, England: Cambridge University Press.

Kaplan, S.J., ed. 1982. "Natural Language." *Sigart Newsletter* 79:27–109.

Kaplan, S.J., and D. Ferris. 1982. "Natural Language in the DP World." *Datamation* 28:114.

Kauffmann, A. 1975. *Introduction to the Theory of Fuzzy Subsets*. Vol. 1. New York: Academic Press.

Kiefer, F. 1982. "The Drive for 'Thinking' Computers: Japan Tries to Race Past U.S." *Christian Science Monitor,* 30 September 1982, p. 1.

Klein, S., and R.F. Simmons. 1963. "A Computational Approach to Grammatical Coding of English Words." *Journal of the ACM* 10(3):334–47.

Klein, S., et al. 1976. "Automatic Novel Writing: A Status Report." 1976. Technical Report. Department of Computer Sciences, University of Wisconsin at Madison.

Knuth, D.E. 1973. *The Art of Computer Programming: Sorting and Searching*. Reading, MA: Addison-Wesley.

Knuth, D.E., and R.W. Moore. 1975. "An Analysis of Alpha-Beta Pruning." *Artificial Intelligence* 6(4):293–96.

Kowalski, R.A. 1979. *Logic for Problem Solving*. Amsterdam: North Holland.

Krutch, J. 1981. *Experiments in Artificial Intelligence for Small Computers.* Indianapolis: Howard W. Sams.

Kuipers, S.J. 1975. "A Frame for Frames." In *Representation and Understanding,* edited by D.G. Bobrow and A. Collins. New York: Academic Press.

Kulikowski, C.A. 1980. "Artificial Intelligence Methods and Systems for Medical Consultation." *IEEE Transactions on Pattern Analysis and Machine Intelligence.*

Kwasny, S.C., and N.K. Sondheimer. 1981. "Relaxation Techniques for Parsing Ill-Formed Input." *American Journal of Computational Linguistics* 7(2):92–108.

Lancaster, F.W. 1978. *Towards Paperless Information Systems.* New York: Academic Press.

Lea, W. 1980. *Trends in Speech Recognition.* Englewood Cliffs, NJ: Prentice-Hall.

Lehnert, W.C. 1978. *The Process of Question Answering: A Computer Simulation of Cognition.* Hillsdale, NJ: Erlbaum.

Lenat, D.B. 1977a. "Automated Theory Formation in Mathematics." *Proceedings of the 5th IJCAI,* Cambridge, MA: 833–42.

———. 1977b. "The Ubiquity of Discovery." *Artificial Intelligence* 9(3).

———. 1982a. "AM: Artificial Intelligence Approach to Discovery in Mathematics as Heuristic Search." In *Knowledge-based Systems in Artificial Intelligence,* edited by R. Davis and D.B. Lenat. New York: McGraw-Hill.

———. 1982b. "Heuristics: The Nature of Heuristics." *Artificial Intelligence* 19(2):189–249.

———. 1983a. "EURISKO: A Program That Learns New Heuristics and Domain Concepts. The Nature of Heuristics III: Program Design and Results." *Artificial Intelligence* 21(1,2):61–99.

———. 1983b. "Theory Formation by Heuristic Search. The Nature of Heuristics II: Background and Examples." *Artificial Intelligence* 21(1, 2): 31–61.

Leverett, B.W., R.G.G. Cattell, S.O. Hobbs, J.M. Newcomer, A.J. Reiner, B.R. Shatz, and W.A. Wulf. 1980. "An Overview of the Production Quality Compiler-Compiler Project." *Computer* 13(8):38–49.

Lewis, H.R., and C.H. Papadimitriou. 1978. "The Efficiency of Algorithms." *Scientific American,* January 1978.

Lindsay, R.K. 1963. "Inferential Memory as the Basis of Machines which Understand Natural Language." In *Computers and Thought,* edited by E.A. Feigenbaum and J. Feldman. New York: McGraw-Hill.

Lindsay, R.K., B.G. Buchanan, E.A. Feigenbaum, and J. Lederberg. 1980. *Applications of Artificial Intelligence for Organic Chemistry: The DENDRAL Project.* New York: McGraw-Hill.

Lovelace, A. 1961. "Notes upon L.F. Menabrea's Sketch of the Analytical Engine Invented by Charles Babbage." In *Charles Babbage and His Calculating Engines,* edited by P. Morrison and E. Morrison. New York: Dover.

McCarthy, J. 1960. "Recursive Functions of Symbolic Expressions and Their Computation by Machine." *Communications of the ACM* 7:184–95.

———. 1980. "Circumscription—A Form of Non-Monotonic Reasoning." *Artificial Intelligence* 13:27–39.

McCarthy, J., and P.J. Hayes. 1969. "Some Philosophical Problems from the Standpoint of Artificial Intelligence." In *Machine Intelligence 4,* edited by B. Meltzer and D. Michie. Edinburgh: Edinburgh University Press.

McCorduck, P. 1979. *Machines Who Think.* San Francisco: Freeman.

McCulloch, W.S., and W. Pitts. 1948. "A Logical Calculus of the Ideas Imminent in Neural Nets." *Bulletin of Mathematical Biophysics* 5.

McDermott, D. 1978. "Planning and Acting." *Cognitive Science* 2:71–109.

McDermott, D., and J. Doyle. 1980. "Non-Monotonic Logic I." *Artificial Intelligence* 13:41–72.

McDermott, J. 1982. "R1: A Rule-based Configurer of Computer Systems." *Artificial Intelligence* 19:39–88.

McDonald, D.B. 1980. "Natural Language Production as a Process of Decision-Making Under Constraints." Ph.D. dissertation, Massachusetts Institute of Technology.

———. 1982. "Understanding Noun Compounds." Ph.D. dissertation, Carnegie-Mellon University.

MACSYMA Group. 1977. "MACSYMA Reference Manual." Technical Report. Massachusetts Institute of Technology.

Malhotra, Ashok. 1975. "Design Criteria for a Knowledge-Based English Language System for Management: An Experimental Analysis." MAC TR 146, Project MAC. Massachusetts Institute of Technology.

Mann, W.C. 1981. "Two Discourse Generators." *Proceedings of the 19th Annual Meeting of the Association for Computational Linguistics.*

Mann, W.C., and J.A. Moore. 1981. "Computer Generation of Multiparagraph English Text." *American Journal of Computational Linguistics* 7(1).

Manna, Z., and R. Waldinger. "A Deductive Approach to Program Synthesis." *ACM Transactions on Programming Languages and Systems* 2(1):542–51.

Marcus, M.P. 1979. "A Theory of Syntactic Recognition for Natural Language." In *Artificial Intelligence: An MIT Perspective,* vol. 1, edited by P.H. Winston and R.H. Brown. Cambridge, MA: MIT Press.

———. 1980. *A Theory of Syntactic Recognition for Natural Language.* Cambridge, MA: MIT Press.

Marr, D. 1982. *Vision.* San Francisco: Freeman.

Martelli, A. 1977. "On the Complexity of Admissible Search Algorithms." *Artificial Intelligence* 8:1–13.

Martelli, A., and U. Montanari. 1973. "Additive And/Or Graphs." *Proceedings of the 3rd IJCAI,* Stanford, CA: 1–11.

———. 1978. "Optimization Decision Trees through Heuristically Guided Search." *Communications of the ACM* 21(12):1025–39.

Meehan, J.R. 1981. "Tale-Spin." In *Inside Computer Understanding: Five Programs Plus Miniatures,* edited by R.C. Schank and C.K. Riesbeck. Hillsdale, NJ: Erlbaum.

Michalski, R.S., J.G. Carbonell, Jr., and T.M. Mitchell, eds. 1986. *Machine Learning.* 2nd ed. Palo Alto, CA: Tioga.

Michalski, R.S., and R.L. Chilansky. 1980. "Learning by Being Told and Learning from Examples: An Experimental Comparison of the Two Methods of Knowledge Acquisition in the Context of Developing an Expert System for Soybean Disease Diagnosis." *International Journal of Policy Analysis and Information Systems* 4:125–61.

Michie, D. 1980. "Knowledge-based Systems." Report 80-1001. University of Illinois at Urbana-Champaign.

Michie, D., ed. 1979. *Expert Systems in the Microelectronic Age.* Edinburgh: Edinburgh University Press.

Miller, G.A., E. Galanter, and K.H. Pribam. 1960. *Plans and the Structure of Behavior.* New York: Holt.

Miller, R., Pople, H., and Myers, J. 1982. "Internist-1: An Experimental Computer-based Diagnostic Consultant for General Internal Medicine." *New England Journal of Medicine* 307(8):468–76.

Minsky, M. 1963. "Steps toward Artificial Intelligence." In *Computers and Thought,* edited by E.A. Feigenbaum and J. Feldman, pp. 406–50. New York: McGraw-Hill.

———. 1967. *Computation: Finite and Infinite Machines.* Englewood Cliffs, NJ: Prentice-Hall.

———. 1975. "A Framework for Representing Knowledge." In *Psychology of Computer Vision,* edited by P. Winston. New York: McGraw-Hill.

———. 1980. "K-Lines." *Cognitive Science.*

Minsky, M., and S. Papert. 1969. *Perceptrons: An Introduction to Computational Geometry.* Cambridge, MA: MIT Press.

Morik, K., and C.-R. Rollinger. 1985. "The Real Estate Agent—Modeling Users by Uncertain Reasoning." *AI Magazine* 6(2):44–52.

Mostow, D.J. 1981. "Mechanical Transformation of Task Heuristics into Operational Procedures." Report No. CS-81-113. Computer Science Department, Carnegie-Mellon University.

Myers, Edith. 1981. "Machines that LISP: New Machines May Become the Personal Computers of Choice for the Artificial Intelligence Community." *Datamation* 27:105.

Newborn, M. 1975. *Computer Chess*. New York: Academic Press.
Newell, A. 1973. "Production Systems: Models of Control Structures." In *Visual Information Processing*, edited by W.G. Chase. New York: Academic Press.
———. 1983. "The Heuristic of George Polya and Its Relation to Artificial Intelligence." In *Methods of Heuristics*, edited by R. Gronar, M. Groner, and W.F. Bischoot. Hillsdale, NJ: Erlbaum.
Newell, A., J.C. Shaw, and H.A. Simon. 1960. "A Variety of Intelligent Learning in a General Problem Solver." In *Self-Organizing Systems*, edited by M.C. Yovits and S. Cameron. Elmsford, NY: Pergamon Press.
———. 1963. "Empirical Explorations with the Logic Theory Machine: A Case Study in Heuristics." In *Computers and Thought*, edited by E.A. Feigenbaum and J. Feldman. New York: McGraw-Hill.
Newell, A., and H.A. Simon. 1963. "GPS: A Program That Simulates Human Thought." In *Computers and Thought*, edited by E.A. Feigenbaum and J. Feldman. New York: McGraw-Hill.
———. 1972. *Human Problem Solving*. Englewood Cliffs, NJ: Prentice-Hall.
———. 1976. "Computer Science as Empirical Inquiry: Symbols and Search." *Communications of the ACM* 19(3):113-26.
Newell, A., and F.N. Tonge. 1960. "An Introduction to Processing Language V." *Communications of the ACM* 3:205-11.
Nii, H.P., and N. Aiello. 1979. "AGE (Attempt to Generalize): A Knowledge-Based Program for Building Knowledge-Based Programs." *Proceedings of the 6th IJCAI*, Tokyo: 645-55.
Nilsson, N.J. 1965. *Learning Machines*. New York: McGraw-Hill.
———. 1980. *Principles of Artificial Intelligence*. Palo Alto, CA: Tioga.
Nishida, T., and S. Doshita. 1983. "An Application of Montague Grammar to English-Japanese Machine Translation." *Proceedings of the Conference on Applied NLP*, Santa Monica, CA.
Norman, D.A. 1981. *Perspectives on Cognitive Science*. Norwood, NJ: Ablex.
Novak, G.S., and A. Araya. 1980. "Research on Expert Problem Solving in Physics." *Proceedings of the 1st Conference of AAAI*, Stanford, CA.
Ogden, C.K., and I.A. Richards. 1947. *The Meaning of Meaning*. New York: Harcourt, Brace.
Paul, R.P. 1981. *Robot Manipulators: Mathematics, Programming and Control*. Cambridge, MA: MIT Press.
Paulos, J.A. 1980. *Mathematics and Humor*. Chicago: University of Chicago Press.
Pearl, J. 1982. "The Solution for the Branching Factor of the Alpha-Beta Pruning Algorithm and its Optimality." *Communications of the ACM* 25(8):559-64.

Peltus, M. 1982. "Artificial Intelligence—Key to the Fifth Generation." *Datamation* 28:114.

Penzins, A.A. 1982. "Friendly Interfaces." *Technology Review* 85:30.

Pereira, F.C.N., and D.H.D. Warren. 1980. "Definite Clause Grammars for Language Analysis—A Survey of the Formalism and a Comparison with Augmented Transition Networks." *Artificial Intelligence* 13(3):231–78.

Peterson, J.L. 1980. "Computer Programs for Detecting and Correcting Spelling Errors." *Communications of the ACM* 23(12):676–87.

Ploya, G. 1957. *How to Solve It*. Princeton, NJ: Princeton University Press.

Pohl, I. 1971. "Bi-directional Search." In *Machine Intelligence 6*, edited by B. Meltzer and D. Michie. New York: American Elsevier.

Pople, H. 1977. "The Formation of Composite Hypotheses in Diagnostic Problem Solving: An Exercise in Synthetic Reasoning." *Proceedings of the 5th IJCAI*, Cambridge, MA, vol. 2: 1030–37.

Post, E.L. 1943. "Formal Reductions of the General Combinatorial Decision Problem." *American Journal of Mathematics* 85:197–268.

Quillian, R. 1968. "Semantic Memory." In *Semantic Information Processing*, edited by M. Minsky. Cambridge, MA: MIT Press.

Quine, W.V. 1961. *From a Logical Point of View*. 2nd ed. New York: Harper & Row.

Quine, W.V., and J. S. Ullian. 1978. *The Web of Belief*. New York: Random House.

Quinlan, J.R. 1979a. "Discovering Rules by Induction from Large Collections of Examples." In *Expert Systems in the Microelectronic Age*, edited by D. Michie, pp. 168–201. Edinburgh: Edinburgh University Press.

———. 1979b. "A Knowledge-based System for Locating Missing High Cards in Bridge." *Proceedings of the 6th IJCAI*, Tokyo.

Raphael, B. 1968. "A Computer Program for Semantic Information Retrieval." In *Semantic Information Processing*, edited by M. Minsky. Cambridge, MA: MIT Press.

Reddy, D.R. 1976. "Speech Recognition by Machine: A Review." *Proceedings of the IEEE* 64.

Reichenberg, H. 1947. *Elements of Symbolic Logic*. New York: Free Press.

Reiger, C., and S. Small. 1979. "Word Expert Parsing." *Proceedings of the 6th IJCAI*, Tokyo: 723–28.

Reingold, E.M., J. Nievergelt, and N. Dao. 1977. *Combinatorial Algorithms: Theory and Practice*. Englewood Cliffs, NJ: Prentice-Hall.

Reinstein, H., and J. Aikens. 1981. "Application Design: Issues in Expert System Architecture." *Proceedings of the 7th IJCAI*, Vancouver, British Columbia, vol. 2: 888–92.

Reiter, R. 1979. "On Reasoning by Default." *Proceedings of TINLAP 2*: 210–18.

———. 1980. "A Logic for Default Reasoning." *Artificial Intelligence* 19:81–132.

Reitman, W., and B. Wilcox. 1976. "Pattern Recognition and Pattern-directed Inferences in a Program for Playing Go." In *Pattern-directed Inference Systems,* edited by D.A. Waterman and F. Hayes-Roth. New York: Academic Press.

———. 1979. "The Structure and Performance of the Interim 2 Go Program." *Proceedings of the 6th IJCAI,* Tokyo.

Rich, E. 1979. "User Modeling via Stereotypes." *Cognitive Science* 3:329–54.

———. 1982. "Programs as Data for Their Help Systems." *Proceedings of the National Computer Conference:* 481–85.

———. 1983. *Artificial Intelligence.* New York: McGraw-Hill.

Rieger, C. 1975. "Conceptual Memory." In *Conceptual Information Processing,* edited by R.C. Schank. Amsterdam: North Holland.

Riesbeck, C.K. 1975. "Conceptual Analysis." In *Conceptual Information Processing,* edited by R.C. Schank. Amsterdam: North Holland.

Roberts, R.B., and I.P. Goldstein. 1977. "The FRL Manual." Technical Report. MIT Artificial Intelligence Laboratory.

Roberts, S.K. 1982. "To Teach a Machine." *Technology Review* 85:22.

Robinson, A.E., D.E. Appelt, B.J. Grosz, G.G. Hendrix, and J.J. Robinson. 1980. "Interpreting Natural Language Utterances in Dialog about Tasks." AI Center TN 210. Menlo Park, CA: SRI International.

Robinson, J.J. 1965. "A Machine-oriented Logic Based on the Resolution Principle." *Journal of the ACM* 12:23.

Rosenblatt, F. 1957. "The Perceptron: A Perceiving and Recognizing Automaton." Project PARA, Cornell Aeronautical Laboratory, Cornell University, Report 85-460-1.

———. 1958. "The Perceptron: A Probabilistic Model for Information Organization and Storage in the Brain." *Psychological Review* 65:358–408.

———. 1962. *Principles of Neurodynamics: Perceptrons and the Theory of Brain Mechanisms.* Washington, DC: Spartan Books.

Rychener, M.D. 1981. "Knowledge-Based Expert Systems: A Brief Bibliography." *Sigart Newsletter* 78.

Sacerdoti, E.D. 1975. "The Nonlinear Nature of Plans." *Proceedings of the 4th IJCAI,* Thilisi, USSR: 206–14.

———. 1977a. "Language Access to Distributed Data with Error Recovery." *Proceedings of the 5th IJCAI,* Cambridge, MA: 196–202.

———. 1977b. *A Structure for Plans and Behavior.* New York: Elsevier.

Samuel, A.L. 1959. "Some Studies in Machine Learning Using the Game of Checkers." *IBM Journal of Research and Development* 3:210–29. (Also in *Computers and Thought,* edited by E.A. Feigenbaum and J. Feldman. New York: McGraw-Hill, 1963.)

Sandewall, E. 1978. "Programming in an Interactive Environment: the 'LISP' Experience." *Computing Surveys* 10(1):35-71.

Schank, R.C. 1972. "Conceptual Dependency: A Theory of Natural Language Understanding." *Cognitive Psychology* 3:552-631.

———. 1975. *Conceptual Information Processing*. Amsterdam: North Holland.

———. 1978. "Identification of Conceptualizations Underlying Natural Language." In *Computer Models of Thought and Language*, edited by R.C. Schank and K. Colby. San Francisco: Freeman.

———. 1980. "Language and Memory." *Cognitive Science* 4:243-84.

Schank, R.C., and R.P. Abelson. 1977. *Scripts, Plans, Goals, and Understanding*. Hillsdale, NJ: Erlbaum.

Schank, R.C., and J.G. Carbonell, Jr. 1979. "Re: The Gettysburg Address: Representing Social and Political Acts." In *Associative Networks: Representation and Use of Knowledge by Computers*, edited by N. Findler. New York: Academic Press.

Schank, R.C., and K. Colby, eds. 1978. *Computer Models of Thought and Language*. San Francisco: Freeman.

Schank, R.C., and D. Nash-Webber, eds. 1975. Proceedings of Theoretical Issues in Natural Language Processing: An Interdisciplinary Workshop in Computational Psychology, Linguistics and Artificial Intelligence.

Schank, R.C., and C.K. Riesbeck, eds. 1981. *Inside Computer Understanding: Five Programs Plus Miniatures*. Hillsdale, NJ: Erlbaum.

Schank, R.C., and Yale A.I. Project. 1975. "SAM—A Story Understander." Research Report 43. Department of Computer Science, Yale University.

Schubert, L. 1975. "Extending the Expressive Power of Semantic Networks." *Proceedings of the 4th IJCAI*, Thilisi, USSR: 158-64.

Schutzer, D. 1985a. "Artificial Intelligence-Based Very Large Data Base Organization and Management." In *Applications in Artificial Intelligence*, edited by S.J. Andriole. Princeton, NJ: Petrocelli Books.

———. 1985b. "The Tools and Techniques of Applied Artificial Intelligence." In *Applications in Artificial Intelligence*, edited by S.J. Andriole. Princeton, NJ: Petrocelli Books.

Searle, J.R. 1969. *Speech Acts*. Cambridge, England: Cambridge University Press.

Selfridge, O.G. 1959. "Pandemonium: A Paradigm for Learning." *Proceedings of the Symposium on Mechanization of Thought Processes*, edited by D. Blake and A. Uttley. London: H.M. Stationery Office.

Shafer, Glenn A. 1976. *A Mathematical Theory of Evidence*. Princeton, NJ: Princeton University Press.

Shannon, C.E. 1950. "Programming a Computer for Playing Chess." *Philosophical Magazine* 41:265-75.

Shapiro, Stuart C. 1979. *Techniques of Artificial Intelligence*. New York: Van Nostrand Reinhold.

Shaw, D. 1985. "NON-VON's Applicability to Three A.I. Task Areas." *Proceedings of the 9th IJCAI*, Los Angeles, CA, vol. 1: 61–73.

Shaw, D., W.R. Swartout, and C. Green. 1975. "Inferring LISP Programs from Examples." *Proceedings of the 4th IJCAI*, Thilisi, USSR: 260–67.

Shortliffe, E.H. 1976. *Computer-based Medical Consultations: MYCIN*. New York: Elsevier.

Shortliffe, E.H., and B.G. Buchanan. 1975. "A Model of Inexact Reasoning in Medicine." *Mathematical Biosciences* 23:351–79.

Shortliffe, E.H., and B.G. Buchanan, eds. 1984. *Rule-based Expert Systems: The MYCIN Experiments of the Stanford Heuristic Programming Project*. Reading, MA: Addison-Wesley.

Shortliffe, E.H., B.G. Buchanan, and E.A. Feigenbaum. 1979. "Knowledge Engineering for Medical Decision Making: A Review of Computer-based Clinical Decision Aids." *Proceedings of the IEEE* 67:1207–24.

Sidner, C.L. 1978. "The Use of Focus as a Tool for Disambiguation of Definite Noun Phrases." *Proceeding of TINLAP 2*.

———. 1979. "Disambiguating References and Interpreting Sentence Purpose in Discourse." In *Artificial Intelligence: An MIT Perspective*, edited by P.H. Winston and R.H. Brown. Vol. 1. Cambridge, MA: MIT Press, pp. 233–52.

Siklossy, L., and J. Roach. 1979. "Proving the Impossible Is Possible: Disproofs Based on Hereditary Partitions." *Proceedings of the 6th IJCAI*, Tokyo, Japan.

Simmons, R.F. 1972. *Computations from the English*. Englewood Cliffs, NJ: Prentice-Hall.

———. 1978. "Semantic Networks: Their Computation and Use for Understanding English Sentences." In *Computer Models of Thought and Language*, edited by R.C. Schank and K.M. Colby. San Francisco: Freeman.

Simmons, R.F., and J. Slocum. 1972. "Generating English Discourse from Semantic Networks." *Communications of the ACM* 15(10):891–905.

Simon, H.A. 1974. "How Big Is a Chunk?" *Science*, pp. 482–88.

———. 1981. *The Sciences of the Artificial*. 2nd ed. Cambridge, MA: MIT Press.

Simon, H.A., and J. B. Kadane. 1975. "Optimal Problem-solving Search: All-or-None Solutions." *Artificial Intelligence* 6(3):235–47.

Simon, H.A., and G. Lea. 1974. "Problem Solving and Rule Induction: A Unified View." In *Knowledge and Cognition*, edited by L. Gregg. Hillsdale, NJ: Erlbaum, pp. 105–27.

Simon, H.A., and L. Siklossy. 1972. *Representation and Meaning*. Englewood Cliffs, NJ: Prentice-Hall.

Slocum, J. 1981. "A Practical Comparison of Parsing Strategies for Machine Translation and Other Natural Language Purposes." Ph.D. dissertation, University of Texas at Austin.

Smith, R.G., and P. Friedland. 1980. "A User's Guide to the Unit System." Tech. Report. Heuristic Programming Project, Stanford University.

Smith, R.G., T.M. Mitchell, R.A. Chestek, and B.G. Buchanan. 1977. "A Model for Learning Systems." *Proceedings of the 5th IJCAI*, Cambridge, MA.

Sridnaran, N.S. 1978. *Artificial Intelligence* 11. Special issue on Applications to the Sciences and Medicine.

Stallman, R.M., and G.J. Sussman. 1977. "Forward Reasoning and Dependency-directed Backtracking in a System for Computer-aided Circuit Analysis." *Artificial Intelligence* 9(2):135–96.

Stanier, A. 1975. "BRIBIP: A Bridge Bidding Program." *Proceedings of the 4th IJCAI*, Thilisi, USSR.

Steele, G.L. 1984. *COMMON LISP*. Bedford, MA: Digital Press.

Steele, G.L., and G.J. Sussman. 1980. "Design of a LISP-based Microprocessor." *Communications of the ACM* 11:628–45.

Stefik, M. 1979. "An Examination of a Frame-Structured Representation System." *Proceedings of the 6th IJCAI*, Tokyo, vol. 2: 845–52.

———. 1981. "Planning and Meta-Planning (MOLGEN: Part 1)." *Artificial Intelligence* 16(2):111–39.

Stefik, M., J. Aikens, R. Balzer, J. Benoit, L. Birnbaum, F. Hayes-Roth, and E.D. Sacerdoti. 1982. "The Organization of Expert Systems." *Artificial Intelligence* 18:135–73.

Stefik, M., and D.G. Bobrow. 1986. "Programming: Themes and Variations." *A.I. Magazine* 6(4):40–62.

Stefik, M., D.G. Bobrow, S. Mittal, and L. Conway. 1983. "Knowledge Programming in LOOPS." *A.I. Magazine* 3(4):3–15.

Stefik, M., et al. 1982. "The Organization of Expert Systems: A Prescriptive Tutorial." VLSI-82-1. Xerox, Palo Alto Research Center.

Strat, T.M. 1984. "Continuous Belief Functions for Evidential Reasoning." *Proceedings of the Conference of AAAI*, 308–13.

Struble, W.T. 1982. "The Year of the Robot." *Technology Review* 85:87.

Summers, P. 1977. "A Methodology for LISP Program Construction from Examples." *Journal of the ACM* 24:161–75.

Sussman, G.J. 1973. "A Computational Model of Skill Acquisition." A.I. Technical Report 297. A.I. Lab, Massachusetts Institute of Technology.

———. 1975. *A Computer Model of Skill Acquisition*. Cambridge, MA: MIT Press.

Sussman, G.J., and D. McDermott. 1972. "Why Conniving Is Better Than Planning." Technical Report, MIT A.I. Memo 2655A. Massachusetts Institute of Technology.

Swartout, W.R. 1981. "Explaining and Justifying Expert Consulting Programs." *Proceedings of the 7th IJCAI,* Vancouver, British Columbia: 812–22.

Swinehart, D., and R. Sproull. 1971. "SAIL." Technical Report 57.2. Stanford AI Project, Stanford University.

Szolovits, P., and S.G. Pauker. 1978. "Categorical and Probabilistic Reasoning in Medical Diagnosis." *Artificial Intelligence* 11:115–54.

Tate, A. 1977. "Generating Project Networks." *Proceedings of the 5th IJCAI,* Cambridge, MA: 888–93.

"Teaching a Machine the Shades of Gray." *Science News,* 17 January 1981, p. 38.

Tennant, H. 1981. *Natural Language Processing.* Princeton, NJ: Petrocelli Books.

"A 'Thinking' Robot Is Invented at Center at Coast University." *New York Times,* 25 February 1982, p. 14.

Thompson, B.H. 1980. "Linguistic Analysis of Natural Language Communication with Computers." *Proceedings of the 8th International Conference on Computational Linguistics,* Tokyo, pp. 190–201.

Tong, R.M., D.E. Shapiro, J.S. Dean, and B.P. McCune. 1983. "A Comparison of Uncertainty Calculi in an Expert System for Information Retrieval." *Proceedings of the 8th IJCAI,* Karlsruhe, West Germany.

Turing, A. 1963. "Computing Machinery and Intelligence." In *Computers and Thought,* edited by E.A. Feigenbaum and J. Feldman. New York: McGraw-Hill.

Tversky, A., and D. Kahneman. 1974. "Judgement under Uncertainty: Heuristics and Biases." *Science,* 185:1124–31.

———. 1982. "Subjective Probability: A Judgement of Representativeness." In *Judgement under Uncertainty: Heuristics and Biases,* edited by D. Kahneman, P. Slovic, and A. Tversky. Cambridge, England: Cambridge University Press.

Uttal, Bro. 1982. "Here Comes Computer Inc." *Fortune,* 4 October 1982, p. 82.

Van Melle, W. 1980. "A Domain Independent System That Aids in Constructing Knowledge Bases." Ph.D. dissertation, Computer Science Department, Stanford University. Rep. STAN-CS-80-820.

Van Melle, W., A.C. Scott, J.S. Bennett, and M.A. Peairs. 1981. "The EMYCIN Manual." Technical Report. Heuristic Programming Project, Stanford University.

Vere, S. 1981. *Planning in Time: Windows and Durations for Activities and Goals.* Pasadena, CA: JPL.

Walker, D.E. 1976. *Speech Understanding Research.* Amsterdam: North Holland.

Waltz, D.L. 1972. "Generating Semantic Descriptions from Drawings of

Scenes with Shadows." AI-TR-271, Project MAC MIT. Massachusetts Institute of Technology.

———. 1975a. "Natural Language Access to a Large Data Base." In *Advance Papers of the International Joint Conference on Artificial Intelligence.* Cambridge, MA: MIT Press.

———. 1975b. "Understanding Line Drawings of Scenes with Shadows." In *The Psychology of Computer Vision,* edited by P. Winston. New York: McGraw-Hill.

———. 1977. "Natural Language Interfaces." *Sigart Newsletter* 61:16–64.

———. 1978. "An English Language Question-answering System for a Large Relational Data Base." *Communications of the ACM* 21(7):526–39.

———. 1982a. "Artificial Intelligence." *Scientific American,* October 1982, p. 118.

———. 1982b. "The State of Art in Natural Language Understanding." In *Strategies for Natural Language Processing,* edited by W.G. Lehnert and M.H. Ringle. Hillsdale, NJ: Erlbaum, pp. 3–32.

Waltz, D.L., ed. 1978. *Theoretical Issues in Natural Language Processing 2.* New York: Association for Computing Machines.

Warren, D.H.D., and L.N. Pereira. 1977. "Prolog—The Language and Its Implementation Compared to LISP." *Proceedings of the Symposium on Artificial Intelligence and Programming Languages.* Sigplan Notices 12(8) and Sigart Newsletter 64.

Waterman, D.A., and F. Hayes-Roth. 1978. *Pattern-directed Inference Systems.* New York: Academic Press.

Weaver, W. 1955. "Translation." In *Machine Translation of Languages,* edited by Locke and A.D. Booth. New York: Technology Press of MIT and Wiley, pp. 15–23.

Webber, B.L., and T.W. Finn. 1982. "Tutorial on Natural Language Interfaces, Part 1—Basic Theory and Practice." *Proceedings of the 2nd Conference of AAAI,* Pittsburgh, PA.

Weischedel, R.M., and N.K. Sondheimer. 1981. "A Framework for Processing Ill-formed Input." TM H-00519. Blue Bell, PA: Sperry Univac.

Weiss, S.M., and C.A. Kulikowski. 1979. "EXPERT: A System for Developing Consultation Models." *Proceedings of the 6th IJCAI,* Tokyo, vol. 2: 942–47.

Weizenbaum, J. 1966. "ELIZA—A Computer Program for the Study of Natural Language Communication between Man and Machine." *Communications of the ACM* 9(1):36–44.

Whitehead, A.N., and B. Russell. 1950. *Principa Mathematica,* 2nd ed. Cambridge, England: Cambridge University Press.

Wilensky, R. 1978. "Why John Married Mary: Understanding Stories Involving Recurring Goals." *Cognitive Science* 2:235–66.

———. 1981. "PAM." In *Inside Computing Understanding,* edited by R.C. Schank and C.K. Riesbeck. Hillsdale, NJ: Erlbaum.

———. 1982. "Talking to UNIX in English: An Overview of UC." *Proceedings of the 2nd Conference of AAAI,* Pittsburgh, PA.

Wilks, Y.A. 1972. *Grammar, Meaning and the Machine Analysis of Language.* London: Routledge and Kegan Paul.

———. 1973. "An Artificial Intelligence Approach to Machine Translation." In *Computer Models of Thought and Language,* edited by R.C. Schank and K.M. Colby. San Francisco: Freeman.

———. 1975a. "Preference Semantics." In *Formal Semantics of Natural Language,* edited by E.L. Keenan. Cambridge, England: Cambridge University Press.

———. 1975b. "A Preferential, Pattern-Seeking Semantics for Natural Language." *Artificial Intelligence* 6:53–74.

Winograd, T. 1972. *Understanding Natural Language.* New York: Academic Press.

———. 1973. "A Procedural Model of Language Understanding." In *Computer Models of Thought and Language,* edited by R.C. Schank and K.M. Colby. San Francisco: Freeman, pp. 152–86.

———. 1975. "Frame Representation and the Declarative-Procedural Controversy." In *Representation and Understanding,* edited by D.G. Bobrow and A. Collins. New York: Academic Press.

———. 1978. "On Primitives, Prototypes, and Other Semantic Anomalies." *Proceedings of TINLAP 2:* 25–32.

———. 1983. *Language as a Cognitive Process: Syntax.* Reading, MA: Addison-Wesley.

Winston, P.H. 1975a. "Learning Structural Descriptions from Examples." In *The Psychology of Computer Vision,* edited by P.H. Winston. New York: McGraw-Hill.

———. 1975b. *The Psychology of Computer Vision.* New York: McGraw-Hill.

———. 1979. "Learning by Creating and Justifying Transfer Frames." In *Artificial Intelligence: An MIT Perspective,* edited by P.H. Winston and R.H. Brown. Cambridge, MA: MIT Press.

———. 1980. "Learning and Reasoning by Analogy." *Communications of the ACM* 23(12):689–703.

———. 1984. *Artificial Intelligence.* 2nd ed. Reading, MA: Addison-Wesley.

Winston, P.H., and B. Horn. 1984. *LISP.* Reading, MA: Addison-Wesley.

Winston, P.H., and R.H. Brown, eds. 1979. *Artificial Intelligence: An MIT Perspective.* Vols. 1 and 2. Cambridge, MA: MIT Press.

Wong, H.K.T., and J. Mylopoulos. 1977. "Two Views of Data Semantics: Data Models in Artificial Intelligence and Database Management." *Infor* 15(3):344–83.

Woods, W.A. 1970. "Transition Network Grammars for Natural Language Analysis." *Communications of the ACM* 13:591–606.

———. 1973. "Progress in Natural Language Understanding: An Application to Lunar Geology." *Proceedings of AFIPS* 42:442–50.

———. 1975. "What's in a Link: Foundations for Semantic Networks." In *Representation and Understanding*, edited by D.G. Bobrow and A. Collins. New York: Academic Press.

———. 1980. "Cascaded ATN Grammars." *American Journal of Computational Linguistics* 6(1):1–12.

Yasaki, E.K. 1981. "AI: More than a Science: Teknowledge Inc. Has Taken upon Itself the Missionary Role of Spreading the Good Word on Knowledge Engineering, Expert Systems, and Artificial Intelligence." *Datamation* 27:63.

Yovits, M.C., G.T. Jacobi, and G.D. Goldstein. 1962. *Self-organizing Systems*. Washington, DC: Spartan Books.

Zadeh, L.A. 1965. "Fuzzy Sets." *Information and Control* 8:338–53.

———. 1975. "Fuzzy Logic and Approximate Reasoning." *Synthese* 30:407–28.

———. 1978. "PRUF—A Meaning Representation Language for Natural Languages." *International Journal of Man-Machine Studies* 10.

———. 1983. "Common Sense Knowledge Representation Based on Fuzzy Logic." *Computer* 16(10):61–67.

———. 1986. "A Simple View of the Dempster-Shafer Theory of Evidence and Its Implication for the Rule of Combination." *A.I. Magazine* 6(2):85–90.

Zue, V.W., and R.M. Schwartz. 1980. "Acoustic Processing and Phonetic Analysis." In *Trends in Speech Recognition*, edited by W.A. Lea. Englewood Cliffs, NJ: Prentice-Hall, pp. 101–24.

Index

A* algorithm, 74–75
Abduction, 44
Abstraction, 43
Abstraction spaces, 82, 138
ABSTRIPS, 9, 83
ACE, 10, 134
ACRONYM, 181, 195
Active values, 58
Agendas, 75
A. I. languages, 122–23
AKO (A Kind Of), 28
Algorithms, 195
ALPHA, 205
Alpha-beta pruning, 78–79
Alvey project, 211
AM, 91
Ambiguity, in language, 147–48, 151, 153
Analogical reasoning, 9, 43
Anaphora, 163
AND-OR networks, 70, 81
Antibiotic prescription, using MYCIN, 25, 37, 40, 59, 61, 87
APL, 123
APPEND, 98, 118
ART, 198, 200
Artificial intelligence
  applications of, 130–94, 223–51
  architecture, 3–7
  attributes, 2–7
  commercialization of, 10–12
  definition of, 1–2
  goals, 3–4
  history, 7–12
  role of computers, 3–5
  theories and concepts, 13–17
Association lists, 105
Associative processor, 215
ATOMCAR, 109
ATOMCDR, 109

Atoms, definition of, 96–97
Augmented Transition Network (ATN), 159–60
Automatic programming, 223
Average branching factor, 172

Backchaining or backward chaining, 54–56, 136, 195
Backtracking, 131, 162
BACON, 225
Bayes' rule, 37–40, 50–51, 62, 98–99, 142–43
Belief functions, 37, 59
Best-first search, 73
Bidirectional search, 56
Binding, 46–48
Blackboard, 83, 167–68, 195
Blocks world, 9, 88
Bottom-up parsing, 153
Bound variables, 103
Branch and bound, 75
Breadth-first search, 72

CAR, 98
Case grammars, 162
CAT, 10
CDR, 98
CENTAUR, 58
Certainty factors, 25, 60–61
Chaining, backward and forward, 52–57
Character recognition, 174
Chemical synthesis, 79–81
Chess, 4, 6, 8, 9, 67
Chomsky grammars, 157–59
Chunk, of knowledge, 24, 214
Classification, 7, 67, 142–46, 174
Clause form, 45–46, 120
CLS (Concept Learning System), 88
CMOS, 211

Cognitive science, 3, 44
Combinatorial explosion, 74
COMMON LISP, 95
Common sense reasoning, 41–44, 67
Compilers, 94
Conceptual dependency, 160–61, 195
COND, 104
Condition-action, 23
Conditional probability, 143
Conflict resolution, 53
Conjunction, 45
Conjunctive normal form, 45–46
CONNIVER, 123
CONS, 98
Consequent mode, 54
Constraint satisfaction, 58, 84, 184
Context-free grammars, 158
Context sensitive, 157–58
Contradiction, 45, 52
Convolution, 183
Credit assignment, 92
Cut, 116–20

DARPA, 167, 181, 206
Data-driven programming, 56, 195
Decision process, 145–46
Decomposition problems, 68
Deduction, 42–44
Deep sentence structure, 160–61, 195
Default reasoning, 41, 44
DELTA, 205
Demons, 28–29, 162
Dempsters rule, 66
DENDRAL, 9, 10, 79–81, 134
Depth-first search, 50, 72
DIAMOND, 148
Difference reduction, 75–76
DIPMETER ADVISOR, 10, 134
Disbelief, 59
Discovery, 91–92
Discrimination network, 145–46
Disjunction, 46
Divide and Conquer, 68
Dynamic typing, 201

Edge processing, 183
Education, 226
8-puzzle, 14–15, 69
EL, 84
Ellipsis, 163
EMYCIN, 22, 55–56
Endorsements, 41–42
ESPRIT, 214

EURISKO, 91–92
EVAL, 103
Evaluation functions, 76–79
Evaluation operator, in LISP, 103
Event-driven processing, 169
Evidential reasoning, 40, 65
EXPERT, 200
Expert systems, 86, 131–42, 232–46
Expert system shells, 86, 137
EXPLODE, 109
EXPRs, 100

Fallacy, 20
Feature detection, feature extraction, 183
FEXPRs, 100
Fifth generation, 205
First-order logic, 18, 21
Formal reasoning, 44–52
FORTH, 123, 193
FORTRAN, 110, 122, 153–57
Forward chaining, 52–54, 195
Frame-based reasoning, 57–59
Frame problem, 92
Frames, 27–31
Franz Lisp, 95
Functions, 21
Future prospects, 205–21
FUZZY, 122
Fuzzy logic, 37, 41, 60–61

Games, game tree, 8
Gbytes, 4
Generalization, 28–29, 43, 88
Generalized cylinders, 185–86
Generate and test, 73
Goal-directed processing, 54, 162, 195
GPS (General problem solver), 8, 76, 83
Grammars, 157–59
Graph search, 72–81
Guessing, 84

HACKER, 82, 84
HAIL, 10
HARPY, 167, 170–72, 195
HEARSAY, 56, 167, 169–70, 172, 195
Heterarchy, 9
Heuristics, 195
Heuristic search, 68
Hierarchical planning, 81–82

INDEX

Higher-order predicate logic systems, 22, 41–42
Hill climbing, 73
History, of A.I., 7–10
Horn Clause, 45–46
Human intelligence, 1, 215
Human-machine interaction, 151–52
HWIM, 167, 172
Hypothesis-driven, 54

Icons, 176
If-added demons, 29
If-needed demons, 29
If-removed demons, 29
If-then rules, 23, 52
Illumination, in analyzing line drawings, 187
Image analysis, 174–87
Image understanding, 174–87
IMPLODE, 109
Induction, 37
Inductive probability, 37
Inference engine, 5, 7, 13
Inheritance, 28
Instantiation, 46, 121
INTELLECT, 10, 148
Interactive processing, 95
INTERLISP, 95, 123, 195
INTERPLAN, 82, 84
Interpretors, 23
IPL, 8
ISA hierarchy, 28
Island processing, 169–72

Kanji, 172
KEE, 58, 126, 134, 198, 200
Kernal language (KL 0), 205
Kernal language (KL 1), 205
KES, 129, 200
Keyword matching, 106
KLONE, 22
Knowledge bases, 6, 13
Knowledge craft, 198
Knowledge engineering, 202–3, 133, 137
Knowledge representation, 14–17

Lambda functions, 102
LAST, 103
Learning, 86–93
Learning by analogy, 91
Learning by being told, 91
Learning by examples, 87

Learning by self-sufficient discovery, 91
Least-commitment strategy, 69, 84
LENGTH, 103
Lexicons, 165
LIFER, 162
Likelihood ratio, 62
Linear assumption, 84
LISP, 8, 45–110, 198
LISP machines, 123–29
LIST, 98
List processing, 45–110, 114–16
List structures, 99–100
Logical programming, 110–22
Logic systems, 18
LOGLISP, 122
LOOPS, 58, 126, 134, 198

Machine perception, 142–46
MACLISP, 95, 123
MACSYMA, 9
MAPCAR, 102
Matching, 105–10
Mbytes, 4
MCC, 206
Means-ends analysis, 75–76
Metalevel reasoning, 44
Meta rules, 5–6
Methods, 58
MICROPLANNER, 9
MINMAX game theory, 77
MITI, 190
Model-based reasoning, 195
Modified attachment, 163
Modus ponens, 20, 43
MOLGEN, 83, 84
Multiple word senses, 147–48, 163
MYCIN, 25, 37, 40, 59, 61, 87, 134, 136

Natural language, 146–63
Natural language interface, 148–51
Natural language processing, 146–63
Natural language understanding, 146–63
Nearest neighbor, 74
Nearly decomposable, 68, 83
Necessity measure, 65–66
Neural nets, 3–4, 86
NOAH, 83–84
Nonhierarchical planning, 82
Noun-noun modification, 153, 163
NP-complete, 74–75

Object graph, 187
Object-oriented paradigm, 135
Odds likelihood form, 62
Operators, 21
Opportunistic planning, 83
OPS, 21–22, 26, 52, 55–56, 134, 198, 200
Optical flow, 185

Painting problem, 68–69
PAM, 197
Parallel machines, 215–16
Parallel processing, 215–16
Parse trees, 153
Parsing, 153
Partitioned semantic networks, 32, 35
Pattern recognition, 142
Perception, 142
Perceptron, 86, 144
Phonetics, 165
Phonology, 165
Phrase structure grammars, 158, 162
Physical symbols, 176
Pixels, 176
Plan-generate-test, 80–81
PLANNER, 9, 56, 123
Planning, 58–60, 81–86
Plausibility, 65
Plausible inference, 3
Plausible reasoning, 4, 69, 84
POP, 123
POPLER, 123
POPLOG, 123
Pragmatics, 153, 165
Predicate calculus, 18–23
Predicate logic, 18–23
Predicates, 20–21, 104
Primal sketch, 176–77
Primitive semantics, 160–62
Probabilistic reasoning, 59–67
Probability, 37, 143
Problem solving, 67–71
Procedural reasoning, 43
Production graph, 187
Production rule systems, 23–27, 136
PROG, 104
Programmers workbench, 223
PROLOG, 18, 45, 51, 56, 110–22, 198
Property inheritance, 28–29, 32–34
Property lists, 32–34, 105
Propositional logic, 18–20
Prosodics, 166
PROSPECTOR, 4, 32, 40, 61–64

Prototypes, 58, 199
Pruning, 80–81
PSIM, 205
Psychology, relationship to A.I., 3, 44
PUFF, 10, 134

Quantifier, 21
Question-answering, 9, 146–48
Q LISP, 123
Quoting in LISP, 101–2

Rapid prototyping, 201
Recursion, 22–23
Refinement strategies, 50–51
Reflectivity representations, 186
Refutation, 45–46
Regular grammar, 158
Representation, 14–17
Resolution, 45–52, 120–22
Resolution theorem proving, 45–52, 120–22
Restaurant frame and script, 29–30
REVERSE, 103
Risk, 128
ROBOT, 10
Robotics, 188–94
Robot programming systems, 259–62
R1 (XCON), 10
ROSIE, 197
Rote learning, 87
Rule-based systems, 23–27, 136
Rule models, 23–27
Rules, 53

SACON, 25
SAIL, 122, 181
SAINT, 9
SAM, 197
Scene analysis, 178
Scripts, 29–31, 161–63
Search, 72–81
  alpha-beta, 78
  best-first, 73
  branch and bound, 75
  breadth-first, 72
  definition of, 72–73
  depth-first, 72
  heuristic pruning, 81
  hill climbing, 73
  minimax, 77
Segmentation, 183
Selective forgetting, 92

Semantic networks, 31–35
Semantics, 160–62, 165
SET, 97–98
SETQ, 97–98
S-expression, 96
Shadow analysis, 187
Shafter-Dempster measures, 66
SHRDLU, 9, 153–54
Situation-action rules, 23
Sketch, 176–77
Slot and filler structures, 28
Smalltalk, 135
Society of the Mind, 9
SODA, 148
Software engineering, 199
Speech understanding, 164–74
State space model, 67
State space search, 67, 160
Statistical inference, 137
Stereotypes, 161
Strategic Computing Program, 206
STRIPS, 82
Structured programming, 199
STUDENT, 9
SUBS, 103
SUBSTITUTE, 103
Substitution, 46, 103, 163–64
Support, 65–66
SUR, 167
Surface sentence structure, 160–61
Symbolic integration, 9
Symbolic processing, 95, 195
Symbolic reasoning, 95
Syntax, 18, 159–60, 165
Synthesizer, 172–74

TATR, 197
Tautology, 20, 52

TEAM, 148–50
TEIRESIAS, 87
Template-driven, 195
Texture, 187
Theorem proving, 45–46, 83
Tic-tac-toe, 15–16
TIMM, 200
Top-down parsing, 153
Top-down reasoning, 199
Top-down refinement, 82
Training sequence, 91
Transformational grammar, 157–59
Transition networks, 159–60
Translation, 147
Transparent reasoning, 5–6
Traveling salesman problem, 74–75
Tree-search, 72–76
Truth table, 19
Turing test, 1, 146–47

Uncertainty, reasoning with, 59–67
Unification, 121

Values for LISP atoms, 96
Variable binding, 50
Vision, 174–87
Vision understanding, 174–87
VLSI, 176, 183, 206

Waltz algorithm, 183–84
Waltz junction labels and line labels, 183–84
Weak methods, 8, 67
Well-formed formulas (WFF's), 18–20

Zeta LISP, 95

Q
335
.S4116
1987

CANISIUS COLLEGE LIBRARY
Q335 .S4116 1987 c.1
Artificial intellige

3 5084 00197 0451

Q 335 .S4116 1987 $39.95
Schutzer, Daniel, 1940-
Artificial intelligence

PAID 8/ /

MAR - 5 1989

MAY 1 7 1999

DEC 1 5 2000

MAY 1 8 2001   OCT 1 6 2002

MAY 1 3 2002

MAY 1 0 1997

CANISIUS COLLEGE LIBRARY
BUFFALO, N.Y.

NOV 1 7 1992